Empire Builders Series: Masterclasses in Business and Law

Brick by Brick

ALSO BY AUTHORSDOOR GROUP

Empire Builders Series: Masterclasses in Business and Law

Expert Insights Into Business Strategy and Legal Acumen

Brick by Brick: The Entrepreneur's Guide to Constructing a Company

Mark Your Territory: Navigating Trademarks in the Modern Marketplace

From Idea to Empire: Mastering the Art of Business Planning

From Idea to Empire: Abridged Edition

Beyond the Pen: Copyright Strategies for Modern Creators

Legal Ink: Navigating the Legalese of Publishing

The Empire Blueprint Series: Case Studies for Business Success

Strategies to Grow, Innovate, and Leave a Lasting Legacy

70 Case Studies in Vision, Strategy, and Personal Branding

70 Case Studies in Leadership, Innovation, and Resilience

74 Case Studies in Growth, Digital presence, and Legacy Building

AuthorsDoor Series: *Publisher & Her World*

The Surprisingly Simple Truth Behind Extraordinary Results

AuthorsDoor Advanced Series: *Publisher & Her World*

Adventures in Publishing and the Creation of Super Brands

AuthorsDoor Masterclass Series: *Publisher & Her World*

The Essential Keys to Unlocking Unstoppable Growth

Empire Builders Series: Masterclasses in Business and Law

Brick by Brick

The Entrepreneur's Guide to Constructing a Company

L. A. MOESZINGER

AuthorsDoor Group
an imprint of The Ridge Publishing Group

Brick by Brick: The Entrepreneur's Guide to Constructing a Company

https://www.AuthorsDoor.com
https://www.RidgePublishingGroup.com

Credit: This book was reviewed for grammatical accuracy with the assistance of ChatGPT, an Artificial Intelligence tool developed by OpenAI. We utilized ChatGPT to ensure clarity and correctness throughout the text, enhancing the reading experience while preserving the author's original voice. The integration of this advanced technology played a crucial role in maintaining the linguistic precision of each chapter.

Library of Congress Control Number: 2024920980

Brick by Brick: The Entrepreneur's Guide to Constructing a Company / by L. A. Moeszinger

ISBN 978-1-956905-28-1 (e-book)
ISBN 978-1-956905-27-4 (softcover)

1. Business & Economics / Entrepreneurship. 2. Business & Economics / New Business Enterprises. 3. Business & Economics / Small Business. 4. Business & Economics / Management. 5. Business & Economics / Information Management. I. Title. II. Series.

Printed in the United States of America

To all the dreamers who dare to lay the first stone, may this guide help you build your visions into realities.

AuthorsDoor Group
Coeur d'Alene, Idaho

INTRODUCTION TO THE AUTHORSDOOR LEADERSHIP PROGRAM

The AuthorsDoor Leadership Program, separate from the Builders Empire Series, is a new initiative designed to empower authors and publishers with the skills to effectively sell books. It features three tailored series: (1) AuthorsDoor Series: *Publisher & Her World*, (2) AuthorsDoor Advanced Series: *Publisher & Her World*, and (3) AuthorsDoor Masterclass Series: *Publisher & Her World*; each series is meticulously structured to guide participants from foundational concepts to advanced strategies in selling books, book by book, in a chronological format. The courses, offered for free on our YouTube channels—Publisher & Her World at Ridge Publishing Group, AuthorsDoor Group: Publisher & Her World, and Authors Red Door #Shorts—complement the books and workbooks, each providing unique and valuable teachings.

Explore additional resources to enhance your journey:

- Follow our blog at AuthorsRedDoor.com.
- Subscribe to our Newsletters at AuthorsDoor.com.
- Join our AuthorsDoor Strategy Forum Facebook Group.
- Connect with our Facebook Page at AuthorsDoor Group.
- Become a fan on our social media channels @AuthorsDoor1.

For feedback or questions, contact us at info@authorsdoor.com. We are here to support your journey from writing to successfully selling your books.

Warm regards,

L. A. Moeszinger #PubHerWorld

Contents

PART 4: TOOLS FOR GROWTH

Introduction

Laying the Foundation for Entrepreneurial Success

Welcome aboard the entrepreneurial express, destination: your business empire! "Brick by Brick: The Entrepreneur's Guide to Constructing a Company" isn't just a book; it's your battle armor in the thrilling, yet peril-riddled world of entrepreneurship. Here, you'll find everything from the nuts and bolts of starting your business to the jet fuel that will propel your fledgling venture into the stratosphere of success.

Embarking on Your Business Odyssey

Embarking on an entrepreneurial journey isn't for the faint-hearted—it's an exhilarating roller coaster ride that demands guts, gumption, and a smidge of cunning. This book is meticulously crafted to guide you through the entrepreneurial maze, from concocting your initial business idea to dodging the Minotaurs of market mishaps. Whether you're a wide-eyed novice with a dream and a sketch or a seasoned entrepreneur aiming to redefine the rules, this guide is your trusty compass.

Building From the Ground Up

Before you race ahead, let's talk foundations. The first chapters are like the dating phase with your business structure and legal setup—critical if you don't fancy a messy breakup (or lawsuit). You'll dive into the sexy world of business structures, tiptoe through the regulatory minefields, and flirt with financial frameworks. It's all about setting up strong, so your business doesn't crumble at the first sign of trouble.

Launching Like a Pro (and Keeping the Engine Running)

Next, we catapult into the market launch—think of it as your business's debutante ball, where first impressions matter. You'll learn how to primp your offerings and charm the heck out of your target market. But what about after the launch party? Stay tuned for insider secrets on keeping the momentum, scaling your business, and not just surviving but thriving in the corporate jungle.

Riding the Wave of Future Trends

As the future unfurls at warp speed, with tech novelties and consumer whims changing faster than a chameleon on a disco ball, this book keeps you clued in. You'll explore how to harness AI without losing your humanity, make blockchain your buddy, and turn sustainability from a buzzword into your business's superpower.

A Toolkit Packed With Entrepreneurial Wizardry

Each chapter is peppered with checklists, smart tips, and relatable anecdotes, ensuring you have the practical mojo to tackle every entrepreneurial challenge. Think of "Brick by Brick" as your Swiss Army knife in the wild terrains of business—ready to deploy at a moment's notice.

Let the Adventure Begin

"Brick by Brick" isn't just preparing you to build a business; it's priming you to launch an empire. As we chart this course together, prepare to be enlightened, entertained, and possibly exasperated (in a good way). Gear up, future tycoon—your empire awaits, and the blueprint to greatness lies within these pages. Let's start building, one witty, wise brick at a time.

Entrepreneurial Mindset

Embarking on the entrepreneurial journey is not just about having a groundbreaking idea or access to capital—it begins with cultivating the right mindset. This foundational section explores the mental frameworks and attitudes that are essential for any entrepreneur looking to build a resilient and thriving business.

Cultivating Resilience and Grit

- **Understanding Resilience**: We introduce the concept of resilience as the ability to bounce back from setbacks and failures, which are inevitable in any entrepreneurial venture. We discuss how resilience is not an inherent trait but a skill that can be developed with practice and persistence.
- **The Role of Grit**: We emphasize the importance of grit, defined as passion and perseverance for long-term goals. Grit enables entrepreneurs to maintain their commitment and enthusiasm over years, despite challenges and temporary failures.

Adopting a Growth Mindset

- **Growth vs. Fixed Mindset**: We contrast a growth mindset, which embraces challenges and views failures as opportunities for growth, with a fixed mindset, which avoids challenges and views failures as a reflection of one's inherent abilities. We highlight why a growth mindset is critical for entrepreneurial success.
- **Practical Tips for Developing a Growth Mindset**: We provide actionable advice for fostering a growth mindset, such as setting learning goals, embracing challenges, and persisting in the face of setbacks.

Embracing Risk and Uncertainty

- **Managing Risk**: We discuss strategies for managing risk effectively, rather than avoiding it. We encourage entrepreneurs to assess risks intelligently, prepare contingency plans, and always calculate the potential downsides.

- **Coping with Uncertainty**: We offer techniques for dealing with the uncertainty that comes with starting and running a business, such as staying informed, being flexible in planning and execution, and maintaining financial buffers.

Innovative Thinking and Continuous Learning

- **Fostering Innovation**: We detail how entrepreneurs can foster an environment of innovation within their startups by encouraging creativity, experimentation, and questioning the status quo.
- **Commitment to Continuous Learning**: We stress the importance of continuous learning and self-improvement. Recommend habits such as reading widely, attending workshops and seminars, and seeking feedback from peers and mentors.

Building Emotional Intelligence

- **Understanding Emotional Intelligence**: We define emotional intelligence and explain its importance in entrepreneurship for managing oneself and relating to others effectively.
- **Developing Emotional Intelligence**: We provide strategies for improving key components of emotional intelligence, including self-awareness, self-regulation, motivation, empathy, and social skills.

Networking and Relationship Building

- **The Power of Networking**: We discuss how building a broad network of relationships can provide support, foster opportunities, and enhance business growth.
- **Effective Networking Strategies**: We offer tips for effective networking, such as being genuine, offering value, and maintaining relationships over time.

By the end of Part One, readers will understand that the right entrepreneurial mindset is as crucial as a solid business plan. They will learn how to cultivate mental habits that foster resilience, encourage innovation, manage risk, and ultimately drive their business forward successfully. This mindset will set the stage for the detailed strategies and practical advice provided in the subsequent parts of "Brick by Brick: The Entrepreneur's Guide to Constructing a Company."

Common Pitfalls and How to Avoid Them

Starting a new venture is fraught with challenges and potential missteps. Part Two is dedicated to identifying common entrepreneurial pitfalls and providing strategic advice on how to sidestep these obstacles, ensuring a smoother path to business success.

1. Lack of Clear Vision and Planning

- **Pitfall**: Many entrepreneurs jump into businesses without a clear, long-term vision and without adequate planning. This can lead to misaligned goals, wasted resources, and business failure.
- **Avoidance Strategy**: Develop a comprehensive business plan that includes a clear vision statement, detailed market analysis, and a robust financial forecast. Regularly review and adjust your plan to remain aligned with your business goals.

2. Underestimating Financial Requirements

- **Pitfall**: A common mistake is underestimating the amount of capital required to start and sustain the business until it becomes profitable. This can lead to cash flow crises that cripple business operations.
- **Avoidance Strategy**: Perform thorough financial planning, including realistic revenue forecasts and expense budgets. Consider worst-case scenarios and ensure you have adequate financial buffers or access to additional funding.

3. Ignoring Customer Feedback

- **Pitfall**: Neglecting the voice of the customer can lead to products or services that do not meet market needs, resulting in poor sales and customer dissatisfaction.

- **Avoidance Strategy**: Establish continuous feedback mechanisms to gather insights from your customers. Use this data to iterate on your offerings and enhance customer satisfaction continuously.

4. Ineffective Marketing

- **Pitfall**: Weak or misaligned marketing strategies can fail to attract the target audience, wasting both time and resources.
- **Avoidance Strategy**: Develop a marketing strategy based on thorough market research. Utilize a mix of marketing channels best suited to reach and engage your target demographic. Monitor the effectiveness of different strategies and adapt as necessary.

5. Poor Hiring Decisions

- **Pitfall**: Hiring the wrong people, or hiring too quickly, can lead to poor team dynamics, inefficiency, and high turnover rates.
- **Avoidance Strategy**: Take the time to hire the right people who not only have the necessary skills but also fit the company culture. Implement structured hiring processes and consider involving multiple team members in the hiring decisions.

6. Overlooking Legal and Regulatory Requirements

- **Pitfall**: Entrepreneurs sometimes neglect the importance of complying with legal and regulatory requirements, which can result in fines, penalties, or severe operational disruptions.
- **Avoidance Strategy**: Prioritize legal compliance from the start. Consult with legal experts to ensure all business activities comply with local, state, and federal laws. Keep informed about changes in regulations that may affect your business.

7. Scaling Too Quickly

- **Pitfall**: Premature scaling, or scaling without proper foundations, can overwhelm your business processes, leading to compromised product quality or service delivery.

- **Avoidance Strategy**: Scale your business methodically. Ensure that you have the operational capability and infrastructure to support growth without compromising on quality or customer service.

8. Failure to Adapt

- **Pitfall**: Sticking rigidly to the original plan without adapting to market changes can make your business irrelevant.
- **Avoidance Strategy**: Remain flexible and open to change. Regularly scan the business environment for new trends and be ready to pivot your strategies in response to new opportunities and threats.

By understanding and preparing for these common pitfalls, entrepreneurs can enhance their chances of success and steer their ventures through the turbulent waters of business with greater assurance and capability. This proactive approach is not about avoiding failure at all costs but about learning to navigate the challenges intelligently and resiliently.

Success Stories and Case Studies

Learning from those who have navigated the entrepreneurial path successfully can provide invaluable insights and inspiration. This section showcases a selection of success stories and case studies, highlighting key lessons from entrepreneurs who have turned their startups into thriving businesses.

1. Technology Innovators: The Story of Dropbox

- **Background**: Dropbox, founded by Drew Houston and Arash Ferdowsi, transformed the way people store and share files online.
- **Challenges Overcome**: Early challenges included fierce competition and skepticism about cloud storage security.
- **Success Factors**: Strategic partnerships, a focus on user-friendly design, and effective viral marketing tactics, including a referral program that significantly boosted user growth.
- **Lesson**: Leveraging simple, user-centric solutions and innovative marketing can carve out a niche even in competitive markets.

2. Retail Revolution: The Rise of Warby Parker

- **Background**: Warby Parker disrupted the traditional eyewear industry with its direct-to-consumer model.
- **Challenges Overcome**: Tackling industry giants with entrenched retail networks and overcoming consumer skepticism about buying glasses online.
- **Success Factors**: A strong brand ethos of affordability and social responsibility, a home try-on program, and exceptional customer service.
- **Lesson**: Addressing industry pain points and enhancing the customer experience can disrupt established industries.

3. Social Impact: TOMS Shoes' One for One Model

- **Background**: TOMS Shoes, founded by Blake Mycoskie, introduced a novel social enterprise model with its One for One campaign—donating a pair of shoes for every pair sold.
- **Challenges Overcome**: Scaling a business model based on social impact without sacrificing profitability.
- **Success Factors**: Building a strong emotional connection with customers, effective storytelling, and maintaining a commitment to social impact alongside business growth.
- **Lesson**: Integrating social responsibility into your business model can differentiate your brand and drive consumer loyalty.

4. Tech and Fashion Fusion: The Stitch Fix Algorithm

- **Background**: Stitch Fix revolutionized personal styling through data science, combining personal stylists with powerful algorithms.
- **Challenges Overcome**: Balancing human intuition with algorithmic recommendations and scaling personalized services.
- **Success Factors**: Innovative use of technology to enhance customer experience, data-driven decision-making, and scalable logistics.

- **Lesson**: Innovative application of technology can transform traditional services, offering personalized experiences at scale.

5. Food Industry Game-Changer: Impossible Foods

- **Background**: Impossible Foods developed plant-based meat substitutes that mimic the taste and texture of real meat, targeting not just vegetarians but also meat eaters.
- **Challenges Overcome**: Scientific and technical challenges in product development, public perception, and regulatory approvals.
- **Success Factors**: Robust R&D, strategic marketing to position their offerings alongside traditional meat products, and partnerships with high-profile restaurants.
- **Lesson**: Addressing environmental and health concerns through product innovation can create new markets and change consumer behaviors.

Each of these case studies demonstrates how understanding market needs, innovating boldly, and persistently addressing challenges can lead to remarkable business successes. These stories not only provide practical lessons but also inspire aspiring entrepreneurs to think creatively and act courageously, reinforcing the notion that with the right approach and mindset, they too can achieve great things in the business world.

Personal Journey

Behind every entrepreneur's journey lies a compelling personal story filled with lessons, motivations, and insights. This section delves into the importance of understanding and embracing your personal motivations for starting a business, which can sustain you through challenges and inspire others.

The Role of Personal Motivation in Entrepreneurial Success

- **Fuel for Perseverance**: Personal motivation acts as the driving force that keeps entrepreneurs pushing forward despite setbacks. It's the deep-seated 'why' that gives clarity and strength during times of uncertainty.

- **Alignment with Goals**: When personal motivations align with business goals, it creates a powerful synergy that enhances passion, commitment, and satisfaction in the entrepreneurial journey.

Understanding Your 'Why'

- **Self-Reflection**: Encourage entrepreneurs to engage in self-reflection to understand their true motivations. Whether it's the desire to solve a particular problem, change an industry, achieve financial independence, or make a significant social impact, knowing one's 'why' is crucial.
- **Vision and Mission Development**: Use this understanding to craft a vision and mission that reflect your personal beliefs and passions. This not only guides your business strategy but also helps communicate your purpose to customers, partners, and employees.

Sharing Personal Stories

- **Connect with Your Audience**: Personal stories resonate with audiences, making your business relatable and your brand memorable. Sharing your journey can build trust and foster a stronger connection with customers and stakeholders.
- **Inspire and Lead by Example**: As an entrepreneur, your story can inspire and mentor others. By openly discussing the challenges and successes, you provide real-world guidance and encouragement to aspiring entrepreneurs.

Case Study: The Founder of Patagonia

- **Background**: Yvon Chouinard, founder of Patagonia, started as an avid climber and environmentalist, which led him to develop climbing equipment that would minimize environmental damage.
- **Motivation**: His passion for the outdoors and commitment to environmental conservation drove him to create a company that reflects these values.

- **Impact**: Patagonia's commitment to sustainability has not only influenced industry standards but also created a loyal customer base that shares the company's environmental ethos.

Integrating Personal Values with Business Practices

- **Ethical Business Practices**: Consider how personal values like integrity, fairness, and responsibility can be integrated into your business practices. This alignment can differentiate your business in a competitive marketplace.
- **Sustainable Growth**: Personal motivation aligned with ethical business practices leads to sustainable growth, as it ensures decisions are not just profit-driven but are also socially and environmentally conscious.

Continual Growth and Adaptation

- **Lifelong Learning**: Consider the importance of continual learning and adaptation, not just in business, but personally. The evolution of your personal goals and motivations can lead to new business opportunities and areas of expansion.
- **Feedback and Adaptation**: Regularly solicit feedback and be open to change. Adaptation based on personal growth and changing motivations can lead to renewed business strategies and innovations.

By understanding and harnessing your personal journey and motivations, you provide a foundation of authenticity and passion for your business. This section not only encourages entrepreneurs to explore and articulate their personal 'why' but also shows how these deep motivations can be seamlessly integrated into their business's broader mission, driving success and fulfillment in the entrepreneurial adventure.

Navigating the Digital Landscape

In today's fast-paced world, digital fluency is not just an advantage—it's a necessity. In Part Three we explore how entrepreneurs can effectively navigate the digital landscape to enhance their business operations, reach a wider audience, and stay competitive in an increasingly connected world.

Embracing Digital Transformation

- **Understanding Digital Transformation**: We define digital transformation as the integration of digital technology into all areas of a business, fundamentally changing how you operate and deliver value to customers. It's about more than just using new technologies; it's about revolutionizing your business model and operations.
- **Benefits of Digital Transformation**: We discuss the various benefits, including improved efficiency, greater market reach, enhanced customer experiences, and increased agility in responding to market changes.

Building a Strong Online Presence

- **Website and SEO**: We stress the importance of having a professional website that serves as the digital storefront for your business. Discuss how search engine optimization (SEO) is critical to increasing visibility and attracting more organic traffic.
- **Social Media Mastery**: We guide on choosing the right social media platforms that align with the business's target audience and marketing goals. We offer strategies for engaging content, regular updates, and interaction with followers to build a loyal online community.
- **E-commerce Opportunities**: For retail businesses, we discuss the importance of e-commerce capabilities. Offer insights into setting up online shopping systems, secure payment gateways, and user-friendly shopping experiences.

Leveraging Digital Marketing Tools

- **Content Marketing**: We explain how valuable and relevant content can attract and retain a clearly-defined audience, ultimately driving profitable customer action.
- **Email Marketing**: We describe how email marketing remains one of the most effective digital marketing tools for reaching and engaging customers, offering tips for crafting compelling campaigns and automating email communications.

- **Data Analytics**: We highlight the role of data analytics in understanding customer behaviors, preferences, and trends. We discuss tools that can help entrepreneurs measure performance and make data-driven decisions.

Protecting Digital Assets

- **Cybersecurity Measures**: We discuss the critical importance of cybersecurity in protecting business and customer data. Provide basic cybersecurity strategies, such as using secure networks, regular software updates, and strong passwords.
- **Legal Compliance**: We cover the legal aspects of operating online, including data protection laws, copyright rules, and e-commerce regulations.

Future-Proofing Your Business Digitally

- **Innovative Technologies**: We keep an eye on emerging technologies such as AI, blockchain, and IoT, and consider their potential impact on your business. We discuss how staying ahead of technological trends can provide new opportunities for innovation and competitive advantage.
- **Adapting to New Consumer Behaviors**: As digital technologies evolve, so do consumer behaviors. We encourage ongoing adaptation and learning to meet changing consumer expectations and capitalize on new digital opportunities.

Digital Skills Development

- **Training and Resources**: We emphasize the importance of continually upgrading digital skills, both for the entrepreneur and their team. We recommend resources for training, such as online courses, workshops, and webinars.

Navigating the digital landscape effectively requires more than just technical know-how; it requires a strategic approach to integrate digital technology into every facet of your business. Part Three provides the tools and knowledge necessary to harness the power of digital transformation, ensuring your business not only survives but thrives in the digital age.

Global Perspective

In today's interconnected world, adopting a global perspective is crucial for entrepreneurial success. Part Three also delves into the significance of thinking globally, understanding international markets, and leveraging global opportunities to scale your business beyond domestic borders.

Embracing Globalization

- **Understanding Globalization**: We define globalization in the context of business as the expansion of operations and strategies across international borders. Discussing how globalization can lead to increased market size, diversified risk, and access to new talent and technologies.
- **Benefits of a Global Approach**: We highlight the advantages of engaging with international markets, such as access to new customer bases, increased brand recognition, and the opportunity for competitive advantage through differentiation.

Analyzing International Markets

- **Market Research**: We stress the importance of conducting thorough market research to understand cultural nuances, consumer behavior, economic conditions, and regulatory environments in different countries. Providing strategies for gathering reliable data and interpreting it effectively.
- **Cultural Sensitivity**: We discuss the need for cultural sensitivity and adaptability in marketing and customer service. Offering insights into local customs, traditions, and business practices to avoid cultural missteps and foster positive relationships.

Strategies for International Expansion

- **Entry Modes**: We outline various modes of entering international markets, including exporting, franchising, joint ventures, and wholly-owned subsidiaries. Discussing the pros and cons of each approach, helping entrepreneurs choose the most suitable strategy based on their business model and goals.

- **Partnerships and Alliances**: We emphasize the role of strategic partnerships and alliances in facilitating smoother entry into foreign markets. Suggesting ways to identify potential partners and negotiate mutually beneficial agreements.

Navigating Challenges

- **Regulatory Challenges**: We address the complexities of navigating different regulatory frameworks and legal systems. Advising on compliance with international trade regulations, tariffs, and local laws.
- **Logistical Challenges**: We discuss the logistical challenges of operating across borders, including supply chain management, shipping, and handling international payments. Offering solutions to streamline these processes and reduce inefficiencies.

Leveraging Technology for Global Operations

- **Digital Tools**: We highlight how digital tools and platforms can facilitate global expansion, from cloud computing enabling seamless data access across geographies to e-commerce platforms opening up global sales opportunities.
- **Communication Technologies**: We discuss the importance of reliable communication technologies in managing international teams and maintaining strong customer relations.

Building a Global Mindset

- **Continuous Learning**: We encourage ongoing learning about global markets and international business trends. Recommending resources such as global business news platforms, international trade organizations, and cross-cultural training programs.
- **Diversity and Inclusion**: We advocate for diversity and inclusion within the organization to enrich understanding of global perspectives and enhance decision-making.

Ethical Considerations

- **Global Responsibility**: We discuss the ethical implications of global business operations, including sustainability, corporate social responsibility, and ethical labor practices. Encouraging businesses to adopt practices that not only comply with international standards but also contribute positively to global communities.

By adopting a global perspective, entrepreneurs can transform their businesses into international players, tapping into expansive markets and diverse resources. Part Three equips readers with the knowledge and strategies needed to navigate the complexities of international expansion and operate successfully on a global stage.

Interactive Components

Incorporating interactive components into your business strategy can significantly enhance learning, engagement, and practical application of concepts discussed throughout "Brick by Brick: The Entrepreneur's Guide to Constructing a Company." Part Four explores how various interactive elements can be utilized to deepen understanding and foster a more dynamic relationship between your business and its stakeholders.

Why Interactive Components Matter

- **Enhanced Engagement**: Interactive elements keep users engaged by making learning or using a product more hands-on and experiential.
- **Improved Retention**: People tend to retain information better when they are actively involved in the learning process through interactive experiences.
- **Feedback Opportunities**: Interactive components often allow for immediate feedback, which can be invaluable for continuous improvement and adaptation.

Types of Interactive Components

- **Digital Tools and Platforms**: Integrate interactive tools such as customer relationship management (CRM) systems, enterprise resource planning (ERP) software, or custom apps that encourage active user engagement and data collection.
- **Interactive Websites and E-commerce Platforms**: Design websites with interactive features like chatbots, quizzes, polls, or calculators that help in personalizing the user experience and providing valuable insights into customer preferences and behaviors.
- **Social Media Interactivity**: Utilize social media platforms to create interactive content such as live streams, polls, contests, and Q&A sessions, fostering a community around your brand and enhancing customer relationships.
- **Virtual and Augmented Reality Experiences**: Employ VR and AR to create immersive experiences for customers, whether for virtual product trials, interactive tours, or educational purposes.
- **Gamification**: Incorporate game-like elements in non-game contexts, such as point systems, leaderboards, or achievement badges, to increase user engagement and loyalty, particularly in learning environments or user platforms.

Implementing Interactive Components

- **Assess Needs and Goals**: Determine what you aim to achieve with interactive components, whether it's increasing user engagement, collecting data, or providing education. This will guide the type of interactivity you implement.
- **User-Friendly Design**: Ensure that interactive elements are easy to use and accessible to all users, regardless of their tech savviness or physical abilities. This might involve user testing and feedback loops to refine usability.
- **Integration with Overall Strategy**: Interactive elements should be seamlessly integrated into your overall business and marketing strategy.

They should complement and enhance your existing processes and customer interactions.

- **Data Security and Privacy**: When implementing interactive tools that collect user data, ensure compliance with data protection laws and regulations. Clearly communicate your data privacy policies to your users.

Monitoring and Evaluation

- **Track Engagement and Usage**: Use analytics tools to monitor how users interact with your components, which features are most used, and where users may be having issues.
- **Gather User Feedback**: Actively seek out user feedback on interactive elements to understand their effectiveness and areas for improvement.
- **Iterate and Improve**: Be prepared to make ongoing adjustments to your interactive components based on user feedback and analytics to ensure they remain relevant and effective.

Examples of Successful Interactive Implementations

- Throughout this book, we provide case studies or examples of businesses that have successfully integrated interactive components, highlighting the strategies used and the outcomes achieved.

Interactive components are more than just technological enhancements; they are a strategic tool that can transform the way you engage with your customers and other stakeholders. By thoughtfully implementing these elements, you can create more meaningful interactions, gather valuable insights, and build a loyal community around your brand.

Future-Proofing Your Business

In an era of rapid technological advancement and shifting market dynamics, future-proofing your business is not just advantageous—it's imperative. The Bonus Chapter provides entrepreneurs with strategic insights and practical steps to ensure their businesses remain relevant, competitive, and capable of thriving in an uncertain future.

Understanding Future-Proofing

- **Definition and Importance**: We define future-proofing as the process of anticipating the future and developing methods to minimize the effects of shocks and stresses of future events on a business. Discussing its importance in allowing businesses to seize new opportunities and avoid pitfalls as industries evolve.
- **Key Areas of Focus**: We highlight critical areas for future-proofing, including technology adoption, flexible business models, workforce development, and innovation strategies.

Leveraging Technology

- **Stay Technologically Agile**: We emphasize the need to stay abreast of emerging technologies that could disrupt or enhance your industry. Encouraging the adoption of new technologies that improve efficiency, customer interaction, and product quality.
- **Invest in Robust IT Infrastructure**: We discuss the importance of investing in scalable and secure IT infrastructure that can support growth and adapt to new technological advancements without extensive overhauls.

Adapting to Market Changes

- **Continuous Market Research**: We advocate for ongoing market research to keep track of evolving customer preferences, emerging market trends, and competitive dynamics. This enables businesses to adapt their products and marketing strategies in response to new data.

- **Diversification**: We recommend diversifying product lines, markets, and revenue streams to reduce dependence on a single source of income, which can buffer the business against market fluctuations.

Cultivating a Flexible Business Model

- **Business Model Innovation**: We encourage regular reviews and iterations of the business model to respond to new challenges and opportunities. This may involve pivoting services or products, exploring new market segments, or adopting different revenue models.
- **Scalability and Modularity**: We suggest designing business processes that are scalable and modular, allowing for parts of the business to evolve independently without disrupting the core operations.

Enhancing Workforce Capability

- **Foster a Culture of Learning**: Build a culture that values continuous learning and adaptability, encouraging employees to gain new skills and stay current with industry developments.
- **Flexible Work Arrangements**: For example, implement flexible work policies that can adapt to future changes in the workforce and workplace norms, such as remote work technologies and practices.

Driving Innovation

- **Encourage Innovation**: Create an environment that encourages creativity and experimentation. This could include setting aside resources for research and development, sponsoring hackathons, or collaborating with academic institutions.
- **Customer-Centric Innovation**: Keep the focus on innovation that addresses customer needs, using feedback loops to ensure that development efforts align with market demands.

Building Resilience

- **Risk Management**: Develop a comprehensive risk management plan that identifies potential threats, assesses their impact, and outlines strategies to mitigate these risks.

- **Crisis Management Plans**: Have in place robust crisis management protocols to deal with unexpected events, ensuring quick recovery and continuity of operations.

Ethical and Sustainable Practices

- **Sustainability**: Embed sustainability into the core of the business operations to appeal to increasingly environmentally-conscious consumers and comply with regulatory standards.
- **Ethical Standards**: Maintain high ethical standards in all business practices, which fosters trust and long-term loyalty among stakeholders.

By proactively future-proofing their businesses, entrepreneurs can navigate the challenges of tomorrow more effectively. This chapter not only provides a roadmap for enduring success but also ensures that the business remains agile, responsive, and forward-looking in its strategic approach.

Encouragement and Motivation

As we close "Brick by Brick: The Entrepreneur's Guide to Constructing a Company," it's important to reflect on the journey you're about to undertake or may already be navigating. This final section is designed to provide encouragement and motivation, reinforcing the resilience and persistence required for successful entrepreneurship.

Celebrating the Entrepreneurial Spirit

- **Acknowledge the Courage**: Starting and running a business requires courage. By choosing this path, you've demonstrated remarkable bravery and ambition. Recognize and celebrate this significant personal achievement.
- **The Value of Perseverance**: We emphasize that perseverance is perhaps the most critical trait of successful entrepreneurs. Encouraging readers to stay the course, even when faced with setbacks. Every challenge is an opportunity to learn, grow, and come back stronger.

Cultivating Optimism and Resilience

- **Maintain a Positive Outlook**: We encourage maintaining a positive yet realistic outlook. Optimism is a powerful tool for mental and emotional resilience, helping you navigate through uncertainties and difficulties with a constructive perspective.

- **Build Resilience**: Resilience isn't innate—it's built through experiences. Each obstacle you overcome not only strengthens your business but also enhances your ability to handle future challenges.

Drawing Inspiration from Others

- **Learn from Others**: Reminding entrepreneurs that they are not alone. Many have walked this path and have stories of both failure and success. Encouraging them to seek out mentors, join entrepreneurial networks, and learn from others' experiences and insights.

- **Share Your Story**: We motivate readers to share their own journeys. Every entrepreneurial story is unique and can serve as inspiration and a learning resource for others. Engaging with a community can also provide support and encouragement.

Embracing Lifelong Learning

- **Commit to Continuous Improvement**: The end of this book is just the beginning of an ongoing learning journey. We encourage a commitment to lifelong learning—whether through further reading, courses, workshops, or practical experience.

- **Stay Updated**: The business world is dynamic, with new technologies, trends, and regulations continually emerging. Staying informed and adaptable is crucial for sustained success.

Setting Realistic Goals and Celebrating Milestones

- **Set Achievable Goals**: We guide readers to set realistic, measurable, and timely goals. Breaking larger objectives into smaller, manageable milestones can help maintain motivation and focus.

- **Celebrate Small Wins**: It's important to celebrate all victories along the way, no matter how small. These celebrations reinforce positive momentum and remind you why you embarked on this journey.

Final Words of Motivation

- **Believe in Yourself**: We encourage readers to believe in themselves and their vision. Confidence, backed by preparation and knowledge, will empower them to make decisions boldly and stand firm in their convictions.
- **Keep the Passion Alive**: Reminding entrepreneurs to keep their passion alive. It's this passion that likely spurred the decision to start a business, and it will be crucial in propelling the business forward.

As you step forward from this book into the practical world of building and growing your business, remember that the journey of entrepreneurship is both challenging and rewarding. It is a path of personal and professional growth, and each step you take builds not just your business, but also your legacy. Keep moving forward, keep learning, and let your entrepreneurial spirit shine brightly.

Are you ready to get started? Read on . . .

PART ONE

Foundation First

Welcome to Part One: Foundation First, where your business journey begins not with a single step, but with a solid foundation. Think of this section as the concrete base of your entrepreneurial skyscraper, where every decision affects the integrity of everything that comes next. Here, you'll dive deep into choosing the right business structure, untangling legal must-knows, and plotting economic viability like a seasoned architect of industry. From erecting strong organizational frameworks to ensuring compliance across various state lines, get ready to lay down the groundwork that's as crucial as the cornerstone of any building. Buckle up, future moguls—let's build this from the ground up!

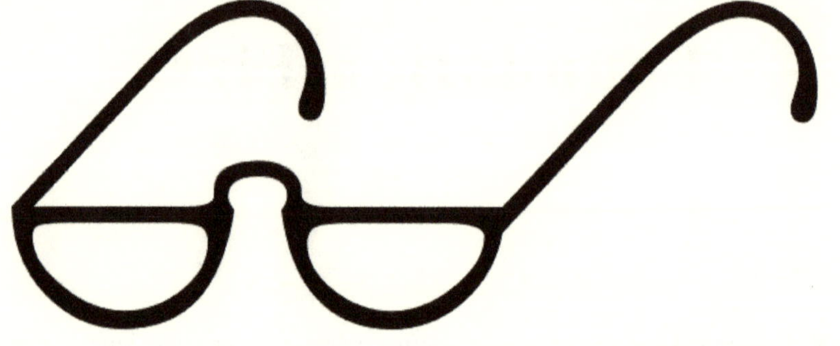

CHAPTER ONE

Choosing the Right Business Structure: A Blueprint for Entrepreneurs

"Choosing the right business structure is the first critical decision of many that shape the future of your enterprise. It's not just paperwork; it's the architecture of your ambition."— MARK CUBAN, ENTREPRENEUR AND INVESTOR

Welcome to the starting line of your entrepreneurial journey—the crucial decision point where you select the foundation for your business empire. This initial choice, far from being merely procedural, sets the trajectory for your venture's future. It impacts not only the daily operations but also the strategic maneuvers you will be able to execute as your business evolves. Choosing the right business structure is essential because it determines how you will navigate the regulatory landscape, manage financial liabilities, and optimize your tax obligations.

In this opening section, we will explore the profound significance of selecting an appropriate business structure. It's a decision that goes beyond administrative formalities; it's about setting a strategic direction for your venture. The structure you choose influences every critical aspect of your business—from your ability to attract and secure investment to how you can scale operations and manage risks. It affects your personal liability, how much tax you pay, and your capacity to make meaningful business decisions.

Whether you're a solo freelancer contemplating a simple sole proprietorship or an ambitious entrepreneur aiming for significant market presence, understanding the various business structures available is crucial. This chapter will serve as your definitive guide, helping you navigate through the complex considerations involved in this decision. We'll discuss the different types of business structures such as Sole Proprietorships, Partnerships, LLCs, S-Corps, C-Corps, and the increasingly popular B-Corps. Each has its unique advantages and challenges, tailored to different business needs and goals.

By the end of this section, you'll not only recognize the importance of meticulously choosing your business structure but also understand how this choice is integral to your long-term success. We'll equip you with the knowledge to assess which structure aligns best with your entrepreneurial vision and personal risk tolerance. Armed with this understanding, you'll be prepared to lay the most solid foundation possible for your business, enabling not just startup but sustainable growth and success in the competitive business landscape.

Let's begin this foundational chapter by delving deep into the strategic significance of each business structure, preparing you to make an informed and impactful decision that will shape the future of your business.

Overview of Business Structures

As you embark on your entrepreneurial venture, one of the first and most critical decisions you will make is choosing the right business structure. This choice not only impacts your day-to-day operations but also influences your financial health, personal liability, and potential for growth. Each business structure offers unique benefits and comes with specific limitations. In this section, we will provide an expansive overview of the various business structures available, helping you to understand their distinct characteristics and how they align with different business objectives.

Sole Proprietorship: This is the simplest and most straightforward form of business ownership, ideal for individuals who intend to operate alone. It is incredibly easy to establish, requiring minimal paperwork and regulatory hurdles. A sole proprietorship offers the owner complete control over all decisions and the ability to quickly adapt to changes. However, this comes with the significant drawback of unlimited personal liability—meaning personal assets are at risk if the business incurs debt or legal issues. Taxation is straightforward, as business income is treated as personal income.

Partnership: Partnerships are formed when two or more individuals decide to go into business together. There are several types of partnerships—general partnerships, limited partnerships, and limited liability partnerships—each offering different levels of liability and involvement in business operations. General partnerships allow for shared decision-making and profits, but also shared liability. Limited partnerships and limited liability partnerships provide some partners with protection against personal liability. This structure encourages collaboration but requires robust partnership agreements to manage responsibilities and resolve potential conflicts.

Limited Liability Company (LLC): An LLC provides its owners, known as members, with limited liability while allowing the flexibility of being taxed as either a sole proprietorship, partnership, or corporation, depending on the number of members and elections made. This structure is highly appealing because it shields personal assets from business debts and legal actions, yet it is more flexible and less formally structured than a corporation. LLCs are favored by small to medium-sized businesses that seek protection with minimal formality.

S-Corporation: An S-Corp is a special type of corporation that offers pass-through taxation, meaning the business's profits and losses can be passed through to the owner's personal tax return, thus avoiding double taxation. However, S-Corps have strict criteria regarding the number and type of allowable shareholders, which may limit investment opportunities. They provide limited liability protection, separating personal assets from corporate debts or lawsuits.

C-Corporation: C-Corporations are the most formal and structured of business entities, suitable for businesses that anticipate significant growth or plan to go public. They offer the strongest liability protection but are subject to double taxation—first on corporate profits and again on dividends paid to shareholders. Despite the tax implications, this structure supports raising capital through the issuance of publicly traded stock.

B-Corporation: B-Corps are designed for for-profit entities that want to consider society and the environment in addition to profit. These corporations are certified to meet rigorous standards of social and environmental performance, accountability, and transparency. For entrepreneurs committed to ethical practices and sustainability, B-Corps offer a way to structure a business that aligns closely with these values.

The subsequent sections will delve deeper into each of these structures, providing a detailed analysis of their legal implications, taxation considerations, and operational specifics. By thoroughly understanding each option, you will be better equipped to choose a business structure that not only suits your immediate needs but also supports your long-term ambitions, ensuring your business is built on a solid and suitable foundation.

Assessing Your Business Needs

Selecting the ideal business structure is a foundational decision that has far-reaching implications for the trajectory and health of your enterprise. This decision impacts your legal obligations, tax liabilities, operational flexibility, and your ability to secure funding and grow. In this section, we provide a comprehensive framework to help you assess your specific business needs, ensuring that the structure you choose aligns perfectly with both your immediate requirements and your long-term goals.

Clarifying Your Business Objectives: Begin by articulating your business vision and objectives. What are your aspirations for your business? Are you aiming for rapid growth with the intention to eventually go public, or do you envision a small, stable venture that you control closely? Your business structure can significantly influence your ability to achieve these goals. For instance, a corporation might be suitable for those seeking to expand and bring in numerous investors, whereas a sole proprietorship could be ideal for someone planning to operate independently.

Evaluating Liability Concerns: One of the most critical considerations in choosing a business structure is understanding the level of personal liability you are willing to assume. If your business involves considerable risk, such as selling physical products or providing services prone to litigation, protecting personal assets becomes crucial. Structures like LLCs and corporations provide liability protection, shielding your personal assets from business debts and legal issues. Conversely, sole proprietorships and partnerships can leave your personal assets vulnerable, a significant factor to consider based on your risk tolerance.

Decoding Tax Implications: Each business structure comes with distinct tax implications. It's essential to comprehend how these can impact your finances. Sole proprietorships and partnerships feature pass-through taxation, where profits are taxed once at the personal income level, potentially saving on taxes but offering less flexibility for business growth through retained earnings. Corporations are taxed separately from the owners, which can mean double taxation of dividends but allows for reinvestment of profits and potential tax advantages under certain conditions.

Assessing Funding Strategies: Your ability to attract investment can be heavily influenced by your choice of business structure. If raising capital is a priority, consider structures that are investor-friendly. For instance, C-corporations are ideal for attracting venture capital or going public due to their ability to issue various types of stock and have unlimited shareholders. Understand the limitations and possibilities each structure offers for equity investment and shareholder arrangements.

Planning for Flexibility and Scalability: Consider how your business may need to evolve in the future. Some structures offer more flexibility than others in terms of scaling operations, adding partners, or exiting the business. LLCs, for example, allow for an unlimited number of members and can offer attractive flexibility for changing membership or different classes of interests without extensive procedural hurdles.

Understanding Administrative Burdens: Each business structure comes with its own set of administrative and compliance obligations. Corporations require strict adherence to formalities such as holding annual meetings, maintaining detailed records, and filing extensive paperwork. Simpler structures like sole proprietorships require less formal administration but offer less protection and structure.

Seeking Professional Guidance: Given the complexities involved in choosing the right business structure, consulting with professionals such as accountants, tax advisors, and lawyers is crucial. These experts can offer tailored advice that considers all aspects of your business plan and personal circumstances, helping to navigate the legal nuances and tax strategies that best suit your business.

By meticulously considering these factors, you will be well-equipped to select a business structure that supports your business's current needs while paving the way for future success and stability. This thorough assessment will act as a strategic compass, guiding your decisions and helping to establish a robust foundation for your business endeavors.

Detailed Analysis of Each Structure

Understanding the specifics of each business structure is crucial for making an informed choice that aligns with your business goals, financial considerations, and risk tolerance. This section offers an in-depth examination of the primary types of business entities, including their legal ramifications, tax implications, and operational characteristics. By thoroughly understanding the advantages and constraints of each option, you will be better equipped to select the structure that best supports your business aspirations.

Sole Proprietorship:

- **Legal Simplicity**: This is the most straightforward business entity, where the business and the owner are legally the same. It requires the least amount of paperwork to set up and few ongoing formalities, making it a low-barrier entry option for new entrepreneurs.

- **Taxation**: The owner reports business income and losses on their personal tax returns, simplifying the tax process. While this setup avoids the complexity of corporate tax structures, it also offers limited opportunities for tax planning that might benefit larger businesses.
- **Liability**: The owner has unlimited personal liability for all business debts and obligations, which means personal assets like a home or car could be at risk if the business incurs debt or faces lawsuits.
- **Suitability**: Best for individuals operating low-risk businesses who prefer simplicity and full control, without the need for external funding or resources.

Partnership:

- **Legal Structure**: Consists of two or more individuals who come together to share the profits and risks of a business. It's imperative to have a well-defined partnership agreement that outlines each partner's contributions, responsibilities, profit sharing, and conflict resolution mechanisms.
- **Taxation**: Offers pass-through taxation where profits and losses are reported on the personal tax returns of the partners, thus avoiding the double taxation applicable to traditional corporations.
- **Liability**: In general partnerships, all partners share unlimited liability for business debts, which can extend to their personal assets. Limited partnerships and LLPs can offer some partners liability protections, contingent upon the nature of their involvement.
- **Suitability**: Suitable for businesses where two or more individuals wish to combine their expertise, resources, and networks, and are comfortable with shared decision-making.

▶ A Limited Partnership Agreement can be found in the **Appendix**. If you are interested in receiving an electronic copy of this document, please email us at documents@AuthorsDoor.com with the subject line "Request for Limited Partnership Agreement." Upon receiving your email, we will promptly send you a Microsoft Word copy of the document. **Disclaimer:** Please note that all agreements are provided for informational purposes only and should not be construed as legal advice. We recommend consulting with a qualified attorney to ensure that any legal documents or decisions are tailored to your specific circumstances.

Limited Liability Company (LLC):

- **Legal Flexibility**: Combines the liability protection of a corporation with the operational flexibility and tax benefits of a partnership. Ownership can include individuals, corporations, and other LLCs.
- **Taxation**: Members can choose to be taxed as a sole proprietorship, partnership, or corporation, allowing for significant flexibility in financial planning and tax reporting.
- **Liability**: Protects members from personal liability for business debts, which means personal assets are safeguarded against business failures or lawsuits.
- **Suitability**: Ideal for owners seeking liability protection combined with minimal formalities. It is particularly appealing to medium-sized businesses or those facing moderate business risks.

▶ An LLC Operating Agreement and Management Agreement can be found in the **Appendix**. If you are interested in receiving an electronic copy of these documents, email us at documents@AuthorsDoor.com with the subject line "Request for LLC Operating Agreement and Management Agreement." Upon receiving your email, we will promptly send you a Microsoft Word copy of the documents. **Disclaimer:** Please note that all agreements are provided for informational purposes only and should not be construed as legal advice. We recommend consulting with a qualified attorney to ensure that any legal documents or decisions are tailored to your specific circumstances.

S-Corporation:

- **Legal Considerations**: Provides limited liability protection while allowing business profits and losses to be passed directly to shareholders' personal tax returns, thereby avoiding double taxation at the corporate level.

- **Taxation**: Requires adherence to specific IRS rules, including restrictions on the number and type of shareholders (limited to 100, all of whom must be U.S. citizens or residents).
- **Liability**: Shareholders are generally not personally liable for business debts and liabilities.
- **Suitability**: Attractive to small business owners who qualify for S status and wish to avoid the double taxation of C-Corporations while still enjoying the benefits of corporate structure.

C-Corporation:

- **Legal Formalities**: Requires compliance with stringent regulatory standards, including maintaining a board of directors, conducting annual meetings, and keeping detailed records.
- **Taxation**: Faces double taxation, where the corporation pays taxes at the corporate level, and shareholders pay taxes on dividends. This structure, however, facilitates reinvestment and capital accumulation.
- **Liability**: Offers the most robust protection against personal liability for shareholders, shielding personal assets from corporate debts and legal challenges.
- **Suitability**: Best suited for businesses that anticipate significant growth, require substantial capital investment, or plan to trade publicly.

▶ Articles of Incorporation and Bylaws can be found in the **Appendix**. If you are interested in receiving an electronic copy of these documents, email us at documents@AuthorsDoor.com with the subject line "Request for Articles of Incorporation and Bylaws." Upon receiving your email, we will promptly send you a Microsoft Word copy of the documents. **Disclaimer:** Please note that all agreements are provided for informational purposes only and should not be construed as legal advice. We recommend consulting with a qualified attorney to ensure that any legal documents or decisions are tailored to your specific circumstances.

B-Corporation:

- **Legal Requirements**: Must adhere to rigorous standards of social and environmental performance, transparency, and accountability. This involves undergoing a specific certification process that assesses the company's impact on workers, the community, the environment, and customers.
- **Taxation**: Subject to the same taxation rules as C-Corporations, with the additional requirement to report on their social and environmental impact.
- **Liability**: Provides the same level of personal asset protection as C-Corporations.
- **Suitability**: Ideal for mission-driven businesses that aim to make a positive impact while operating in a for-profit framework.

This detailed exploration helps you appreciate the nuances of each business structure, guiding your decision-making process to ensure that your chosen entity not only meets your current needs but also supports your strategic vision for the future. The next sections will integrate this knowledge with practical steps for setting up your chosen structure and navigating potential challenges in the business environment.

Case Studies

Understanding the practical applications of different business structures can significantly inform your decision-making process. This section delves into detailed case studies that showcase how various business structures have been effectively utilized across diverse industries. Each case study explores the background, strategic decisions, challenges, and outcomes associated with these structures, offering real-world insights and lessons learned.

Case Study 1: From Freelancer to Protected Entrepreneur

- **Background**: A freelance graphic designer, initially operating as a sole proprietor, experienced significant growth in clientele, including high-profile corporate clients. With increased revenue came greater liability risks, especially with contracts involving larger firms.
- **Decision**: To mitigate personal liability and formalize the business, the designer transitioned to a Limited Liability Company (LLC).
- **Outcome**: The LLC not only protected personal assets from business liabilities but also enhanced the business's credibility, facilitating contracts with larger companies and improving access to business loans. This transition also offered tax flexibility, allowing the designer to optimize financial outcomes.

Case Study 2: Scaling a Tech Startup with Venture Capital

- **Background**: A tech startup initially structured as an S-Corporation to benefit from pass-through taxation and protect the founders' personal assets as they developed their prototype and entered the market.
- **Decision**: As the startup's need for capital grew and it looked towards scaling, it converted into a C-Corporation to accommodate more investors and prepare for a potential Initial Public Offering (IPO).
- **Outcome**: This restructuring attracted significant venture capital investment due to the favorable conditions for equity distribution and investor protection inherent in a C-Corporation. The C-Corporation status eventually facilitated a successful IPO, providing the liquidity and capital necessary for major expansion.

Case Study 3: Legal Firm's Shift to Limited Liability Partnership (LLP)

- **Background**: Partners at a longstanding law firm were increasingly uncomfortable with the unlimited liability associated with a general partnership, especially given the high stakes of legal practice.

- **Decision**: The firm transitioned to an LLP, which limited each partner's liability to their own actions and their direct involvement in the firm, without altering the operational or tax benefits of the partnership model.
- **Outcome**: The new structure protected partners' personal assets against liabilities created by other partners' actions, which not only secured the partners' personal financial security but also helped retain top talent who valued this protective measure.

Case Study 4: Embracing Corporate Social Responsibility through B-Corp Certification

- **Background**: A consumer goods company committed to sustainable practices faced the challenge of differentiating itself in a crowded market and demonstrating its commitment to social and environmental responsibility authentically.
- **Decision**: The company pursued and achieved B-Corporation certification, adhering to stringent standards of social and environmental performance, accountability, and transparency.
- **Outcome**: The certification boosted the company's reputation and brand loyalty among eco-conscious consumers. It also opened doors to new business partnerships and markets focused on sustainability, driving revenue growth and enhancing the company's competitive edge.

Case Study 5: Family-Owned Business Structures for Succession Planning

- **Background**: A family-owned restaurant chain needed a business structure that would facilitate easy ownership transfers between family members and avoid the complexities of double taxation on business profits.
- **Decision**: The family chose to structure the business as an S-Corporation, which provided favorable pass-through taxation benefits and facilitated easier management of shares within the family.
- **Outcome**: This decision allowed for smooth generational transitions of ownership, maintaining family control over the business while managing tax liabilities efficiently. The structure also supported clear and

structured business governance, which is crucial in family-run businesses to avoid conflicts and ensure professional management.

These case studies illustrate the strategic considerations behind choosing a business structure and the direct impact of these decisions on business operations, growth, and sustainability. By examining these real-world applications, you can better assess which business structure might align best with your business's specific needs and goals, thereby setting a strong foundation for success.

Choosing the Right Structure for You

With a comprehensive understanding of different business structures and insights drawn from real-world applications, the next crucial step is determining the best structure for your own business. This section provides a detailed framework to guide you through the decision-making process. By considering your business's specific needs, goals, and operational preferences, you can identify the most suitable business structure that aligns with your strategic vision.

Step 1: Articulate Your Business Goals

- Begin by clarifying your business objectives. Are you aiming for rapid growth, or do you prefer a stable, manageable operation? Do you plan to go public, or is keeping the business in the family a priority? These considerations will influence your choice of structure by aligning it with your long-term vision.

Step 2: Analyze Legal Liability Concerns

- Evaluate the potential risks and liabilities associated with your business activities. If you are entering a high-risk industry, or if there's substantial personal risk involved, opting for a structure that offers liability protection, such as an LLC or a corporation, may be necessary to protect personal assets and ensure peace of mind.

Step 3: Assess Tax Implications

- Different structures have distinct tax advantages and obligations. A sole proprietorship or partnership offers pass-through taxation, which might be beneficial for smaller businesses looking to minimize their tax burden.

Conversely, corporations are taxed separately from their owners and can benefit from corporate tax rates, which may be advantageous for businesses planning significant reinvestment of profits.

Step 4: Consider Future Growth and Expansion

- Think strategically about your business's capacity for growth. If attracting investors or scaling quickly is in your business plan, structures like C-corporations may offer more advantages due to their ability to issue various types of shares and attract foreign or institutional investors.

Step 5: Evaluate Operational and Administrative Requirements

- Reflect on your willingness and ability to manage the administrative duties associated with different business structures. Corporations require a significant amount of record-keeping, operational processes, and compliance with regulations, which can be resource-intensive. If simplicity is valued, a sole proprietorship or partnership may be more appropriate.

Step 6: Seek Professional Advice

- Engage with business consultants, tax advisors, and legal professionals who can provide insights tailored to your specific situation. Their expertise can help clarify the implications of each business structure and ensure that you are making the best decision based on accurate, personalized information.

Step 7: Decision-Making

- With all the information and professional advice at your disposal, make a well-informed decision that best suits your business's needs and your personal circumstances. Consider not only the immediate benefits but also how the structure will serve your business as it evolves.

Step 8: Implementation and Ongoing Review

- Once you have selected a business structure, undertake the necessary steps to officially establish your business. This involves registering with relevant authorities, completing required paperwork, and meeting any legal stipulations. After implementation, it's crucial to continually review and assess the structure's effectiveness against your business's performance and evolving goals. This adaptive approach will help you remain responsive to changes and ensure that your business structure continues to support your operations effectively.

By methodically working through these steps, you will equip yourself to choose a business structure that not only meets your current requirements but also supports your future ambitions. This proactive and informed approach will lay a strong foundation for your business's success, providing the stability and flexibility needed to navigate the complexities of your industry.

Setting Up Your Business Structure

Now that you have selected the optimal business structure for your entrepreneurial goals, the next critical step is the effective implementation of this structure. Proper setup is essential to ensure your business operates legally, remains compliant with regulatory requirements, and is structured to minimize potential risks. This section outlines a comprehensive process to establish your business entity, from registration to compliance, providing a step-by-step guide to getting started on the right footing.

Step 1: Register Your Business Name

- **Action**: Begin by conducting a thorough name availability search to ensure that the business name you've chosen isn't already in use or trademarked by another entity. Once confirmed, register the business name with your state's business registry. This may include filing a 'Doing Business As' (DBA) if you plan to operate under a name different from your officially registered name.
- **Importance**: This step secures your business name legally, protecting your brand identity and preventing others from registering the same name. It establishes your business's legal presence and can be crucial for brand marketing and consumer recognition.

Step 2: Obtain Federal and State Tax IDs

- **Action**: Apply for an Employer Identification Number (EIN) from the Internal Revenue Service (IRS), which will serve as your federal tax ID. Additionally, if your business requires collecting sales tax or you have employees, you'll likely need a state tax ID from your state's department of revenue.
- **Importance**: These tax IDs are fundamental for all your business dealings, including opening bank accounts, hiring employees, and complying with tax regulations. They are essential identifiers for your business in the governmental and financial ecosystem.

Step 3: File Organizational Documents

- **Action**: Depending on your chosen structure, submit the necessary foundational documents to the state. This includes Articles of Incorporation for corporations, Articles of Organization for LLCs, and partnership agreements for partnerships.
- **Importance**: These documents officially establish the existence of your business under law, setting forth the basic structure, governance rules, and operational guidelines. They are legally required to formally define the nature and structure of your business.

Step 4: Draft Internal Agreements

- **Action**: Prepare and finalize internal governance documents such as articles of incorporation and bylaws for corporations or operating agreements for partnerships and LLCs. These should detail management frameworks, fiscal policies, member roles and responsibilities, and procedures for handling internal disputes.
- **Importance**: These agreements ensure that all parties involved in the business have clear expectations about operations, responsibilities, and profits distribution. They play a crucial role in preventing misunderstandings and conflicts among founders and stakeholders.

Step 5: Obtain Licenses and Permits

- **Action**: Research and secure all necessary local, state, and federal licenses and permits required for your specific business activities. This can vary widely depending on the industry, location, and the nature of your business operations.
- **Importance**: Obtaining the correct licenses and permits is critical for operating your business legally. Failure to comply can result in fines, sanctions, or even the forced closure of your business.

Step 6: Set Up Financial Accounts

- **Action**: Open a dedicated business banking account to separate your personal finances from your business dealings. Consider setting up credit lines and merchant services if your business will accept credit and debit card transactions. Implementing a reliable accounting system or software to manage your finances effectively is also advisable.
- **Importance**: Maintaining separate accounts for personal and business finances simplifies tax reporting, enhances financial management, and contributes to your business's credibility and professionalism.

Step 7: Plan for Compliance and Ongoing Management

- **Action**: Develop a routine for ongoing legal and financial compliance. This includes regular reviews of your tax obligations, renewals of licenses and permits, and adherence to any annual reporting or filing requirements specific to your business structure.
- **Importance**: Proactive compliance planning helps ensure that your business does not incur penalties or legal issues, maintains a good standing with regulatory authorities, and operates smoothly without disruptions.

By following these detailed steps, you can set up your business structure with confidence, knowing that you have addressed all the critical legal, financial, and operational aspects required for a strong start and sustained success.

Quick Tips and Recap

As we wrap up our discussion on choosing the right business structure, here are the essential takeaways to remember:

- **Define Your Goals**: Clearly outline your business objectives to choose a structure that best supports your aims.
- **Assess Risks**: Opt for a structure that protects personal assets from business liabilities.
- **Tax Considerations**: Choose a structure that offers tax benefits suitable for your financial strategy.
- **Plan for Growth**: Select a structure flexible enough to accommodate future expansion.
- **Legal Compliance**: Understand and manage the legal requirements associated with your chosen structure.
- **Professional Advice**: Consult with experts to align your business structure with legal standards and business goals.
- **Register Your Business**: Secure your business name and obtain all necessary IDs and licenses.
- **Separate Finances**: Maintain distinct personal and business finances for simpler management.
- **Stay Compliant**: Keep licenses and permits up to date, and stay on top of tax obligations and filings.
- **Regular Evaluations**: Periodically review your business structure to ensure it continues to meet your evolving needs.

This summary encapsulates the key points for setting up your business structure efficiently, ensuring you build a robust foundation for your business's ongoing success.

CHAPTER TWO

Navigating the Legal Landscape: What Every Entrepreneur Needs to Know

"Understanding the legal landscape isn't just about avoiding pitfalls; it's about finding opportunities where others see obstacles. The best entrepreneurs know that legal preparedness is a strategic asset."
— RICHARD BRANSON, FOUNDER OF VIRGIN GROUP

Ahoy there, intrepid entrepreneur! Ready to set sail across the choppy waters of legal compliance? Consider this chapter your trusty navigational chart, steering you clear of the perilous cliffs of litigation and guiding you through the foggy realms of regulatory demands. Legalities might not quicken the pulse like your big business ideas do, but think of them as the rules of the road that keep your enterprise cruising smoothly.

We'll demystify the jargon and break down the essential statutes, because knowing your legal ABCs is just as crucial as your business model. From copyrights to contracts, and patents to privacy policies, we'll cover the gamut to ensure you're not just compliant, but savvy about the laws that can affect your business's course.

Whether you're a sole proprietor or the next startup unicorn, understanding the legal landscape is non-negotiable. This chapter won't just help you dodge legal bullets; it'll arm you with the knowledge to turn legal foresight into competitive advantage. Let's turn you into a legal eagle, ready to soar above the competition with the confidence that comes from being fully informed and impeccably compliant.

Understanding Business Law Basics

Embarking on an entrepreneurial journey without a fundamental understanding of business law is like setting sail without a map; it's essential to know the legal landscape to navigate your business to success effectively. This introductory section aims to demystify the complexities of business law, breaking down intricate legal terms and concepts into digestible, actionable insights. Here, you'll learn about the crucial aspects of business law that directly impact the operation, stability, and growth of your business.

The Importance of Choosing the Right Legal Structure

- **Overview**: The legal structure of your business affects everything from daily operations to taxes, and from your personal liability to your ability to raise capital. It's one of the first and most important decisions you will make.

- **Exploration of Business Structures**: We'll delve into the details of various business structures including sole proprietorships, partnerships, limited liability companies (LLCs), S-corporations, and C-corporations. Each has distinct advantages and disadvantages depending on your business goals and context.

- **Criteria for Selection**: This section will guide you through selecting the appropriate structure by evaluating factors such as risk exposure, financial practices, administrative burden, and future growth plans.

Navigating Tax Obligations

- **Fundamentals of Business Taxation**: Gain an understanding of the tax implications associated with each business structure. Knowing how taxation works can help you in planning financial strategies more effectively and can impact your bottom line significantly.
- **Compliance Strategies**: Learn how to stay compliant with various tax obligations at federal, state, and local levels. We'll cover key tax filing dates, essential deductions, and strategies to avoid common pitfalls like underpayment and late filing penalties.

Understanding Regulatory Requirements

- **General Business Regulations**: An overview of standard federal and state regulations that affect most businesses, including employment laws, anti-discrimination policies, environmental regulations, and consumer protection laws.
- **Industry-Specific Legislation**: Detailed explanation of how to identify and comply with regulations that are unique to your specific industry, whether it's financial services, health care, manufacturing, or another sector.

Licenses and Permits

- **Determining Your Needs**: Practical advice on how to identify the specific licenses and permits your business requires based on its activities and location. This might include everything from a basic business operation license to specialized permits for constructions, health operations, or environmental activities.
- **Procedure for Acquisition**: Step-by-step guidance on the application process for obtaining the necessary licenses and permits, including where to go, the costs involved, and typical timeframes for processing.

Effective Documentation Practices

- **Importance of Keeping Records**: Emphasize the critical role that good documentation plays in protecting your business legally and financially. Proper record-keeping can be a lifeline in the event of legal disputes or when facing audits.
- **Documentation Strategies**: Best practices for managing and maintaining records, from digital backups to secure storage systems. Tips on what documents to keep, how long to retain them, and how to organize records for easy access and compliance.

By the end of this chapter, you will have a foundational understanding of the legal intricacies involved in running a business. This knowledge not only helps in ensuring compliance and minimizing legal risks but also serves as a critical component in laying a robust foundation for the future growth and success of your venture. Armed with this understanding, you can confidently make informed decisions that align with both your business objectives and legal requirements.

Intellectual Property Rights

In the competitive landscape of entrepreneurship, intellectual property (IP) stands as a cornerstone of innovation and brand differentiation. Understanding and effectively managing IP rights can not only safeguard your creations but also provide significant leverage in achieving competitive advantage. This section delves deeply into the various types of intellectual property, outlining effective strategies for protection, and demonstrating how to utilize these assets to enhance your business's market position.

Exploring the Types of Intellectual Property

- **Patents**: Patents are crucial for protecting inventions and innovative processes, granting the inventor exclusive rights to use, sell, or manufacture the invention for a limited period, generally 20 years from the filing date. This subsection will guide you through the criteria for patentability, the process of obtaining a patent, and the strategic importance of patents in protecting technological and product advancements.

- **Trademarks**: Trademarks protect logos, names, and other symbols that distinguish your goods or services from those of others. They are vital for maintaining the identity and reputation of your brand. Here, we will discuss the process of trademark registration, ongoing maintenance requirements, and strategies for enforcing trademark rights against unauthorized use.
- **Copyrights**: Copyrights protect original artistic and literary works—everything from books and articles to music and software. Copyright protection is automatic upon the creation and fixation of the work in a tangible medium, lasting for the life of the author plus 70 years in most jurisdictions. This section will explain how to effectively secure copyright protection and enforce rights, including licensing and dealing with copyright infringement.
- **Trade Secrets**: Trade secrets encompass formulas, practices, processes, designs, instruments, or compilations of information that provide a business advantage over competitors who do not know or use them. Protection strategies involve confidentiality agreements, secure information practices, and understanding the legal remedies available in case of misappropriation.

Strategies for Protecting Intellectual Property

- **Proactive Protection Measures**: Developing a comprehensive IP strategy is essential for safeguarding your assets. This includes conducting regular IP audits, securing appropriate IP registrations, and implementing effective surveillance systems to monitor and detect potential infringements.
- **Legal Frameworks and Enforcement**: Familiarize yourself with the legal frameworks that support IP rights and the enforcement mechanisms available. This includes understanding how to initiate legal proceedings for IP violations, the types of legal remedies available, such as

injunctions and damages, and the potential for criminal prosecution in severe cases of infringement.

- **Global IP Considerations**: For businesses operating internationally or planning to expand overseas, it's crucial to secure IP rights in foreign jurisdictions. This subsection will cover the basics of international IP law, including key treaties and conventions that can help protect your intellectual property worldwide.

Leveraging Intellectual Property in Business

- **Monetization Strategies**: Intellectual property can significantly enhance revenue through licensing deals, franchising opportunities, and strategic alliances. We will explore various models for IP monetization, highlighting key considerations in negotiation and contract drafting.
- **Strategic Alliances and Partnerships**: Using IP to forge strategic partnerships can amplify your business's capabilities and access to markets. Learn how to leverage your IP portfolio to attract and secure beneficial business partnerships.
- **Competitive Intelligence**: Utilizing IP as a tool for competitive intelligence involves understanding the IP activities of competitors to anticipate market shifts and align your innovation pipeline accordingly. This proactive approach can help you stay ahead in the industry and navigate around potential IP conflicts.

By the end of this chapter, you will be equipped with a solid foundation in managing and protecting your intellectual property. More importantly, you'll understand how to strategically employ IP assets to fortify your business's market position, ensuring that your innovations and creative outputs significantly contribute to your business success and growth.

Contracts and Agreements

Navigating the intricacies of contracts and agreements is essential for any business, as these documents legally bind parties to their obligations and outline the framework for business relationships. Effective contracts reduce risks, clarify expectations, and provide a clear path for resolving disputes. This section aims to deepen your understanding of the contractual process, from creation and negotiation to management and enforcement, ensuring that your agreements protect your interests and contribute to the smooth operation of your business.

Fundamentals of Contract Law

- **Core Elements**: Every contract must include certain fundamental elements: an offer, acceptance, consideration (an exchange of value), and mutual consent. We will explore these components in detail, explaining how they interact to form legally binding agreements.
- **Types of Contracts**: Gain insights into different types of contracts used in business environments, including sales contracts, service agreements, lease agreements, partnership agreements, and confidentiality agreements. Each type serves specific purposes and requires particular clauses to be effective.

Drafting Effective Contracts

- **Language and Clarity**: Learn the importance of using precise, clear language to avoid ambiguities that can lead to legal disputes. This subsection will offer guidelines on drafting contracts that are both comprehensive and understandable to all parties involved.
- **Critical Clauses**: Delve into essential clauses that should be included in most business contracts, such as scope of work, payment terms, confidentiality, dispute resolution mechanisms, termination conditions, and liability limitations. Understanding these clauses will help you construct robust agreements that safeguard your business interests.

Negotiation Techniques

- **Preparation and Strategy**: Effective negotiation is key to developing contracts that benefit all parties. We will cover strategies for successful negotiation, including preparation techniques, understanding the counterpart's needs, and tactics for reaching a favorable outcome.
- **Avoiding Negotiation Pitfalls**: Learn to identify and steer clear of common negotiation errors such as poor preparation, emotional decision-

making, and failing to listen to the other party. This guidance will help you maintain professionalism and ensure productive negotiations.

Managing Contracts

- **Oversight and Performance Monitoring**: Once a contract is in place, managing its execution is crucial. This section provides strategies for overseeing contract performance, ensuring that all parties meet their obligations, and addressing issues as they arise.
- **Modifications and Renewals**: Understand the procedures for modifying contracts in response to changing business conditions and managing renewals. This includes how to negotiate extensions, incorporate new terms, and terminate agreements when necessary.

Resolving Disputes and Enforcing Agreements

- **Dispute Resolution Options**: Examine the various methods for resolving contractual disputes, including negotiation, mediation, arbitration, and litigation. Each option offers different advantages and considerations, and choosing the right path can help preserve business relationships and minimize costs.
- **Enforcement Strategies**: Discuss the legal mechanisms available to enforce contracts, including seeking injunctive relief and damages for breach of contract. Knowledge of these enforcement tools is vital to protect your legal rights and ensure compliance with agreed terms.

By the end of this chapter, you will have a comprehensive toolkit for managing contracts throughout their lifecycle—from drafting and negotiating to fulfillment and eventual renewal or termination. Armed with this knowledge, you can approach contracts with confidence, knowing that your agreements are not only legally sound but also aligned with your business goals and operational strategies. This foundation will help you mitigate risks, foster strong business relationships, and maintain a competitive edge in your market.

▶ An Indemnity Agreement can be found in the **Appendix**. If you are interested in receiving an electronic copy of this document, email us at documents@AuthorsDoor.com with the subject line "Request for Indemnity

Agreement." Upon receiving your email, we will promptly send you a Microsoft Word copy of the document. **Disclaimer:** Please note that all agreements are provided for informational purposes only and should not be construed as legal advice. We recommend consulting with a qualified attorney to ensure that any legal documents or decisions are tailored to your specific circumstances.

Employment Law

Mastering the intricacies of employment law is essential for any business owner to ensure compliance, mitigate risks, and foster a supportive work environment. This section provides a comprehensive exploration of the legal framework governing employment relationships, offering detailed insights into everything from the hiring process to employee management and termination. By understanding these laws, you can protect your business from legal disputes and create a workplace that supports both employee satisfaction and productivity.

Introduction to Employment Law

- **Basic Principles**: Begin with an overview of the foundational principles of employment law, including the critical distinction between employees and independent contractors, which affects both tax obligations and liability.
- **Key Legislation**: Discuss major federal laws such as the Fair Labor Standards Act (FLSA), which regulates minimum wage, overtime, and child labor; the Americans with Disabilities Act (ADA), which addresses workplace discrimination based on disability; and the Family and Medical Leave Act (FMLA), which ensures leave for family and medical reasons. Also, explore relevant state-specific laws that may impose additional requirements.

Hiring Practices

- **Compliance in Hiring**: Examine legal considerations during the hiring process, including crafting nondiscriminatory job postings, conducting interviews, performing background checks, and ensuring all hiring practices comply with equal opportunity laws.

- **Drafting Employment Agreements**: Detail the essential components of employment contracts, such as job responsibilities, compensation, benefits, confidentiality obligations, and conditions for termination, to avoid future disputes and clarify expectations.

▶ An Employment Agreement—At Will Employment, Confidential Information, Invention Assignment, and Arbitration Agreement—can be found in the **Appendix**. If you are interested in receiving an electronic copy of this document, email us at documents@AuthorsDoor.com with the subject line "Request for Employment Agreement." Upon receiving your email, we will promptly send you a Microsoft Word copy of the document. **Disclaimer:** Please note that all agreements are provided for informational purposes only and should not be construed as legal advice. We recommend consulting with a qualified attorney to ensure that any legal documents or decisions are tailored to your specific circumstances.

Development of Workplace Policies

- **Creating an Employee Handbook**: Guide on how to develop a comprehensive employee handbook that clearly communicates workplace policies and procedures. This document should cover everything from the standard code of conduct and dress code to more complex issues like anti-discrimination policies, harassment policies, and safety protocols.
- **Ensuring Compliance**: Discuss the importance of aligning your workplace policies with current laws and regulations and provide strategies for regularly updating these policies as laws evolve.

Rights and Responsibilities in the Workplace

- **Employee Rights**: Offer an in-depth look at the rights afforded to employees, including the right to fair wages, a safe work environment, freedom from discrimination, and privacy protections.

- **Employer Obligations**: Outline the legal obligations of employers, such as accommodating employees with disabilities, managing various types of leave entitlements, and handling employee grievances and complaints in a lawful manner.

Performance Management and Termination

- **Managing Employee Performance**: Share best practices for effectively managing employee performance, including setting clear performance metrics, conducting regular reviews, and providing constructive feedback.
- **Procedures for Lawful Termination**: Navigate the complex process of employee termination, highlighting the differences between firing at-will employees and those under contract, managing layoffs with sensitivity and legality, and how to conduct a termination meeting to minimize the risk of legal repercussions.

Resolving Disputes and Handling Legal Challenges

- **Internal Dispute Resolution**: Introduce effective methods for resolving workplace disputes internally, such as mediation and arbitration, to maintain morale and prevent external legal challenges.
- **Facing Legal Actions**: Prepare business owners for the possibility of legal actions stemming from employment issues, discussing how to respond to lawsuits, the role of legal representation, and the potential outcomes of such disputes.

Through this detailed exploration of employment law, business owners can gain the necessary knowledge to navigate the legal challenges associated with managing a workforce. This section aims to equip you with the tools needed to create legally compliant, fair, and effective employment practices that support both the operational needs of your business and the rights of your employees, ultimately contributing to a stable and productive work environment.

Online Business Laws

As the digital economy expands, mastering the complex landscape of online business laws is crucial for any entrepreneur aiming to capitalize on the growth of e-commerce and digital services. This section addresses the specialized legal considerations necessary for operating in the online space. From navigating e-commerce regulations to ensuring compliance with digital copyright laws, data privacy standards, and consumer protection laws, this detailed guide will help you manage legal risks and maintain the integrity and reputation of your online business.

E-Commerce Regulations

- **Introduction to E-Commerce Law**: Begin with a comprehensive overview of the regulatory environment governing e-commerce, detailing the key legal frameworks that impact online transactions, digital contracts, and consumer rights.
- **Navigating Jurisdictional Issues**: Discuss the complexities of jurisdiction in the online realm, where businesses may need to comply with laws from multiple states or countries. Learn to identify which legal standards apply to your transactions and how to effectively manage compliance across different regulatory landscapes.
- **Payment Processing and Online Tax Obligations**: Explore the legal requirements related to online payment systems, including security standards and obligations under financial regulations. Address the challenges of internet sales tax, focusing on how to correctly collect, report, and remit taxes in various jurisdictions, particularly in light of recent legislative changes affecting online sales.

Intellectual Property in the Digital Space

- **Protecting Digital Assets**: Offer strategies for safeguarding intellectual property online, including securing copyright for digital content, trademarks for online brands, and patents for unique digital products and processes.

- **Infringement and Enforcement**: Provide practical advice on monitoring and protecting your intellectual property against online infringement. Learn how to enforce your rights through mechanisms such as the Digital Millennium Copyright Act (DMCA) takedown notices and litigation when necessary.

Privacy and Data Protection

- **Drafting Effective Privacy Policies**: Guide the creation and implementation of robust privacy policies that comply with stringent regulations like the General Data Protection Regulation (GDPR) and the California Consumer Privacy Act (CCPA).
- **Ensuring Data Security**: Highlight the importance of maintaining high standards of data security to protect sensitive customer information. Discuss compliance with specific legal standards, such as the Health Insurance Portability and Accountability Act (HIPAA) for medical information and the Payment Card Industry Data Security Standard (PCI DSS) for payment data.

Consumer Protection in the Online Environment

- **Truthful Online Advertising**: Examine legal standards for advertising and marketing online, ensuring that all promotional materials are honest, transparent, and non-deceptive to uphold consumer trust and comply with trade regulations.
- **Managing Returns and Refunds**: Explain the legal frameworks governing return and refund policies, which are vital for consumer rights and satisfaction. Detail how to formulate and communicate these policies clearly to customers to avoid disputes and ensure compliance with the law.

Emerging Legal Issues in Digital Commerce

- **Legal Aspects of Cryptocurrency and Blockchain**: Delve into the burgeoning area of cryptocurrency and blockchain, discussing the legal implications for online transactions, including issues of security, transparency, and regulatory compliance.

- **Artificial Intelligence in E-Commerce**: Consider the legal challenges associated with using artificial intelligence and machine learning in online business operations, such as automated decision-making processes, data usage, and potential biases, ensuring adherence to emerging regulations and ethical standards.

This section aims to equip you with a deep understanding of the legal issues unique to online businesses and provide actionable strategies to address these challenges. By adhering to these guidelines, you can operate your digital ventures confidently and compliantly, securing a competitive edge in the rapidly evolving online marketplace.

Navigating Regulatory Compliance

In the business world, adhering to regulatory compliance is not just about avoiding legal pitfalls; it's about demonstrating commitment to ethical practices and enhancing trust among stakeholders. This section focuses on the essential aspects of regulatory compliance, offering a detailed guide for entrepreneurs to understand, navigate, and effectively manage the regulations that impact their businesses. From understanding the basis of various compliance requirements to implementing strategies for maintaining ongoing compliance, this section will help you ensure that your business operations are both lawful and ethical.

Understanding the Scope of Regulatory Compliance

- **Comprehensive Overview**: Begin with an introduction to the regulatory landscape that affects different aspects of business operations, including finance, environment, health and safety, and industry-specific regulations.
- **Key Regulatory Bodies**: Identify and discuss the major regulatory agencies that govern business practices in your jurisdiction, such as the Securities and Exchange Commission (SEC), Environmental Protection Agency (EPA), and the Occupational Safety and Health Administration (OSHA), and what their mandates mean for your business.

Strategies for Ensuring Compliance

- **Risk Assessment**: Learn how to conduct thorough risk assessments to identify areas of your business that are most vulnerable to compliance issues. This proactive approach helps prioritize compliance efforts and allocate resources more effectively.
- **Compliance Programs**: Develop and implement comprehensive compliance programs tailored to your business's specific needs. This includes creating policies, procedures, and controls to guide operations and ensure adherence to applicable laws and regulations.
- **Training and Education**: Understand the importance of training your employees on compliance standards and procedures. Regular training ensures that staff are up-to-date on the latest regulatory requirements and understand their roles in maintaining compliance.

Monitoring and Auditing

- **Regular Audits**: Set up regular auditing schedules to review compliance practices and identify areas for improvement. Audits can be internal or involve third-party firms that specialize in regulatory compliance.
- **Continuous Monitoring**: Implement systems for continuous monitoring of compliance, using technology to streamline the process and provide real-time insights into potential issues before they become significant problems.

Dealing with Non-Compliance

- **Identifying Breaches**: Learn how to quickly identify and respond to compliance breaches. This includes establishing clear procedures for investigating potential violations and taking corrective actions.
- **Legal Consequences**: Understand the potential legal consequences of non-compliance, from fines and penalties to more severe repercussions like business closures or criminal charges.
- **Crisis Management**: Develop effective crisis management strategies to address compliance failures. This involves managing communications

with regulatory bodies, the public, and other stakeholders to mitigate damage and restore trust.

Staying Updated with Regulatory Changes

- **Keeping Informed**: Stay informed about changes in laws and regulations that affect your industry. This can be achieved through subscriptions to relevant legal and industry publications, memberships in professional organizations, and attending seminars and workshops.
- **Adapting to Changes**: Outline strategies for swiftly adapting business operations to meet new regulatory requirements, ensuring continuous compliance.

By mastering these aspects of regulatory compliance, you will not only protect your business from legal risks but also build a reputation for reliability and integrity. This section aims to transform regulatory compliance from a daunting obligation into a strategic asset that enhances operational efficiencies and boosts consumer and investor confidence.

Legal Risk Management and Prevention

Legal risks can derail even the most well-planned business strategies, making an effective legal risk management and prevention framework essential for safeguarding your business's future. This section delves deeply into identifying, assessing, managing, and mitigating the myriad legal risks that businesses face today. By instituting robust risk management practices, you can proactively address potential legal challenges, ensuring smooth operational continuity and compliance with all relevant laws and regulations.

Understanding Legal Risks

- **Types of Legal Risks**: Start by mapping out the various legal risks associated with running a business. These include contractual risks, compliance risks, employment law risks, intellectual property risks, and risks from potential litigation.
- **Risk Identification Process**: Introduce systematic processes for identifying risks, such as legal audits, stakeholder interviews, and the use

of technology to monitor compliance and operational activities. This foundational step is critical for developing a proactive risk management strategy.

Developing a Comprehensive Risk Management Plan

- **Strategy Formulation**: Develop a comprehensive legal risk management plan that outlines strategies for mitigating each identified risk. This plan should integrate with your overall business strategies and be adaptable to changing legal environments.
- **Policies and Procedures**: Create detailed policies and procedures that guide actions in specific risk scenarios. These should encompass areas like contract negotiation, regulatory compliance, intellectual property management, and employment practices.
- **Ongoing Review and Adaptation**: Emphasize the importance of regularly reviewing and updating the risk management plan to reflect new legal developments and business realities. This ensures that the plan remains effective over time.

Implementing Preventative Measures

- **Proactive Legal Audits**: Schedule regular legal audits to proactively examine and improve all areas of your business operations. These audits help identify vulnerabilities before they can evolve into serious legal issues.
- **Employee Training and Engagement**: Invest in comprehensive training programs to ensure that all employees understand their legal responsibilities and the importance of strict adherence to company policies and regulations. Engaged and well-informed employees are your first line of defense against legal risks.
- **Robust Documentation Practices**: Maintain meticulous documentation of all business activities. Proper record-keeping is crucial for compliance, provides invaluable evidence in legal disputes, and supports effective audit processes.

Early Detection and Issue Resolution

- **Systems for Early Detection**: Implement early detection systems that continuously monitor for signs of legal issues. These might include compliance tracking tools, regular reports from department heads, and feedback mechanisms for employees and customers.
- **Access to Legal Expertise**: Maintain relationships with legal professionals who specialize in relevant areas of law. Quick access to expert advice is vital for addressing potential issues swiftly and effectively.
- **Crisis Management Protocols**: Develop a clear, actionable crisis management plan that outlines procedures for dealing with legal emergencies. This plan should include detailed communication strategies, steps for damage control, and protocols for legal consultation and representation.

Enhancing Compliance and Reducing Exposure

- **Compliance Enhancements**: Strengthen your compliance frameworks to exceed minimum legal standards. This proactive approach not only reduces the risk of legal issues but also positions your business as a trustworthy and reliable entity.
- **Strategic Risk Transfer**: Explore options for transferring risk where possible, such as through insurance, outsourcing certain operations, or contractual indemnities.

By the conclusion of this section, you will have a robust toolkit for managing legal risks in a comprehensive, proactive manner. Implementing these strategies will protect your business from potential disruptions and liabilities, thereby enhancing its stability, compliance, and overall success in a complex legal landscape. This proactive approach to legal risk management will empower you to navigate challenges confidently, turning potential threats into opportunities for reinforcing your business's resilience and integrity.

Quick Tips and Recap

As we conclude this chapter on navigating the legal landscape for entrepreneurs, here are some succinct tips and a recap of key points to ensure your business remains compliant and legally sound:

- **Understand Your Business Structure**: Choose the appropriate business structure (e.g., LLC, S-Corp, Partnership) to optimize tax benefits, liability protection, and operational flexibility.
- **Protect Intellectual Property**: Secure and defend your intellectual property through patents, trademarks, copyrights, and trade secrets to maintain competitive advantage and brand integrity.
- **Draft Comprehensive Contracts**: Ensure all business agreements are clear, legally binding, and include essential clauses to avoid ambiguity and potential disputes.
- **Stay Compliant with Employment Laws**: Familiarize yourself with employment laws to manage hiring, workplace policies, employee rights, and termination processes legally and ethically.
- **Adapt to Online Business Regulations**: Understand and comply with e-commerce laws, digital copyright norms, privacy policies, and data protection requirements if your business operates online.
- **Implement Robust Risk Management**: Regularly assess and manage legal risks through audits, employee training, and effective policies to prevent legal issues before they arise.
- **Keep Documentation Thorough and Organized**: Maintain detailed records of all business operations and legal compliance to support audits and legal proceedings.
- **Monitor Regulatory Changes**: Stay updated on legal and regulatory changes affecting your industry to ensure continuous compliance and adapt your business practices accordingly.

- **Seek Legal Advice**: Consult with legal professionals to navigate complex legal issues, draft documents, and ensure that your business meets all regulatory requirements.
- **Develop a Crisis Management Plan**: Prepare for potential legal disputes with a solid crisis management plan that includes immediate steps, communication strategies, and contact information for legal support.

These tips are designed to help you build a legally resilient business that can not only withstand legal scrutiny but also thrive in a competitive business environment. Remember, legal preparedness is not just about risk avoidance; it's about creating a foundation that supports sustainable growth and success.

CHAPTER THREE

Economic Foundations: Assessing Your Business Viability

"Evaluating the economic viability of your business idea is the cornerstone of entrepreneurial success. It's not just about having capital; it's about knowing how, when, and where to allocate it to maximize your return." — WARREN BUFFETT, CEO OF BERKSHIRE HATHAWAY

Welcome to the economic boot camp for entrepreneurs, where we crunch more than just numbers—we crunch reality. Before you invest your life's savings or woo that investor with deep pockets, let's ensure your business isn't just a castle in the air. This chapter is your fiscal fitness test, designed to stretch your understanding of market demands, financial forecasting, and the all-important break-even analysis.

We'll dive into the exhilarating world of cash flow calculations, profit margins, and capital requirements. Think of it as your personal business health check-up. You wouldn't run a marathon without a medical, right? Well, launching a business without assessing its economic viability is like running blindfolded on a treadmill—lots of action, but going nowhere fast.

From exploring startup costs to predicting revenue streams, we'll equip you with the tools to gauge the financial pulse of your enterprise. By the end of this chapter, you'll not only know if your business idea holds water but also how deep and how far it can sail. So, tighten your seatbelt and put on your thinking cap; it's time to turn those dreams into financially viable realities.

Understanding Market Demand

Launching a successful business starts with a clear understanding of market demand. This essential first step involves conducting comprehensive market research to verify that there is a sustainable market for your product or service. By deeply understanding who your customers are, what they need, and how they behave, you can tailor your business to meet those needs effectively. This section guides you through detailed methodologies for assessing market demand, enabling you to build a business that is responsive to market dynamics and poised for success.

Introduction to Market Research

- **Purpose of Market Research**: Explain the significance of market research in verifying the feasibility of your business idea. Market research connects your business concept with the realities of the marketplace.
- **Types of Market Research**: Distinguish between primary and secondary research. Primary research involves collecting new data directly from sources such as potential customers, while secondary research involves analyzing existing data from reports, studies, and other publications.

Conducting Effective Market Research

- **Primary Research Methods**: Delve into methods like surveys, focus groups, and one-on-one interviews. These techniques allow you to gather firsthand insights into customer needs, preferences, and purchase behaviors. Learn how to design effective surveys, select focus group participants, and conduct meaningful interviews.
- **Secondary Research Utilization**: Explore how to leverage existing data from industry reports, market analysis studies, and competitive analyses. This form of research helps you understand broader market trends, the competitive landscape, and potential market segments.

Analyzing Industry Trends

- **Identifying Trends**: Teach how to spot and interpret trends that could impact your business, both currently and in the future. This involves analyzing industry reports and market data to extract relevant trends.
- **Adapting to Market Changes**: Offer strategies for adapting your business model to capitalize on these trends, ensuring long-term relevance and competitiveness in a shifting market.

Defining and Understanding Your Target Market

- **Market Segmentation**: Guide through the process of dividing a market into clear segments based on various factors, including demographics, psychographics, and behavior. Effective segmentation is key to targeting the right customers.
- **Developing Customer Personas**: Illustrate how to create detailed customer personas based on segmentation. These personas help in visualizing the ideal customer, making it easier to tailor marketing and product development strategies to meet specific needs.

Testing and Validating Market Demand

- **Market Testing Techniques**: Introduce methods such as creating a minimum viable product (MVP), running pilot tests, or launching beta versions to test how your target market responds to your product or service.

- **Feedback Collection and Iteration**: Stress the importance of collecting feedback from these initial offerings and using it to refine your product or service. This iterative process is crucial for making adjustments based on actual customer needs and behaviors.

Using Data to Make Informed Decisions

- **Data Analysis and Decision Making**: Discuss how to analyze the data collected through various research methods and use this information to make informed strategic decisions. This includes deciding whether to proceed with a business launch, pivot the business model, or even abandon the business idea based on the strength of market demand.

By the end of this section, you will possess a thorough understanding of how to assess market demand effectively. This knowledge enables you to launch your business with confidence, equipped with evidence-based strategies that align with real-world market needs and customer expectations. This solid foundation in market research not only minimizes the risk of business failure but also sets the stage for dynamic growth and adaptation in an ever-evolving marketplace.

Startup Costs and Capital Requirements

A comprehensive understanding of startup costs and capital requirements is essential for any entrepreneur looking to establish a new business. This section delves into the financial underpinnings necessary for launching a successful enterprise, offering a detailed exploration of various expenses and the avenues available for securing the necessary capital. By accurately calculating and effectively managing your startup costs, you can lay a robust financial foundation that supports sustainable business operations and growth.

Detailed Analysis of Startup Costs

- **Comprehensive Cost Breakdown**: Begin with a thorough identification of all potential startup expenses. These may include but are not limited to costs associated with legal fees, licensing, equipment and technology purchases, initial inventory, facility leases, marketing and advertising expenses, and salaries or wages during the startup phase.

- **Fixed versus Variable Costs**: Differentiate between fixed costs, which remain constant regardless of business activity (e.g., rent, salaries, utility bills), and variable costs, which fluctuate with the level of business activity (e.g., raw materials, shipping costs). Understanding these differences is crucial for precise budgeting and financial forecasting.
- **One-time versus Recurring Expenses**: Distinguish between one-time expenses, such as purchasing major equipment or paying for initial setup fees, and ongoing operational expenses like monthly utilities, rent, and payroll. This distinction helps in projecting cash flow and planning for financial sustainability.

Estimating Total Capital Requirements

- **Initial Cost Calculation**: Provide guidance on how to calculate total startup costs by aggregating all identified expenses. This figure represents the initial capital required to launch the business effectively.
- **Future Cash Flow Projections**: Discuss the importance of projecting future cash flows by estimating expected revenues and comparing them against anticipated ongoing expenses. This exercise helps in determining when the business may require additional funding to support operations or expansion.

Exploring Funding Options

- **Personal Savings**: Analyze the advantages and potential risks associated with using personal savings for business funding. While this method can simplify the startup process by avoiding debt, it also risks personal financial security.
- **Debt Financing**: Explore traditional debt financing options such as bank loans, lines of credit, and Small Business Administration (SBA) loans. Offer insights into the criteria required for securing these funds, including a solid business plan, a good credit score, and sometimes collateral.

- **Equity Financing**: Introduce equity financing options through angel investors and venture capitalists. Detail the process of attracting these investors, including crafting compelling pitches and understanding the trade-offs related to equity dilution and investor expectations.
- **Alternative Funding Sources**: Cover innovative funding methods like crowdfunding, grants, and participation in startup incubators and accelerators. Each of these options can offer unique advantages and challenges, depending on the business model and specific funding needs.

Strategies for Effective Financial Management

- **Budgeting**: Instruct on how to create a detailed budget that encompasses all startup and operational expenses. A well-structured budget is critical for monitoring financial performance and ensuring fiscal responsibility.
- **Expense Tracking and Control**: Highlight the importance of continuously monitoring expenses and comparing actual spending against budgeted projections. This vigilance helps in identifying potential overspending areas and opportunities for cost savings, ensuring the business remains on a financially viable path.

By the end of this section, you will not only understand how to identify and calculate the costs associated with starting and running your business but also how to secure and manage the capital needed to finance these activities. Armed with this knowledge, entrepreneurs can confidently navigate the financial aspects of business setup and operations, enhancing their prospects for long-term success and stability in the marketplace.

Revenue Streams and Profitability

For any business, the creation and management of revenue streams are vital to achieving and sustaining profitability. This section delves into the complexities of identifying potential revenue streams, formulating effective pricing strategies, and optimizing profitability, providing a comprehensive guide for entrepreneurs to secure the financial health of their ventures.

Exploring Revenue Stream Opportunities

- **Diversity in Revenue Models**: Begin with an overview of the necessity of diversifying income sources. Discuss the various revenue models available to businesses, including direct sales, subscription models, licensing, franchising, and advertising-based revenue. Each model comes with unique advantages and challenges, which should align with your business objectives and market dynamics.
- **Innovative Revenue Strategies**: Explore innovative revenue generation methods that may not be traditional but offer significant growth potential, such as offering freemium products, participating in affiliate marketing programs, or utilizing data monetization strategies. These modern approaches can provide competitive advantages and new customer acquisition channels.

Developing a Comprehensive Pricing Strategy

- **Key Pricing Factors**: Examine the critical factors that influence pricing decisions, including production and operational costs, competitive landscape, customer demand, and market conditions. This understanding is crucial for setting prices that not only cover costs but also appeal to your target market.
- **Advanced Pricing Techniques**: Detail a range of pricing techniques such as cost-plus pricing, value-based pricing, psychological pricing, penetration pricing, and dynamic pricing. Highlight the advantages and pitfalls of each, providing scenarios where each technique might be most effective.
- **Psychological Influences on Pricing**: Introduce psychological pricing strategies that can influence customer perception and encourage purchase decisions, such as charm pricing ($9.99 vs. $10.00) or using high-priced items to enhance the attractiveness of lower-priced options.

Maximizing Profitability

- **Profit Margin Analysis**: Educate on calculating and interpreting various profit margins—gross, operating, and net margins—each offering insights into different aspects of business efficiency and financial health. This analysis helps pinpoint areas for cost optimization and operational improvements.

- **Cost Reduction Techniques**: Offer strategies for reducing costs without compromising quality or customer satisfaction. Discuss optimizing supply chain management, utilizing technology for automation, and renegotiating supplier contracts as ways to lower expenses and thereby enhance profitability.
- **Revenue Enhancement Methods**: Explore techniques to increase revenue, such as upselling and cross-selling, refining marketing strategies, expanding into new markets, and improving customer loyalty and retention rates. These methods can significantly boost the average revenue per customer and expand the overall market base.

Financial Forecasting and Goal Setting

- **Projecting Future Performance**: Guide on using historical data, market analysis, and forecasting techniques to project future financial performance. Effective forecasting can aid in setting realistic, measurable financial goals and preparing for future market fluctuations.
- **Setting and Adjusting Financial Goals**: Discuss the importance of establishing clear, achievable financial targets based on thorough analysis and market forecasts. Emphasize the need for flexibility in goal setting, allowing for adjustments as market and business conditions evolve.

By thoroughly exploring these elements, this section equips you with the necessary knowledge and tools to effectively manage and optimize your revenue streams and pricing strategies. Understanding these financial components allows you to position your business for profitable growth, ensuring you have the financial resources necessary to achieve long-term success in a competitive marketplace.

Cash Flow Analysis

Effective cash flow management is critical for the survival and growth of any business. It provides a detailed snapshot of the financial health of your enterprise, indicating whether the business is generating enough cash to meet its obligations and invest in growth opportunities. This section offers an exhaustive guide to understanding, tracking, and optimizing cash flow, ensuring that you can sustain operations and make informed financial decisions.

Fundamentals of Cash Flow

- **Definition and Importance**: Define cash flow as the net amount of cash being transferred into and out of a business. Highlight its importance in measuring the liquidity, flexibility, and overall financial performance of your enterprise.
- **Components of Cash Flow**: Break down the components of cash flow into three categories: operational cash flow (cash generated from primary business activities), investment cash flow (cash used for and from investments in assets), and financing cash flow (cash exchanged between the company and its owners, creditors).

Constructing a Cash Flow Statement

- **Step-by-Step Construction**: Provide a detailed guide on how to compile a cash flow statement. This involves documenting all cash inflows from sales or services, investments, and financing activities, as well as all cash outflows that include business expenses, asset purchases, and repayments of debt.
- **Utilization of Accounting Software**: Recommend various accounting tools and software solutions that can streamline the creation and ongoing management of cash flow statements, enhancing accuracy and efficiency.

Analyzing Cash Flow Data

- **Trend Identification**: Teach how to analyze the data from cash flow statements to identify trends, patterns, and anomalies. This analysis helps predict future cash flow scenarios based on historical data and current business activities.

- **Financial Ratios and Metrics**: Discuss crucial cash flow ratios and metrics such as the operating cash flow ratio, free cash flow, and net cash flow. Explain how these indicators can provide deeper insights into the business's operational efficiency and financial stability.

Enhancing Cash Flow Management

- **Optimizing Inflows**: Explore strategies to enhance cash inflows, including tightening credit terms, offering early payment discounts to customers, and enhancing revenue streams through upselling or cross-selling.
- **Controlling Outflows**: Provide techniques for managing and minimizing cash outflows. Suggestions might include optimizing inventory management, renegotiating terms with suppliers and creditors, and prioritizing expenditures.
- **Future Cash Planning**: Emphasize the importance of forecasting future cash flows. This involves projecting future inflows and outflows based on business forecasts, seasonal trends, and economic conditions, allowing for strategic business planning and investment.

Navigating Cash Flow Challenges

- **Identifying Common Pitfalls**: Highlight common cash flow management challenges such as overexpansion, high overhead costs, or poor debtor management. Discuss how these can be mitigated or avoided to maintain a healthy cash flow.
- **Addressing Cash Shortages**: Offer solutions for managing periods of cash shortfall, including arranging for lines of credit, optimizing payment cycles, or liquidating non-essential assets.
- **Emergency Preparedness**: Discuss the importance of maintaining a cash reserve or emergency fund to manage unexpected financial disruptions without compromising the operational capabilities of the business.

By the end of this section, you will have a robust understanding of how to manage cash flow effectively within your business. You will be equipped with the skills to not only maintain adequate liquidity but also to use cash flow analysis as a strategic tool for financial planning and business development. This knowledge ensures that you can navigate the ebbs and flows of business finance, keeping your enterprise resilient in the face of financial challenges and poised for future growth.

Break-even Analysis

Break-even analysis is an essential financial tool that enables entrepreneurs to determine when their business will start to make a profit, effectively balancing expenses with revenues. This crucial analysis helps in making informed decisions about pricing, scaling, and managing business operations. In this section, we delve deeper into the process and significance of conducting a thorough break-even analysis, equipping you with the necessary skills to evaluate the financial viability of your business endeavors.

Introduction to Break-even Analysis

- **Concept and Significance**: Define break-even analysis as the method to calculate the point at which total revenues equal total costs, resulting in neither profit nor loss. It is vital for validating the economic feasibility of business models, setting financial targets, and strategizing business operations.
- **Value to Entrepreneurs**: Emphasize its utility in assessing how many units of a product or service need to be sold to cover costs, aiding in both short-term financial management and long-term business planning.

Steps to Conduct a Break-even Analysis

- **Identifying Costs**: Begin with identifying all costs associated with the business. Distinguish between fixed costs (unchanging with output levels, such as rent, salaries, and administrative expenses) and variable costs (fluctuate with production volume, such as materials and direct labor).

- **Determining Sales Price and Contribution Margin**: Calculate the selling price per unit of your product or service and subtract the variable cost per unit to find the contribution margin per unit. This figure represents the portion of each sale that contributes to covering fixed costs and generating profit.
- **Calculating the Break-even Point**: Breakeven Point (in units)=Total Fixed CostsContribution Margin per UnitBreakeven Point (in units)=Contribution Margin per UnitTotal Fixed Costs. This formula will yield the number of units that must be sold to reach the break-even point, allowing you to gauge the sales volume needed to begin achieving profitability.

Strategic Uses of Break-even Analysis

- **Pricing Decisions**: Utilize break-even analysis to inform pricing strategies. Understand how altering the price per unit affects the break-even volume, helping to balance competitive pricing with profitable margins.
- **Financial Forecasting and Budgeting**: Incorporate break-even points into financial projections and budgets to better manage cash flows and financial resources, ensuring that the business remains on a stable financial footing.
- **Risk Evaluation and Management**: Assess the financial risk of new and existing business ventures by understanding how variations in market conditions, costs, or pricing could impact the break-even point.

Challenges in Applying Break-even Analysis

- **Sensitivity to Market Changes**: Acknowledge that break-even analysis is sensitive to changes in market conditions, such as fluctuations in consumer demand or variations in material costs. Regular updates and revisions are necessary to keep the analysis relevant.
- **Managing Fixed Costs**: Discuss the importance of managing fixed costs as a strategy to lower the break-even point, thereby reducing the volume of sales needed to start generating profits.

- **Dynamic Business Environments**: Consider the complexities of applying break-even analysis in dynamic business environments where product mixes, market strategies, and competitive landscapes are constantly evolving.

Enhancing Break-even Analysis with Real-world Examples

- **Case Studies**: Provide detailed case studies illustrating how real businesses have successfully used break-even analysis to make strategic decisions in product launches, pricing adjustments, and during economic downturns.
- **Practical Tips**: Offer practical tips for effectively applying break-even analysis, including how to gather accurate cost data, predict realistic sales volumes, and adjust assumptions based on market feedback.

By the end of this section, you will not only understand how to perform a break-even analysis but also appreciate its critical role in strategic financial planning and risk management. This knowledge will empower you to make informed decisions that enhance the financial stability and profitability of your business, supporting sustainable growth in competitive markets.

Financial Forecasting

Financial forecasting is an indispensable tool for navigating the uncertainties of business, providing insights into future financial conditions and helping to shape strategic decisions. In this section, we explore the intricacies of creating detailed financial forecasts that encompass revenue, expenses, and profitability assessments. By developing a robust forecasting model, you can prepare your business to meet future challenges and capitalize on potential opportunities.

Essentials of Financial Forecasting

- **Definition and Strategic Value**: Define financial forecasting as the practice of predicting a business's future financial outcomes by analyzing historical data and current market trends. Highlight its critical role in guiding strategic planning, optimizing resource allocation, and enhancing investor confidence.

- **Core Elements of a Financial Forecast**: Detail the key components of a financial forecast, including income projections, balance sheet forecasts, cash flow estimates, and planned capital expenditures. Each component plays a vital role in painting a comprehensive picture of the business's financial future.

Developing a Financial Forecast

- **Gathering Historical Data**: Emphasize the importance of accurate historical data as the foundation of any reliable forecast. This includes sales figures, operational costs, cash flows, and other financial statements.
- **Incorporating Market Analysis**: Discuss how external factors such as economic indicators, industry trends, and competitive dynamics should influence the forecasting process. This broader market analysis helps adjust projections to reflect potential market shifts.
- **Projecting Revenues and Expenses**: Provide methodologies for estimating future revenues by analyzing sales trends, market potential, and pricing strategies. Similarly, outline approaches for forecasting expenses, considering both fixed and variable costs and anticipating changes due to strategic decisions or market conditions.

Technological Tools and Methods

- **Forecasting Software and Applications**: Introduce advanced software and tools that facilitate financial forecasting. These technologies can help automate data analysis, improve accuracy, and save time.
- **Scenario Planning and Sensitivity Analysis**: Advocate for the use of scenario planning and sensitivity analysis to explore different financial outcomes based on varying assumptions. This approach allows businesses to prepare for best-case, worst-case, and most likely scenarios, enhancing strategic flexibility.

Refining and Utilizing Financial Forecasts

- **Iterative Refinement**: Stress the need for continuously updating forecasts as new financial data becomes available and as the business environment evolves. Regular updates ensure that forecasts remain relevant and reliable.

- **Feedback Mechanisms**: Set up systems to regularly compare forecasted results with actual performance. This feedback loop is crucial for understanding discrepancies and refining future forecasts.
- **Strategic Decision-Making**: Illustrate how well-crafted financial forecasts can inform critical business decisions, from expanding operations and entering new markets to adjusting pricing strategies and managing inventory levels.

Risk Management and Decision Support

- **Identifying Financial Risks**: Use financial forecasts to identify potential financial risks and vulnerabilities. This proactive risk assessment helps in devising effective mitigation strategies.
- **Supporting Funding and Investment Decisions**: Explain how credible financial forecasts can support funding initiatives, providing potential investors and lenders with clear evidence of the business's future profitability and growth prospects.

Avoiding Common Forecasting Errors

- **Guarding Against Bias**: Warn against common biases like overoptimism in sales projections or underestimation of potential costs, which can distort the financial outlook.
- **Flexibility in Forecasting**: Encourage maintaining flexibility in forecasts to accommodate unexpected changes in the business landscape, ensuring that your business can adapt quickly to new challenges and opportunities.

By mastering financial forecasting, entrepreneurs can ensure that their business decisions are grounded in a thorough understanding of potential future financial landscapes. This section equips you with the knowledge to develop, refine, and implement effective financial forecasts, turning them into a strategic asset for your business.

Risk Assessment and Mitigation

Risk management is a crucial pillar in the architecture of any successful business, safeguarding its assets, reputation, and operational capabilities. This section delves into the detailed processes of identifying, evaluating, and managing various risks that could potentially disrupt business activities. By cultivating a robust risk management framework, entrepreneurs can not only protect their ventures from potential setbacks but also position them for sustained growth and stability.

Foundations of Risk Management

- **Defining Risk Management**: Introduce risk management as the systematic process of identifying, assessing, and responding to risks in a way that aligns with business objectives and minimizes losses. Emphasize its critical role in ensuring business continuity and financial health.
- **Categories of Business Risks**: Elaborate on different types of risks that businesses face, including strategic risks (related to business strategy and model), compliance risks (related to legal and regulatory obligations), financial risks (related to the company's financial structure and transactions), operational risks (related to operational and administrative procedures), and environmental risks (related to the physical environment).

Identifying and Analyzing Risks

- **Risk Identification Techniques**: Outline practical methods for risk identification, such as SWOT analysis (Strengths, Weaknesses, Opportunities, Threats), scenario planning, and stakeholder interviews. Stress the importance of a comprehensive approach that considers both internal operations and external market dynamics.
- **Risk Analysis Methods**: Discuss how to evaluate the identified risks by considering their likelihood and potential impact. Introduce quantitative techniques like probabilistic modeling and qualitative approaches such as expert judgment to assess risks.

Strategizing Risk Mitigation

- **Prioritizing Risks**: Guide on how to prioritize risks based on their severity and the business's ability to respond. This prioritization helps in allocating resources efficiently and effectively.
- **Mitigation Strategies**: Develop specific strategies for each major risk, which might include risk avoidance, reduction, transfer (through insurance or outsourcing), or acceptance (for minor risks). Provide examples of how each strategy can be applied in different business contexts.

Implementation of Risk Controls

- **Control Solutions**: Implement suitable control measures tailored to the specific nature of prioritized risks. This might involve physical controls (security measures, safety systems), procedural controls (audits, checks, training programs), and technological controls (data encryption, cybersecurity measures).
- **Monitoring and Continuous Improvement**: Establish ongoing monitoring mechanisms to ensure the effectiveness of risk controls and make adjustments as necessary. Highlight the importance of a dynamic risk management process that evolves with the business and its environment.

Integrating Risk Management into Corporate Strategy

- **Strategic Integration**: Stress the necessity of integrating risk management into the overall corporate strategy to ensure that it supports business objectives and does not operate in isolation.
- **Building a Risk-Aware Culture**: Advocate for the development of a risk-aware culture within the organization, where employees at all levels understand the importance of risk management and are encouraged to participate actively in identifying and managing risks.

Technological Advancements in Risk Management

- **Utilizing Technology**: Introduce advanced technologies that can aid in risk management, such as big data analytics, artificial intelligence, and automated monitoring systems. These technologies can provide deeper insights, predict potential risks more accurately, and enhance the speed and effectiveness of the risk management process.

Case Studies and Real-World Applications

- **Practical Examples**: Conclude with case studies that demonstrate successful risk management strategies implemented by other businesses. These real-world examples can provide valuable lessons and actionable insights for entrepreneurs.

By the end of this section, entrepreneurs will have a thorough understanding of how to implement and maintain an effective risk management framework. This knowledge empowers business owners to not only protect their enterprises from potential threats but also to enhance decision-making processes and strategic planning, contributing to the long-term success and resilience of their business.

Quick Tips and Recap

As we wrap up this chapter on assessing the economic foundations of your business, here are some key takeaways and quick tips to help ensure your business's viability and financial health:

- **Understand Market Demand**: Ensure there is a strong demand for your product or service before moving forward. Use both primary and secondary market research to validate your business concept.
- **Calculate Startup Costs**: Clearly identify and categorize your startup costs, including both one-time and ongoing expenses. Understand how these costs impact your initial capital requirements.
- **Diversify Revenue Streams**: Explore multiple revenue models to find the best fit for your business. Diversification can help stabilize income and reduce financial risk.

- **Set Realistic Pricing**: Develop a pricing strategy that covers costs and aligns with market expectations. Use break-even analysis to inform your pricing decisions.
- **Manage Cash Flow Effectively**: Regularly monitor your cash inflows and outflows. A positive cash flow is crucial for sustaining business operations.
- **Perform Break-even Analysis**: Know how many units you need to sell to cover your costs. This analysis is essential for understanding the financial feasibility of your business.
- **Forecast Financially**: Use historical data and market analysis to forecast future financial performance. Accurate financial forecasting aids in strategic planning and risk management.
- **Assess and Mitigate Risks**: Continuously identify and assess potential risks. Develop strategies to mitigate significant risks to ensure business stability.
- **Stay Informed and Flexible**: Keep abreast of market and economic changes that can affect your business. Flexibility in your business model and financial planning can help you adapt quickly to changing circumstances.
- **Seek Expert Advice**: Don't hesitate to consult with financial experts. Professional advice can help you avoid common pitfalls and make informed financial decisions.

By incorporating these practices into your business planning and operations, you can build a financially sound enterprise that is well-equipped to navigate the challenges of the market and capitalize on opportunities for growth and success.

CHAPTER FOUR

Organizational Architecture: Structuring for Success

"Good business structure is not just about the hierarchy; it's about creating an environment where every piece and every person knows exactly where they fit in the puzzle of success." — JACK WELCH, FORMER CEO OF GENERAL ELECTRIC

Welcome to the drafting table where we architect your business's backbone! This isn't just about who sits where or who reports to whom. It's about designing an organizational structure that supports your business goals like steel beams in a skyscraper. Whether you're a solopreneur or planning to be the next Google, how you organize your team can make or break your enterprise.

In this chapter, we'll map out the blueprints of successful organizational structures—from flat and agile to hierarchical and robust. You'll learn how to align your business structure with your strategic objectives, ensuring that every team member not only knows their role but thrives in it. We'll cover the nuts and bolts of roles and responsibilities, departmental divisions, and how to build a flow of communication that doesn't bottleneck at the top.

Think of this as playing Tetris with human resources: every piece must fit perfectly to create a seamless line of efficiency and productivity. By the end of this chapter, you'll have a solid framework on which to build your business empire, one block at a time. Get ready to turn those organizational charts from a tangled mess into a masterclass in business engineering!

Foundations of Organizational Structure

The organizational structure of a business is a critical framework that defines how activities such as task allocation, coordination, and supervision are directed toward the achievement of organizational goals. This section delves into the foundational concepts of organizational structure, exploring various forms and their implications for business efficiency and effectiveness. By understanding these principles, businesses can establish a structure that supports their strategic objectives, fosters effective communication, and enhances overall performance.

Introduction to Organizational Structure

- **Definition and Importance**: Define organizational structure as the system that outlines how certain activities are directed to achieve the goals of an organization. These activities include roles, responsibilities, and authority which are crucial for decision-making processes. Emphasize why a thoughtfully designed structure is essential for maintaining clarity in reporting relationships, optimizing workflows, and enhancing operational efficiency.
- **Key Elements of Organizational Structure**: Describe the fundamental elements that constitute an organizational structure:
    - **Work Specialization**: The degree to which organizational tasks are divided into separate jobs. Each segment of a job is completed by an individual or a department specializing in that segment.

- **Departmentalization**: The basis on which jobs are grouped together to form departments. Common forms include functional, product, geographic, and customer departmentalization.
- **Chain of Command**: A control mechanism dedicated to making sure the right people are in the right jobs and tasks are carried out correctly. It includes the concepts of authority, responsibility, and accountability.
- **Span of Control**: The number of subordinates a manager can efficiently and effectively direct. Wider spans of control reduce the levels of hierarchy.
- **Centralization and Decentralization**: The degree to which decision-making is concentrated at a single point in the organization. Centralization refers to decision authority being located near the top, while decentralization involves delegating authority to lower levels.
- **Formalization**: The extent to which jobs within the organization are standardized and the activities of employees are governed by rules and procedures.

Exploring Types of Organizational Structures

- **Functional Structure**: Detail how this structure groups people with similar occupational specialties together into departments. Discuss advantages such as efficiencies from grouping similar specialties and skills together, and disadvantages like the potential for creating silos within an organization.
- **Divisional Structure**: Describe how this structure consists of separate business units or divisions. Each division has its resources and functions and operates semi-autonomously. Outline benefits such as flexibility and clearer performance assessments, and drawbacks such as duplication of resources and efforts across divisions.

- **Matrix Structure**: Explain this hybrid structure that combines two structures, typically functional and divisional, to leverage the benefits of both. Discuss how it facilitates resource sharing and functional expertise but can also lead to conflicts due to dual reporting lines.
- **Flatarchy Structure**: Introduce this less hierarchical structure commonly found in startups and smaller companies, which eliminates many middle management levels to flatten the managerial hierarchy. Highlight how it promotes faster decision-making and increased flexibility, but may lead to management challenges as the organization grows.

Selecting an Appropriate Structure

- **Alignment with Business Goals**: Emphasize the importance of aligning the organizational structure with the business's strategic goals to promote efficiency and effectiveness. For instance, a tech startup might benefit from a flat structure to foster innovation, whereas a multinational corporation might require a matrix structure to manage its diverse product lines and regional units efficiently.
- **Consideration for Adaptability**: Stress the need for structures to be adaptable to accommodate growth and changes in the external business environment. Suggest regular reviews of the organizational structure to ensure it continues to meet the needs of the business.

This foundational overview equips business leaders with the insights needed to critically assess and choose an organizational structure that not only meets the current needs of their business but also supports its future growth and success. By carefully considering these elements, businesses can craft a structure that optimizes operations, supports clear communication, and enhances strategic execution.

Aligning Structure with Strategy

Aligning your organizational structure with your business strategy is essential for operational success and achieving strategic objectives. This section examines how to design an organizational structure that supports and enhances your strategic goals, ensuring that the company's operational framework facilitates rather than hinders its ambitions. By thoughtfully aligning structure with strategy, businesses can improve efficiency, enhance adaptability, and better position themselves for sustainable growth.

Understanding the Interplay Between Strategy and Structure

- **Strategic Foundations**: Start by defining what constitutes a business strategy—these are the plans and decisions that guide a company towards its long-term goals. Discuss how a clear and focused strategy provides the blueprint for organizational design, influencing the choice of structure that best supports achieving these goals.
- **Importance of Alignment**: Emphasize the critical importance of ensuring that the organizational structure is in sync with the business strategy. Alignment enhances efficiency, improves clarity in roles and responsibilities, and ensures that resources are allocated correctly to support strategic objectives.

Evaluating Strategic Needs

- **Identifying Strategic Objectives**: Outline the process for clearly defining the strategic objectives of the business. Whether focusing on growth, innovation, efficiency, or customer intimacy, each objective may necessitate a different organizational approach.
- **Operational Requirements Analysis**: Assess the key operational activities required to fulfill strategic objectives. This involves examining the current organization of tasks, the efficacy of information flows, and the effectiveness of decision-making processes within the company.

Selecting the Appropriate Organizational Structure

- **Functional Structure for Operational Efficiency**: Recommend a functional structure if the strategic focus is on enhancing operational efficiency through specialization and economies of scale. This structure is particularly advantageous for organizations looking to deepen expertise and streamline processes within specific domains.
- **Divisional Structure for Market Responsiveness**: Suggest adopting a divisional structure for companies focusing on diversification or geographic expansion. This setup supports local market responsiveness and can be tailored to fit varying consumer preferences and regional characteristics.
- **Matrix Structure for Dynamic Environments**: Propose a matrix structure for organizations that operate in highly dynamic and competitive industries where flexibility and rapid response are paramount. This dual-reporting structure can foster innovation and accelerate decision-making by blending functional and product-based characteristics.
- **Flat Structure for Innovation-Driven Firms**: Advocate for a flat or flatarchy structure for startups and SMEs where innovation and agility are crucial. This less hierarchical setup encourages faster decision-making and closer interactions between management and operational staff, fostering an entrepreneurial culture.

Implementing and Managing Structural Changes

- **Detailed Transition Planning**: Provide a detailed plan for transitioning from the current organizational structure to the chosen one. This plan should address key areas such as stakeholder engagement, timeline of implementation, and anticipated challenges.
- **Support and Training for Staff**: Highlight the importance of adequately preparing and supporting employees through structural changes. Training programs should be instituted to familiarize staff with their new roles and responsibilities, ensuring a smooth transition and continuity of operations.

Continual Evaluation and Adaptation

- **Ongoing Structural Review**: Set a protocol for the regular review of the organizational structure to ensure it remains aligned with any shifts in business strategy. This adaptability is crucial as external market conditions and internal business objectives evolve.
- **Feedback and Adjustment Mechanisms**: Implement robust feedback mechanisms that allow employees to express concerns and suggest improvements regarding the organizational structure. Such feedback is invaluable for making iterative adjustments and maintaining alignment with business goals.

By meticulously aligning organizational structure with strategic objectives, companies can create a coherent and efficient operation that is well-equipped to navigate the complexities of the business environment. This section provides the frameworks and tools necessary to achieve and maintain this alignment, thereby enhancing the company's capability to execute its strategy effectively and achieve its long-term goals.

Designing Roles and Responsibilities

Effective organizational performance hinges significantly on the clarity and precision of roles and responsibilities assigned to each team member. This section explores the intricacies of designing roles that align seamlessly with the organizational structure and strategic objectives, ensuring that each employee is positioned to contribute optimally to the company's success. By meticulously crafting and assigning roles, businesses can enhance operational efficiency, foster employee engagement, and support sustainable growth.

Core Principles of Role Design

- **Alignment with Strategic Objectives**: Begin by underscoring the importance of aligning individual roles with the broader strategic goals of the organization. Each role should be designed to directly support specific aspects of the business strategy, ensuring that every employee's efforts contribute to overarching objectives.

- **Clarity and Definition**: Emphasize the necessity for roles to be clearly defined to prevent overlap and ensure comprehensive coverage of all necessary tasks. Responsibilities should be articulated clearly and distinctly to avoid ambiguities that can lead to inefficiencies or conflicts.

Systematic Approach to Defining Roles and Responsibilities

- **Role Identification**: Outline the process for identifying essential roles within the organization, guided by the chosen organizational structure. Whether operating within a functional, divisional, matrix, or flat structure, understanding the structure's demands is crucial for determining the required roles.
- **Job Analysis**: Detail the job analysis process, which involves collecting information about the tasks associated with each role, the conditions under which the job is performed, and the necessary qualifications. This thorough analysis is foundational in crafting roles that are both effective and efficient.
- **Crafting Job Descriptions**: Translate job analysis data into precise job descriptions. These should include the job title, purpose, list of key duties, responsibilities, working conditions, and performance evaluation standards.
- **Differentiating Roles**: Ensure that roles are distinctly differentiated to avoid redundancy and confusion. This differentiation is critical in defining clear lines of authority and responsibility, which are essential for smooth operations and accountability.

Integrating Roles within the Organizational Framework

- **Departmental Integration**: Align roles within departments to ensure that the organizational structure facilitates efficient workflows and effective communication. Each department should be structured to support both the vertical (hierarchical) and horizontal (collaborative) dynamics of the organization.
- **Encouraging Cross-Functional Collaboration**: In structures that benefit from cross-functional teams, such as matrix or flat structures,

design roles to foster collaboration across different functional areas. Specify collaboration points and communication protocols to enhance interdisciplinary teamwork and innovation.

Adapting Roles to Organizational Dynamics

- **Incorporating Flexibility**: Design roles with an inherent flexibility to accommodate future changes in the business environment or strategic direction. This adaptability allows the organization to respond swiftly to new challenges or opportunities without the need for extensive restructuring.
- **Ongoing Role Evaluation**: Implement mechanisms for continuous evaluation of role effectiveness against performance metrics and strategic alignment. Adjust and refine roles based on feedback and changing organizational needs.

Empowering Employees within Their Roles

- **Autonomy and Empowerment**: Wherever feasible, provide employees with autonomy in their roles. This empowerment, when coupled with clear responsibilities, can significantly enhance job satisfaction, motivation, and productivity.
- **Professional Development**: Embed opportunities for professional growth and skill advancement within roles. This focus on development helps maintain a skilled and adaptable workforce, ready to meet the evolving demands of the business and industry.

By ensuring that roles and responsibilities are meticulously designed, clearly communicated, and regularly evaluated, organizations can create a work environment that is both productive and fulfilling for employees. This strategic approach to role design not only supports operational efficiency but also enhances employee alignment with the company's goals, driving collective success.

Creating Departmental Divisions

The strategic organization of a company into well-defined departments is pivotal for enhancing operational efficiency, fostering specialized expertise, and aligning with overarching business goals. This section delves into the intricacies of departmentalization, outlining how to structure divisions effectively to support communication flows, streamline operations, and promote scalability within the organizational framework.

Understanding Departmentalization

- **Significance of Departmental Divisions**: Begin with an overview of the critical role that departmental divisions play in an organization. These divisions help in segregating functions, concentrating expertise, and improving resource management, which collectively enhances organizational efficiency and responsiveness.
- **Goals of Departmentalization**: Explain that the primary goals of creating departments are to foster specialization, enhance coordination within and across functions, and build a structure that can dynamically scale with the business's growth and evolving market demands.

Approaches to Departmentalization

- **Functional Departmentalization**: Describe organizing departments by common functions or practices, such as Human Resources, Finance, Marketing, and Production. This approach benefits organizations by cultivating depth in specialized areas, leading to proficiency and operational efficiency.
- **Product-based Departmentalization**: Discuss the structuring of departments around specific products or product lines, suitable for companies with diverse or complex product portfolios. This method allows for focused strategy development, product management, and marketing efforts tailored to the specific needs of each product category.
- **Geographic Departmentalization**: Outline the advantages of organizing departments based on geographic regions, particularly effective for organizations operating in diverse locales with varying

cultural, economic, and regulatory environments. This structure supports localized management that is responsive to regional demands and opportunities.

- **Customer-based Departmentalization**: Explain the segmentation of departments to cater to specific customer groups or market segments. This form of departmentalization is advantageous for organizations with diverse customer bases, allowing for tailored strategies that address distinct customer needs and preferences.

Strategic Design of Departments

- **Assessment of Organizational Needs**: Emphasize the importance of thoroughly assessing the company's strategic objectives and operational needs to determine the most suitable departmental structure. This assessment should consider factors such as the size of the organization, the nature of its products or services, and its market environment.
- **Alignment with Business Objectives**: Ensure that the departmental structure aligns seamlessly with the organization's strategic goals. Each department should have defined roles that directly contribute to the company's broader objectives, ensuring that all efforts are coordinated and synergistic.
- **Selection of Departmental Leadership**: Discuss the critical role of department heads who must possess not only expertise in their specific areas but also strong leadership qualities to manage teams, inspire performance, and drive departmental and organizational success.

Integrating and Managing Departmental Divisions

- **Fostering Inter-departmental Collaboration**: Highlight strategies to encourage collaboration and communication between departments. Techniques might include cross-functional teams, integrated communication platforms, and corporate initiatives that require joint departmental input.
- **Continuous Evaluation and Adaptation**: Advocate for regular reviews of the departmental structure to gauge its effectiveness in meeting

organizational goals. Adjustments should be made as necessary to respond to internal shifts and external market changes, ensuring the structure remains optimal over time.

Addressing Common Challenges

- **Preventing Silos**: Tackle the issue of departmental silos, which can isolate departments and hinder organization-wide collaboration and efficiency. Recommend strategies such as setting overlapping goals, cross-departmental projects, and rotational job assignments to mitigate silo effects.
- **Balancing Autonomy and Oversight**: Offer insights on maintaining a balance between granting departments autonomy to innovate and implement strategies while ensuring they adhere to central organizational policies and goals.

Through thoughtful departmentalization, organizations can achieve a balance of specialization, efficiency, and adaptability, making them well-equipped to meet current demands and future challenges. This section provides a comprehensive guide for business leaders to design and implement effective departmental structures that align with strategic business goals and foster an integrated, collaborative corporate environment.

Optimizing Communication Flows

Effective communication is the lifeline of any organization, ensuring that information flows efficiently across various levels and departments. In this section, we explore strategies for designing and maintaining optimal communication flows within an organization. This involves structuring communication channels that promote clarity, foster collaboration, and enhance overall organizational responsiveness.

Importance of Efficient Communication

- **Overview and Benefits**: Begin with an overview of why effective communication is crucial for any organization. Efficient communication enhances collaboration, improves decision-making, fosters a positive corporate culture, and ultimately drives business success.

- **Challenges in Communication**: Address common communication challenges that organizations face, such as information silos, message distortion, and delays in communication flow, which can hinder responsiveness and operational efficiency.

Structuring Communication Channels

- **Vertical Communication**: Discuss the importance of vertical communication, which includes both downward communication from management to employees and upward communication from employees to management. Highlight how this ensures that directives and corporate policies are clearly communicated and that feedback and insights from employees reach the executive levels.
- **Horizontal Communication**: Explain the role of horizontal communication—communication that occurs between departments or among employees within the same department. Emphasize how this type of communication is essential for coordinating activities, sharing resources, and solving problems collaboratively.
- **Diagonal Communication**: Introduce diagonal communication, which occurs across different levels and departments, bypassing the traditional hierarchical routes. This can speed up problem-solving and innovation by connecting various parts of the organization directly.

Techniques to Enhance Communication

- **Open Communication Culture**: Advocate for the development of an open communication culture where employees feel valued and are encouraged to express ideas and concerns. This can be fostered through regular open-door policies, town hall meetings, and transparent leadership practices.
- **Use of Technology**: Highlight how modern communication tools such as instant messaging apps, collaboration platforms, and intranets can

facilitate more efficient and immediate communication across all levels of the organization.

- **Regular Updates and Meetings**: Discuss the importance of regular updates and scheduled meetings, which can help keep everyone aligned with the organization's goals and current on key projects and initiatives.

Monitoring and Improving Communication

- **Feedback Mechanisms**: Implement mechanisms for monitoring the effectiveness of communication strategies, such as feedback surveys and suggestion boxes. These tools can help identify areas where communication may be breaking down and require improvement.
- **Training and Development**: Emphasize the importance of ongoing training programs that teach effective communication skills, including active listening, clear writing, and presentation skills. These programs should be designed to enhance communication capabilities at all organizational levels.
- **Continuous Evaluation and Adaptation**: Recommend establishing a continuous evaluation process to assess the efficiency of communication channels and practices. This involves revisiting communication strategies regularly and making necessary adjustments to address new challenges or changes within the organization.

By meticulously planning and regularly evaluating communication strategies, organizations can ensure that information flows smoothly and efficiently across all levels and departments. This not only enhances day-to-day operations but also contributes to a more agile and responsive organizational structure, capable of adapting to changes and seizing opportunities in a dynamic business environment.

Implementing the Organizational Design

Once an organizational structure has been thoughtfully planned and designed, the next crucial step is implementation. This section delves into the practical aspects of rolling out a new organizational structure, detailing the strategies, tools, and considerations necessary to ensure a smooth transition and successful integration of the new design within the company.

Preparation for Implementation

- **Strategic Communication**: Start by discussing the importance of communicating the new organizational structure to all stakeholders effectively. This involves explaining the reasons behind the change, how it aligns with the company's goals, and what benefits it is expected to bring. Clear communication can help in managing resistance and garnering support.
- **Aligning Systems and Processes**: Outline the need to align existing systems and processes with the new structure. This may include updating software systems, modifying workflows, and revising operational processes to fit the new organizational framework.

Phased Roll-out

- **Pilot Testing**: Recommend starting with a pilot test of the new structure in a single department or for a small project. This allows the organization to identify potential issues and make necessary adjustments before a full-scale implementation.
- **Staged Implementation**: Discuss the benefits of a staged implementation, where the new structure is rolled out gradually across the organization. This phased approach can help manage the transition more effectively, allowing time for adjustments and minimizing disruptions to operations.

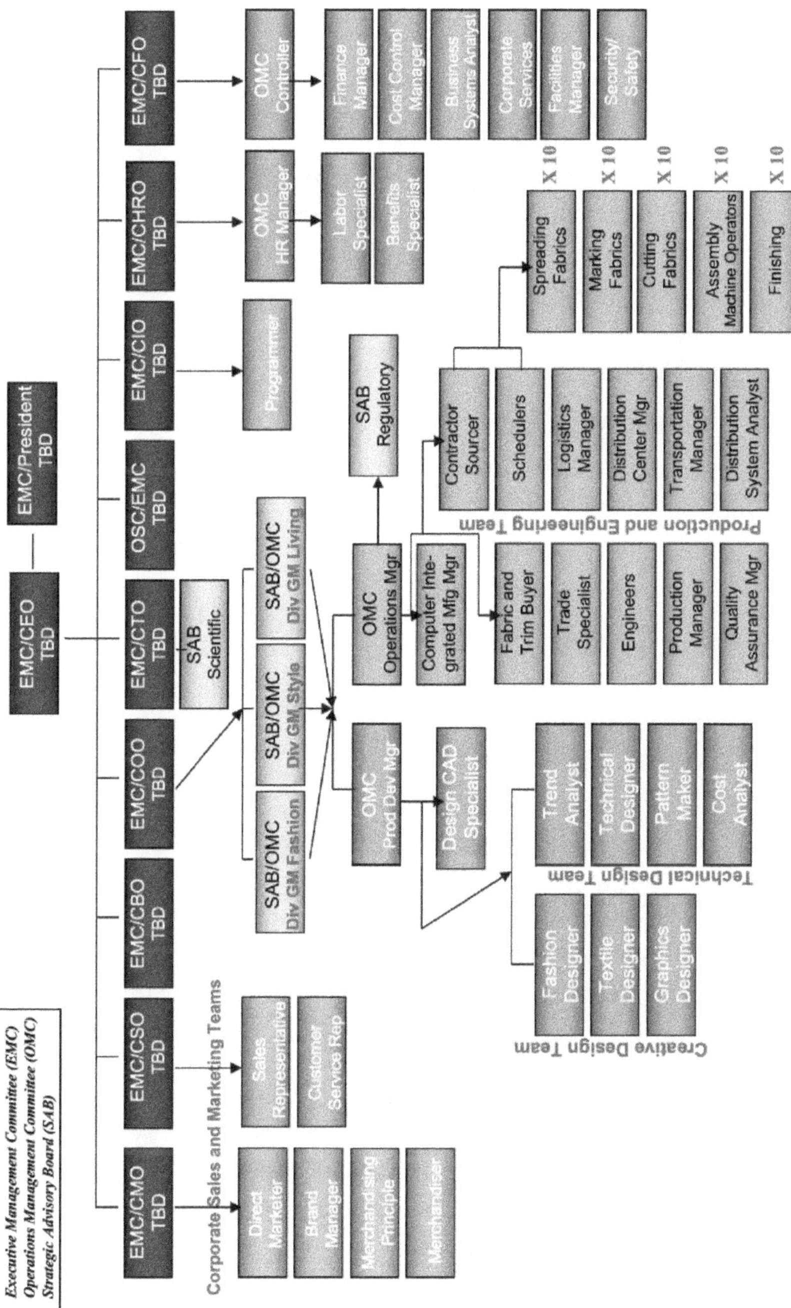

Figure 1: Sample Organization Chart

Managing Change

- **Change Management Framework**: Introduce a formal change management framework to guide the implementation process. This should include strategies for dealing with employee resistance, methods for effective change communication, and techniques for engaging employees throughout the transition.
- **Training and Support**: Highlight the critical role of training and ongoing support during the implementation phase. Provide comprehensive training to all employees to help them understand their new roles and responsibilities within the new structure. Ongoing support, such as help desks or dedicated change agents, can assist in addressing any questions or issues that arise during the transition.

Monitoring and Feedback

- **Real-time Monitoring**: Set up mechanisms to monitor the implementation in real-time. This allows the management team to track progress, assess the impact of changes, and quickly address any challenges or resistance that may surface.
- **Feedback Loops**: Establish robust feedback loops to gather input from employees at all levels. This feedback is invaluable for understanding how the changes are being perceived and for making necessary adjustments to the implementation plan.

Evaluating and Adjusting the New Structure

- **Evaluation Metrics**: Define clear metrics to evaluate the effectiveness of the new organizational structure. These could include performance metrics, employee satisfaction scores, and operational efficiency indicators.
- **Continuous Improvement**: Emphasize the need for continuous improvement. Based on the evaluation, make necessary adjustments to the organizational structure to better align with the company's strategic objectives and operational needs.

Legal and Ethical Considerations

- **Compliance Checks**: Ensure that the new organizational structure complies with all relevant laws and regulations. This includes labor laws, industry-specific regulations, and corporate governance standards.
- **Ethical Implications**: Consider the ethical implications of organizational changes, especially those that might affect employee job security, privacy, and workplace dynamics.

Implementing a new organizational structure is a complex and dynamic process that requires careful planning, effective communication, and rigorous management of change. By following a structured approach as outlined in this section, businesses can ensure that their new organizational design is not only successfully implemented but also capable of driving long-term success and adaptation in an evolving market landscape.

Evaluating and Evolving Organizational Structures

An organizational structure is not a static entity; it requires ongoing evaluation and adjustment to remain effective as the business evolves and external conditions change. This section focuses on the methodologies and best practices for continuously assessing the effectiveness of an organizational structure and making necessary adaptations to ensure it supports the organization's sustained success and strategic objectives.

Importance of Ongoing Evaluation

- **Adaptive Organization**: Stress the importance of an adaptive organizational structure that can respond to internal changes and external market dynamics. A flexible structure ensures that the organization remains competitive and relevant.
- **Alignment with Strategic Goals**: Emphasize that regular evaluations are crucial to ensure that the organizational structure continually aligns with the company's strategic goals. Misalignments can lead to inefficiencies, decreased employee satisfaction, and hindered growth.

Evaluation Techniques

- **Performance Metrics**: Introduce specific performance metrics used to evaluate the effectiveness of the organizational structure. These might include financial performance, employee productivity metrics, customer satisfaction ratings, and operational efficiency indicators.
- **Employee Feedback**: Discuss the value of gathering feedback from employees at all levels through surveys, interviews, and focus groups. Employee insights can provide a ground-level view of the structural impacts on day-to-day operations and job satisfaction.
- **External Assessments**: Recommend periodic external assessments by consultants or industry experts who can provide unbiased opinions on the efficiency and effectiveness of the organizational structure.

Adaptation Strategies

- **Incremental Adjustments**: Describe how making small, incremental adjustments to the organizational structure can help manage changes without causing major disruptions. This approach allows for continuous improvement and is less risky compared to large-scale restructurings.
- **Reorganization Initiatives**: Outline scenarios where more significant reorganization might be necessary, such as post-merger integrations, major shifts in market conditions, or new strategic directions. Provide a framework for planning and implementing these larger-scale changes.

- **Change Management Practices**: Reinforce the need for robust change management practices to support structural adjustments. This includes preparing change management plans, communicating changes effectively across the organization, and providing support and training to employees during transitions.

Leveraging Technology for Evaluation

- **Data Analytics Tools**: Highlight the use of advanced data analytics tools that can help in measuring the impact of organizational structures on business performance. These tools can analyze large volumes of data to identify patterns and insights that might not be apparent through manual evaluations.

- **Simulation Software**: Discuss the benefits of using simulation software to model changes in organizational structure and predict potential impacts before they are implemented. This can help in making informed decisions about structural adjustments.

Creating a Culture of Continuous Improvement

- **Leadership Involvement**: Emphasize the role of leadership in fostering a culture of continuous improvement regarding organizational structure. Leaders should champion the use of evaluations and adjustments as part of the normal business rhythm.

- **Employee Involvement**: Encourage involving employees in the evaluation and evolution process. This inclusion not only makes employees feel valued but also harnesses their firsthand experiences and ideas for improving organizational effectiveness.

Ethical and Legal Considerations

- **Ethical Management of Changes**: Address the ethical considerations in managing organizational changes, particularly those affecting job roles, employment terms, and privacy.

- **Regulatory Compliance**: Ensure that all structural changes comply with legal and regulatory requirements, which can vary by geography and industry.

By regularly evaluating and adapting its organizational structure, a company can maintain its operational effectiveness, foster innovation, and respond dynamically to new challenges and opportunities. This ongoing process ensures that the structure of the organization evolves in line with its strategic objectives and the changing business landscape.

Quick Tips and Recap

As we conclude this chapter on organizational architecture and structuring for success, here are some key takeaways and quick tips to ensure your organizational structure effectively supports your business goals:

- **Align Structure with Strategy**: Always ensure that your organizational structure aligns with your strategic objectives. Misalignment can lead to inefficiencies and obstacles in achieving business goals.
- **Clear Roles and Responsibilities**: Define clear roles and responsibilities to avoid confusion and overlap. Ensure every employee understands their duties and how they contribute to the organization.
- **Choose the Right Structure**: Select an organizational structure that fits your business size, strategy, and market. Whether functional, divisional, matrix, or flat, each has its benefits and challenges.
- **Foster Effective Communication**: Develop efficient communication channels across all levels of the organization. Proper communication flow is crucial for operational success and employee satisfaction.
- **Implement Gradually**: When rolling out a new organizational structure, consider a phased approach to manage the transition smoothly and allow for adjustments based on initial feedback.
- **Regular Evaluation**: Continuously evaluate the effectiveness of your organizational structure to ensure it remains aligned with business needs and market conditions. Adjust as necessary to maintain flexibility and responsiveness.

- **Involve Your Team**: Engage employees in the design and evaluation of the organizational structure. Their input can provide valuable insights and increase buy-in for structural changes.
- **Use Technology**: Leverage modern tools and software for designing, implementing, and evaluating your organizational structure. Technology can offer data-driven insights and support more informed decision-making.
- **Prepare for Resistance**: Anticipate and manage resistance to organizational changes through effective communication, education, and involvement of employees at all levels.
- **Promote Continuous Improvement**: Cultivate a culture of continuous improvement where organizational structure adjustments are part of regular business operations, not just one-time changes.

By following these tips, you can ensure that your organizational structure not only meets current needs but is also poised to adapt to future challenges and opportunities, supporting sustained business growth and success.

CHAPTER FIVE

Regional Compliance: Adapting to State-specific Business Laws

"Understanding and adapting to regional compliance isn't just a legal duty; it's a competitive edge that allows your business to operate smoothly and expand confidently into new territories."
— Indra Nooyi, former CEO of PepsiCo

Buckle up, entrepreneurs! You're about to take a whirlwind tour through the patchwork quilt of state-specific business laws. It's like a road trip through the United States, but instead of snapping selfies, you'll be collecting essential legal knowledge to keep your business running smoothly across different jurisdictions.

This chapter is your navigational guide through the diverse landscape of regional regulations. From the sunny shores of California, where privacy laws reign supreme, to the bustling streets of New York, where business regulations are as dense as the city itself, understanding these nuances is crucial. We'll explore how to tailor your business practices not just to survive but to thrive under varied legal climates.

Forget one-size-fits-all strategies; this is about custom-fitting your business suit to meet local standards. You'll learn how to dodge legal pitfalls and leverage regional advantages, turning local laws from hurdles into stepping stones. By the end of this chapter, you'll be as adept at navigating state compliance as a local taxi driver is at dodging traffic—effortlessly and efficiently. Get ready to localize your strategy and globalize your mindset!

Introduction to Regional Compliance

Navigating the complex landscape of state-specific business laws in the United States can seem daunting for any entrepreneur. Each state has its own set of rules and regulations, affecting everything from environmental standards to employment laws, consumer protection to corporate taxes. This introductory section provides a broad overview of the diversity in legal frameworks across states and why understanding these differences is crucial for running a successful business.

Diverse Legal Landscapes

- **Variability Across States**: Begin with an explanation of how and why business laws vary significantly from one state to another. Factors influencing these variations include local economic priorities, cultural differences, political climates, and historical precedents.
- **Key Areas of Legal Difference**: Highlight major areas where state laws tend to differ, including:
    - **Labor Laws**: Such as minimum wage requirements, worker's compensation, and termination procedures.
    - **Environmental Regulations**: Including state-specific standards for pollution control, waste management, and resource conservation.

- **Tax Regulations**: Detailing differences in state corporate taxes, sales taxes, and special tax incentives for businesses.
- **Consumer Protection Laws**: Covering state variations in laws related to consumer rights, product liability, and advertising.

Implications for Businesses

- **Operational Impact**: Discuss how these legal differences can impact various aspects of business operations. For example, labor laws affect human resource management, environmental regulations might influence production processes, and tax laws can impact financial planning.
- **Strategic Importance**: Emphasize the strategic importance of understanding and complying with these laws to avoid legal pitfalls, financial penalties, and potential damage to a company's reputation. Compliance is not just about adhering to the law but is a strategic imperative that can confer competitive advantage.

The Need for Compliance Awareness

- **Continuous Learning and Adaptation**: Stress the need for entrepreneurs to continuously educate themselves about the legal requirements in each state where they operate. The dynamic nature of laws means that what is compliant today may not necessarily remain so tomorrow.
- **Resource Allocation for Compliance**: Advise on the necessity of allocating adequate resources towards ensuring compliance, including investing in legal counsel and compliance officers who can navigate and keep track of these complex, evolving regulations.

Setting the Stage for Compliance Strategy

- **Introduction to Compliance Strategies**: Preview the upcoming sections that will delve deeper into effective strategies for managing multi-state operations, industry-specific challenges, and risk management, all designed to help businesses not only meet but leverage compliance for business success.

This section sets the foundation for understanding the critical role of state-specific compliance in the broader context of business operations and strategic planning. It prepares the reader for a deeper exploration of how to effectively navigate this fragmented legal landscape, ensuring that their business practices are not only lawful but also strategically optimized for regional success.

Strategies for Multi-state Operations

Operating a business across multiple states presents unique challenges due to the varying legal landscapes in each jurisdiction. This section discusses strategies for effectively managing and harmonizing these differences to ensure compliance and operational efficiency. By adopting a proactive approach to multi-state operations, businesses can mitigate risks and capitalize on regional opportunities.

Understanding Multi-state Compliance

- **Comprehensive Legal Audits**: Begin with the importance of conducting comprehensive legal audits to understand the specific requirements in each state where the business operates. This involves a detailed analysis of local laws and regulations that impact business activities, such as employment laws, environmental regulations, and tax obligations.
- **Centralized Legal Database**: Recommend establishing a centralized database that contains all state-specific legal requirements relevant to the business. This resource should be accessible to key personnel and updated regularly to reflect changes in the law.

Harmonizing Operations Across States

- **Standardization vs. Localization**: Discuss the balance between standardizing operations to maintain consistency and localizing practices to comply with state-specific laws. Identify areas where standardization is possible and beneficial, and recognize situations where customization is necessary.
- **Flexible Policy Frameworks**: Suggest developing flexible policy frameworks that can be easily adapted to meet different state

requirements. This includes creating modular policies that can be adjusted based on local regulations without compromising the core operational standards of the business.

Implementing Compliance Mechanisms

- **Use of Technology**: Highlight the role of advanced technology in managing multi-state compliance. Technologies such as compliance management software can help track changes in state laws, manage deadlines for regulatory filings, and ensure that all parts of the business remain compliant with local requirements.
- **Training and Development**: Emphasize the importance of ongoing training for employees, particularly those in managerial or operational roles that span multiple states. Training programs should focus on understanding and managing the complexities of multi-state operations, including how to apply corporate policies in different legal environments.

Risk Management Strategies

- **Regular Compliance Reviews**: Advise on setting up regular reviews of compliance status across all states to identify potential risks or areas of non-compliance before they become problematic. These reviews should involve cross-functional teams to ensure comprehensive coverage of all areas of the business.
- **Legal Risk Assessment**: Encourage conducting periodic legal risk assessments to evaluate the potential impact of non-compliance on the business. This includes assessing the financial, operational, and reputational risks associated with failing to meet state-specific legal standards.

Leveraging Regional Expertise

- **Local Legal Expertise**: Recommend partnering with local legal experts or consultants who specialize in state-specific laws. These experts can provide valuable insights and guidance on local compliance, reducing the burden on the central legal team.

- **Decentralized Compliance Teams**: Consider the benefits of creating decentralized compliance teams located in key states. These teams can provide on-the-ground support for local operations and ensure faster response times to state-specific legal changes.

By adopting these strategies, businesses can effectively manage the challenges of operating across multiple state jurisdictions. These approaches not only ensure compliance with diverse legal requirements but also enhance operational efficiency and foster a proactive culture of compliance throughout the organization.

Industry-Specific Regulator Challenges

Different industries face unique regulatory landscapes that can vary significantly from state to state. This section explores the challenges and strategies for navigating these industry-specific regulations, providing insights into how businesses in sectors like healthcare, finance, real estate, and technology can achieve compliance while optimizing their operational strategies.

Understanding Industry-Specific Regulations

- **Overview of Variance**: Begin by outlining how and why regulations vary significantly across industries and states. For instance, healthcare companies must navigate HIPAA compliance, while financial institutions deal with a different set of regulations like the Dodd-Frank Act on a state-by-state basis.
- **Critical Sectors Explored**:
    - **Healthcare**: Discuss stringent patient privacy laws, medical licensing requirements, and insurance regulations, which can differ greatly across states.
    - **Finance**: Cover compliance with state-specific banking regulations, securities laws, and consumer financial protection standards.
    - **Real Estate**: Explore zoning laws, property rights, and real estate licensing requirements that vary locally.

    - **Technology**: Address data privacy laws like California's CCPA, along with varying state laws on issues like cybersecurity and e-commerce.

Strategies for Managing Regulatory Challenges

- **Comprehensive Regulatory Mapping**: Recommend developing a comprehensive map of all relevant state-specific regulations affecting the industry. This should include keeping track of upcoming legislative changes that could impact operations.
- **Engagement with Regulatory Bodies**: Advise on establishing a proactive relationship with state regulatory bodies. Regular engagement can help businesses stay ahead of potential regulatory changes and even influence policy development.
- **Customized Compliance Programs**: Encourage the creation of customized compliance programs that address the specific requirements of each state where the business operates. This may involve specialized compliance teams or software solutions tailored to industry-specific needs.

Leveraging Technology for Compliance

- **Regulatory Technology Solutions**: Highlight the use of regulatory technology (RegTech) solutions that can streamline compliance across states. These technologies can automate compliance processes, track regulatory changes, and ensure that the business meets all applicable legal requirements efficiently.
- **Data Management Systems**: Discuss the importance of robust data management systems, especially for industries like healthcare and finance, where data sensitivity is paramount. Such systems help ensure that customer or patient data is handled according to varied state laws.

Training and Adaptability

- **Employee Training Programs**: Emphasize the need for comprehensive training programs that educate employees on the nuances of state-specific and industry-specific regulations. Well-informed employees are crucial for maintaining compliance at the operational level.

- **Adaptability in Processes**: Suggest implementing adaptable processes that can quickly adjust to changes in regulatory environments. This flexibility can be crucial for industries facing frequent legislative updates.

Risk Assessment and Mitigation

- **Continuous Risk Monitoring**: Propose continuous monitoring of compliance risks as part of the organization's risk management strategy. This includes regular audits and assessments to ensure that all aspects of the business comply with state and industry regulations.
- **Crisis Management Plans**: Discuss the importance of having a crisis management plan in place to address potential compliance failures. Such plans should outline steps for mitigating damage, legal or otherwise, and for communicating with stakeholders during a compliance crisis.

By understanding and addressing the unique regulatory challenges of their industry, businesses can better navigate the complex and often fragmented regulatory environment across different states. This proactive approach not only ensures compliance but also positions the company to take full advantage of its operational and strategic capabilities within each state's regulatory framework.

Risk Management and Compliance Resources

Effective risk management and access to the right compliance resources are essential for navigating the complex landscape of state-specific business laws. This section outlines how businesses can identify potential compliance risks and leverage various resources to maintain adherence to regional regulations effectively.

Identifying Compliance Risks

- **Risk Identification Processes**: Start by discussing the importance of identifying compliance risks as part of the organization's broader risk management strategy. Detail the processes for assessing risks associated with non-compliance, including financial penalties, operational disruptions, and reputational damage.

- **Risk Assessment Tools**: Recommend using specific tools and methodologies for risk assessment, such as compliance audits, SWOT analyses (Strengths, Weaknesses, Opportunities, Threats), and regulatory compliance software that can help track and manage regulatory changes.

Leveraging Compliance Resources

- **Compliance Teams**: Advise on the formation or enhancement of internal compliance teams dedicated to managing state-specific legal requirements. These teams should include legal experts familiar with the regulatory environments of the states in which the company operates.
- **External Consultants and Legal Experts**: Discuss the benefits of engaging with external consultants and legal experts who specialize in state-specific regulations. These professionals can provide insights and guidance that complement the internal team's expertise.
- **Training Programs**: Emphasize the importance of ongoing training programs for employees, particularly those directly involved in compliance-related processes. Training should cover relevant state laws and best practices for maintaining compliance.

Utilizing Technology and Tools

- **Compliance Management Software**: Highlight the advantages of investing in compliance management software that can help businesses monitor regulatory changes, manage documentation, and ensure that compliance tasks are completed on time.
- **Online Resources and Databases**: Point to valuable online resources, including state government websites, legal databases, and industry-specific forums, where businesses can find up-to-date information on regional compliance requirements.

Developing Compliance Policies and Procedures

- **Policy Development**: Guide businesses on developing robust compliance policies that reflect the complexities of operating in multiple states. These policies should be clear, accessible to all employees, and regularly updated to reflect new legal developments.
- **Procedure Implementation**: Discuss the implementation of procedures that operationalize the compliance policies. This includes setting up reporting systems, compliance checklists, and review processes that ensure ongoing adherence to legal standards.

Evaluating Compliance Resources

- **Resource Evaluation**: Encourage regular evaluations of the effectiveness of the utilized compliance resources and tools. This can help ensure that the business is using the most efficient, cost-effective solutions available and adapting to new challenges as they arise.
- **Feedback and Improvement**: Recommend establishing feedback mechanisms that allow employees to report on the utility of compliance resources and suggest improvements. This feedback can be crucial for continuously refining the approach to compliance.

By proactively managing compliance risks and effectively leveraging both internal and external resources, businesses can ensure that they meet all necessary legal requirements while maintaining operational efficiency. This strategic approach to compliance not only prevents legal issues but also builds a strong foundation for business growth and reputation management across various states.

Case Studies and Practical Insights

Learning from both successful compliance strategies and cautionary tales of regulatory pitfalls is essential for businesses navigating the complex tapestry of state-specific laws. This section presents case studies that illustrate the consequences of both effective and poor compliance practices, providing practical insights and valuable lessons learned.

Successful Compliance Strategies

- **Case Study 1: Proactive Adaptation in Healthcare**: Detail a healthcare company that successfully navigated the intricate web of state-specific health regulations by implementing a robust compliance program. Highlight how the company used advanced regulatory tracking tools to stay ahead of changes, and how its investment in continuous employee training minimized the risk of non-compliance.
- **Case Study 2: Technology Firm Leveraging Local Expertise**: Explore a technology firm that excelled in managing privacy laws across different states by building a network of local legal experts. Illustrate how this approach not only ensured compliance but also fostered innovations that were compliant with state-specific regulations, giving the company a competitive edge.

Failures in Compliance and Lessons Learned

- **Case Study 3: Retail Chain's Oversight Leads to Fines**: Analyze a retail chain that faced significant fines and reputational damage due to non-compliance with employment laws in several states. Discuss the lack of centralized compliance policies and how the failure to adapt to local labor laws led to legal challenges. Emphasize the importance of uniform policy frameworks that are flexible enough to incorporate state-specific requirements.
- **Case Study 4: Financial Missteps Due to Inadequate Risk Management**: Review a financial services company that suffered operational disruptions and financial losses from failing to comply with state-specific licensing requirements. Point out the gaps in risk assessment and the absence of adequate monitoring systems that could have preempted these compliance issues.

Extracting Lessons and Best Practices

- **Analysis of Success Factors**: From the successful case studies, extract key factors such as the importance of proactive legal tracking, the benefits of local expertise, and the strategic advantage of ongoing training and technology in ensuring compliance.

- **Understanding Pitfalls to Avoid**: From the failure case studies, identify common pitfalls like inadequate risk management, poor adaptation of policies to local contexts, and the consequences of reactive rather than proactive compliance strategies.
- **Implementing Best Practices**: Offer guidelines on implementing the successful strategies observed in the case studies, such as developing comprehensive compliance frameworks, investing in technology and expert resources, and fostering a culture of compliance throughout the organization.

By examining these case studies, businesses can gain a clearer understanding of the tangible impacts of compliance strategies and the critical importance of adapting to the legal nuances of each state. These real-world examples serve as both a warning and a guide, helping businesses to devise robust compliance strategies that mitigate risks and enhance their operational success across diverse regulatory landscapes.

Quick Tips and Recap

As we conclude our exploration of adapting to state-specific business laws, here are some essential tips and a recap to help streamline your compliance strategies across different jurisdictions:

- **Stay Informed**: Regularly update yourself and your compliance team on changes in state laws that affect your business. Utilize reliable sources and legal alerts to stay ahead.
- **Leverage Technology**: Invest in compliance management software to help track and manage state-specific regulations efficiently. This technology can save time and reduce errors in compliance processes.
- **Consult Local Experts**: Engage with local legal experts or consultants who specialize in the specific regulations of the states where you operate. Their insights can prove invaluable.

- **Implement Flexible Policies**: Develop compliance policies that are broad enough to cover general principles but flexible enough to adapt to specific state requirements.
- **Conduct Regular Audits**: Schedule regular compliance audits to ensure that all areas of your business meet state laws. Use the findings to strengthen your compliance efforts.
- **Train Your Team**: Regularly train your employees, especially those in compliance-sensitive positions, to ensure they understand the regulatory requirements and their roles in maintaining compliance.
- **Build a Compliance Culture**: Foster a culture that values compliance and ethical behavior. This can reduce risks and enhance your company's reputation.
- **Use Case Studies**: Learn from the successes and failures of others through case studies. Apply these lessons to your own business to avoid similar pitfalls.
- **Create a Risk Management Plan**: Develop a comprehensive risk management plan that includes strategies for identifying, assessing, and mitigating compliance risks.
- **Stay Proactive**: Always be proactive rather than reactive in your compliance efforts. Anticipating changes and preparing in advance can save your business from costly penalties and legal issues.

By following these tips, you can effectively navigate the complex landscape of state-specific regulations and build a resilient, compliant organization that is well-equipped to operate successfully across multiple states.

PART TWO

Building Your Business

Welcome to Part Two: Building Your Business, where the real fun begins! Think of this as assembling your entrepreneurial LEGO set. Each brick represents a crucial piece of your business—from crafting a memorable brand to navigating the intricate world of corporate governance. Here, we're not just stacking blocks aimlessly; we're meticulously constructing a fortress that's robust, resilient, and ready for anything the business world throws at it. As we delve into the mechanics of operational excellence and strategic alignments, you'll learn how to turn a blueprint of ideas into a towering edifice of enterprise. Get your hard hats ready, it's time to build not just a business, but a legacy.

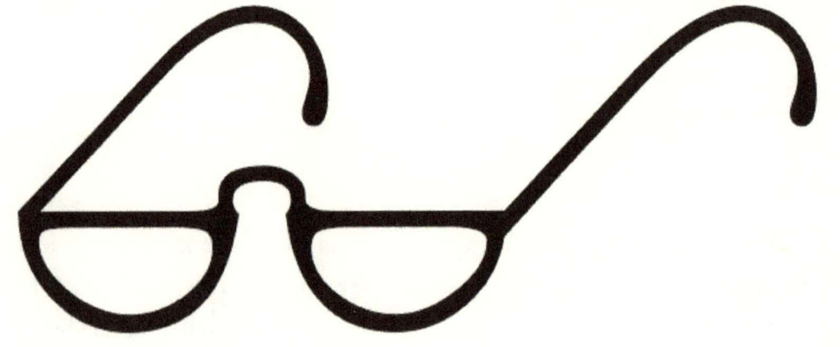

CHAPTER SIX

Branding Your Business: Crafting a Memorable Name and Image

"Your brand is the single most important investment you can make in your business."— STEVE JOBS, CO-FOUNDER OF APPLE INC.

Welcome to the world of branding, where your business not only gets a name but also a personality that could either be the life of the party or the wallflower! This chapter isn't about slapping on a catchy name and a flashy logo; it's about birthing an identity that resonates with your target market as profoundly as their favorite childhood memories.

Dive into the art and science of branding where we navigate the nuances of creating a name that sticks and an image that captivates. We'll explore the psychology behind color choices, font styles, and logo designs that aren't just pretty, but have the pulling power of a thousand magnets. You'll learn how to weave your core values and unique selling propositions into a brand narrative that speaks directly to the hearts (and wallets) of your customers.

Think of this as dressing your business for success. Just like you wouldn't wear flip-flops to a black-tie event, your business needs to show up in the market dressed appropriately for its audience. By the end of this chapter, you'll have a toolkit to create a brand that's not only seen and heard but remembered and revered. Ready to make your business the icon of your industry? Let's get branding!

The Fundamentals of Branding

Welcome to the foundational building block of your business's identity—branding. In this section, we'll delve into what branding really means and why it's crucial for your business's success. By understanding the core elements of branding, you'll be equipped to develop a powerful brand that resonates with your audience and distinguishes your business in the competitive market.

What is Branding?

- **Definition and Scope**: Branding is more than just a name or a logo; it encompasses the entire experience your customers have with your business. It involves the design, message, and personality that you convey in every interaction. Effective branding creates memorable impressions and fosters long-term relationships.
- **Components of a Brand**: Discuss the key components that make up a brand:
    - **Name**: The foundational piece that captures the essence of your business.
    - **Logo**: A visual symbol that represents your business in its simplest form.
    - **Color Palette**: The selection of colors used consistently in all branding materials, influencing mood and brand perception.

  - **Typography**: The style of text used across all communications, reinforcing the personality of the brand.
  - **Voice and Tone**: The consistent way your brand communicates with its audience, whether through written or spoken word.

Importance of Branding

- **Differentiation**: Branding sets your business apart from competitors by highlighting unique traits and value propositions. It tells your customers what they can expect from your products or services that they can't get elsewhere.
- **Customer Recognition**: A strong brand is immediately recognizable, which increases the likelihood of customer preference and loyalty. This recognition builds over time through consistent branding efforts across all customer touchpoints.
- **Building Trust and Loyalty**: Well-crafted branding helps build trust with your audience. Trust leads to customer loyalty, as customers are more likely to return to a brand that they believe is reliable and aligns with their values.
- **Supporting Advertising and Marketing**: Effective branding amplifies your marketing efforts. It provides a coherent identity for your advertising campaigns, which can improve their effectiveness and efficiency.

Psychology Behind Branding

- **Emotional Connection**: Discuss how brands connect on an emotional level with customers by aligning their brand message with the values and desires of their target audience. This emotional connection makes the brand more appealing and can drive decision-making.
- **Perception and Association**: Explain how customers often make purchasing decisions based on their perception of the brand rather than based solely on product features. A strong brand can elevate a product or service by imbuing it with additional value through positive associations.

Setting the Stage for Brand Development

- **Strategic Foundation**: Emphasize the necessity of approaching branding with a strategic mindset. Branding should not be an afterthought; it needs to be integrated into the business planning process from the outset.
- **Aligning Brand with Business Objectives**: Ensure that the development of your brand aligns with your overall business objectives. The brand should reflect where you want your business to go and how you want it to be perceived.

This introduction sets the stage for a deeper exploration into the specific aspects of branding, such as developing a brand name and designing a visual identity, which are covered in the following sections. By grasping these fundamentals, you will be better equipped to create a brand that effectively communicates the essence of your business to your target audience.

Developing a Brand Name

Choosing the right name for your business is a crucial decision that can have a significant impact on its success. The brand name is often the first encounter potential customers have with your company, and it sets the tone for all future interactions. In this section, we delve into the process of creating a brand name that is not only memorable but also embodies the essence of your business and resonates with your target audience.

Understanding the Importance of a Good Name

- **First Impression**: Explain how a brand name functions as the initial handshake between your business and potential customers, setting expectations and beginning the relationship.
- **Market Differentiation**: Discuss how a unique and catchy name can help your business stand out in a crowded marketplace, making it easier for customers to remember and recommend.

Criteria for an Effective Brand Name

- **Memorability**: A great brand name should be easy to remember. This often means keeping it short, simple, and catchy.
- **Relevance**: The name should reflect your business's identity, mission, or value proposition, connecting intuitively with your core products or services.
- **Scalability**: Consider future growth possibilities; the name should be versatile enough to encompass potential expansion in products, services, or geographies.
- **Legibility and Pronunciation**: Ensure the name is easy to read and pronounce in your primary market areas to avoid confusion and enhance brand recall.
- **Legal Availability**: Emphasize the importance of checking the legal availability of a name to ensure it is not already trademarked or in heavy use within your industry.

Steps to Developing a Brand Name

- **Brainstorming Session**: Start with a brainstorming session involving key stakeholders. Use prompts such as key business values, unique selling propositions, and target audience characteristics to generate a wide range of ideas.
- **Narrowing Down the List**: Filter the initial list by considering factors like relevance, memorability, and scalability. Use customer feedback, if possible, to gauge public reaction to potential names.
- **Cultural Considerations**: For businesses planning to operate internationally, it's crucial to evaluate how a name translates across different languages and cultures to avoid negative connotations or misunderstandings.
- **Trademark Research**: Once a shortlist is created, conduct thorough trademark research to ensure the name can be legally used without infringement on existing trademarks.

Finalizing Your Brand Name

- **Testing and Feedback**: Test the final contenders for the brand name with a broader audience segment to gather feedback on their appeal and any unintended interpretations.
- **Making the Decision**: Based on feedback and comprehensive evaluation, make an informed decision on the brand name that best represents your business and has the potential to grow with it.

Registering the Name

- **Legal Registration**: Guide through the process of legally registering the brand name as a trademark to protect it from use by others. Discuss the importance of securing domain names and social media handles early in the process to maintain consistency across all platforms.

By carefully selecting a brand name that meets these criteria, you create a solid foundation for your business identity and marketing efforts. A well-chosen name not only captures the essence of what your business stands for but also plays a critical role in its overall branding strategy.

Designing a Compelling Logo and Visual Identity

A strong visual identity is pivotal for a brand's recognition and emotional connection with its audience. This section delves into the creation of a logo and the broader visual elements that make up a brand's identity, explaining how these elements work together to convey the brand's message and values effectively.

Importance of a Strong Visual Identity

- **Immediate Recognition**: Discuss how a logo serves as the face of your company, offering instant recognition in a sea of competitors. A well-designed logo can evoke emotions and associations with your brand almost instantaneously.
- **Consistency Across Touchpoints**: Emphasize the role of a cohesive visual identity in maintaining consistency across various customer touchpoints, from your website and social media to packaging and

advertising. Consistency helps reinforce brand memory and can enhance trust and loyalty.

Elements of Visual Identity

- **Logo Design**: The logo should be simple yet memorable, versatile enough to work across various media and sizes, and appropriate for the industry and audience.
- **Color Palette**: Colors play a crucial role in branding by conveying emotions and setting the tone for how customers perceive the brand. Discuss the psychology of colors and how to choose a palette that aligns with the brand's personality and values.
- **Typography**: The choice of fonts should complement the brand's character and be legible across different platforms. Explain the impact of typography on brand perception and the importance of selecting typefaces that reflect the brand's essence.
- **Imagery and Iconography**: Guide on the use of additional visual elements like photographs, illustrations, and icons that support the brand narrative and enhance visual communication.

Designing Your Logo

- **Concept Development**: Begin the logo design process by translating the brand's core attributes, values, and personality into visual elements. This may involve mood boards, sketches, and early drafts to visualize concepts.
- **Simplicity and Clarity**: Stress the importance of simplicity in logo design to ensure clarity and recognition. A simple logo often translates better across different sizes and mediums.
- **Versatility**: Ensure the logo is versatile, looking as good on a small piece of merchandise as it does on a large billboard. Test the logo in various contexts to guarantee its effectiveness.
- **Feedback and Revisions**: Gather feedback from various stakeholders and potential customers to refine the logo design. Use this feedback to

make adjustments that sharpen the logo's ability to communicate the brand's message.

Implementing the Visual Identity

- **Brand Guidelines**: Develop comprehensive brand guidelines that dictate how all aspects of the brand's visual identity should be used, including logo placement, color usage, typography, and imagery. These guidelines ensure consistency across all marketing materials and communications.
- **Training and Communication**: Train your team on the importance of adhering to these guidelines and communicate these standards to any partners or vendors who might use your branding elements.

Evolving Your Visual Identity

- **Regular Updates**: Recognize that visual identities may need to evolve to stay relevant. Schedule regular reviews of your branding to ensure it continues to resonate with your audience and remains effective in an ever-changing market landscape.

By carefully crafting a compelling logo and a cohesive visual identity, you create a powerful brand image that can significantly impact your business's market presence. This visual identity becomes a key tool in building brand recognition, fostering customer loyalty, and differentiating your business in a competitive environment.

Crafting Your Brand Narrative

A strong brand narrative is essential for connecting with your audience on a deeper level. This section explores how to craft a compelling brand story that integrates your core values and unique selling propositions into a cohesive narrative that resonates with customers, influences perceptions, and drives loyalty.

The Power of Storytelling in Branding

- **Emotional Connection**: Begin by discussing the importance of storytelling in creating an emotional connection with your audience. A good story can humanize your brand, making it more relatable and memorable to your customers.
- **Differentiation**: Explain how a unique brand narrative can set your business apart from competitors by highlighting what makes you special in a way that facts and figures alone cannot.

Components of a Strong Brand Narrative

- **Origin Story**: Share the origins of your business, focusing on what inspired you to start the company, the challenges you've faced, and the milestones you've achieved. This not only adds authenticity but also builds an emotional rapport with your audience.
- **Mission and Vision**: Clearly articulate your brand's mission and vision. Discuss how these elements reflect your business's values and aspirations, and how they resonate with your target market.
- **Customer-Centric Stories**: Incorporate stories that focus on the customers, such as testimonials, case studies, or user-generated content. These narratives should illustrate how your products or services have positively impacted your customers' lives.

Developing Your Brand Narrative

- **Identify Key Messages**: Pinpoint the key messages you want to convey through your narrative. These should align with your brand's core values and the primary benefits of your products or services.
- **Consistency Across Platforms**: Ensure that your brand narrative is consistent across all platforms, from your website and social media to marketing materials and advertising. Consistency reinforces your brand identity and helps build trust with your audience.

- **Engage and Involve**: Aim to engage your audience by making your narrative interactive. Encourage them to share their own stories related to your brand or participate in community-driven initiatives.

Implementing the Narrative

- **Content Strategy**: Develop a content strategy that supports the dissemination of your brand narrative. Plan how you will tell your story through blogs, social media posts, videos, podcasts, and other marketing materials.
- **Training Staff**: Train your employees, especially customer-facing staff, to understand and effectively communicate your brand narrative. They should be able to embody the brand's values and convey its story authentically and passionately.

Evaluating and Evolving Your Narrative

- **Feedback and Adaptation**: Regularly gather feedback from your audience to see how your brand narrative is being received. Use this feedback to refine and adapt your story as needed to ensure it remains relevant and engaging.
- **Evolution with Growth**: As your business grows and evolves, so should your brand narrative. Update your story to reflect new products, services, milestones, or shifts in market dynamics.

By effectively crafting and communicating a brand narrative, you transform your business from just another company into a beloved brand. This narrative becomes a powerful tool in shaping how customers perceive and interact with your brand, fostering loyalty and driving long-term success.

Implementing and Maintaining Your Brand

After developing a brand name, visual identity, and narrative, the next crucial step is to implement these elements consistently across all aspects of your business and maintain them over time. This section outlines strategies for effective brand implementation and ongoing maintenance to ensure your brand remains strong and cohesive as your business grows.

Implementing Your Brand Strategy

- **Brand Integration Across Touchpoints**: Discuss the importance of integrating your brand elements consistently across every customer touchpoint. This includes digital presence (website, social media), marketing materials (brochures, business cards), product packaging, and customer service interactions.
- **Employee Onboarding and Training**: Highlight the need for comprehensive training for all employees on the brand's values, voice, and visual identity. Employees should understand how to communicate the brand accurately and consistently in their roles.

Maintaining Brand Consistency

- **Creating Brand Guidelines**: Develop detailed brand guidelines that cover all aspects of the brand, including logo usage, color palette, typography, imagery, and the brand's narrative tone. These guidelines ensure that anyone who works on the brand, from internal teams to external partners, maintains consistency.
- **Regular Audits of Brand Usage**: Schedule regular audits to review how the brand is being applied across different channels and materials. This helps identify any deviations from the brand guidelines and correct them promptly.

Adapting and Evolving the Brand

- **Monitoring Market Trends and Feedback**: Keep an eye on evolving market trends and gather customer feedback to understand how your brand is perceived. Use this information to make informed decisions about when and how to make subtle adjustments to your branding without losing the core identity.
- **Flexibility in Brand Guidelines**: While maintaining consistency is key, allow some flexibility in your brand guidelines to enable creative interpretations that can refresh the brand without altering its essence.

Leveraging Technology for Brand Management

- **Digital Asset Management (DAM) Systems**: Implement a DAM system to organize, store, and share branding materials like logos, photos, templates, and brand guidelines. This technology helps maintain consistency as it ensures that all stakeholders have access to the same resources.
- **Brand Management Software**: Consider using brand management software that can help monitor the use of your brand across various platforms and automate the enforcement of brand guidelines.

Engaging Stakeholders in Brand Maintenance

- **Internal Engagement**: Regularly engage with employees to reinforce the importance of the brand and update them on any changes to branding strategies or guidelines.
- **External Partner Collaboration**: Work closely with partners, such as marketing agencies and distributors, to ensure they understand and adhere to your brand guidelines. Provide regular updates and training if necessary.

Reviewing and Refreshing the Brand

- **Scheduled Reviews**: Set a schedule for periodic comprehensive reviews of the brand's performance and relevance. This should involve assessing all brand elements to determine if they still effectively communicate the brand's message and resonate with the target audience.
- **Refreshing the Brand**: Based on the review, decide if a brand refresh is needed. This could involve updating visual elements, tweaking the brand narrative, or overhauling the brand strategy to align with new business objectives or market conditions.

By meticulously implementing and diligently maintaining your brand, you ensure that it remains a strong and consistent force driving your business forward. This ongoing effort helps your brand stay relevant and powerful, capable of supporting your business as it evolves and grows.

Quick Tips and Recap

As we wrap up this chapter on branding your business, here are some concise tips and a quick recap to help ensure your branding efforts are effective and enduring:

- **Be Strategic**: Always start with a clear strategy that aligns your brand with your business objectives and audience expectations.
- **Memorable Name**: Choose a brand name that is not only memorable and unique but also reflects the essence and values of your business.
- **Consistent Visual Identity**: Develop a consistent visual identity that includes a logo, color palette, and typography that are easily recognizable and reflect your brand's personality.
- **Compelling Narrative**: Craft a brand narrative that tells a compelling story about your business, resonating with customers and differentiating you from competitors.
- **Consistency Across Touchpoints**: Ensure that your brand is consistently represented across all touchpoints, from digital platforms to physical packaging, to build trust and recognition.
- **Educate Your Team**: Train all employees on the brand's values, voice, and visual identity to ensure consistent representation in every customer interaction.
- **Brand Guidelines**: Create and maintain detailed brand guidelines to help manage your brand's identity across various channels and ensure consistency.
- **Regular Brand Audits**: Conduct regular audits to check the consistency and effectiveness of your brand across all channels and touchpoints.
- **Stay Adaptive**: Be prepared to evolve your branding as your business grows and as market conditions change, ensuring the brand remains relevant and engaging.
- **Leverage Technology**: Use technology such as digital asset management systems and brand management software to help maintain consistency and efficiency in brand management.

- **Feedback Loop**: Establish mechanisms to collect and analyze feedback from customers and employees on your brand's performance, using insights to make informed adjustments.

By following these tips, you can ensure that your brand not only stands out in the marketplace but also grows along with your business, maintaining relevance and resonance with your target audience over time.

CHAPTER SEVEN

Partnerships and LLCs: Choosing the Right Framework

"Selecting the right business structure, be it a partnership or an LLC, is a foundational decision that defines both your financial journey and your strategic vision." — MICHAEL E. GERBER, AUTHOR AND BUSINESS CONSULTANT

Step right up to the partnership carousel or hop aboard the LLC express! This chapter is about picking the right ride for your business adventure. Whether you're looking to buddy up with a partner or keep it flexible with an LLC, making the right choice is crucial for your business's health and your sanity.

Partnerships are like marriages: full of potential, but they require communication, shared goals, and yes, sometimes even prenups in the form of agreements. We'll dissect the dynamics of partnerships, from general to limited, and guide you through the complexities of joint ventures where two plus two really must equal more than four.

On the flip side, if you're a fan of flexibility and less formality, then LLCs might just be your business soulmate. Here, you'll learn how to enjoy the perks of liability protection without the drama of corporate formalities. We'll explore how to tailor an LLC to fit your business like a glove, maximizing benefits while minimizing headaches.

By the end of this chapter, you'll be equipped to make an informed decision, knowing when to pair up, when to go solo, and how to structure it all for success. Let's dive into the legal fine print with a dose of humor and emerge with a clear plan, shall we?

Understanding Business Partnerships

Embarking on a business partnership is akin to starting a professional marriage. It involves mutual commitment, shared goals, and the understanding that each party's contributions are crucial to the success of the enterprise. This section explores the various types of partnerships, outlining their structures, responsibilities, and potential benefits to help you determine if a partnership is the right choice for your business.

Types of Partnerships

- **General Partnerships (GP)**: In a general partnership, all partners share equal responsibility for managing the business and are equally liable for the debts and obligations it incurs. This type of partnership is straightforward to establish, requiring no formal paperwork or fees in most jurisdictions, though drafting a partnership agreement is highly recommended to clarify roles and responsibilities.
- **Limited Partnerships (LP)**: Limited partnerships consist of at least one general partner and one or more limited partners. The general partner manages the business and assumes liability for its debts, while limited partners contribute capital and share in the profits but do not participate

in daily operations, limiting their liability to the extent of their investment.

- **Limited Liability Partnerships (LLP)**: Often used by professional groups such as lawyers, doctors, and accountants, LLPs protect each partner from debts against the partnership and from the actions of other partners. In an LLP, partners aren't responsible for the misconduct or negligence of their fellow partners.

Legal Implications

- Discuss the legal implications that accompany each type of partnership. This includes the liability each partner faces, the legal obligations for debt and decisions, and how partners are expected to contribute to tax responsibilities. Understanding these facets is crucial for ensuring that all partners are aware of their duties and the potential risks involved.

Benefits of Forming a Partnership

- **Shared Resources**: Partnerships allow for the pooling of resources, including capital, skills, knowledge, and contacts, which can lead to enhanced productivity, innovation, and market reach.
- **Flexibility**: Partnerships offer more flexibility in management and operations compared to corporations. They are generally less regulated and have fewer formalities, allowing partners to negotiate the terms and structure that best suit their needs.
- **Tax Advantages**: Income from the partnership is passed through to the individual partners' tax returns, meaning the partnership itself is not taxed. Each partner pays taxes on their share of the profits at their individual tax rates, avoiding the double taxation commonly associated with corporations.

Considerations Before Forming a Partnership

- **Drafting a Partnership Agreement**: Emphasize the importance of a comprehensive partnership agreement that details profit sharing, responsibilities, dispute resolution methods, and exit strategies. This document is essential for preventing misunderstandings and conflicts among partners.

- **Alignment of Vision and Values**: Partners should share a common business vision and compatible values. Misalignments can lead to conflicts that might jeopardize the business.
- **Exit Strategy**: Plan for the potential dissolution of the partnership, outlining processes for partners wishing to leave or sell their interests. This includes how to handle the departure or death of a partner.

By understanding the different types of partnerships and the responsibilities each entails, potential business partners can make informed decisions about forming a partnership that aligns with their business objectives and personal liability comfort levels. This foundation is crucial for building a successful partnership that fosters growth and withstands the challenges of the business world.

The Ins and Outs of Limited Liability Companies (LLCs)

Limited Liability Companies (LLCs) offer a flexible business structure that combines the pass-through taxation of a partnership with the limited liability protection of a corporation. This section delves into what an LLC is, why it might be the best choice for business owners seeking flexibility and liability protection, and the steps involved in forming and operating an LLC effectively.

What is an LLC?

- **Definition and Basic Structure**: An LLC is a legal form of a business organization that provides limited liability to its owners, known as members. Unlike partnerships, where individual partners can be held responsible for business debts and liabilities, an LLC ensures that members are protected from personal liability for business decisions or actions of the LLC. This protection is akin to that of a corporation, but the LLC enjoys more flexibility and fewer formalities.

Advantages of an LLC

- **Liability Protection**: Members of an LLC are protected from personal liability for business debts and claims. This means that in most cases, their personal assets — like the personal bank account, car, or house — are protected if the LLC faces bankruptcy or lawsuits.
- **Tax Flexibility**: LLCs benefit from pass-through taxation by default, meaning that the business itself is not taxed directly. Instead, profits and losses are passed through to members' personal tax returns, avoiding the double taxation faced by C Corporations.
- **Operational Flexibility**: LLCs are not required to have a board of directors, hold regular board meetings, or keep detailed corporate minutes, as corporations are. This flexibility can be particularly advantageous for smaller companies and startups that wish to remain agile.

Forming an LLC

- **Choosing a Name**: The name of your LLC must be distinguishable from other business names and include "Limited Liability Company" or its abbreviations (LLC or L.L.C.) as part of the name. You will need to check with your state's business filing office to make sure your desired name is available.
- **Filing the Articles of Organization**: This is the primary document required to formally register your LLC with the state. The articles typically include the business name, address, and the names of its members, and are filed with the Secretary of State or equivalent state agency.
- **Operating Agreement**: Although not always legally required, creating an operating agreement is highly recommended. This internal document outlines the LLC's operating procedures, ownership, and profit distributions among members. It serves as an official contract that binds the members to its terms.

Managing an LLC

- **Membership Structure**: LLCs can have one member (single-member LLC) or many members (multi-member LLC). Members can be individuals, corporations, other LLCs, or foreign entities. There are no maximum number limits.
- **Regulatory Requirements**: Depending on your business type and location, your LLC may need to obtain specific business licenses and permits to operate legally. Members should also ensure that they follow any local, state, and federal regulations that apply to their industry.
- **Annual Requirements**: Some states require LLCs to submit an annual report and/or pay franchise fees. It is crucial to understand and comply with your state's specific requirements to maintain good standing and continue operating legally.

Choosing to form an LLC can be advantageous for many business owners due to its liability protection, tax benefits, and operational flexibility. Understanding how to set up and manage an LLC correctly is key to taking full advantage of its structure while ensuring compliance with legal requirements.

Comparing Partnerships and LLCs

When starting a business, choosing the right structure is crucial for both operational success and legal protection. This section provides a detailed comparison between partnerships and Limited Liability Companies (LLCs), helping you understand the key differences and decide which structure might be the best fit for your business needs.

Key Differences

- **Legal Liability**: One of the most significant differences lies in the area of legal liability. In partnerships, partners can be personally liable for the debts and obligations of the business, including actions taken by other partners. In contrast, LLCs offer liability protection where members are typically not personally liable for business debts or legal actions against the company.

- **Tax Treatment**: Both partnerships and LLCs generally offer pass-through taxation, meaning the business itself is not taxed on its profits. Instead, profits and losses are passed through to the owners' personal income tax returns. However, LLCs provide additional flexibility, allowing members to choose to be taxed as a corporation if it proves advantageous.
- **Formalities and Recordkeeping**: Partnerships often require less formal recordkeeping and operational processes than LLCs. While LLCs do not require as many formalities as corporations, they typically demand more documentation than partnerships, such as filing articles of organization and potentially drafting an operating agreement.

Operational Flexibility

- **Management Structure**: In a partnership, decisions are often made jointly by the partners or according to terms set out in a partnership agreement. LLCs offer more flexibility in structuring the management, either managed by members or by designated managers who may not be members of the LLC.
- **Ownership and Investment**: Partnerships may face limitations when it comes to adding new partners or adjusting ownership stakes, usually requiring a new partnership agreement. LLCs provide a simpler mechanism for adding members or changing the percentage of ownership through amendments to the operating agreement or membership interest agreements.

Formation and Dissolution

- **Setting Up**: Forming a partnership can be as simple as starting to do business together, with a formal partnership agreement as optional (though recommended). In contrast, setting up an LLC requires filing formal articles of organization with the state and paying a filing fee.
- **Dissolution**: Dissolving a partnership can sometimes trigger the dissolution of the entire business, depending on the terms of the partnership agreement. LLCs typically offer more continuity, allowing

the business to survive even if a member leaves, provided that the operating agreement specifies such arrangements.

Pros and Cons for Specific Business Scenarios

- **Small and Informal Businesses**: For small ventures with limited risk, a partnership might be sufficient and cost-effective. Its ease of setup and flexibility in operations can be advantageous.
- **Businesses Needing Investment**: For businesses seeking outside investors or those wanting to protect personal assets from business risks, an LLC may be the better choice. The LLC structure can make it easier to bring in investors and offers members protection from personal liability.

Choosing the Right Structure

- Evaluate your business's specific needs, considering factors such as the level of liability protection required, tax implications, the potential need for investment, and the desired complexity of operations. Consult with a legal or financial advisor to understand fully the implications of each option.

This comparative analysis should help clarify the fundamental distinctions between partnerships and LLCs, providing a solid foundation for making an informed decision about the most appropriate business structure for your venture.

Case Studies: Successes and Challenges

Understanding the practical applications and potential pitfalls of different business structures can be greatly enhanced by examining real-world examples. This section presents case studies of both partnerships and LLCs, illustrating how these structures have led to successes or posed challenges in various business scenarios. These stories will help crystallize the concepts discussed earlier and provide actionable insights.

Success in Partnerships

- **Case Study: Creative Agency Partnership**: Explore a case study of a successful general partnership formed by two creative professionals. Highlight how their combined expertise and shared vision led to a thriving business. Discuss how the transparency in operations and joint decision-making facilitated rapid growth and adaptation to market changes. However, also note the measures they took to mitigate potential risks, such as drafting a detailed partnership agreement that outlined roles, profit sharing, and dispute resolution methods.

Challenges in Partnerships

- **Case Study: Restaurant Venture**: Examine a partnership in a restaurant business that faced challenges due to misaligned goals and poor communication. One partner wanted rapid expansion while the other preferred a focus on quality and gradual growth. The lack of a clear partnership agreement led to conflicts and ultimately a costly dissolution of the partnership. Highlight how these issues could have been mitigated with better upfront agreements and regular communication.

Success in LLCs

- **Case Study: Tech Startup LLC**: Discuss a tech startup that opted for an LLC structure to take advantage of liability protection and flexibility in management. The case study should detail how the LLC format attracted investors due to the clear separation between personal and business liabilities and how the flexible management structure allowed for the hiring of an experienced CEO to manage operations, leading to successful scaling of the company.

Challenges in LLCs

- **Case Study: Real Estate LLC**: Present a scenario where an LLC formed for real estate investments ran into problems due to unclear operational roles and responsibilities among members. Despite the liability protection and tax benefits, the LLC faced internal conflicts that hampered decision-making and project advancements. This case should illustrate the importance of a well-crafted operating agreement and the need for clear communication and role definitions within an LLC.

Lessons Learned

- **From Partnerships**: Emphasize the importance of having a solid partnership agreement in place that covers all potential areas of conflict, including the division of labor, financial contributions, profits distribution, and the steps to handle disputes or the exit of a partner.
- **From LLCs**: Highlight the necessity of maintaining proper documentation and clarity in the roles and responsibilities of members to prevent mismanagement and internal conflicts. Also, stress the value of using the flexibility of the LLC structure to adapt to changing business needs and market conditions.

Each case study serves as a learning tool, providing insights into how different business structures can influence the outcomes and sustainability of a business. By understanding these real-world applications and challenges, prospective business owners can better prepare themselves for the complexities of business formation and management.

Making the Right Choice for Your Business

Choosing between a partnership and an LLC is a critical decision that will influence your business's legal framework, operational dynamics, and long-term viability. This section provides guidance on how to assess your specific business needs and make an informed choice that aligns with your goals and risk tolerance. It will help you navigate the decision-making process with practical steps and considerations.

Assessing Your Business Needs

- **Consider Business Goals**: Reflect on what you hope to achieve with your business. Are you looking to grow quickly and possibly prepare for an acquisition? Or do you prefer maintaining a small, manageable operation? Your business structure should support your long-term goals.

- **Evaluate Liability Concerns**: Determine your comfort level with personal liability. If protecting personal assets is a priority, an LLC offers clear advantages with its liability protection, unlike a partnership where personal liability can be more exposed.
- **Think About Funding Needs**: If you anticipate needing significant external funding, consider how investors might view your business structure. LLCs are often more attractive to investors because they provide liability protection and flexible profit distribution options.

Understanding Tax Implications

- **Tax Flexibility of LLCs**: LLCs offer the option to be taxed as a sole proprietor, partnership, or corporation, providing significant flexibility depending on your financial goals and the specifics of your business.
- **Pass-through Taxation in Partnerships**: Partnerships benefit from pass-through taxation without the flexibility of choosing an alternative tax structure, which might be simpler but less advantageous under certain conditions.

Operational Complexity and Costs

- **Simplicity in Partnerships**: Partnerships can be easier and less costly to set up and maintain, especially if fewer formalities suit your business style and administrative capabilities.
- **Regulatory Requirements for LLCs**: While LLCs require more formal setup and ongoing compliance, such as filing articles of organization and potentially more complex accounting, they provide greater structure and protection.

Drafting the Necessary Agreements

- **Partnership Agreements**: If opting for a partnership, draft a comprehensive partnership agreement that includes provisions for managing disagreements, distributing profits and losses, and handling the departure or addition of partners.

- **Operating Agreements for LLCs**: For LLCs, create a detailed operating agreement that outlines member roles, capital contributions, profit sharing, and management structure, among other operational protocols.

Consulting with Professionals

- **Seek Legal and Financial Advice**: Before finalizing your decision, consult with legal and financial professionals. They can provide personalized advice based on the latest laws and regulations applicable to your specific circumstances and location.
- **Ongoing Review and Adjustment**: Business needs and legal environments change, so periodically review your business structure to ensure it continues to serve your best interests. Be prepared to adjust as necessary to accommodate growth or changes in the law.

By carefully considering these aspects and seeking appropriate counsel, you can choose a business structure that not only meets your current needs but also supports your future ambitions. Whether you choose a partnership for its simplicity and direct control or an LLC for its flexibility and protection, understanding the implications of each framework allows you to make a strategic decision that positions your business for success.

Quick Tips and Recap

As we wrap up our exploration of choosing the right business framework through partnerships and LLCs, here are some key takeaways and quick tips to guide your decision-making process:

- **Assess Your Needs**: Clearly define your business goals, operational needs, and risk tolerance to determine which structure best aligns with your objectives.
- **Understand Liability**: Remember that LLCs offer liability protection that shields personal assets, whereas partnerships may expose personal assets to business debts and legal actions.

- **Consider Tax Implications**: Evaluate the tax benefits and responsibilities of each structure. LLCs offer tax flexibility, while partnerships are strictly pass-through entities.
- **Evaluate Funding Requirements**: Consider future capital needs; LLCs are typically more attractive to investors due to their structured management and limited liability.
- **Prepare for Formalities**: Be aware that LLCs require more formal setup and ongoing compliance than partnerships, which may influence your choice depending on your capacity to handle administrative tasks.
- **Draft Clear Agreements**: Whether choosing a partnership or an LLC, have comprehensive agreements in place (partnership agreements for partnerships and operating agreements for LLCs) to outline operational procedures and reduce potential conflicts.
- **Consult Professionals**: Seek advice from legal and financial experts to ensure that your chosen structure complies with current laws and meets your business needs effectively.
- **Plan for the Future**: Regularly review your business structure to ensure it continues to meet your evolving business needs and adjust as necessary.

By keeping these tips in mind, you can make a well-informed decision on the business structure that not only suits your current situation but also supports your long-term business vision and growth.

CHAPTER EIGHT

Boardroom Basics: Essentials of Corporate Governance

"Good corporate governance is about 'intellectual honesty' and not just sticking to rules and regulations, capital flows where it is welcome and stays where it is well treated."— WALTER WRISTON, FORMER CEO OF CITIBANK

Welcome to the big leagues, where the boardroom is the battleground and corporate governance the rulebook! This chapter isn't about snooze-worthy statutes; it's about mastering the chess game of executive oversight, where every move can propel you toward victory or nudge you toward checkmate.

Here, we'll strip down the daunting facade of corporate governance to its bare essentials—transparency, accountability, and effective management. You'll learn the art of balancing power with responsibility, ensuring that your company not only grows but thrives under a watchful eye. From setting up a savvy board of directors to navigating complex shareholder relationships, we're covering all bases to turn you into a governance guru.

Think of corporate governance as the spine of your company: it keeps everything upright and functioning. We'll explore how to implement robust governance structures that support and stabilize your business, prevent legal mishaps, and enhance your reputation in the marketplace. Ready to rule the boardroom? Let's dive into the mechanics of governance that are more exciting than any episode of "Billions."

Fundamentals of Corporate Governance

Corporate governance is the framework of rules, relationships, systems, and processes within and by which authority is exercised and controlled in corporations. It encompasses the mechanisms through which companies, and those in control, are held to account. In this section, we delve into the essential elements of corporate governance: transparency, accountability, and effective management, and explore how they are crucial to business integrity and performance.

Understanding Corporate Governance

- **Definition and Importance**: Corporate governance involves overseeing the management of a company to ensure that it complies with legal and ethical standards, as well as internal bylaws and policies. Good governance ensures that a company is run in a responsible and efficient manner, which is crucial for attracting investment, maintaining company health, and protecting shareholder value.
- **Key Principles**: Introduce the core principles of good corporate governance which include:
    - **Transparency**: Ensuring that actions, decisions, and processes are clear to stakeholders and shareholders alike. This involves regular and accurate reporting of financial and operational results.

- **Accountability**: Holding individuals within the organization accountable for their actions, which helps in reinforcing trust and ethical corporate behavior.
- **Fairness**: Treating all stakeholders equitably and justly, providing equal opportunity for stakeholders to express their opinions and concerns.
- **Responsibility**: Ensuring that the company's resources are managed responsibly and sustainably, focusing on long-term value creation rather than short-term gains.

The Role of Corporate Governance

- **Risk Management**: Discuss how effective governance practices help in identifying and mitigating risks before they can adversely affect the company. This includes compliance risks, operational risks, and strategic risks.
- **Performance Enhancement**: Explain how good governance is directly linked to improved company performance. Companies with strong governance structures tend to make more prudent decisions and have better controls in place, leading to increased operational efficiencies and higher profitability.
- **Stakeholder Assurance**: Highlight how governance frameworks provide security to shareholders and other stakeholders that the management acts in their best interests and aligns with broader business goals.

Governance Frameworks and Models

- **Legal Frameworks**: Provide an overview of the legal frameworks that govern corporate entities, including state and federal laws that regulate securities, employment, and business operations.
- **Internal Controls and Procedures**: Discuss the internal controls and procedures typically used in corporations to enforce governance policies, such as audits, board oversight, and compliance programs.

- **International Standards**: Mention international standards and guidelines for corporate governance, such as those from the OECD (Organization for Economic Co-operation and Development), which provide benchmarks for governance practices globally.

By understanding these fundamentals, business leaders and board members can ensure that their organizations not only comply with mandatory regulations but also exceed them, thereby driving their companies towards sustainable growth and ethical excellence. This strong foundation in corporate governance practices will be critical as we explore further aspects such as the roles and responsibilities of board members, effective meeting strategies, and complex shareholder relations in subsequent sections.

Roles and Responsibilities of the Board of Directors

The board of directors plays a pivotal role in shaping a company's strategic direction and overseeing its management. Understanding the specific roles and responsibilities of the board is crucial for effective corporate governance. This section delves into the composition of the board, the duties of its members, and how these responsibilities impact the company's overall success.

Composition of the Board

- **Diversity and Expertise**: Highlight the importance of having a diverse board in terms of skills, experience, and backgrounds. A well-rounded board is better equipped to oversee complex corporate activities and offer a range of perspectives that can prevent groupthink.
- **Roles within the Board**: Describe the typical roles within a board, including the Chairperson, CEO (if also a board member), Treasurer, and Secretary, and explain the distinct responsibilities associated with each position.

Key Responsibilities of the Board

- **Setting Strategic Direction**: The board is primarily responsible for setting the long-term strategy of the company, aligning it with stakeholders' interests, and ensuring sustainability. This involves crafting strategic goals, and major plans of action, and setting performance objectives.

- **Monitoring Company Performance**: Discuss how the board must regularly monitor the implementation of the strategic plan through performance evaluations of both financial and non-financial outcomes. This involves reviewing management's performance and the overall health of the company.
- **Financial Oversight**: Explain the board's role in overseeing the company's financial integrity. This includes approving annual budgets, ensuring accurate financial reporting, and conducting audits.
- **Risk Management**: Boards are tasked with overseeing the company's risk management policies and procedures. They must ensure that the company has adequate systems to manage its risks, including financial, operational, compliance, and reputational risks.
- **Legal Compliance**: Ensure that the company adheres to all legal requirements and ethical standards. This includes overseeing the company's compliance with employment laws, environmental laws, corporate governance standards, and other statutory regulations.

Enhancing Board Effectiveness

- **Regular Training and Development**: Members should participate in ongoing education to stay updated on governance best practices, industry trends, and regulatory changes.
- **Evaluation of Board Performance**: Incorporate regular assessments of the board's performance and the effectiveness of its governance practices. This might include self-evaluations, peer reviews, or external evaluations.
- **Succession Planning**: Discuss the importance of planning for the succession of senior leaders and board members to ensure stability and continuity within the company.

Challenges in Board Management

- **Managing Conflicts of Interest**: Address how the board should handle conflicts of interest to maintain trust and integrity in its governance. This includes setting policies for disclosing potential conflicts and recusing affected members from relevant decisions.
- **Balancing Roles**: Particularly in cases where the CEO is also a board member, emphasize the need for balance between executive influence and independent oversight by the board.

By fulfilling these roles and responsibilities effectively, the board of directors ensures that the company is governed with a balance of authority and accountability. This not only supports the company's strategic goals but also enhances its reputation and trustworthiness in the eyes of shareholders, employees, and the broader community.

Corporate Governance Principles and Practices Memo

Sample corporate governance principles and practices memo to board members, summarizing their roles and responsibilities:

CORPORATE GOVERNANCE PRINCIPLES AND PRACTICES MEMO

The primary responsibilities of the board of directors of _________________ (the "Company") are to oversee the exercise of corporate powers and to ensure that the Company's business and affairs are managed to meet its stated goals and objectives. The Board recognizes its responsibility to engage, and provide for the continuity of, executive management that possesses the character, skills and experience required to attain the Company's goals and to ensure that nominees for the Board possess appropriate qualifications and reflect a reasonable diversity of backgrounds and perspectives.

Directors will fulfill the following responsibilities and requirements:

- Represent the collective interests of all stockholders of the Company;
- Discharge Board duties in good faith, with due care and in a manner he/she reasonably believes to be in the best interests of the Company;
- Possess independence, objectivity and the highest degree of integrity on an individual and collective basis;
- Be dedicated to understanding the business of the Company and issues presented to the Board;
- Be committed to active, objective, thoughtful, constructive and independent participation at meetings of the Board and its committees;
- Bring to the Board's deliberations their collective breadth of business,

professional and personal experience to represent the interests of shareholders;

- Review fundamental operating, financial and other corporate plans, strategies and objectives;
- Evaluate on a regular and timely basis the qualitative and quantitative performance of the Company and its senior management;
- Review the process of providing appropriate financial and operation information, internally and externally;
- Assure adherence to proper policies of corporate conduct, including compliance with applicable laws, regulations, business and ethical standards;
- Assure compliance with requirements for timely, accurate and complete disclosure of information in filings with the Securities and Exchange Commission such as proxy statements and reports on Form 10-K or 10-Q (e.g., disclosure regarding nominating committee functions and communications between security holders and boards of directors);
- Assure maintenance of proper accounting, financial and other appropriate controls; and
- Evaluate and take steps to improve the overall effectiveness of the Board.

The Board has the responsibility to organize its functions and conduct its business in the manner it deems most effective and efficient, consistent with its duties of good faith, due care and loyalty. In that regard, the Board has adopted a set of flexible policies to guide its governance practices in the future. These practices, set forth below, will be regularly re-evaluated by the Board's Corporate Governance and Nominating Committee in light of changing circumstances in order to continue serving the best interests of shareholders. Accordingly, the summary of current practices is not a fixed policy or resolution by the Board, but merely a statement of current practices that is subject to continuing assessment and change.

1. Size of the Board

The Board of Directors currently has [______] members. The number will vary from time to time depending on circumstances, but the Board's intention is to [maintain its size in a range] between [_____] and [______] members. A significant majority of the Board members are and will continue to be independent directors.

2. Board Definition of What Constitutes Independence for Directors

No relationship between any director and the Company should be of a nature that could compromise the independence of any Board member in governing the affairs of the Company. The determination of what constitutes independence for a director in any individual situation shall be made by the Board in light of the totality of the facts and circumstances relating to such situation, including whether the director is a current or past employee of the Company, and in compliance with the requirements of NASDAQ's applicable listing standards and other applicable rules and regulations.

[3. Independent Lead Director

The Board may elect an independent director to serve as Lead Director. The Lead Director will facilitate and preside over meetings of independent directors in executive session. Also, the Lead Director may serve as the focal point for directors regarding the resolution of any conflicts with the chief executive officer, or with other directors, and for coordinating feedback to the chief executive officer on behalf of directors regarding business issues and corporate governance.]

4. Number of Committees

The present Board committees are: the Audit Committee, the Compensation Committee and the Corporate Governance and Nominating Committee. Members of all committees are non-employees of the Company and shall be "independent" under applicable NASDAQ guidelines. The Board considers its current committee structure to be appropriate but the number and scope of committees may be revised as appropriate to meet changing conditions and needs.

5. Board Member Criteria

The Corporate Governance and Nominating Committee is responsible for reviewing the appropriate skills and characteristics required of directors in the context of prevailing business conditions and composition of the Board. The qualifications to be considered in the selection of director nominees include the extent of experience in business, trade, finance or management; the extent of knowledge of regional and national business affairs; and the overall judgment to advise and direct the Company in meeting its responsibilities to stockholders, customers, employees and the public. The objective is to have a Board that brings to the Company a variety of perspectives and skills derived from high quality business and professional experience.

6. Procedure for Selecting New Director Candidates

The Board is responsible for selecting its members, subject to shareholder approval, but delegates the screening process to the Corporate Governance and Nominating Committee. The Corporate Governance and Nominating Committee is expected to work closely with the chief executive officer to determine the characteristics and qualifications desired in new members of the Board and to make recommendations of candidates to the entire Board.

7. Board Member Orientation

Orientation materials will be made available and appropriate meetings will be held to acquaint new directors with the business, history, current circumstances, key issues and top managers of the Company.

8. Frequency of Board Meetings; Attendance

Currently, the Board has [_____] regular meeting each year, with additional meetings as required. The Board considers its current meeting schedule to be adequate, but the number of regular meetings may be adjusted as necessary to meet changing conditions and needs. A calendar of Board meetings will be developed and circulated as far in advance as practicable. Members are expected to attend all meetings barring special circumstances.

9. Briefing Materials Distributed in Advance

As much information and data as practical on the meeting agenda items and the Company's financial performance is sent to Board members in advance of Board and Committee meetings.

10. Executive Sessions of Independent Directors

At each meeting of the Board, the agenda includes time for an executive session with only independent directors and the chief executive officer present, and time for another executive session of independent directors without the chief executive officer present. The chairperson may participate in all executive sessions.

11. Board Access to Senior Management

All Board members have access to senior management, with the expectation that such contact would be minimally disruptive to the business operation of the Company. The chief executive officer is encouraged to invite to Board meetings senior managers who can provide additional insight into business matters being discussed and those with high future potential who should be given personal exposure to members of the Board.

12. Assignment of Committee Members

The Corporate Governance and Nominating Committee is responsible for reviewing and recommending to the Board the assignment of directors to various committees, subject to applicable membership requirements to ensure diversity of Board member experience and variety of exposure to the affairs of the Company.

13. Frequency and Length of Committee Meetings

Generally, committees meet in conjunction with regular Board meetings. Committee chairpersons may also call meetings when they deem it necessary. Committee meetings may be as frequent and as long as needed.

14. Committee Agenda

The agenda for Committee meetings is developed by Committee Chairpersons in consultation with appropriate members of management. The agenda for each meeting is circulated in advance and Committee members may suggest additional items for consideration.

15. Assessing the Board's Performance

The Corporate Governance and Nominating Committee will conduct an annual assessment of the overall effectiveness of the organization of the Board and the Board's performance of its governance responsibilities. The Committee will report its findings to the whole Board for discussion.

16. Directors Who Change Their Job Responsibilities

A Board member, including the chief executive officer, who ceases to be actively employed in his/her principal business or profession, or experiences other changed circumstances that could pose a conflict of interest, diminish his/her effectiveness as a Board member, or otherwise be detrimental to the Company, is expected to offer his/her resignation to the Board. The Board in its discretion will determine whether such member should continue to serve as a director for an unexpired term or any future terms.

17. Term Limits/Retirement Age

No term limits for directors have been established. The Board expects that no member of the Board shall stand for reelection after his or her 70th birthday.

18. Selection of the Chairman and Chief Executive Officer

The Board elects the chairman and chief executive officer in the manner and based on the criteria that it deems appropriate and in the best interests of the Company given the circumstances at the time of such election.

19. Formal Evaluation of the Chief Executive Officer

Each year, the chairpersons of the Corporate Governance and Nominating Committee and the Compensation Committee will conduct a formal evaluation of the chief executive officer's performance based on appropriate quantitative and qualitative criteria.

20. Succession Planning

The chief executive officer will annually review succession planning with the Compensation and Executive Development Committee, and provide the Board with a continuing current recommendation as to succession in the event of that officer's termination of employment, disability or death.

21. Board Interaction with Institutional Investors, the Media and Customers

The responsibility for communications and relationships on behalf of the

Company with institutional investors, the media, and customers should be management's.

22. Authorization Guidelines

The Board will establish, and periodically update, guidelines for authorization of expenditures or other corporate actions, including the acquisition or disposition of capital assets, and these will periodically be reviewed with management.

▶ If you are interested in receiving an electronic copy of this document, please email us at documents@AuthorsDoor.com with the subject line "Request for Corporate Governance Principles and Practices Memo." Upon receiving your email, we will promptly send you a Microsoft Word copy of the document. **Disclaimer:** Please note that all agreements are provided for informational purposes only and should not be construed as legal advice. We recommend consulting with a qualified attorney to ensure that any legal documents or decisions are tailored to your specific circumstances.

Effective Board Meetings and Decision-Making

Effective board meetings are crucial for making strategic decisions and overseeing the company's management. This section explores how to conduct board meetings that not only comply with governance standards but also foster productive discussions and decisive actions.

Planning and Preparing for Board Meetings

- **Scheduling and Frequency**: Discuss the importance of regular board meetings, typically held quarterly or as needed, to address ongoing business and emergent issues. Planning meetings in advance ensures that all members have adequate time to prepare.
- **Agenda Setting**: Emphasize the role of the Chairperson in setting the agenda, in consultation with other board members and senior management. The agenda should prioritize strategic issues and include routine governance items, ensuring a focus on critical business matters.
- **Preparation of Materials**: Highlight the necessity of distributing meeting materials, such as financial reports, performance reviews, and briefing documents, well in advance. This allows board members

sufficient time to review and come prepared to engage in meaningful discussions.

Conducting the Meeting

- **Opening Procedures**: Outline standard opening procedures, including the establishment of a quorum, approval of previous meeting minutes, and introductory remarks by the Chair.
- **Discussion and Debate**: Encourage open and structured discussions where all members have the opportunity to express their views. Effective moderation by the Chair is crucial to manage time and maintain focus on agenda items.
- **Decision-Making**: Explain the decision-making process, which may include voting on resolutions or consensus-building, depending on the company's bylaws. Ensure that all decisions are recorded in the meeting minutes for transparency and accountability.

Roles of Key Participants

- **Chairperson**: The Chairperson plays a critical role in guiding the meeting, facilitating discussions, ensuring that the agenda is followed, and that all relevant issues are addressed. They also ensure that the meeting environment is conducive to open communication and effective decision-making.
- **Board Members**: All members should come prepared, participate actively in discussions, and make decisions based on informed judgments and the best interests of the company.
- **Secretary**: The Secretary of the board ensures that the meeting is properly documented, including recording decisions and action items, and that all corporate records are maintained accurately.

Enhancing Meeting Effectiveness

- **Use of Technology**: Consider the use of board management software to organize and distribute meeting materials, schedule meetings, record minutes, and track action items.

- **Executive Sessions**: Include executive sessions where board members meet privately without the presence of management to discuss sensitive issues, personnel performance, or other confidential matters.
- **Feedback and Continuous Improvement**: Regularly solicit feedback from board members on the meeting process and outcomes to identify areas for improvement. Continuous refinement of meeting practices can enhance the overall effectiveness of the board.

Legal and Ethical Considerations

- **Compliance**: Ensure all meetings comply with legal and ethical standards, including those related to confidentiality, conflicts of interest, and fiduciary duties. Adherence to these standards protects the company and individual board members from legal repercussions.

By focusing on the structure, participation, and procedures of board meetings, companies can enhance their governance practices and make more effective strategic decisions. Well-run board meetings are essential for maintaining corporate health and achieving long-term success.

Managing Board Dynamics and Shareholder Relations

Navigating the complexities of board dynamics and shareholder relations is crucial for maintaining a healthy corporate governance environment. This section explores strategies for managing interactions within the boardroom and between the board and shareholders to ensure effective communication, cooperation, and compliance with governance standards.

Understanding Board Dynamics

- **Composition and Diversity**: Discuss the importance of having a diverse board in terms of expertise, experience, and backgrounds to enrich decision-making processes and bring different perspectives to the table.
- **Conflict Management**: Address strategies for managing conflicts of interest and interpersonal conflicts within the board. Highlight the

importance of establishing clear guidelines and procedures for conflict resolution to maintain a functional and cohesive board.

- **Building Cohesion**: Explore ways to foster a collaborative atmosphere within the board through team-building activities, strategic retreats, and regular informal gatherings. Such initiatives can enhance mutual respect and improve collaborative decision-making.

Effective Communication with Shareholders

- **Transparency and Disclosure**: Emphasize the importance of transparency in communications with shareholders. Regularly sharing financial reports, strategic decisions, and governance practices helps build trust and ensures that shareholders feel informed and valued.
- **Engagement Strategies**: Discuss different strategies for engaging with shareholders, such as annual meetings, special briefings, newsletters, and interactive platforms where shareholders can express concerns and provide feedback.
- **Handling Shareholder Proposals and Concerns**: Provide guidance on how to effectively address shareholder proposals and concerns in compliance with legal requirements and best practices. This includes setting formal procedures for submitting proposals and timely responses from the board.

Legal and Regulatory Compliance

- **Compliance with Securities Laws**: Outline the board's responsibility to ensure that the company complies with all applicable securities laws, which include regulations on public disclosures, insider trading, and shareholder rights.
- **Annual and Special Meetings**: Detail the legal requirements for conducting annual general meetings (AGMs) and special meetings, including notice periods, agendas, voting procedures, and documentation.

Shareholder Activism

- **Understanding Activism**: Explain shareholder activism and its impact on corporate governance. Discuss how active shareholders can influence governance and strategic decisions through proposals, voting, or public campaigns.
- **Proactive Engagement**: Advocate for proactive engagement with activist shareholders to understand their perspectives and concerns, potentially integrating valuable insights into governance practices and business strategy.

Crisis Management

- **Preparedness and Response**: Highlight the importance of having a crisis management plan that includes clear roles for the board and mechanisms for quick and effective communication with shareholders during crises.
- **Role of the Board in Crises**: Discuss the critical role the board plays in overseeing the management's response to crises and communicating with shareholders to manage expectations and maintain confidence.

By effectively managing board dynamics and maintaining strong relationships with shareholders, companies can enhance their governance structures and foster an environment of trust and cooperation. This, in turn, supports the company's stability and long-term success, ensuring that it remains resilient in the face of challenges and responsive to the needs of its stakeholders.

Legal and Ethical Considerations in Governance

Navigating the legal and ethical landscapes is crucial for maintaining effective corporate governance. This final section outlines the responsibilities of the board in ensuring compliance with legal standards and upholding high ethical practices. It also discusses how adherence to these standards not only protects the company but also strengthens its reputation and operational success.

Compliance with Laws and Regulations

- **Understanding Regulatory Requirements**: Detail the board's responsibility to ensure that the company complies with all applicable laws and regulations, including corporate, securities, labor, environmental, and antitrust laws. Emphasize the need for continuous education and awareness among board members regarding these regulations.
- **Role of Compliance Programs**: Discuss the importance of establishing and maintaining robust compliance programs that monitor and enforce regulatory requirements. Highlight how these programs should be integrated into the company's overall risk management strategy.

Ethical Standards and Corporate Integrity

- **Establishing a Code of Ethics**: Advocate for the development and enforcement of a corporate code of ethics that outlines expected behaviors and ethical practices for all employees, management, and board members. This code serves as a foundation for decision-making and interactions within and outside the company.
- **Handling Ethical Dilemmas**: Provide guidelines on how the board should address ethical dilemmas and conflicts of interest. Stress the importance of transparency and fairness in handling such issues to maintain trust and integrity within the company.

Board Oversight and Accountability

- **Audit Committees**: Explain the critical role of audit committees in overseeing financial reporting processes and internal controls, ensuring accuracy, and preventing fraud. Discuss the composition and functions of an effective audit committee.
- **Evaluating Board Performance**: Highlight the necessity for regular evaluation of board performance to ensure that governance objectives are being met. Discuss methodologies for assessing board effectiveness, such as self-evaluations, peer reviews, or engagement of external consultants.

- **Transparency in Board Decisions**: Stress the importance of transparency in board decision-making processes. Ensure that shareholders and stakeholders have access to information about board activities and decisions, fostering a culture of openness and accountability.

Legal Liabilities and Protections

- **Understanding Director Liability**: Outline the potential legal liabilities that board members face in their roles, including breaches of fiduciary duties. Discuss legal protections available, such as indemnification and directors' and officers' (D&O) insurance, to mitigate these risks.
- **Reporting and Disclosure Obligations**: Detail the board's responsibilities regarding financial and operational reporting, including the need to ensure that disclosures are complete, accurate, and timely. Discuss the legal implications of failing to meet these disclosure obligations.

Promoting a Culture of Ethics and Compliance

- **Leading by Example**: Encourage board members to lead by example by adhering to the highest standards of ethics and compliance. This leadership approach helps cultivate a corporate culture that values ethical behavior and compliance throughout the organization.
- **Continuous Improvement**: Advocate for ongoing improvements to governance practices based on changes in laws, industry standards, and company operations. Encourage adaptability and forward-thinking in governance practices to anticipate and respond to new challenges.

By adhering to stringent legal and ethical standards, the board of directors ensures that the company not only meets its regulatory obligations but also operates with integrity. This commitment to legal compliance and ethical behavior is essential for building a reputable and sustainable business that can navigate the complexities of the modern corporate environment.

Quick Tips and Recap

To ensure effective corporate governance and successful management within the boardroom, here are some essential tips and a recap of the key points discussed in this chapter:

- **Understand Key Governance Principles**: Always keep the core principles of transparency, accountability, fairness, and responsibility at the forefront of governance activities.
- **Roles and Responsibilities**: Ensure clarity regarding the roles and responsibilities of each board member, including the distinct roles of the Chairperson, CEO, and other key officers.
- **Effective Meetings**: Conduct well-organized board meetings with clear agendas and pre-distributed materials to facilitate informed discussions and decisions.
- **Manage Dynamics and Relationships**: Pay attention to board dynamics and shareholder relations. Address conflicts of interest and strive for a cooperative atmosphere in the boardroom.
- **Legal Compliance**: Stay informed about the legal obligations affecting your business, including corporate, securities, and employment laws, and ensure all board decisions comply with these regulations.
- **Ethical Leadership**: Develop and enforce a strong code of ethics. Lead by example to promote a culture of integrity and ethical behavior throughout the organization.
- **Regular Evaluations**: Implement regular performance evaluations for the board and individual members to assess effectiveness and identify areas for improvement.
- **Risk Management**: Maintain robust risk management strategies and ensure that the board actively oversees the implementation and effectiveness of these strategies.

- **Communication is Key**: Keep open and transparent communication with stakeholders to enhance trust and support for the board's strategic decisions.
- **Adapt and Evolve**: Stay adaptable and be prepared to evolve governance practices in response to new challenges, regulatory changes, or shifts in the business environment.

By following these tips, boards can enhance their governance practices, support sustainable business growth, and maintain high standards of integrity and compliance. This not only protects the company legally and financially but also strengthens its reputation in the marketplace.

CHAPTER NINE

Keeping Records Clean: Managing Corporate Documentation

"Effective record keeping is a cornerstone of corporate success. It's not just about staying organized; it's about ensuring the integrity of your business for decisions that shape its future." — MICHAEL BLOOMBERG, FOUNDER OF BLOOMBERG L.P.

Welcome to the world where paperwork isn't just a chore; it's an art. Step into the archives of any thriving business, and you'll find a meticulous mosaic of records, from board minutes to tax receipts. This isn't just about keeping the auditors happy—it's about crafting a legacy of transparency and order that could rival the Library of Congress.

In this chapter, we're rolling up our sleeves and diving into the filing cabinets of corporate America. Learn the ins and outs of document management that won't just save you during tax season but could also be your knight in shining armor during a legal joust. We'll tackle everything from the exhilarating world of annual reports to the adrenaline-pumping thrill of compliance filings.

Forget the image of a dusty, paper-laden office; modern document management is sleek, digital, and as cutting-edge as it gets. We'll show you how to streamline your records, protect sensitive information, and turn your business's paper trail into a goldmine of organized intelligence. Ready to become a black belt in the dojo of documentation? Let's get those records straight!

The Importance of Proper Documentation

In the realm of business, maintaining accurate and comprehensive documentation is not merely a bureaucratic necessity but a cornerstone of corporate integrity and operational efficiency. This section explores the pivotal reasons why proper documentation is crucial for every business, from legal compliance to strategic decision-making.

Legal Compliance and Audit Preparedness

- **Regulatory Requirements**: Many industries are subject to specific regulatory requirements that mandate the maintenance of certain records. Failure to comply can result in legal penalties, fines, or more severe consequences.
- **Audit Readiness**: Accurate documentation ensures that a business is always ready for internal or external audits. Auditors rely heavily on well-organized records to verify the accuracy of financial reports and compliance with laws and regulations.

Facilitating Financial Transparency

- **Tracking Financial Transactions**: Detailed records of financial transactions help in tracking the inflow and outflow of funds, crucial for managing budgets, forecasting, and financial planning.
- **Preventing Fraud**: Comprehensive documentation acts as a deterrent to fraudulent activities. When employees know that all transactions are

well-documented and subject to scrutiny, the likelihood of fraudulent behavior diminishes.

Historical Accuracy and Institutional Memory

- **Business Continuity**: Proper documentation preserves the institutional memory of a company, which is invaluable during transitions in management or ownership. It ensures continuity by providing a detailed account of past business operations.
- **Strategic Decision Making**: Historical data, preserved through meticulous record-keeping, serves as a foundation for strategic planning. Analyzing past trends and outcomes helps in making informed decisions about the future.

Enhancing Operational Efficiency

- **Streamlining Processes**: Organized documentation streamlines various business processes, from onboarding new employees to executing marketing strategies and customer service.
- **Quick Access to Information**: Efficiently managed records allow for quick retrieval of information, which is crucial during time-sensitive periods such as project deadlines or legal disputes.

Building Corporate Reputation

- **Stakeholder Confidence**: Transparent and accessible records bolster stakeholder confidence. Investors, lenders, and partners are more likely to trust and engage with businesses that demonstrate a commitment to thorough record-keeping.
- **Legal Protection**: In the event of legal challenges, comprehensive documentation can protect the company by providing evidence that can support its positions and practices.

Documentation as a Strategic Asset

- **Leveraging Data for Competitive Advantage**: Beyond compliance and operational necessity, well-organized data can be analyzed to uncover business insights and opportunities, turning records into a strategic asset that drives competitive advantage.

By understanding these multifaceted benefits, businesses can appreciate that proper documentation is not just a compliance requirement but a fundamental practice that supports legal integrity, operational excellence, and strategic prowess. This foundational perspective sets the stage for exploring the specific types of corporate records that businesses must manage effectively, which is covered in the following section.

Types of Corporate Records

Effective management of corporate documentation encompasses a variety of records, each serving distinct functions and subject to specific regulatory requirements. This section outlines the major types of corporate records, providing insight into their significance and the standard practices for maintaining them.

Board Meeting Minutes

- **Purpose and Importance**: Minutes from board meetings document the discussions and decisions made by the board of directors. They serve as a legal record and are crucial for transparency and accountability.
- **Best Practices**: Ensure that minutes are detailed enough to capture the essence of discussions and rationales for decisions. Store them securely and make them accessible to authorized personnel only.

Draft Corporate Minutes

The style of minutes is determined in large part by the personal preferences of the chairman of the board, the corporate secretary, and other senior management of the corporation, and the directors, as well as by tradition within the company.

[NAME OF CORPORATION]
NOTICE OF MEETING OF THE BOARD OF DIRECTORS
______________, 20__

Pursuant to the call of the [office of person calling the meeting [check Bylaws to see who may call meetings of the Board] of [Name of Corporation], a [State] corporation (the "Company"), notice is hereby given that a [regular/special] meeting of the Board of

Directors will be held on ____ day, ________, 20__, commencing at ______ [a.m./p.m.] at the offices of the Company at ____.

The proposed agenda for the meeting is as follows:

1.
2.
3.

Dated: ______________, 20__

____
Secretary

**WAIVER OF NOTICE AND CONSENT
TO HOLDING OF A SPECIAL MEETING
OF THE BOARD OF DIRECTORS
OF
[NAME OF CORPORATION]**

The undersigned, constituting the entire Board of Directors of [Name of Corporation], a [State] corporation (the "Company"), hereby waive notice and consent to the holding of the Special Meeting of the Board of Directors of the Company on ___________, 20__ at the offices of the Company. The undersigned further agree that any business transacted at such meeting shall be valid, legal and of the same force and effect as though said meeting were held after notice duly given.

Dated: ___________, 20__

____
Director

____
Director

____
Director

____
Director

**MINUTES OF A REGULAR MEETING
OF THE BOARD OF DIRECTORS OF**

____

A regular meeting of the Board of Directors (the "Board") of [Name of Corporation], a [State] corporation (the "Company"), was held at the Company's offices located at ____ on ____ day, __________, 20__, at _____ [a.m./p.m.].

DIRECTORS PRESENT:

____

DIRECTORS ABSENT:

____

OTHERS PRESENT:

____

CALL TO ORDER

____________ served as Chairman of the meeting, and ___________ acted as Secretary of the meeting. The Chairman called the meeting to order and announced that a quorum of directors was present and the meeting, having been duly convened, was ready to proceed with business.

APPROVAL OF MINUTES

The Board reviewed the minutes of the meeting held __________, 20__. After discussion, upon motion duly made, seconded and unanimously approved, the following resolution was adopted:

RESOLVED, that the minutes of the meeting of the Board held _________, 20__ be, and they hereby are, approved in the form distributed to the members of the Board.

[INCLUDE GENERAL DESCRIPTION OF MATTERS DISCUSSED BY THE BOARD, INCLUDING RESOLUTIONS COVERING MATTERS REQUIRING BOARD APPROVAL.]

ADJOURNMENT

There being no further business to come before the meeting, the meeting was adjourned at _____ [a.m./p.m.].

Respectfully submitted,

____

Secretary

ACTION OF THE BOARD OF DIRECTORS OF
[NAME OF CORPORATION]
BY UNANIMOUS WRITTEN CONSENT

The undersigned, being all the members of the Board of Directors of [Name of Corporation], a [California] corporation, do hereby consent by this writing, to take the following action, to adopt the following resolutions, and to transact the following business of the corporation:

ELECTION OF OFFICERS

RESOLVED, that the following named persons are elected to the offices set forth opposite their names [at the annual compensation for services to be rendered to the corporation set forth opposite their titles] to serve until the next annual meeting of the Board of Directors or until their successors are duly elected:

Name	**Officer**	**[Annual Compensation]**
__________________	______________	_________________
__________________	______________	_________________
__________________	______________	_________________
__________________	______________	_________________

RATIFICATION

RESOLVED, that the [contract/lease agreement] executed on behalf of the corporation by [Name] on _________________, 20__ attached hereto and marked Exhibit ___ is hereby confirmed, ratified, and approved as action taken by and for the corporation.

RESOLVED FURTHER, that all actions taken by officers of the corporation on behalf of the corporation [since the last meeting of the Board of Directors] [since ______________, 20__] are hereby confirmed, ratified, and approved as actions taken by and for the corporation.

AUTHORIZATION

RESOLVED, that the officers of the corporation are hereby authorized and directed for and on behalf of the corporation to take such action and execute such documents as they deem necessary or advisable in order to carry out and perform [the purposes of the foregoing resolutions] [the proper duties of their offices].

The undersigned hereby consent to the foregoing resolutions and direct that this Written consent be filed with the minutes of the proceedings of the Board of Directors of this corporation and that pursuant to Section 307(b) of the General Corporation Law of the State of California [and the Bylaws of this corporation] said resolutions shall have the same force and effect as if they were adopted at a meeting at which the undersigned were personally present.

Dated: ____________, 20__

____
Director

____
Director

____
Director

____
Director

▶ An Annual Meeting document package—Resolutions of Board of Directors, Notice of Annual Meeting, Proxy Statement, Proxy, Script, Inspector of Election Oath, Certified List of Shareholders, Certificate of Mailing, Ballot, and Minutes of Annual Meeting—can be found in the **Appendix**. If you are interested in receiving an electronic copy of these documents, please email us at documents@AuthorsDoor.com with the subject line "Request for Annual Meeting Document Package." Upon receiving your email, we will promptly send you a Microsoft Word copy of the documents. **Disclaimer:** Please note that all agreements are provided for informational purposes only and should not be construed as legal advice. We recommend consulting with a qualified attorney to ensure that any legal documents or decisions are tailored to your specific circumstances.

Financial Records

- **Types of Financial Documents**: Include invoices, receipts, payroll data, bank statements, and ledgers. These documents are vital for financial tracking, reporting, and auditing.
- **Retention and Management**: Maintain financial records for a minimum period as required by law, typically seven years, to support tax filings and potential audits. Use secure, organized systems for storage.

Contracts and Legal Agreements

- **Scope**: This encompasses all binding agreements into which the company enters, including with suppliers, customers, and employees.
- **Documentation Practices**: Store contracts in a manner that ensures they are easily accessible for review and renewal. Track key dates such as expiration and renewal terms.

Compliance Filings

- **Regulatory Documents**: These are filings that companies must submit to comply with legal and regulatory requirements, such as annual reports, tax returns, and environmental compliance documents.
- **Handling Procedures**: Establish systematic procedures for preparing, reviewing, and submitting compliance documents to ensure timeliness and accuracy.

Employee Records

- **Content**: Employee records include personal information, employment contracts, performance reviews, and disciplinary documentation.
- **Privacy and Security**: Given the sensitive nature of these documents, ensure they are stored securely and that access is restricted to authorized personnel to comply with privacy laws.

Intellectual Property Documentation

- **Types and Relevance**: Includes patents, trademarks, copyrights, and trade secrets. Proper documentation supports the protection and enforcement of intellectual property rights.
- **Management Strategy**: Regularly update records to reflect current statuses, renewals, and ongoing litigation if applicable.

Annual Reports

- **Overview**: Annual reports provide a comprehensive summary of a company's financial health, operational success, and strategic direction over the fiscal year.
- **Utility**: They are used not just for regulatory compliance but also as a tool for communicating with shareholders, investors, and other stakeholders.

Digital Records

- **Emerging Importance**: With the increasing shift to digital operations, managing electronic documents and ensuring their integrity has become paramount.
- **Digital Best Practices**: Implement robust data management systems, regular backups, and strong cybersecurity measures to protect digital records.

By categorizing and understanding the different types of corporate records, businesses can establish tailored management practices that ensure each category is handled appropriately. This not only aids in compliance and operational efficiency but also supports strategic decision-making and enhances corporate transparency.

Document Management Systems

In today's digital age, managing corporate documentation efficiently demands the use of sophisticated document management systems (DMS). These systems not only streamline the storage, retrieval, and archiving of documents but also enhance security and compliance. This section explores various aspects of document management systems, highlighting how they can transform your corporate record-keeping into a seamless, secure, and scalable process.

Introduction to Document Management Systems

- **Definition and Functionality**: A Document Management System is a software solution designed to store, manage, and track electronic documents and images of paper-based information captured through the use of a document scanner. DMS technology helps in organizing all business documents and data in one place, making them easily accessible and manageable.
- **Key Features**: Discuss the essential features of a good DMS, including document indexing, search capabilities, access controls, version control, and audit trails. These features facilitate quick retrieval of documents and ensure that changes are tracked and unauthorized access is prevented.

Benefits of Implementing a DMS

- **Enhanced Security**: Detail how DMS solutions provide robust security features such as encryption, secure access permissions, and regular backups to protect sensitive corporate information from unauthorized access and data breaches.
- **Improved Compliance**: Explain how DMS can aid in compliance with regulatory requirements by ensuring that documents are stored and managed in a manner that meets legal standards, including retention schedules and secure disposal of sensitive information.
- **Operational Efficiency**: Highlight how automating document management processes reduces manual handling, minimizes errors, and saves time and resources. A DMS can significantly speed up document retrieval times and improve overall organizational productivity.

- **Scalability**: Discuss the scalability of DMS solutions, which can grow with the business, accommodating increasing amounts of data and more complex document management needs without compromising performance or security.

Choosing the Right Document Management System

- **Assessing Needs**: Start by assessing your company's specific needs based on the volume of documents, types of documents, and workflow requirements. Consider factors such as the number of users, the need for remote access, and integration capabilities with other software systems.
- **Vendor Selection**: Provide guidelines on selecting a suitable vendor, including checking vendor reputation, support and service terms, security features, and compliance with industry standards.
- **Implementation Considerations**: Outline key considerations for implementing a DMS, such as migration of existing documents into the system, training for employees, and setting up adequate technical support. Discuss the importance of a phased rollout to minimize disruptions to regular business operations.

Maintaining a Document Management System

- **Regular Updates and Maintenance**: Emphasize the importance of keeping the DMS software updated to benefit from improved features, security updates, and bug fixes. Regular maintenance ensures the system operates efficiently and continues to meet organizational needs.
- **Monitoring and Evaluation**: Suggest establishing regular reviews and audits of the DMS to evaluate its effectiveness, user satisfaction, and compliance with document management policies and procedures. Feedback from these evaluations can guide further refinements and enhancements.

Implementing a robust document management system can significantly improve the way a company manages its corporate documentation, turning a potential administrative burden into a strategic asset that supports business operations, ensures compliance, and enhances decision-making.

Best Practices for Record Keeping

Effective record keeping is not only a regulatory requirement but also a crucial component of a company's operational excellence. This section outlines best practices for managing corporate documentation, ensuring that records are accurate, secure, and easily accessible, thus facilitating better decision-making and compliance.

Developing a Record Keeping Policy

- **Establish Clear Guidelines**: Create comprehensive guidelines that outline what documents should be kept, how they should be organized, where they should be stored, and for how long. This policy should be aligned with legal requirements and business needs.
- **Regular Updates**: Keep the record-keeping policy updated to reflect changes in regulatory requirements, business operations, and technological advancements.

Organizing Documents

- **Categorization and Indexing**: Organize documents in a systematic manner, categorizing them by type, purpose, or department. Utilize indexing systems within your document management software to facilitate easy searching and retrieval.
- **Version Control**: Implement version control procedures to keep track of changes made to important documents. This ensures that everyone in the organization uses the most current version of a document and can access previous versions when necessary.

Security Measures

- **Access Controls**: Define who has access to various types of documents, especially sensitive ones, to minimize the risk of unauthorized access. Use roles and permissions features in your document management system to enforce these controls.

- **Data Protection**: Protect documents from unauthorized access, alteration, and deletion by implementing strong security measures such as encryption, secure user authentication, and regular security audits.

Retention and Disposal

- **Retention Schedules**: Adhere to legal and operational document retention schedules. Keep documents for the period required by law and business needs, and no longer, to avoid unnecessary storage costs and potential security risks.
- **Secure Disposal**: When documents are no longer needed, dispose of them securely to prevent the risk of confidential information leaks. Use methods like shredding for paper records and secure deletion for digital files.

Audit and Compliance

- **Regular Audits**: Conduct regular audits of your record-keeping practices to ensure compliance with your record-keeping policy and legal requirements. Audits help identify gaps in document management and areas for improvement.
- **Compliance Checks**: Continuously monitor compliance with relevant laws and regulations to ensure that your record-keeping practices meet all legal standards and industry best practices.

Training and Awareness

- **Employee Training**: Regularly train employees on the importance of proper document management, how to use document management systems, and their specific roles in maintaining records.
- **Awareness Programs**: Implement awareness programs that highlight the significance of security and compliance in record keeping.

Leveraging Technology

- **Adopt Advanced Tools**: Use advanced document management tools that offer features like automated backup, disaster recovery, and advanced search capabilities. This technology not only enhances efficiency but also improves compliance and data security.

By following these best practices, companies can ensure that their record keeping is not just a passive compliance exercise but a proactive strategy that enhances organizational efficiency, reduces risk, and supports strategic decision-making.

Transitioning to a Paperless Office

Moving towards a paperless office is not just an environmentally friendly choice but also a strategic business decision that can lead to increased efficiency, reduced costs, and improved security. This section provides a roadmap for companies looking to transition from traditional paper-based record-keeping to a digital-first approach, highlighting the benefits and outlining the key steps involved.

Benefits of Going Paperless

- **Cost Reduction**: Minimize expenses related to printing, storing, and managing paper documents. Going paperless can significantly reduce the need for physical storage space and the associated costs.
- **Increased Efficiency**: Digital documents can be accessed and shared quickly and easily, eliminating the time spent searching through physical files. Automation of document processes can further streamline operations and reduce manual tasks.
- **Enhanced Security**: Digital documents are easier to secure and back up in multiple locations, reducing the risk of loss due to physical damage or theft.
- **Environmental Impact**: Reduce your company's carbon footprint by decreasing paper use, which contributes to conservation efforts and aligns with corporate sustainability goals.

Planning the Transition

- **Assess Current Practices**: Start by assessing current document management practices and identifying the types of documents that are still maintained in paper form. Understand the workflows associated with these documents to determine how they can be digitized.

- **Set Clear Objectives**: Define clear objectives for the transition, including timelines, budget constraints, and specific outcomes you aim to achieve, such as cost savings or improved access to information.

Choosing the Right Tools

- **Document Management Software**: Select appropriate document management software that meets your company's needs. Consider factors such as scalability, security features, ease of use, and compatibility with existing systems.
- **Scanning Solutions**: Invest in robust scanning solutions that can handle the volume and variety of documents you need to digitize. Ensure that the scanners are capable of producing high-quality digital copies.

Implementing the Paperless System

- **Digitize Existing Records**: Begin the process of digitizing existing paper records. Prioritize documents based on frequency of access and importance.
- **Revise Document-Related Policies**: Update your document management policies and procedures to reflect the new digital-first approach. This includes revisions to how documents are created, stored, shared, and disposed of.
- **Integration into Workflows**: Integrate digital document management into daily workflows. Ensure that all employees are trained on the new systems and understand how to access and manage digital documents.

Managing Change

- **Training and Support**: Provide comprehensive training for all employees on how to use the new document management system. Offer ongoing support to address any issues that arise during the transition.
- **Monitor and Adapt**: Continuously monitor the effectiveness of the paperless system and be ready to make adjustments as needed. Solicit

feedback from users to improve the system and resolve any challenges that emerge.

Ensuring Legal Compliance

- **Regulatory Considerations**: Ensure that the digital management system complies with all relevant regulations concerning document retention, privacy, and data security. This may involve consulting with legal experts to verify compliance.

By methodically planning and executing the transition to a paperless office, companies can not only enjoy operational benefits but also position themselves as modern, eco-conscious businesses. This shift not only supports internal efficiency but also enhances the company's reputation in an increasingly environmentally aware marketplace.

Quick Tips and Recap

As we conclude our exploration of managing corporate documentation, here are some essential tips and a quick recap to ensure your records are clean, compliant, and effectively managed:

- **Emphasize the Importance of Documentation**: Recognize that proper documentation is crucial for legal compliance, financial transparency, and historical accuracy.
- **Categorize Documents Systematically**: Organize documents into clear categories and maintain them using a consistent filing system, whether digital or physical.
- **Implement a Document Management System (DMS)**: Adopt a DMS that fits your business needs to streamline management, enhance security, and improve access to documents.
- **Follow Best Practices for Record Keeping**: Develop and regularly update a comprehensive record-keeping policy, use categorization, indexing, and version control, enforce strict access controls to protect sensitive information, adhere to legal retention schedules, and securely dispose of outdated documents.

- **Plan and Execute the Transition to a Paperless Office**: Assess current practices, set objectives for going paperless, choose the right digital tools, train employees on new systems, and monitor implementation to optimize the process.
- **Ensure Legal Compliance**: Stay informed about regulatory requirements for document retention and privacy. Regularly review and adjust your document management practices to remain compliant.
- **Prepare for Audits**: Maintain documentation in an audit-ready manner, ensuring all records are easily accessible and accurately maintained to facilitate smooth audit processes.

CHAPTER TEN

Financial Frameworks: Effective Capital Management

"Capital isn't scarce; vision is. Effective capital management aligns financial resources with visionary goals to turn ambitions into reality."— SAM WALTON, FOUNDER OF WALMART AND SAM'S CLUB

Dive into the vault of financial wisdom in this pivotal chapter, where every dollar counts and mismanagement is more villainous than a soap opera antagonist. Welcome to the high-stakes world of capital management, where being penny-wise doesn't mean being pound-foolish, and a well-managed wallet is the secret to enduring business prosperity.

In this finance-fueled adventure, we'll unravel the mysteries of capital allocation, budgeting, and cash flow management. Learn how to juggle expenses, investments, and profits with the dexterity of a Wall Street trader. Whether you're bootstrapping a startup or navigating the financial seas of a multinational, mastering your monies is a must.

Forget dry, daunting spreadsheets; think of this as your guide to the financial strategies that spark growth and stability. We'll show you how to squeeze every ounce of value from your capital with savvy risk assessments and strategic funding choices that ensure your business isn't just surviving but thriving. Ready to turn your financial fears into fiscal finesse? Let's make your money work as hard as you do.

Principles of Capital Management

Capital management is a critical aspect of financial stewardship that dictates the longevity and health of a business. This section delves into the foundational principles of capital management, exploring how businesses can effectively balance risk with returns, optimize their capital structure, and align capital allocation with their strategic objectives to foster growth and stability.

Understanding Capital Management

- **Definition**: Capital management involves the strategic planning, allocation, and control of financial resources to maximize a business's value. It ensures that a business can meet its operational needs, fulfill its financial obligations, and pursue its long-term goals.
- **Objective**: The primary objective is to create sustainable value for shareholders by managing the company's capital efficiently while minimizing financial risk.

Balancing Risk and Return

- **Risk Assessment**: Discuss the importance of assessing the risks associated with different types of investments and financial strategies. Companies must understand the potential returns and the risks to make informed decisions.
- **Optimal Risk-Reward Ratio**: Explain strategies for achieving an optimal balance between risk and return. This includes diversification of

investments, prudent financial planning, and continuous market analysis to adapt strategies as necessary.

Optimizing Capital Structure

- **Debt vs. Equity**: Analyze the advantages and disadvantages of using debt versus equity financing. The decision impacts a company's balance sheet, cost of capital, and overall financial flexibility.
- **Leverage**: Detail how leverage (using borrowed capital for investment) can amplify returns but also increase risk. Discuss how companies determine the right level of leverage based on their risk tolerance, market conditions, and operational needs.

Strategic Capital Allocation

- **Allocation Framework**: Present frameworks for capital allocation that align with business strategy and operational requirements. This involves prioritizing investments in projects and ventures that yield the best returns relative to their risk.
- **Performance Monitoring**: Highlight the importance of monitoring the performance of allocated capital to ensure it meets targeted returns and supports strategic objectives. This includes regular review and reallocation based on performance outcomes and shifting market dynamics.

Long-Term Strategic Alignment

- **Aligning with Business Goals**: Emphasize how capital management should be tightly aligned with the company's long-term strategic goals. Whether expanding into new markets, investing in research and development, or enhancing operational capacities, the deployment of capital must support overarching business objectives.
- **Sustainability Considerations**: Discuss the growing importance of considering sustainability in capital allocation decisions. This includes investing in environmentally and socially responsible ventures and practices that ensure long-term profitability and compliance with global standards.

By adhering to these principles, businesses can ensure that their capital management strategies not only protect against undue risk but also position the company for successful growth and profitability. This foundation sets the stage for further discussions on specific capital management practices such as budgeting, cash flow management, and risk assessment in subsequent sections.

Budgeting and Financial Planning

Effective budgeting and financial planning are cornerstones of sound capital management. This section explores the techniques and processes essential for crafting budgets that support business operations while driving strategic initiatives. It also delves into financial planning practices that ensure long-term financial health and operational stability.

Importance of Budgeting

- **Foundation for Financial Control**: Budgets serve as a foundational tool for financial control, allowing businesses to forecast and manage their financial resources effectively.
- **Decision-Making Tool**: They provide a framework for decision-making, helping businesses prioritize expenditures and align them with strategic goals.

Creating an Effective Budget

- **Revenue Forecasting**: Begin with accurate revenue forecasting, which involves analyzing historical data, market trends, and current economic conditions to project future revenues.
- **Cost Estimation**: Accurately estimate costs, considering both fixed and variable expenses. This involves detailed analysis to ensure that all potential costs are accounted for, including direct costs, operational expenses, and overheads.
- **Profit Projections**: Utilize revenue forecasts and cost estimates to project profits. This helps in setting realistic financial goals and assessing the potential financial health of the business.

Financial Planning Techniques

- **Short-term vs. Long-term Planning**: Distinguish between short-term financial planning, which focuses on immediate operational needs, and long-term planning, which is oriented towards strategic goals and growth initiatives.
- **Capital Expenditure Planning (CapEx)**: Plan for capital expenditures by evaluating the returns on investment of high-value assets and their alignment with long-term strategic goals.
- **Contingency Planning**: Include provisions for unexpected events or economic downturns, ensuring the business can continue operations under various scenarios.

Budget Review and Adjustment

- **Regular Review Cycles**: Implement regular review cycles to compare actual financial performance against the budget. This allows for timely adjustments in response to deviations or unforeseen circumstances.
- **Flexible Budgeting**: Embrace flexible budgeting techniques that allow for modifications in response to dynamic market conditions and business needs.

Integrating Budgets with Business Strategy

- **Strategic Alignment**: Ensure that the budget supports the overarching business strategy. This requires collaboration across departments to align financial resources with strategic projects and operational requirements.
- **Stakeholder Involvement**: Involve key stakeholders in the budgeting process to garner insights and foster commitment across the organization.

Utilizing Technology in Budgeting

- **Software Solutions**: Employ budgeting software and financial planning tools that provide real-time data, analytical capabilities, and scenario planning features. These tools enhance accuracy in forecasting and improve efficiency in the budgeting process.

- **Data Analytics**: Leverage data analytics to gain deeper insights into spending patterns, cost drivers, and potential savings opportunities. This data-driven approach supports more informed financial decisions.

By adhering to these budgeting and financial planning practices, businesses can maintain tight control over their finances, reduce risk, and ensure that they are well-positioned to meet both current operational needs and future strategic objectives.

Cash Flow Management

Effective cash flow management is essential for maintaining the liquidity needed to fund daily operations and long-term growth initiatives. This section delves into key strategies for managing cash flow, ensuring that businesses have the resources necessary to meet their financial obligations and capitalize on opportunities as they arise.

Understanding Cash Flow

- **Definition and Importance**: Cash flow represents the net amount of cash and cash-equivalents being transferred into and out of a business. Proper management is crucial as it affects the business's ability to cover payroll, purchase inventory, and invest in new opportunities without incurring unnecessary debt.
- **Components of Cash Flow**: Break down the three main components of cash flow: operational cash flow (day-to-day business activities), investing cash flow (assets and investment activities), and financing cash flow (how debt and equity are managed).

Strategies for Optimizing Cash Flow

- **Accelerating Receivables**: Implement strategies to accelerate incoming cash, such as offering discounts for early payment, reducing payment terms, and utilizing electronic invoicing to speed up the billing process.
- **Managing Payables**: Efficiently manage outgoing cash by negotiating better payment terms with suppliers, prioritizing payments based on their

financial impact, and ensuring timely payment practices to avoid penalties.

- **Inventory Management**: Optimize inventory levels to avoid tying up excess capital in unsold stock while ensuring there are enough goods to meet customer demand.

Cash Flow Forecasting

- **Forecasting Techniques**: Discuss the importance of accurate cash flow forecasting in predicting future cash positions. This involves historical data analysis, understanding market cycles, and predicting external impacts on cash flow.
- **Tools and Software**: Highlight the use of specialized software and tools that can help in creating more accurate and dynamic cash flow forecasts.

Maintaining a Cash Reserve

- **Importance of Liquidity**: Stress the importance of maintaining an adequate level of cash reserves to cover unexpected expenses or economic downturns.
- **Calculating Reserve Needs**: Provide guidelines on how to calculate the appropriate level of reserves based on historical cash flow fluctuations and potential market risks.

Leveraging Financing Options

- **Short-term Financing**: Explore options like lines of credit or short-term loans that can be used to smooth out cash flow irregularities.
- **Long-term Financing Strategies**: Discuss the strategic use of long-term financing to fund larger projects or expansions that have the potential to increase future cash flows.

Monitoring and Adjusting

- **Regular Review and Adjustment**: Emphasize the need for regular reviews of cash flow management strategies to ensure they remain effective as business conditions change.

- **Key Performance Indicators (KPIs)**: Identify critical KPIs related to cash flow, such as days sales outstanding (DSO), days payable outstanding (DPO), and cash conversion cycle, to monitor financial health and operational efficiency.

Effective cash flow management not only ensures that a business can meet its current obligations but also positions it for future growth and stability. By implementing these strategies, businesses can maintain sufficient liquidity to operate effectively even in the face of financial uncertainties.

Investment Strategies and Capital Allocation

Effective capital allocation and strategic investment decisions are pivotal for maximizing returns and supporting sustainable business growth. This section delves into how businesses can manage their investments wisely, ensuring that every dollar spent contributes positively to the company's strategic objectives.

Principles of Capital Allocation

- **Understanding Capital Allocation**: Define capital allocation as the process of deciding how to deploy the organization's financial resources to achieve maximum return on investment. This involves not only investing in new assets and projects but also reallocating resources across existing assets and divisions.
- **Balancing Short-term and Long-term Goals**: Discuss the importance of balancing short-term operational needs with long-term strategic investments to ensure sustained growth and stability.

Investment Decision-Making

- **Capital Budgeting**: Introduce capital budgeting techniques such as Net Present Value (NPV), Internal Rate of Return (IRR), and Payback Period as tools to evaluate potential investments. Explain how these metrics help determine the financial viability and strategic alignment of investment projects.

- **Risk Assessment**: Highlight the need for thorough risk assessment when making investment decisions. Discuss how to identify, quantify, and mitigate financial and operational risks associated with new investments.

Diversification Strategies

- **Portfolio Diversification**: Explain the concept of diversification in capital allocation. Discuss how investing in a variety of projects and markets can reduce risk and stabilize returns over time.
- **Sector and Geographic Diversification**: Encourage diversification across different sectors and geographies to protect the business from sector-specific or region-specific downturns.

Optimizing Return on Investment

- **Performance Monitoring**: Stress the importance of ongoing monitoring and evaluation of investment outcomes. Discuss how regular performance reviews can help refine investment strategies and ensure that they continue to meet the company's strategic goals.
- **Reinvestment Strategies**: Explore strategies for reinvesting profits back into the business. Discuss how effective reinvestment can fuel innovation, improve operational efficiency, and drive future growth.

Stakeholder Engagement in Investment Decisions

- **Involving Key Stakeholders**: Outline the benefits of involving key stakeholders, including investors, board members, and senior management, in the investment decision-making process. Discuss how their insights and expertise can enhance decision quality.
- **Communication and Transparency**: Emphasize the importance of clear communication and transparency with stakeholders regarding investment strategies and outcomes to maintain trust and support.

Leveraging Financial Partnerships

- **Strategic Partnerships**: Discuss how forming strategic partnerships can provide additional capital and expertise for investment opportunities.

Highlight the potential for synergies and access to new markets or technologies through partnerships.

- **Joint Ventures**: Explore the role of joint ventures as a strategy for sharing risk and combining resources for larger or more complex investments.

By adhering to these strategies, businesses can ensure that their investment decisions are well-considered, strategically aligned, and optimized for both risk and return. This comprehensive approach to investment and capital allocation is essential for driving growth, enhancing competitive advantage, and building long-term shareholder value.

Risk Management in Finance

Navigating the financial landscape requires a solid understanding of both risk management and the variety of funding options available to sustain and grow a business. This section discusses how to effectively manage financial risks and explores the diverse sources of funding that can be leveraged to support business objectives.

Understanding Financial Risk Management

- **Importance of Risk Management**: Emphasize the crucial role of risk management in safeguarding the business's financial health and ensuring stability in the face of economic fluctuations and market volatility.
- **Identifying Risks**: Outline the process for identifying potential financial risks, including credit risks, liquidity risks, market risks, and operational risks.
- **Assessing Risks**: Discuss methodologies for assessing the likelihood and potential impact of identified risks, using tools such as risk matrices or financial models.
- **Mitigating Risks**: Provide strategies for mitigating risks, such as diversifying investment portfolios, improving debt management, using hedging instruments, and establishing strong internal controls.

Exploring Funding Options

- **Debt Financing**: Detail the use of loans, credit lines, and bonds as common methods of debt financing. Discuss the advantages and disadvantages of each, including potential impacts on cash flow and financial leverage.
- **Equity Financing**: Explore equity financing options such as issuing new shares of stock. Discuss how this can provide capital without incurring debt, but may dilute existing ownership and earnings per share.
- **Alternative Funding Sources**:
    - **Venture Capital**: Explain how venture capital can provide significant funding for high-growth potential businesses, usually in exchange for equity and active involvement in business management.
    - **Crowdfunding**: Discuss the rise of crowdfunding platforms as a way to raise funds from a large number of people, typically via the internet. Highlight different types of crowdfunding, such as rewards-based, equity-based, and debt-based crowdfunding.

Integrating Funding with Growth Strategies

- **Aligning Funding with Business Phases**: Explain how different funding options are better suited to different stages of a business's growth, from startup phase (seed and venture capital) to expansion phase (public offerings and corporate bonds).
- **Strategic Considerations for Funding**: Discuss how to choose the right funding option based on the business's strategic goals, risk profile, and market conditions. Emphasize the importance of considering the cost of capital and potential return on investment.

Maintaining Financial Flexibility

- **Financial Planning**: Stress the importance of maintaining financial flexibility to take advantage of emerging opportunities or to navigate unexpected challenges.

- **Building Reserves**: Discuss the significance of building cash reserves as a buffer against financial uncertainties and to provide funding for opportunistic investments.

Effective Communication with Stakeholders

- **Transparency with Investors and Lenders**: Highlight the necessity of maintaining transparency with investors and lenders about the company's financial status, risk management practices, and use of funds to build trust and ensure continued support.

By mastering the intricacies of risk management and understanding the spectrum of funding options available, businesses can make informed decisions that not only protect against potential downsides but also position them for successful growth and expansion. This strategic approach to financial management ensures that companies remain robust and responsive in the ever-changing business environment.

Quick Tips and Recap

- **Emphasize Proactive Capital Management**: Regularly assess and adjust your capital management strategies to balance risk with return, ensuring sustainable business growth and financial health.
- **Utilize Effective Budgeting Practices**: Develop and maintain detailed budgets that forecast revenue, manage costs, and allocate resources to align with strategic business goals.
- **Prioritize Cash Flow Management**: Implement robust cash flow management practices to maintain liquidity, manage day-to-day operations, and fund strategic initiatives without relying excessively on external financing.
- **Make Informed Investment Decisions**: Use capital budgeting tools like NPV and IRR to evaluate investment opportunities rigorously, ensuring they meet strategic objectives and offer acceptable risk-adjusted returns.
- **Adopt Comprehensive Risk Management**: Identify, assess, and mitigate financial risks through diversification, hedging, and

establishing strong internal controls to protect the business's assets and earnings.

- **Explore Diverse Funding Options**: Understand and utilize a mix of funding sources including debt, equity, and alternative financing to optimize your capital structure and support different stages of business growth.
- **Maintain Financial Flexibility**: Keep your financial options open by managing debt levels, building cash reserves, and staying informed about new funding opportunities to adapt quickly to market changes or operational needs.
- **Ensure Stakeholder Engagement and Transparency**: Regularly communicate with stakeholders about your financial strategies, risk management, and use of funds to maintain trust and support for your financial decisions.

By adhering to these principles and practices, businesses can enhance their financial frameworks, ensuring they not only survive but thrive in the competitive and ever-changing business landscape.

PART THREE

Expanding Horizons

Welcome to Part Three: Expanding Horizons, where the entrepreneurial spirit meets the pioneer's ambition. Here, the business world is your oyster, and you're armed with the pearl of innovation. This section is not just about stretching geographical boundaries; it's about catapulting your business into new realms of opportunity. From penetrating new markets to harnessing the power of technology and collaborations, we dive deep into strategies that transform local champions into global contenders. Prepare to push the envelope and broaden your business vistas—it's time to take your enterprise beyond the familiar and into the extraordinary. Let's turn those local landmarks into global legacies!

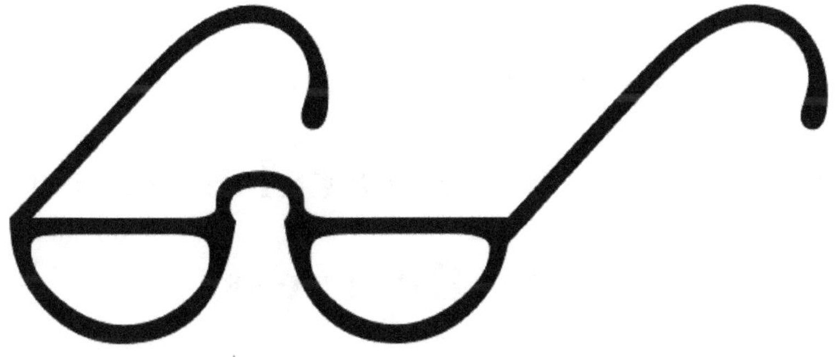

CHAPTER ELEVEN

Adapting to Change: Managing Structural Shifts in Your Business

"Embracing change within your business structure isn't just about survival; it's about seizing opportunities to innovate and lead in your industry."— SATYA NADELLA, CEO OF MICROSOFT

Ah, change—the only constant in the business world, and yet it catches us by surprise every time, like an unexpected plot twist in your favorite soap opera. This chapter is all about rolling with the punches, bending without breaking, and turning every curveball into a home run. Whether you're scaling up, scaling down, or just shifting sideways, mastering the art of structural shifts is crucial.

We'll explore the ins and outs of navigating business metamorphoses, from mergers and acquisitions to rebranding and restructuring. Learn how to reassess and realign your organizational architecture without losing your balance—or your mind. It's about being as flexible as a gymnast and as resilient as a cockroach in the corporate jungle.

Forget about merely surviving changes; we're here to show you how to thrive. You'll discover how to anticipate shifts, prepare your team, and maintain operational integrity even when the business landscape looks like a game of Jenga in overdrive. Strap in, grab your change management toolkit, and let's make adaptability your business's new superpower.

Understanding the Dynamics of Change

Change is an inevitable part of the business landscape, often driven by forces both within and outside the organization. This section explores the various types of organizational changes and the underlying factors that necessitate these transformations, providing a foundational understanding of the dynamics at play.

Types of Organizational Changes

- **Mergers and Acquisitions (M&A)**: M&A can drastically alter a company's structure, market position, and strategic direction. These changes are typically pursued to achieve synergies, expand market reach, or acquire new technologies.
- **Downsizing**: Sometimes necessary during economic downturns or due to organizational restructuring, downsizing involves reducing the company's workforce or operations to improve efficiency and reduce costs.
- **Expansion**: Whether opening new locations, entering new markets, or increasing the product line, expansion requires adjustments in organizational structure and resource allocation.
- **Rebranding**: This involves changing the corporate image, which can affect customer perception and requires internal changes to align with the new brand identity.

- **Restructuring**: Restructuring may involve revamping internal structures, processes, or technologies to improve efficiency, effectiveness, and competitiveness.

Driving Forces Behind Change

- **Market Conditions**: Shifts in consumer demand, economic downturns, or increased competition can force businesses to adapt their strategies and operations.
- **Technological Advancements**: Rapid technological changes may necessitate updates to equipment, processes, or products to stay relevant and competitive.
- **Regulatory Changes**: New or changing regulations can require adjustments in operations, compliance measures, or business models to ensure legal compliance.
- **Leadership Transitions**: New leadership can bring different strategic visions, prompting changes in organizational structure or business direction.

Impacts of Change

- **Operational Impacts**: Structural changes often impact day-to-day operations. Understanding these impacts is crucial for managing transitions smoothly and maintaining productivity.
- **Cultural Impacts**: Changes, especially major ones like mergers or rebranding, can significantly affect organizational culture. Managing the cultural integration or transformation is key to successful change implementation.
- **Financial Impacts**: Most changes have financial implications, whether through the cost of implementation, the impact on revenue, or changes in financial management strategies.

Managing Expectations and Perceptions

- **Stakeholder Communication**: Effective communication with stakeholders—including employees, customers, and investors—is essential during times of change. Clear, transparent communication helps manage expectations and reduce uncertainty.

- **Building Trust**: Maintaining or rebuilding trust is critical, especially if changes are extensive or involve significant disruptions. Trust is built through consistent, honest communication and by involving stakeholders in the change process.

Understanding these dynamics allows business leaders to anticipate the challenges associated with change and to develop strategies that leverage change for growth and improvement. This foundational knowledge sets the stage for deeper exploration into strategic planning for change, ensuring that the business remains resilient and adaptable in a constantly evolving environment.

Strategic Planning for Change

Effective management of change requires not just reactive measures but proactive strategic planning. This section delves into the critical role of strategic planning in adapting to and capitalizing on change, providing a framework for anticipating future shifts and creating strategies that enhance organizational resilience and agility.

The Role of Strategic Planning in Change Management

- **Proactive vs. Reactive Planning**: Emphasize the benefits of proactive planning which allows organizations to anticipate changes and prepare strategies in advance, rather than reacting hastily to market forces or internal pressures.
- **Aligning Strategy with Vision**: Strategic planning should align with the long-term vision of the organization, ensuring that changes contribute to the broader business goals and objectives.

Developing a Strategic Change Plan

- **Environmental Scanning**: Regularly conduct environmental scans to identify emerging trends, potential threats, and new opportunities in the industry. Tools like PESTEL analysis (Political, Economic, Social,

Technological, Environmental, Legal) can provide comprehensive insights.

- **Scenario Planning**: Use scenario planning to anticipate possible future scenarios and develop flexible strategies to handle various outcomes. This helps in preparing for uncertainties effectively.
- **Risk Assessment**: Integral to strategic planning is the assessment of risks associated with potential changes. Identify the risks each scenario presents and plan mitigative actions to minimize negative impacts.

Setting Objectives and Key Results

- **SMART Goals**: Define specific, measurable, achievable, relevant, and time-bound goals that guide the change process and provide clear benchmarks for success.
- **Key Performance Indicators (KPIs)**: Establish KPIs to monitor progress and measure the effectiveness of implemented changes. These indicators help in adjusting strategies as needed to achieve desired outcomes.

Engaging Stakeholders in the Planning Process

- **Inclusive Approach**: Include key stakeholders in the planning process to gather diverse insights and foster a sense of ownership and commitment to the strategic plan.
- **Communication Strategy**: Develop a comprehensive communication strategy that keeps all stakeholders informed about the reasons for changes, the benefits expected, and the roles individuals will play in the process.

Implementing the Strategic Plan

- **Phased Implementation**: Implement changes in phases to minimize disruption and allow for adjustments based on interim feedback and outcomes.

- **Change Leadership**: Identify or develop change leaders within the organization who can drive the change process, motivate others, and address resistance effectively.

Feedback Loops and Continuous Improvement

- **Regular Review Meetings**: Hold regular meetings to review the progress of the strategic plan and make necessary adjustments. This ensures that the plan remains relevant and effective in the face of ongoing changes.
- **Learning Organization**: Foster a culture that views change as an opportunity for learning and growth. Encourage feedback and lessons learned from past changes to improve future strategic planning processes.

Strategic planning for change is not a one-time effort but a continuous process that requires adaptability, foresight, and engagement across the organization. By effectively planning for change, businesses can not only survive but thrive in dynamic environments, turning potential challenges into opportunities for innovation and growth.

Implementing Structural Changes

Successfully implementing structural changes within an organization demands careful planning, strong leadership, and clear communication. This section focuses on the processes and best practices for executing changes effectively, ensuring minimal disruption and achieving the desired outcomes.

Developing a Change Implementation Plan

- **Detailed Action Plan**: Create a comprehensive action plan that outlines the steps needed to implement the change, including timelines, resources required, and responsibilities assigned to team members.
- **Integration with Daily Operations**: Ensure that the plan integrates smoothly with existing operations to avoid unnecessary disruptions. Consider how the changes will affect daily activities and plan for a transition period.

Role of Leadership in Change Management

- **Vision and Commitment**: Leaders must clearly communicate the vision behind the change and demonstrate commitment to the process. Their attitude can significantly influence how the rest of the organization responds to the change.
- **Support and Guidance**: Leaders should be accessible, providing support and guidance to employees throughout the transition. They play a crucial role in motivating the team and addressing any concerns that arise.

Communicating the Change

- **Transparent Communication**: Maintain transparency with all stakeholders about the reasons for the change, the benefits it aims to achieve, and how it will be implemented. Clear communication can help manage expectations and mitigate resistance.
- **Regular Updates**: Provide regular updates on the progress of the change implementation. This keeps everyone informed and helps maintain momentum and engagement from all parties involved.

Managing Resistance to Change

- **Identify Resistance**: Recognize areas where resistance is likely to occur and understand the reasons behind it. Resistance often stems from fear of the unknown or a sense of loss.
- **Address Concerns**: Actively address these concerns through discussions, training sessions, and demonstrations of how the change will benefit individuals and the organization as a whole.

Employee Engagement and Involvement

- **Inclusive Approach**: Involve employees in the change process as much as possible. This can include seeking their input during the planning phase and involving them in decision-making.

- **Training and Development**: Provide adequate training and development opportunities to help employees acquire the skills needed for new processes or technologies introduced by the change.

Monitoring and Adjusting

- **Feedback Mechanisms**: Implement mechanisms for collecting feedback from employees at various stages of the implementation process. Feedback is crucial for identifying issues early and making necessary adjustments.
- **Performance Monitoring**: Monitor the performance of the change implementation against predefined metrics and KPIs. This helps determine if the change is meeting its objectives and what adjustments may be needed for better results.

Celebrating Milestones

- **Recognition and Rewards**: Recognize and celebrate milestones as the organization progresses through the change. This can boost morale and reinforce the benefits of the change, encouraging continued support and effort from the team.

Implementing structural changes is a dynamic process that requires flexibility, persistence, and a deep understanding of the organizational culture. By following these best practices, organizations can enhance their capacity to adapt, ultimately leading to a more resilient and agile business model.

Tools and Techniques for Effective Change Management

Effective change management requires a robust toolkit that includes proven methodologies and practical techniques to guide organizations through transitions. This section explores various tools and frameworks that can aid businesses in managing change effectively, ensuring smooth implementation and minimizing disruptions.

Change Management Models

- **Kotter's 8-Step Change Model**: Introduce Kotter's model which provides a sequential approach starting with creating urgency, forming powerful coalitions, creating a vision for change, and communicating the vision. The model emphasizes the need for short-term wins, consolidating gains, and anchoring changes in corporate culture.
- **ADKAR Model**: Explain the ADKAR model, which focuses on individual change management through five key goals: Awareness, Desire, Knowledge, Ability, and Reinforcement. This model is particularly effective for ensuring that changes are embraced at the employee level.

Project Management Tools

- **Gantt Charts**: Utilize Gantt charts to plan and visualize the timeline of change projects, tracking progress against key milestones and deadlines.
- **Critical Path Method (CPM)**: Employ CPM to identify the longest sequence of dependent activities and estimate the shortest possible project duration to focus efforts on critical tasks that impact the project timeline.

Stakeholder Analysis Tools

- **Stakeholder Maps**: Create stakeholder maps to identify and categorize stakeholders by their level of influence and interest in the change. This helps in tailoring communication strategies to different groups and engaging them effectively.
- **Power/Interest Grid**: Use the Power/Interest Grid to prioritize stakeholder concerns and expectations, which can guide the allocation of resources in managing stakeholder relationships.

Communication Strategies

- **Regular Briefings**: Establish a schedule of regular briefings to keep stakeholders informed and engaged throughout the change process.

- **Feedback Loops**: Implement continuous feedback loops using surveys, interviews, and informal discussions to gather input and assess the sentiment around the changes.

Resistance Management Techniques

- **Resistance Workshops**: Conduct workshops to address concerns, dispel myths, and gather insights directly from those resistant to change.
- **Change Champions**: Identify and empower change champions within the organization who can advocate for the benefits of the change and assist their peers through the transition.

Cultural Alignment Strategies

- **Cultural Assessments**: Perform cultural assessments to understand the existing organizational culture and identify aspects that may support or hinder the proposed changes.
- **Cultural Adjustment Plans**: Develop plans to adjust the organizational culture in alignment with new values and behaviors introduced by the change.

Training and Support Systems

- **Customized Training Programs**: Develop customized training programs to equip employees with the necessary skills and knowledge to adapt to new systems, processes, or technologies.
- **Support Desks**: Set up support desks or help lines to provide ongoing assistance and resolve issues as employees transition to new ways of working.

By employing these tools and techniques, organizations can manage the complexities associated with change more effectively. These resources not only facilitate smoother transitions but also help in achieving the desired outcomes of change initiatives, ensuring that the organization remains adaptive and competitive in a rapidly evolving business environment.

Sustaining Success Post-Change

Successfully implementing structural changes is only the first step; sustaining those changes and integrating them into the fabric of the organization is equally crucial. This section explores strategies to ensure that the new changes are not only accepted but also thrive, contributing to long-term organizational success and resilience.

Evaluating Change Impact

- **Performance Metrics**: Establish clear metrics to evaluate the success of the change based on predefined objectives. This could include financial performance, productivity measures, customer satisfaction scores, or employee engagement levels.
- **Regular Reviews**: Schedule regular review meetings to assess the progress of the change initiatives against these metrics. This allows for ongoing adjustments and fine-tuning to optimize outcomes.

Reinforcing Changes

- **Continuous Reinforcement**: Utilize various reinforcement mechanisms such as ongoing training, communication, and recognition programs to help make the changes stick. This includes celebrating successes and quick wins to build momentum and positive perceptions of the change.
- **Feedback Mechanisms**: Implement robust feedback systems that allow employees to share their experiences and concerns post-change. This feedback should be actively used to address any issues and adapt strategies as necessary.

Cultural Integration

- **Aligning with Organizational Culture**: Ensure that the changes are aligned with the core values and behaviors of the organization. If necessary, undertake initiatives to evolve the organizational culture to better support the new changes.
- **Leadership Role Modeling**: Encourage leaders at all levels to model behaviors that reflect the changes. Leadership alignment is critical in

legitimizing changes and integrating them into the organizational culture.

Building Resilience and Flexibility

- **Developing Adaptive Capabilities**: Foster an environment that values learning and flexibility. Encourage employees to develop skills and behaviors that support adaptability and resilience.
- **Change Preparedness**: Equip the organization with the tools and mindset to handle future changes. This includes building a change-ready culture where change is expected and embraced as part of the organizational life.

Long-term Strategic Focus

- **Strategic Alignment**: Continuously align change initiatives with the organization's long-term strategic goals. Ensure that every change moves the organization closer to achieving its broader objectives.
- **Sustainability Considerations**: Factor sustainability into the change process, ensuring that changes contribute positively to the organization's long-term sustainability goals, whether they are environmental, social, or economic.

Leveraging Technology

- **Technology Utilization**: Maximize the use of technology to support the new changes. This can include digital tools to enhance communication, collaboration, and data analysis which are vital for maintaining the efficacy and relevance of changes over time.

By following these strategies, organizations can not only implement changes effectively but also ensure that these changes deliver lasting benefits. This ongoing commitment to nurturing and refining change initiatives helps to solidify the gains achieved, ensuring they contribute to the organization's enduring success and adaptability in an ever-changing business environment.

Quick Tips and Recap

- Understand the various types of organizational changes such as mergers, acquisitions, downsizing, expansion, and restructuring, and recognize the forces driving these changes including market dynamics, technological advances, and internal growth strategies.
- Embrace strategic planning as a proactive measure to anticipate and prepare for potential changes, using tools like environmental scanning and scenario planning to map out future possibilities and responses.
- Implement structural changes effectively by developing a detailed action plan, engaging strong leadership to guide the process, and maintaining open and transparent communication with all stakeholders to manage expectations and reduce resistance.
- Utilize proven change management tools and techniques such as Kotter's 8-Step Change Model and the ADKAR Model to structure the change process; employ project management tools like Gantt charts and the Critical Path Method to monitor progress and keep changes on track.
- Sustain the implemented changes by continuously reinforcing the new practices through training, support, and cultural integration; regularly review and adjust the changes based on performance metrics and feedback to ensure they remain aligned with the organization's long-term goals and adapt to evolving external and internal conditions.
- Cultivate a resilient organizational culture that is flexible, adaptable, and prepared to handle future changes, emphasizing the importance of continuous learning, strategic alignment, and sustainability considerations in solidifying long-term success.

By following these guidelines, your organization can effectively navigate and manage structural shifts, ensuring that changes lead to improvement and innovation rather than disruption and setback.

CHAPTER TWELVE

Equity Essentials: Handling Stock and Ownership Complexities

"Understanding equity and stock ownership complexities is crucial for navigating the corporate landscape effectively and ensuring all stakeholders thrive." — JAMIE DIMON, CEO OF JPMORGAN CHASE

Step into the Wall Street of your business, where shares are more than just numbers—they are tickets to your entrepreneurial roller coaster! Here in the land of equity, every stock certificate is a plot twist, and ownership stakes are the main characters. This chapter will help you navigate the intricate ballet of buying, selling, and managing shares without stepping on any financial toes.

Whether you're issuing stock for the first time or juggling the interests of multiple shareholders, we'll break down the complex dance into manageable steps. Learn how to align shareholder interests with business goals, handle the delicate art of equity dilution, and avoid the common pitfalls that can lead to shareholder revolts. From crafting transparent shareholder agreements to understanding the impact of stock options on your control over the company, this section will equip you with the savvy to manage your equity like a seasoned maestro.

So, tighten your grip on that gavel—whether you're convening a board meeting or negotiating a buyout, the power of equity management is at your fingertips. Let's turn those complex ownership challenges into strategic advantages that propel your business forward!

Basics of Equity and Stock Issuance

Understanding the fundamentals of equity and the mechanisms of stock issuance is crucial for any business owner looking to navigate the complexities of corporate ownership. This section delves into the core concepts of equity, different types of stock, and the initial steps involved in issuing shares.

Understanding Equity

- **Definition of Equity**: Equity represents ownership in a company. It is the shareholders' stake that signifies their claim on the company's assets and earnings.
- **Types of Equity**: Differentiate between equity types such as common stock, which typically carries voting rights and a claim on profits via dividends, and preferred stock, which often has priority over common stock in dividend payments and asset liquidation but may not carry voting rights.

Types of Stock

- **Common Stock**: Discuss the features of common stock, including the rights to vote on corporate matters and receive dividends. Highlight how common stockholders are last in priority when it comes to asset distribution upon liquidation.
- **Preferred Stock**: Explain the benefits of preferred stock, such as fixed dividends and priority over common stock in asset distribution. Discuss

its various configurations, including convertible and cumulative preferences.

Process of Issuing Stock

- **Initial Public Offering (IPO)**: Outline the process of an IPO, from the decision-making and preparation phase, involving financial audits and regulatory compliance, to the actual public offering where shares are sold to the public.
- **Private Placement**: Discuss private placement as an alternative to an IPO for raising capital by selling stocks or bonds to private investors rather than the public market. Highlight the advantages, such as fewer regulatory requirements and greater speed in securing funding.

Legal and Regulatory Considerations

- **Securities Regulation**: Introduce the securities regulations that govern the issuance of stock, emphasizing the need for compliance with rules set by bodies such as the Securities and Exchange Commission (SEC) in the United States.
- **Documentation and Disclosure**: Discuss the importance of proper documentation, including the prospectus during an IPO, which must disclose essential information about the business, its finances, and the risks involved to potential investors.

Preparing for Stock Issuance

- **Financial Audits**: Emphasize the need for comprehensive financial audits to ensure that all financial statements are accurate and transparent before stock issuance.
- **Choosing Financial Partners**: Explain the role of financial partners, such as investment banks, in helping to structure the offering, set the price, and market the shares to potential investors.

By establishing a solid foundation in the basics of equity and stock issuance, businesses can better prepare to enter the public markets or secure private investment effectively. This knowledge is crucial for navigating the initial phases of expanding ownership and setting the stage for successful financial growth and stability.

Managing Shareholder Relations

Effectively managing shareholder relations is crucial for maintaining a stable and supportive investment environment. This section discusses strategies for building and sustaining positive relationships with shareholders, ensuring their interests are aligned with the company's strategic goals.

Importance of Shareholder Relations

- **Building Trust**: Emphasize the importance of trust between shareholders and the company's management. Trust is fundamental to investor confidence and can significantly affect the company's ability to raise capital and its overall market perception.
- **Transparency and Communication**: Highlight the need for transparency in all communications with shareholders. Regular, clear, and honest communication can prevent misunderstandings and mitigate potential conflicts.

Effective Communication Strategies

- **Regular Updates**: Implement a system for regular updates via newsletters, emails, or online portals that keep shareholders informed about company performance, key decisions, and future plans.
- **Annual Meetings**: Discuss the role of annual shareholder meetings as a platform for direct interaction. These meetings allow shareholders to ask questions, express concerns, and provide feedback directly to the board and management.
- **Crisis Communication**: Outline strategies for communication during crises, ensuring that shareholders are informed about what is happening, what the company is doing in response, and what steps are being taken to mitigate the situation.

Aligning Interests with Business Goals

- **Shareholder Engagement**: Involve shareholders in discussions about the company's strategic direction to ensure that their interests are considered in decision-making processes.
- **Dividend Policies**: Explain how establishing clear and consistent dividend policies can help align shareholders' financial returns with company performance, thus maintaining their support and investment.

Handling Shareholder Disputes

- **Proactive Conflict Resolution**: Introduce mechanisms for identifying and addressing shareholder concerns before they escalate into disputes. This could include regular feedback sessions and dedicated communication channels for investor grievances.
- **Legal Framework**: Provide information on the legal frameworks that govern shareholder rights and the company's obligations. Understanding these can help in navigating disputes and ensuring that resolutions are compliant with regulatory standards.

Tools and Technologies

- **Investor Relations (IR) Platforms**: Utilize modern IR platforms that offer tools for disseminating information, managing communications, and gathering shareholder feedback efficiently.
- **Social Media**: Leverage social media and other online platforms to maintain an ongoing dialogue with shareholders and the broader market, making the company's activities and achievements more visible and accessible.

By prioritizing effective shareholder relations management, companies can foster a loyal and supportive investor base that is more likely to back the company during both prosperous and challenging times. This commitment to open dialogue and mutual interest alignment not only enhances corporate governance but also contributes to the long-term success of the organization.

Equity Dilution and Its Impacts

Equity dilution occurs when a company issues new shares, reducing the ownership percentage of existing shareholders. This section explores the concept of equity dilution, its potential impacts on shareholders, and strategies for managing it effectively to maintain investor confidence and company valuation.

Understanding Equity Dilution

- **Definition and Causes**: Define equity dilution as the decrease in existing shareholders' ownership percentages due to the issuance of additional shares. Common causes include raising capital through new equity, conversion of convertible securities, and stock option exercises.
- **Calculating Dilution**: Discuss how to calculate the extent of dilution and its impact on share value and ownership structure. Include examples to illustrate how dilution affects earnings per share (EPS) and control over company decisions.

Impacts of Dilution

- **Impact on Share Value**: Explain how dilution can affect share value by spreading earnings over a larger number of shares, potentially reducing the value of each share if the capital raised does not result in proportional growth.
- **Control and Voting Power**: Highlight the impact on shareholders' control and voting power within the company. Dilution can diminish individual shareholders' influence on corporate governance and strategic decisions.

Communicating About Dilution

- **Transparency with Shareholders**: Emphasize the importance of being transparent with shareholders about the reasons for dilution and how it is expected to benefit the company. Clear communication can help mitigate negative perceptions and potential dissatisfaction.

- **Disclosure Practices**: Outline best practices for disclosure, ensuring that all regulatory requirements are met and that shareholders are fully informed about changes to the share structure.

Strategies to Manage Equity Dilution

- **Minimizing Unnecessary Dilution**: Discuss strategies to minimize dilution, such as using debt financing where appropriate or issuing new shares at a price that accurately reflects the company's value to prevent excessive dilution.
- **Offering Preemptive Rights**: Consider offering preemptive rights to existing shareholders, allowing them the opportunity to purchase new shares proportionate to their existing holdings to maintain their ownership percentage.
- **Using Dilution as a Strategic Tool**: Describe scenarios where dilution might be strategically beneficial, such as in acquisitions or in attracting key employees through stock option plans. The long-term benefits (e.g., acquiring a competitive business or securing a talented executive team) may outweigh the short-term impacts of dilution.

Long-Term Planning

- **Incorporating Anti-dilution Provisions**: Include anti-dilution provisions in agreements with investors, which can adjust the conversion rates or prices to protect them from future equity dilution.
- **Regular Review of Equity Plan**: Regularly review and adjust the equity compensation plan to ensure it aligns with the company's long-term strategic goals and market conditions, minimizing undue dilution while attracting and retaining talent.

By understanding and strategically managing equity dilution, companies can protect existing shareholders' interests while securing the capital and resources needed for growth. Effective management of dilution not only supports a company's financial health but also builds and maintains trust with its investors.

Stock Options and Incentives

Stock options and other equity-based incentives are powerful tools for attracting, retaining, and motivating employees. This section explores the mechanics of stock options, the benefits they offer to both employees and employers, and how to effectively manage these incentives to align with company goals.

Understanding Stock Options

- **Definition and Types**: Define stock options as contracts that give employees the right, but not the obligation, to buy shares of the company at a predetermined price, known as the exercise or strike price, within a specific time period. Differentiate between the two main types: incentive stock options (ISOs) and non-qualified stock options (NSOs).
- **Benefits to Employees**: Discuss how stock options can serve as a form of compensation that aligns employees' interests with the success of the company, potentially leading to substantial financial reward if the company's stock price increases.

► A Stock Purchase Agreement can be found in the **Appendix**. If you are interested in receiving an electronic copy of this document, email us at documents@AuthorsDoor.com with the subject line "Request for Stock Purchase Agreement." Upon receiving your email, we will promptly send you a Microsoft Word copy of the document. **Disclaimer:** Please note that all agreements are provided for informational purposes only and should not be construed as legal advice. We recommend consulting with a qualified attorney to ensure that any legal documents or decisions are tailored to your specific circumstances.

Setting Up an Employee Stock Option Plan (ESOP)

- **Plan Design**: Outline the steps to design an ESOP, including determining eligibility, the total number of shares to be included in the plan, the vesting schedule, and the exercise price.
- **Legal and Regulatory Considerations**: Highlight the legal requirements and tax implications for both employers and employees

when establishing and participating in an ESOP. Emphasize the importance of complying with securities laws and regulations.

Advantages of Offering Stock Options

- **Attracting Talent**: Emphasize how stock options can make a compensation package more attractive to high-caliber candidates who might seek to share in the company's growth potential.
- **Employee Retention**: Discuss how vesting schedules can incentivize employees to remain with the company longer, reducing turnover and retaining valuable expertise.
- **Enhancing Employee Motivation and Performance**: Explain how giving employees a stake in the company's success can boost motivation, increase productivity, and foster a stronger alignment with corporate goals.

Managing Equity-Based Incentives

- **Communicating Value to Employees**: Provide strategies for effectively communicating the value and potential benefits of stock options to employees, ensuring they understand how options work and the conditions under which they can benefit.
- **Regular Review and Adjustments**: Advocate for regular reviews of the ESOP to ensure it continues to meet the strategic needs of the business and remains competitive and fair, especially in changing market conditions.
- **Balancing Dilution and Incentives**: Address the need to balance the issuance of stock options with the potential for equity dilution, ensuring that the interests of both shareholders and option holders are considered.

Challenges and Considerations

- **Market Volatility**: Discuss the impact of market volatility on the perceived value of stock options and how companies can manage expectations during downturns.

- **Cost Recognition**: Highlight the need for companies to recognize the cost of issuing stock options, which can impact financial statements and investor perceptions.

By leveraging stock options and other equity-based incentives effectively, companies can not only enhance their recruitment and retention strategies but also create a workforce that is deeply invested in the organization's success. This alignment of interests between the company and its employees helps drive sustained growth and innovation.

Handling Complex Equity Challenges

Navigating the complex landscape of equity management involves more than just distributing shares; it requires addressing intricate scenarios that can significantly impact the company's ownership structure and shareholder relations. This section discusses how to handle complex equity challenges such as buybacks, stock splits, shareholder disputes, and restructuring ownership, providing strategies to manage these situations effectively.

Stock Buybacks

- **Purpose and Impact**: Explain the reasons behind stock buybacks, such as increasing the value of remaining shares, distributing excess cash to shareholders, or adjusting the capital structure.
- **Implementation**: Discuss the methods of conducting buybacks, including open market purchases and tender offers, along with the regulatory considerations and market conditions that influence this decision.

Stock Splits and Reverse Splits

- **Rationale**: Clarify why companies might undertake stock splits or reverse splits, often to make shares more accessible to investors by adjusting the share price or to meet stock exchange listing requirements.
- **Effects on Shareholders**: Detail how splits affect shareholders, emphasizing that while the total value of their holdings remains the

same, the psychological perception of more affordable shares can boost market interest.

Managing Shareholder Disputes

- **Common Causes**: Identify common causes of shareholder disputes, such as disagreements over dividend policies, strategic decisions, or management performance.
- **Resolution Strategies**: Offer strategies for resolving disputes, including mediation, arbitration, or, in some cases, legal action. Highlight the importance of maintaining open lines of communication and transparent decision-making processes to prevent disputes.

Restructuring Ownership

- **Reasons for Restructuring**: Discuss scenarios that might necessitate ownership restructuring, such as preparing for acquisitions, divestitures, or transitioning from private to public ownership.
- **Approach**: Outline the steps involved in restructuring ownership, including valuation assessments, negotiation with stakeholders, and alignment with overall strategic objectives.

Legal and Regulatory Compliance

- **Navigating Compliance**: Emphasize the importance of adhering to legal and regulatory requirements when modifying equity structures, conducting buybacks, or handling disputes.
- **Documentation and Reporting**: Explain the necessity for meticulous documentation and timely reporting to regulatory authorities to ensure compliance and maintain corporate integrity.

Preventive Measures and Best Practices

- **Proactive Governance**: Advocate for proactive governance practices, such as regularly reviewing shareholder agreements and corporate bylaws to adapt to changing circumstances and prevent conflicts.
- **Educating Shareholders**: Discuss the importance of educating shareholders about their rights and responsibilities, the company's

strategic direction, and the rationale behind major equity decisions to foster a cooperative relationship.

By effectively managing these complex equity challenges, companies can ensure that their capital structure supports their strategic goals, maintains shareholder confidence, and upholds corporate governance standards. This proactive approach to equity management not only safeguards the company's financial health but also contributes to its long-term success and stability.

Quick Tips and Recap

- **Understand Equity Types**: Familiarize yourself with the different types of equity, including common and preferred stock, to effectively manage stock issuance and shareholder expectations.
- **Maintain Transparent Shareholder Relations**: Foster strong, transparent relationships with shareholders through regular communication, updates, and meetings to ensure alignment and satisfaction with business strategies.
- **Manage Equity Dilution Thoughtfully**: Be strategic about equity dilution; consider its impact on share value and shareholder control, and communicate changes clearly to affected parties.
- **Leverage Stock Options Wisely**: Use stock options and other equity-based incentives as tools to attract, retain, and motivate employees, ensuring they align with long-term company goals.
- **Navigate Complex Equity Challenges**: Tackle complex equity issues like buybacks, stock splits, and shareholder disputes with careful planning, clear communication, and adherence to legal and regulatory requirements.
- **Proactively Adjust Ownership Structures**: Be prepared to adjust ownership structures in response to business growth, market changes, or strategic shifts, ensuring all changes support the overall business objectives.

- **Ensure Legal and Regulatory Compliance**: Always ensure compliance with legal and regulatory frameworks to maintain corporate integrity and avoid legal repercussions.
- **Educate and Engage Stakeholders**: Continuously educate and involve stakeholders in major decisions and changes regarding equity to foster trust and cooperative relationships.

By following these tips, you can effectively manage your company's equity complexities, turning potential challenges into opportunities for strategic advantage and sustained business growth.

CHAPTER THIRTEEN

Going National: Strategies for Multi-state Expansion

"Expanding nationally requires understanding that what works in one state may not work in another. Adaptability and local insight are keys to successful multi-state expansion." — HOWARD SCHULTZ, FORMER CEO OF STARBUCKS

Buckle up and prepare your business for a coast-to-coast adventure! In this chapter, we're not just crossing state lines; we're redrawing the map of your business's boundaries. Expanding into multiple states isn't for the faint of heart—it's the corporate equivalent of planning a nationwide tour for a rock band. Each new state is a different venue, with its own set of rules, fans, and peculiar local flavors.

We'll guide you through the labyrinth of logistical, regulatory, and market challenges that come with spreading your business far and wide. Learn how to scout locations with the precision of a seasoned explorer and navigate new regulatory environments like a pro. From understanding regional market trends to adapting your marketing strategies to diverse audiences, this chapter is your handbook for turning local triumphs into national success stories.

With the right approach, your business can go from hometown hero to national sensation. Ready to see your logo on billboards from coast to coast? Let's plot the route, pack your entrepreneurial spirit, and hit the road to multi-state mastery!

Assessing Market Viability Across States

Expanding your business across multiple states requires a thorough understanding of various regional markets. This section discusses how to assess the viability of different markets to ensure that your expansion efforts are both strategic and profitable.

Understanding Regional Market Dynamics

- **Market Research**: Begin with comprehensive market research to understand the demographics, consumer behavior, economic conditions, and cultural nuances of each potential market. Utilize both primary data (surveys, focus groups) and secondary data (industry reports, census data).
- **Competitive Analysis**: Conduct a detailed analysis of the competitive landscape in each state. Identify local competitors, their market share, strengths, and weaknesses. This will help you understand the competitive challenges and opportunities your business might face.

Evaluating Economic and Regulatory Environments

- **Economic Indicators**: Examine economic indicators such as GDP growth rates, employment rates, income levels, and real estate costs to gauge the economic health and consumer spending power in each state.
- **Regulatory Climate**: Assess the regulatory environment in each state. Some states may have more stringent business regulations, higher taxes, or more complex licensing requirements, which could impact your operational costs and business model.

Consumer Preferences and Needs

- **Local Consumer Behavior**: Study local consumer preferences and purchasing behaviors. This can vary significantly across regions and influence product offerings, pricing strategies, and promotional activities.
- **Cultural Sensitivities**: Be aware of cultural differences and sensitivities that may affect consumer response to your products or marketing. Tailoring your approach to align with local values and norms can enhance acceptance and success.

Feasibility and Profitability Analysis

- **Cost-Benefit Analysis**: Conduct a cost-benefit analysis for entering each new state. Consider potential revenue against the costs of expansion, including marketing, logistics, staffing, and compliance with local regulations.
- **Scalability and Growth Potential**: Evaluate the scalability of your business model in each new market. Consider factors such as market size, growth potential, and the ability to scale operations efficiently.

Tools and Resources for Market Assessment

- **Geographic Information Systems (GIS)**: Utilize GIS tools to analyze geographical data that can provide insights into market trends, population density, and consumer demographics.
- **Professional Consultancies**: Consider hiring market research firms or local consultants who understand the regional dynamics and can provide detailed insights and recommendations.

By meticulously assessing each potential market, you can determine where to focus your expansion efforts to maximize success. This strategic approach ensures that your business is well-positioned to meet the diverse needs of new regional markets and can adapt effectively to local conditions and consumer preferences.

Navigating Regulatory and Legal Landscapes

Expanding your business into new states brings with it a complex web of regulatory and legal challenges. This section outlines how to navigate these challenges effectively, ensuring compliance while maintaining operational efficiency.

Understanding State-Specific Regulations

- **Business Registration and Licensing**: Detail the requirements for registering your business and obtaining necessary licenses in each state. This includes understanding state-specific variations in corporate structure, zoning laws, and business operation permits.
- **Taxation Laws**: Explore the tax implications of multi-state operations. Each state has its own tax regime, affecting corporate income taxes, sales taxes, and payroll taxes. Understanding these can significantly impact your financial planning.

Employment Laws

- **Worker Rights and Wages**: Each state has its own set of employment laws, including minimum wage requirements, worker rights, and benefits obligations. Familiarize yourself with these laws to ensure fair and legal treatment of employees across all locations.
- **Hiring Practices**: Discuss how different states may have different regulations regarding hiring practices, including background checks, anti-discrimination policies, and eligibility for employment.

Industry-Specific Regulations

- **Sector-Specific Compliance**: Certain industries may face additional state-specific regulations, such as healthcare, financial services, or education. Identify and understand these to ensure that your business meets all industry standards and legal requirements.
- **Environmental Regulations**: Highlight the importance of compliance with state environmental regulations, which can vary widely and may

impact business operations, especially in industries like manufacturing or agriculture.

Strategies for Managing Legal Complexity

- **Legal Advisory**: Recommend building relationships with legal experts in each state or hiring a multistate legal team that can navigate and manage the diverse legal landscape efficiently.
- **Compliance Programs**: Develop robust compliance programs that include regular audits, employee training, and updates in legal changes to maintain compliance across all states.

Utilizing Technology and Tools

- **Regulatory Technology Solutions**: Leverage technology solutions that provide updates on regulatory changes and help manage compliance documentation and processes efficiently.
- **Centralized Legal Database**: Maintain a centralized database of legal and regulatory information that can be accessed by teams across different states to ensure uniform compliance practices.

Building Local Networks

- **Engaging with Local Authorities**: Establish good relationships with local regulatory bodies and chambers of commerce. These relationships can provide insights into regulatory changes and facilitate smoother business operations.
- **Networking with Other Businesses**: Network with other businesses operating in the region to share best practices and insights related to navigating the state's regulatory environment.

By proactively addressing the regulatory and legal challenges of multi-state expansion, businesses can avoid costly penalties and disruptions, ensuring a smoother transition into new markets. This strategic approach not only aids in compliance but also enhances the business's reputation and operational success in new regions.

Strategic Location Scouting and Setup

Expanding into new states requires careful consideration of where to establish physical presences, such as offices or retail locations. This section discusses the strategic process of location scouting and the key factors involved in setting up successful operations in chosen locations.

Factors in Location Scouting

- **Market Accessibility**: Evaluate the accessibility of each potential location to your target market. Consider factors such as population density, demographic trends, and proximity to major transport networks.
- **Logistics and Supply Chain**: Analyze the logistics of each location, including ease of supply chain management, availability of vendors and partners, and transportation costs. Efficient logistics are crucial for maintaining cost-effective operations.
- **Cost of Business Operations**: Assess the cost implications of each location, which include not only real estate prices but also labor costs, utilities, and local taxes. Opt for locations that offer economic advantages without compromising other strategic factors.
- **Workforce Availability**: Investigate the local labor market to ensure there is a sufficient pool of potential employees with the necessary skills and qualifications. Consider the competitiveness of the labor market and local wage levels.

Setting Up Operations

- **Real Estate Considerations**: Whether leasing or purchasing property, engage local real estate experts to find spaces that best suit your operational needs and budget. Consider the potential for future expansion and the flexibility of the space.
- **Regulatory Compliance**: Ensure that all business activities comply with local zoning laws, building codes, and other regulatory requirements. Engaging with local authorities during the early stages can prevent legal complications later on.

- **Infrastructure Setup**: Plan and execute the setup of necessary infrastructure, including IT systems, telecommunications, and office equipment. Consider the reliability of local utilities and internet services as they are critical for daily operations.

Integration with Local Ecosystems

- **Community Engagement**: Become an active participant in the local community to build brand awareness and foster goodwill. Community involvement can also provide insights into local market preferences and trends.
- **Local Partnerships**: Establish relationships with local businesses, suppliers, and service providers. These partnerships can facilitate smoother operations and integration into the local business community.

Risk Management

- **Risk Assessment**: Conduct thorough risk assessments for each potential location, considering factors such as natural disasters, economic stability, and political climate.
- **Mitigation Strategies**: Develop strategies to mitigate identified risks, such as purchasing insurance, developing contingency plans, and creating flexible business strategies that can adapt to changing circumstances.

Monitoring and Evaluation

- **Performance Metrics**: Set clear performance metrics for new locations to evaluate their success and contribution to overall business objectives.
- **Ongoing Review**: Regularly review the performance of new locations against these metrics, and be prepared to make adjustments to operations, strategy, or even location based on these evaluations.

By taking a strategic approach to location scouting and setup, businesses can ensure that new state expansions not only align with their broader business strategies but are also optimized for success in each local market. This careful planning and execution lay a solid foundation for achieving national presence and recognition.

Adapting Marketing and Branding Strategies

As businesses expand into multiple states, adapting marketing and branding strategies to regional variations becomes critical. This section explores how to tailor your marketing efforts to diverse audiences while maintaining a cohesive brand identity across all locations.

Understanding Regional Market Differences

- **Cultural Nuances**: Recognize and respect cultural differences that might affect consumer behavior and preferences across different states. Tailoring your message to local tastes, values, and traditions can significantly enhance relevance and reception.
- **Consumer Behavior Variations**: Analyze how consumer buying habits vary regionally due to factors like climate, economic status, and lifestyle. This analysis will guide the customization of marketing strategies to fit local demands.

Localizing Marketing Content

- **Customization of Advertising Materials**: Adapt marketing materials such as advertisements, promotional campaigns, and even product packaging to reflect local languages, cultural references, and regional appeals.
- **Digital and Social Media Strategies**: Leverage geo-targeting in digital and social media campaigns to deliver content that is specifically designed for audiences in each state. Utilize local influencers and community figures to enhance outreach and authenticity.

Maintaining Brand Consistency

- **Unified Brand Message**: While customizing content, ensure that the core brand message remains consistent across all markets. This helps in building a strong, recognizable brand identity nationwide.

- **Brand Guidelines**: Establish and disseminate comprehensive brand guidelines that detail the permissible variations in branding elements like logos, colors, and taglines to ensure consistency across all forms of media and locations.

Engaging Local Communities

- **Community Involvement**: Actively participate in local events and sponsor community activities to build brand presence and goodwill. This also provides valuable insights into local consumer attitudes and preferences.
- **Feedback Mechanisms**: Implement systems to gather feedback from local customers to continuously refine and improve marketing strategies based on direct consumer input.

Evaluating Marketing Effectiveness

- **Performance Metrics**: Set specific, measurable goals for each regional marketing campaign and regularly track these against performance metrics such as engagement rates, conversion rates, and ROI.
- **Adaptation and Improvement**: Use the data collected to continuously refine marketing strategies, making adjustments based on what is most effective in each region.

Training and Development

- **Local Marketing Teams**: Where possible, employ marketing professionals from within the local communities who understand the regional market deeply. Provide ongoing training to ensure they are aligned with the overall corporate marketing strategies and have the skills needed to execute them effectively.
- **Cross-Regional Sharing**: Facilitate the sharing of insights and successful strategies between regions to foster innovation and improve overall marketing effectiveness across the company.

By effectively adapting marketing strategies to the unique characteristics of each state while maintaining a unified brand identity, businesses can ensure that their expansion is not only seen but also resonates with the new audiences. This strategic approach to localized marketing will support successful multi-state expansion and long-term growth.

Implementing Robust Operational Frameworks

Expanding into multiple states requires not just strategic marketing and legal compliance, but also a solid operational framework that ensures consistency and efficiency across all new locations. This section outlines the strategies for creating scalable operational systems that support a successful multi-state expansion.

Developing Scalable Operations

- **Centralized vs. Decentralized Operations**: Evaluate the benefits and drawbacks of centralized versus decentralized operational structures. Centralized operations can offer consistency and cost efficiencies, while decentralized operations allow for greater flexibility and local responsiveness.
- **Standardization of Processes**: Implement standardized processes and practices across all locations to ensure operational consistency. This includes uniform training programs, operational procedures, and quality control measures.

Technology Integration

- **Leveraging Technology**: Utilize advanced technology solutions like Enterprise Resource Planning (ERP) systems to integrate business processes across different locations. These systems can help manage logistics, inventory, human resources, and finances on a unified platform.
- **Digital Tools for Communication and Collaboration**: Adopt digital tools that facilitate seamless communication and collaboration across state lines. This could include project management software, virtual meeting platforms, and cloud-based document sharing.

Supply Chain Management

- **Optimizing Supply Chains**: Develop efficient supply chain strategies that cater to the needs of multiple locations. Consider local sourcing to reduce costs and increase supply chain responsiveness.
- **Logistics and Distribution**: Streamline logistics and distribution networks to ensure that products and services are delivered efficiently across all states. Use logistics software to optimize routes and manage deliveries effectively.

Risk Management Across States

- **Identifying and Mitigating Risks**: Identify potential operational risks associated with multi-state expansion, such as supply chain disruptions, regulatory changes, or economic fluctuations. Develop contingency plans to mitigate these risks.
- **Regular Risk Assessments**: Conduct regular risk assessments to stay ahead of potential operational issues and adjust strategies proactively.

Performance Monitoring and Continuous Improvement

- **Setting KPIs and Metrics**: Establish clear key performance indicators (KPIs) and metrics to monitor the performance of operations across all states. These should cover aspects like efficiency, cost management, customer satisfaction, and employee performance.
- **Feedback Loops and Adjustments**: Create feedback loops that allow employees and managers to report issues or suggest improvements. Use this feedback to make continuous adjustments to operations, enhancing effectiveness and adaptability.

Employee Training and Development

- **Consistent Training Programs**: Ensure that all employees, regardless of location, receive consistent training that aligns with the company's standards and practices. This helps in maintaining a uniform service quality and operational approach.

- **Cultural Sensitivity and Adaptation**: Train employees on cultural sensitivity to better understand and respond to the local nuances of each state, which can significantly impact customer service and local team dynamics.

By implementing these robust operational frameworks, businesses can ensure that their expansion efforts are supported by efficient, scalable, and adaptable operations. This foundation not only facilitates smoother transitions into new markets but also supports sustained growth and success across diverse geographic regions.

Quick Tips and Recap

- **Conduct thorough market research** to understand regional differences and assess the viability of each potential expansion area based on local consumer behavior, economic conditions, and competitive landscapes.
- **Navigate state-specific regulatory environments** by understanding and complying with local business registration, licensing, and tax requirements, and consider hiring local legal expertise to aid in compliance.
- **Choose strategic locations** for physical operations by considering market access, logistics, local workforce availability, and overall cost-effectiveness.
- **Adapt marketing and branding strategies** to resonate with local cultures and preferences while maintaining a consistent brand identity across all regions.
- **Implement scalable operational frameworks** that ensure efficiency and consistency across multiple states, leveraging technology like ERP systems for integrated management.
- **Optimize supply chains and logistics** to support efficient distribution and service delivery in new regions.

- **Standardize processes and training** across all locations to ensure consistent operations and service quality, while allowing some flexibility to meet local needs.
- **Regularly monitor performance** using clear KPIs and metrics to assess the success of multi-state operations and make necessary adjustments.
- **Maintain open lines of communication** with local teams and stakeholders to ensure continuous feedback and adaptation to regional market needs.

By following these tips, businesses can effectively manage the complexities of multi-state expansion, ensuring successful integration into new markets and laying a strong foundation for national growth.

CHAPTER FOURTEEN

Tax Tactics: Planning for Compliance and Optimization

"Tax planning is an essential skill for any business leader. Effective tax strategy goes beyond mere compliance; it involves making proactive decisions that can significantly impact your company's financial health."— JOHN D. ROCKEFELLER, AMERICAN BUSINESS MAGNATE

Welcome to the thrilling world of taxes, where the only things certain are death, taxes, and the occasional audit. But fear not! This chapter is your secret weapon for turning a dreary duty into a strategic triumph. Here, we'll transform you from a tax novice into a savvy strategist, navigating the complexities of tax compliance with the finesse of a seasoned accountant on a caffeine high.

Dive deep into the art of tax planning, where every deduction is a brushstroke and every credit is a masterstroke. Learn how to optimize your filings not just to stay on the right side of the law, but to enhance your financial performance. We'll tackle everything from simple deductions to complex incentives that can significantly reduce your taxable income.

Forget the headache of receipts and regulations; think of this as your playbook for minimizing liabilities and maximizing opportunities. Ready to crack the tax code? Let's decode the IRS lingo, uncover hidden savings, and plan your fiscal path like a tax planning prodigy.

Understanding Tax Compliance

Navigating the complexities of tax compliance is crucial for every business. This section explores the essentials of fulfilling tax obligations correctly and efficiently, ensuring legal compliance and minimizing the risk of penalties.

Basics of Tax Compliance

- **Tax Compliance Definition**: Understand tax compliance as adhering to all tax laws and regulations as they apply to your business operations, including accurate reporting of income, expenses, and payments to tax authorities.
- **Importance of Compliance**: Stress the significance of tax compliance in avoiding legal issues, penalties, and damage to your business's reputation. Compliance ensures smooth operations and maintains good standing with tax authorities.

Common Tax Obligations for Businesses

- **Income Tax**: Discuss the requirements for filing business income tax returns, including the need to report all income, deductions, and credits accurately.
- **Payroll Tax**: Outline the obligations related to payroll taxes, which include withholding taxes from employees' salaries and paying employer contributions for Social Security and Medicare.

- **Sales Tax**: Explain the process of collecting, reporting, and remitting sales tax, which may vary significantly between different states and localities.

Understanding Tax Forms and Filings

- **Key Forms**: Introduce key tax forms that businesses typically must handle, such as IRS Form 1120 for corporations, Form 1065 for partnerships, and Schedule C for sole proprietors.
- **Filing Deadlines**: Highlight critical tax filing deadlines to avoid penalties for late submissions. Include annual federal and state tax return deadlines, as well as quarterly estimated tax payment deadlines for businesses and self-employed individuals.

Record Keeping for Tax Purposes

- **Documentation Requirements**: Emphasize the importance of keeping comprehensive and accurate financial records. Explain which documents need to be retained, such as receipts, invoices, payroll records, and previous tax returns.
- **Organizational Tips**: Provide tips for organizing documents in a manner that facilitates easy access and reference, which is particularly useful in the event of an audit.

Utilizing Professional Help

- **When to Hire a Tax Professional**: Advise on situations where it may be beneficial to hire a tax professional, such as dealing with complex tax issues, filing in multiple states, or handling audits.
- **Choosing the Right Advisor**: Offer guidance on selecting a qualified tax advisor or accountant, including checking credentials, experience, and their understanding of your particular industry.

Benefits of Proactive Tax Planning

- **Avoiding Penalties and Interest**: Discuss how proactive tax compliance can help avoid penalties and interest charges associated with late or incorrect filings.

- **Strategic Financial Planning**: Highlight how good tax compliance practices are integral to effective financial planning and can provide insights into financial health and opportunities for cost savings.

By mastering the fundamentals of tax compliance, businesses can ensure they meet all legal obligations and manage their tax affairs efficiently. This foundational understanding is crucial for navigating the broader aspects of tax strategy and planning discussed in the subsequent sections of this chapter.

Strategies for Tax Optimization

Tax optimization involves legally minimizing tax liabilities while maximizing a business's cash flow and profitability. This section explores various strategies to effectively reduce taxes within the bounds of the law, ensuring that businesses can leverage every available benefit.

Understanding Tax Optimization

- **Definition and Importance**: Define tax optimization as the process of analyzing financial situations and planning in a way that reduces tax liability. Emphasize its importance in improving a business's bottom line and increasing operational efficiency.
- **Ethical Considerations**: Highlight the difference between legal tax avoidance (minimization through planning) and illegal tax evasion, stressing the importance of maintaining ethical practices in tax planning.

Utilizing Deductions and Credits

- **Maximizing Deductions**: Discuss how businesses can maximize deductions by accurately tracking and claiming all eligible business expenses, such as office supplies, travel expenses, and depreciation on assets.
- **Leveraging Tax Credits**: Explore specific tax credits available for businesses, such as those for research and development, environmental improvements, or hiring from certain demographics. Explain how these credits can directly reduce tax owed, dollar for dollar.

Strategic Entity Selection

- **Choosing the Right Business Structure**: Examine how the choice of business entity (e.g., sole proprietorship, partnership, corporation, S corporation) affects taxation. Discuss the tax implications of each structure and how choosing the right one can optimize tax outcomes.

- **Re-evaluating Business Structure**: Suggest considering a periodic evaluation of the business structure to ensure it remains the most tax-efficient as the company grows and tax laws change.

Income Shifting Strategies

- **Timing Income and Expenses**: Explain strategies for deferring income to future tax periods and accelerating expenses into the current tax period to reduce taxable income.

- **Using Retirement Plans**: Discuss the benefits of using retirement plans as a tax-deferral strategy, not only for the business owner but also for employees, which can reduce current taxable income through contributions.

Tax-Loss Harvesting

- **Utilizing Losses**: Describe how businesses can use tax-loss harvesting to offset gains by realizing losses on other investments or business activities, which can reduce overall taxable income.

- **Carryforward and Carryback Losses**: Provide information on carrying losses forward to future tax years or back to past tax years to offset taxable income, thereby optimizing tax liabilities over time.

Advanced Tax Planning Techniques

- **Incorporating in Tax-Advantaged States**: Consider the benefits and logistics of incorporating in states with favorable tax laws, which might offer lower corporate tax rates or no state income taxes.

- **International Tax Strategies**: For businesses operating globally, discuss considerations and strategies for managing international tax obligations to optimize the global effective tax rate.

Regular Tax Planning Reviews

- **Annual Reviews**: Recommend conducting annual tax planning reviews with a qualified tax professional to adapt to changes in the business environment, financial status, and tax legislation.

By employing these tax optimization strategies, businesses can ensure they are not only compliant with tax laws but also operating in the most financially efficient manner. This proactive approach to tax planning can significantly enhance a business's ability to invest in growth and innovation.

Leveraging Tax Credits and Incentives

Tax credits and incentives can significantly reduce a company's tax burden and encourage activities in areas such as research, development, and sustainable practices. This section provides an in-depth look at how businesses can identify, qualify for, and effectively utilize these financial benefits.

Overview of Tax Credits and Incentives

- **Definition of Tax Credits**: Explain that tax credits are benefits that directly reduce the amount of tax owed, dollar for dollar, unlike deductions which reduce the amount of income subject to tax.
- **Common Types of Tax Credits**: Introduce common tax credits that businesses might leverage, such as the Research and Development (R&D) Tax Credit, Work Opportunity Tax Credit (WOTC), and energy efficiency credits.

Identifying Eligible Credits and Incentives

- **Conducting a Tax Credit Audit**: Recommend conducting a comprehensive review of all possible tax credits and incentives with a tax professional. This audit can uncover underutilized credits that could save substantial amounts on tax liabilities.
- **Staying Informed on New Opportunities**: Emphasize the importance of staying updated on new and expiring tax credits. Often, tax legislation

introduces temporary incentives that can be beneficial if acted upon quickly.

Steps to Qualify for Tax Credits

- **Understanding Eligibility Requirements**: Detail the specific qualifications for each tax credit, which may include types of activities conducted, expenditures incurred, or the necessity of certain business practices.
- **Documentation and Record-Keeping**: Discuss the critical need for maintaining detailed records that substantiate eligibility for tax credits. This includes financial records, receipts, contracts, and detailed logs of activities.

Maximizing the Benefit of Incentives

- **Strategic Planning for Utilization**: Explore strategies for maximizing the benefit of tax credits, such as timing the recognition of credits to offset peak tax liabilities or combining various incentives to enhance financial outcomes.
- **Recapture of Credits**: Warn about the potential for recapture of certain tax credits if the conditions under which they were granted change and how to plan and mitigate this risk.

Government and Local Incentives

- **Federal vs. State Incentives**: Compare the benefits of federal tax credits with those offered by states, which can vary widely and may be stacked or used in conjunction to maximize savings.
- **Local Economic Development Incentives**: Highlight local incentives aimed at economic development, such as reduced property taxes, grants, or subsidized loans for businesses that contribute positively to the local economy.

Navigating the Application Process

- **Application Procedures**: Guide through the typical application process for claiming tax credits, including required forms and timelines.

- **Leveraging Professional Assistance**: Stress the benefits of using tax professionals or consultants who specialize in tax credits and incentives to ensure compliance and optimal use of available benefits.

Evaluating the Impact on Business Strategy

- **Integrating into Business Planning**: Encourage businesses to integrate potential tax credits into their financial forecasting and strategic planning. Understanding how these benefits affect cash flow and investment decisions can influence broader business strategies.

By effectively leveraging tax credits and incentives, businesses can not only reduce their tax liabilities but also support and finance their strategic initiatives in innovation, workforce development, and environmental sustainability. This proactive approach to tax planning enhances a company's financial performance and competitive edge.

Planning for Audits and Avoiding Penalties

Tax audits are a critical aspect of tax compliance, and preparing adequately for them can prevent significant disruptions and penalties. This section outlines strategies for handling audits efficiently and safeguarding your business against potential penalties and fines.

Understanding the Audit Process

- **What Triggers an Audit**: Explain common triggers for tax audits, including discrepancies between reported figures and industry norms, excessive deductions, and random selections. Understanding these triggers can help in taking preemptive measures to avoid unnecessary scrutiny.

- **Types of Audits**: Distinguish between the different types of tax audits, such as correspondence audits, office audits, and field audits, each varying in complexity and requirements.

Preparing for an Audit

- **Maintaining Impeccable Records**: Emphasize the importance of maintaining accurate and detailed financial records. Well-organized documentation can expedite the audit process and support your filings.
- **Conducting Internal Reviews**: Recommend periodic internal reviews or pre-audit checks to ensure that all financial practices comply with tax laws and to identify any potential issues before they are flagged by an auditor.

Responding to an Audit

- **Timely and Accurate Responses**: Stress the importance of responding promptly and accurately to any requests for information from tax authorities. Delayed or inaccurate responses can complicate the audit process and lead to penalties.
- **Professional Representation**: Consider the benefits of professional representation during an audit, such as a CPA or a tax attorney, who can provide expertise and negotiate on behalf of your business.

Minimizing Penalties

- **Understanding Penalty Assessments**: Discuss different types of penalties that can be assessed, such as for late payments, underpayments, or filing inaccuracies, and the criteria tax authorities use to determine these penalties.
- **Penalty Abatement Strategies**: Introduce strategies for penalty abatement, which can include proving reasonable cause, demonstrating that failures were due to good faith errors, or negotiating payment plans.

Post-Audit Actions

- **Implementing Recommendations**: After an audit, it's crucial to implement any recommendations provided by the auditors to correct procedural or compliance deficiencies.

- **Adjusting Practices**: Based on the audit outcomes, adjust your tax practices and compliance processes to prevent future issues and possibly reduce the risk of subsequent audits.

Leveraging Technology for Compliance

- **Automated Compliance Tools**: Highlight the role of advanced accounting and compliance software that can help ensure accuracy in filings and maintain necessary records effectively.
- **Continuous Monitoring**: Utilize technology to continuously monitor compliance with tax laws, helping to identify and rectify discrepancies in real-time.

Building a Culture of Compliance

- **Training and Awareness**: Develop a culture of compliance within your organization by regularly training employees on tax matters and the importance of accurate reporting.
- **Compliance as a Strategic Priority**: Position tax compliance as a strategic priority at the executive level to ensure it receives the necessary attention and resources.

By being well-prepared and proactive about audits, businesses can navigate this daunting aspect of tax compliance with confidence, minimizing the risk of penalties and maintaining a solid reputation with tax authorities. This strategic approach to audit preparedness can save significant time, costs, and stress, allowing businesses to focus on growth and operational excellence.

Keeping Up with Tax Law Changes

Tax laws are continually evolving, influenced by changes in policy, economic shifts, and legislative updates. Staying informed about these changes is crucial for ensuring compliance and optimizing tax strategies. This section provides guidance on how to stay abreast of tax law changes and incorporate this knowledge into your business planning.

Importance of Staying Informed

- **Adapting to Changes**: Emphasize how staying updated with tax law changes can help your business adapt its strategies to maintain compliance and take advantage of new tax benefits or avoid new liabilities.
- **Proactive Planning**: Discuss the role of proactive tax planning in responding to changes in tax laws, allowing your business to adjust practices and strategies efficiently and effectively.

Sources for Tax Law Updates

- **Government Publications**: Recommend regularly checking publications from the IRS, state tax agencies, and other relevant government bodies which often provide updates on tax laws and guidance on compliance.
- **Professional Tax Advisors**: Highlight the importance of maintaining relationships with professional tax advisors who can provide expert interpretations of how changes affect your business specifically.

Integrating New Tax Laws into Business Operations

- **Review and Assessment**: Set up a regular review process to assess the impact of tax law changes on your business operations. This should include evaluating how updates affect your tax liabilities, deductions, and obligations.
- **Updating Systems and Processes**: Discuss the need to update accounting systems and operational processes to accommodate new tax rules, ensuring that your business remains compliant and that reporting is accurate.

Training and Communication

- **Employee Training**: Provide training for your finance and accounting teams on the latest tax law changes. Ensure they understand the implications of these changes and how to apply them in their roles.

- **Communication Strategies**: Develop communication strategies to keep all stakeholders informed about relevant tax law changes and their impacts on the business. This includes employees, investors, and other key stakeholders.

Using Technology to Stay Current

- **Tax Management Software**: Consider investing in tax management software that offers updates and features aligned with the latest tax laws. These tools can help automate compliance and reduce the risk of errors.
- **Automated Alerts**: Set up automated alerts from reliable tax news sources or through professional services that offer real-time updates on legislative changes affecting your industry.

Strategic Adjustments and Scenario Planning

- **Scenario Planning**: Engage in scenario planning to prepare for potential impacts of significant tax changes. This can help your business foresee the effects of different outcomes and develop flexible strategies to manage them.
- **Adaptive Financial Strategies**: Adjust your financial planning and forecasting models to reflect changes in tax legislation, ensuring that your business remains financially stable and well-positioned for future growth.

Building a Network of Expertise

- **Collaboration and Networking**: Build a network of tax professionals, legal experts, and industry peers who can provide insights and advice on navigating tax law changes. Participating in forums, workshops, and conferences can also provide valuable learning opportunities.

By maintaining a proactive approach to staying informed about tax law changes and effectively integrating this knowledge into business operations, you can ensure that your business not only complies with current laws but also optimizes its tax positions to support ongoing success and stability.

Quick Tips and Recap

- **Stay Proactive with Compliance**: Regularly review your tax compliance status to ensure adherence to all federal, state, and local tax laws.
- **Maximize Deductions and Credits**: Actively seek out and utilize all relevant tax deductions and credits to minimize liabilities and enhance financial performance.
- **Leverage Legal Entity Structures**: Evaluate and choose the most tax-efficient business structure for your operations to optimize tax outcomes.
- **Use Tax-Loss Harvesting**: Take advantage of tax-loss harvesting to offset taxable income and reduce overall tax liability.
- **Prepare for Audits**: Maintain meticulous records and documentation to support all tax filings and deductions, preparing thoroughly for potential audits.
- **Stay Informed on Tax Law Changes**: Regularly update your knowledge of tax laws and changes by consulting with tax professionals, attending relevant training, and using updated tax software.
- **Engage Professional Help**: Utilize tax advisors and accountants to navigate complex tax scenarios and strategic tax planning.
- **Integrate Tax Planning into Business Strategy**: Incorporate tax considerations into your business decision-making processes to ensure all strategies are aligned with tax efficiency goals.
- **Educate Your Team**: Keep your financial and operational teams well-informed about tax responsibilities and updates to empower them with the knowledge needed for compliance and optimization.

By following these tips, businesses can navigate the complexities of tax planning and compliance effectively, turning a potential challenge into a strategic advantage that supports business growth and stability.

CHAPTER FIFTEEN

Risk Management: Safeguarding Your Business

"Risk management is the fine art of navigating uncertainties, protecting your assets while positioning your business for future growth." — SHERYL SANDBERG, TECHNOLOGY EXECUTIVE AND AUTHOR

Welcome to the thrill-seeker's guide to business—also known as risk management. Here, we don't just tiptoe safely around potential pitfalls; we dance confidently through them. Risk management isn't about avoiding danger completely; it's about preparing so well that you almost wish a challenge would come your way, just so you can knock it out of the park!

In this chapter, we'll equip you with the armor and strategy to protect your business empire from the dragons of disaster. Whether those dragons breathe fire in the form of market fluctuations, legal entanglements, or operational hiccups, you'll be ready with a shield in one hand and a plan in the other. Learn how to identify threats before they appear on the horizon, assess their potential impact like a seasoned scout, and deploy countermeasures that are as creative as they are effective.

From crafting airtight insurance policies to establishing strong compliance protocols, and even to managing reputation damage control—think of this as your comprehensive guide to building a fortress around your business. Let's fortify your enterprise and turn risks into opportunities for growth and innovation. Ready to become a risk management champion? Let's dive into the art of safeguarding your business with style and savvy.

Identifying and Assessing Risks

Effective risk management begins with the ability to identify and accurately assess potential risks before they impact the business. This section explores essential techniques for recognizing threats and evaluating their potential severity and likelihood.

Understanding Risk Identification

- **Definition and Importance**: Define risk identification as the process of recognizing potential problems that could negatively affect an organization. Highlight how early identification allows for proactive management and minimizes disruptions.
- **Sources of Risk**: Discuss various sources of risk, including operational, financial, strategic, compliance, and external factors like economic changes or natural disasters.

Techniques for Identifying Risks

- **Brainstorming Sessions**: Conduct regular brainstorming sessions with team members from all levels of the organization to gather diverse perspectives on potential risks.

- **SWOT Analysis**: Utilize SWOT analysis (Strengths, Weaknesses, Opportunities, Threats) to systematically identify risks associated with business operations and the external environment.
- **Industry Analysis**: Keep abreast of industry reports and trends that can help predict sector-specific risks, including technological advancements or regulatory changes.

Assessing Risk

- **Risk Assessment Frameworks**: Introduce frameworks for assessing risk, such as the likelihood and impact matrix, which helps categorize risks based on their potential effect on the business and their probability of occurring.
- **Quantitative and Qualitative Assessments**: Explain the difference between quantitative assessments (using numerical data to measure risk) and qualitative assessments (using descriptions and scenarios to understand risk).

Risk Prioritization

- **Prioritizing Risks**: After risks have been identified and assessed, prioritize them based on their potential impact on the business and the likelihood of occurrence. This helps allocate resources where they are most needed.
- **Continuous Monitoring**: Emphasize the importance of continuously monitoring the business environment as new risks can emerge as the market, technology, and external conditions evolve.

Documentation and Reporting

- **Risk Register**: Develop and maintain a risk register to document identified risks and their assessment. The register should include potential impacts, mitigation strategies, responsible persons, and monitoring mechanisms.

- **Regular Reviews**: Schedule regular reviews of the risk register to update it with new insights, changes in the business environment, or outcomes of risk management efforts.

By effectively identifying and assessing risks, businesses can prepare more robust risk management strategies, ensuring they are better equipped to handle challenges that may arise. This proactive approach not only safeguards the business but also supports strategic decision-making and planning.

Developing Risk Management Strategies

Once risks are identified and assessed, the next critical step is to develop tailored strategies to manage those risks effectively. This section delves into various approaches for managing risks, emphasizing how businesses can choose and implement the most appropriate strategies based on the nature and severity of identified risks.

Foundations of Risk Management Strategies

- **Overview of Risk Management Options**: Introduce the four primary strategies for managing risk: avoidance, reduction, transfer, and acceptance. Explain how the choice of strategy depends on the risk's likelihood and impact.
- **Risk Avoidance**: Describe how avoiding risk involves altering plans to sidestep potential problems entirely, such as choosing not to enter a high-risk market or discontinuing a product line that poses compliance issues.

Risk Reduction

- **Implementing Mitigation Measures**: Focus on risk reduction strategies that involve taking steps to reduce the likelihood or impact of a risk. This could include implementing safety protocols, improving security measures, or investing in technology upgrades.
- **Training and Preparedness**: Highlight the importance of training employees to handle risks effectively and establishing protocols that prepare the organization to deal with potential threats smoothly.

Risk Transfer

- **Insurance**: Discuss how transferring risk often involves using insurance policies to manage potential financial losses by shifting the financial burden to an insurer.
- **Contracts and Partnerships**: Explore how risk can also be transferred through contracts, such as indemnity clauses, or through strategic partnerships where risks are shared among parties.

Risk Acceptance

- **Understanding Acceptable Risks**: Explain when it makes sense to accept a risk, typically when the cost of mitigating the risk exceeds the benefit gained from doing so, or when the likelihood of occurrence is very low.
- **Contingency Planning**: Stress the importance of having contingency plans in place for accepted risks, ensuring that the organization can respond quickly and effectively if those risks materialize.

Implementing Risk Management Plans

- **Action Plans**: Detail the steps to create actionable risk management plans that specify who is responsible for implementing each part of the strategy, timelines for implementation, and the resources required.
- **Integration into Corporate Strategy**: Discuss how risk management strategies should be integrated into the broader corporate strategy to ensure that they align with business objectives and enhance overall organizational resilience.

Monitoring and Revising Strategies

- **Regular Monitoring**: Emphasize the need for ongoing monitoring of risk management strategies to assess their effectiveness and make necessary adjustments.
- **Feedback Loops**: Set up feedback loops that allow continuous learning and adaptation of strategies based on new information or changes in the business environment.

By developing robust risk management strategies, businesses can not only protect themselves against potential threats but also enhance their ability to operate confidently and dynamically in a volatile business landscape. This proactive and strategic approach to risk management supports sustained growth and long-term success.

Insurance and Risk Transfer

Insurance is a critical tool for transferring risk away from the business, providing a financial safety net in case of unexpected events. This section explores the different types of insurance businesses should consider and how to effectively use insurance as part of a broader risk management strategy.

Understanding the Role of Insurance

- **Purpose of Business Insurance**: Define business insurance as a risk transfer mechanism that protects against financial losses from specific risks, such as property damage, liability claims, or business interruption.
- **Benefits of Insurance**: Highlight how insurance not only provides financial protection but also peace of mind, allowing business owners to focus on growth and operations without the constant fear of potential catastrophes.

Types of Business Insurance

- **General Liability Insurance**: Essential for protecting against claims of bodily injury, property damage, and other liabilities that can arise from business operations.
- **Property Insurance**: Covers damage to business property due to events like fire, theft, and natural disasters, ensuring that physical assets are protected.
- **Professional Liability Insurance (Errors and Omissions)**: Crucial for businesses that provide services or advice, protecting against claims of negligence or inadequate work.

- **Product Liability Insurance**: Important for manufacturers and retailers, providing protection against lawsuits arising from damages caused by products.
- **Business Interruption Insurance**: Compensates for lost income and expenses incurred when a business must temporarily cease operations due to a covered event.
- **Cyber Liability Insurance**: Increasingly vital as businesses become more digital, protecting against losses from data breaches and other cyber threats.

Choosing the Right Insurance Coverage

- **Assessment of Needs**: Discuss how businesses should conduct a thorough assessment of their risks to determine the types and levels of insurance needed.
- **Comparison Shopping**: Recommend comparing offers from multiple insurers to find the best coverage terms and rates. Utilize insurance brokers if necessary to navigate complex insurance landscapes.
- **Customization of Policies**: Emphasize the importance of customizing insurance policies to fit specific business needs, ensuring that coverage is neither insufficient nor excessively costly.

Managing Insurance Relationships

- **Working with Insurance Providers**: Outline strategies for building effective relationships with insurance providers, such as maintaining open communication, regular reviews of coverage needs, and prompt reporting of incidents.
- **Claims Management**: Provide guidelines on managing insurance claims, including timely notification, detailed documentation, and active management of the claims process to ensure fair and prompt settlement.

Regular Review and Adjustment

- **Annual Insurance Reviews**: Advocate for annual reviews of insurance policies to adjust coverage as the business grows and its risk profile changes.
- **Adapting to New Risks**: Stress the need to continually assess and adapt insurance coverage in response to emerging risks, such as technological changes or new regulatory environments.

By effectively utilizing insurance as a risk transfer tool, businesses can protect themselves against a wide range of potential threats, ensuring financial stability and continuity in the face of unforeseen challenges. This proactive approach to risk management through insurance not only safeguards the business but also supports its long-term resilience and success.

Building Compliance and Safety Protocols

A robust compliance and safety framework is essential for minimizing risks associated with legal violations, workplace accidents, and other regulatory non-compliance issues. This section discusses how to establish and maintain effective compliance protocols and safety measures to protect your business and ensure it operates within legal and ethical boundaries.

Importance of Compliance and Safety

- **Risk Mitigation**: Emphasize the role of compliance and safety protocols in mitigating risks that could lead to severe financial, legal, or reputational damage.
- **Regulatory Adherence**: Highlight the necessity of adhering to industry-specific regulations and laws to avoid penalties, fines, or legal actions.

Developing Compliance Protocols

- **Understanding Legal Requirements**: Start by gaining a thorough understanding of all relevant local, state, federal, and international laws that affect your business operations. This includes employment laws, environmental regulations, health and safety standards, and industry-specific compliance issues.

- **Creating a Compliance Framework**: Outline steps to develop a compliance framework that includes clear policies and procedures, responsibility assignments, and mechanisms for monitoring and enforcement.
- **Training and Education**: Implement comprehensive training programs for all employees to ensure they understand their compliance obligations and how to fulfill them. Regularly update training materials to reflect any changes in the law or business operations.

Establishing Safety Protocols

- **Risk Assessment**: Conduct regular risk assessments to identify potential safety hazards in the workplace.
- **Preventive Measures**: Develop and implement preventive measures, such as safety equipment, proper ergonomics, and emergency response procedures.
- **Regular Safety Audits**: Schedule regular safety audits to ensure ongoing adherence to safety protocols and to identify areas for improvement.

Integrating Technology

- **Compliance Software Solutions**: Utilize technology, such as compliance management software, to streamline the tracking, management, and reporting of compliance data.
- **Safety Monitoring Technologies**: Employ technologies like surveillance cameras, alarm systems, and hazard detection devices to enhance workplace safety.

Handling Non-Compliance

- **Incident Response Plans**: Develop clear procedures for responding to compliance failures or safety incidents, including immediate corrective actions and strategies for preventing future occurrences.

- **Documentation and Reporting**: Maintain detailed records of compliance efforts and safety incidents to provide evidence of due diligence and to facilitate the analysis of trends or repeated issues.

Engaging with Regulatory Bodies

- **Proactive Engagement**: Maintain open lines of communication with relevant regulatory bodies. Proactively engage with these entities to stay informed about potential regulatory changes and to demonstrate your business's commitment to compliance.
- **Seeking Guidance**: When in doubt, seek guidance from legal experts or consultants who specialize in your industry's regulations to ensure that your compliance and safety protocols meet all legal standards.

Building a Culture of Compliance and Safety

- **Leadership Commitment**: Ensure that leadership actively supports and participates in compliance and safety initiatives, setting a positive tone at the top.
- **Employee Involvement**: Encourage employee involvement in the development and implementation of compliance and safety measures to enhance buy-in and adherence.

By building comprehensive compliance and safety protocols, businesses can significantly reduce the risks of regulatory penalties, workplace accidents, and other associated liabilities. This proactive approach not only protects the company but also reinforces a culture of safety and responsibility throughout the organization.

Crisis Management and Recovery

Effective crisis management is crucial for safeguarding a business during unforeseen events. This section outlines how to develop a comprehensive crisis management plan that encompasses prevention, response, and recovery strategies to ensure the business can withstand and quickly recover from disruptions.

Understanding Crisis Management

- **Definition and Scope**: Define crisis management as the process by which a business plans for and responds to unexpected, disruptive events that could threaten to harm the organization or its stakeholders.
- **Types of Crises**: Identify different types of crises that could impact a business, such as natural disasters, technological failures, financial problems, or reputational damage.

Developing a Crisis Management Plan

- **Prevention Strategies**: Discuss how to implement preventive measures that can reduce the likelihood of a crisis or lessen its impact. This could include regular system backups, diversifying suppliers, or continuous monitoring of financial health.
- **Preparedness**: Create plans that outline specific actions to be taken in response to various types of crises. This should include designated crisis response teams and clear communication channels.

Immediate Response to Crises

- **Activation of the Crisis Plan**: Outline the steps for activating the crisis management plan when an event occurs, including who makes the decision and how it is communicated.
- **Crisis Communication**: Develop a communication strategy that addresses communication with employees, customers, suppliers, regulators, and the public. Effective communication is crucial for managing stakeholder expectations and maintaining trust during a crisis.

Recovery and Business Continuity

- **Business Continuity Plans**: Integrate business continuity strategies into the crisis management plan to ensure critical business functions can continue during and after a crisis.
- **Resource Management**: Plan for the allocation and management of resources during a crisis, including financial resources, human resources, and supply chain resources.

Post-Crisis Analysis and Improvement

- **Debriefing and Learning**: After a crisis, conduct a debriefing session to analyze the effectiveness of the response and identify lessons learned.
- **Plan Updates**: Regularly update the crisis management plan based on insights gained from exercises and actual events. This helps to refine strategies and improve readiness for future crises.

Training and Drills

- **Regular Training**: Conduct regular training sessions for all employees on their roles during a crisis. This ensures everyone knows what is expected of them and how to perform their duties safely and effectively.
- **Simulation Drills**: Perform simulation drills to practice crisis response and refine the crisis management plan. This helps to identify any gaps in the plan and provides a realistic practice environment for the crisis response team.

Leveraging Technology in Crisis Management

- **Technology Solutions**: Utilize technology solutions that can aid in crisis management, such as emergency notification systems, online dashboards for real-time monitoring, and mobile apps for communication.

By establishing a robust crisis management and recovery framework, businesses can ensure they are well-prepared to handle any emergency. This proactive planning not only minimizes the impact of crises when they occur but also enhances the business's resilience, enabling a quicker return to normal operations.

Quick Tips and Recap

- **Identify Potential Risks Early**: Regularly assess and identify potential risks across all aspects of your business to prepare effective mitigation strategies.
- **Develop Comprehensive Risk Strategies**: Employ a mix of risk avoidance, reduction, transfer, and acceptance strategies tailored to the specific risks your business faces.

- **Invest in Adequate Insurance**: Secure appropriate insurance policies to transfer financial risks, including general liability, property, and professional liability insurance.
- **Maintain Compliance**: Build robust compliance and safety protocols to mitigate legal and operational risks and ensure safety in the workplace.
- **Prepare for Crises**: Develop and regularly update a detailed crisis management plan that includes prevention, response, and recovery strategies.
- **Conduct Regular Training and Drills**: Engage employees in regular training and drills to ensure everyone understands their role in managing risks and responding to crises.
- **Utilize Technology**: Leverage technology to enhance your risk management processes, from automated compliance checks to real-time monitoring systems.
- **Regularly Review and Update Plans**: Continuously review and update your risk management, compliance protocols, and crisis plans to adapt to new challenges and changes in the business environment.
- **Engage Experts When Needed**: Consult with legal, insurance, and risk management professionals to ensure your strategies are comprehensive and up-to-date.
- **Promote a Culture of Risk Awareness**: Foster a company culture that emphasizes the importance of risk awareness, preparation, and proactive management among all employees.

By following these tips, businesses can build a strong foundation for managing risks effectively, ensuring they are well-prepared to handle unexpected challenges and protect their assets, reputation, and operational stability.

PART FOUR

Tools for Growth

Welcome to the entrepreneur's treasure chest, Part Four: Tools for Growth, where we transform fledgling enterprises into soaring successes with the right gadgets in our toolkit. This isn't about wielding hammers and nails; it's about mastering the strategic implements that carve paths through the market wilderness and sculpt market leaders from rough business sketches. Here, you'll discover the power tools of business growth—from innovative software that streamlines operations to frameworks that fortify your strategic decisions. Think of this section as your personal growth accelerator, turbocharging your journey from startup to standout. Whether you're looking to scale skyscrapers or just climb the next rung on the ladder, these tools are the jetpack on your entrepreneurial suit. Ready to gear up and grow? Let's dive into the toolbox that turns ambitious visions into tangible victories.

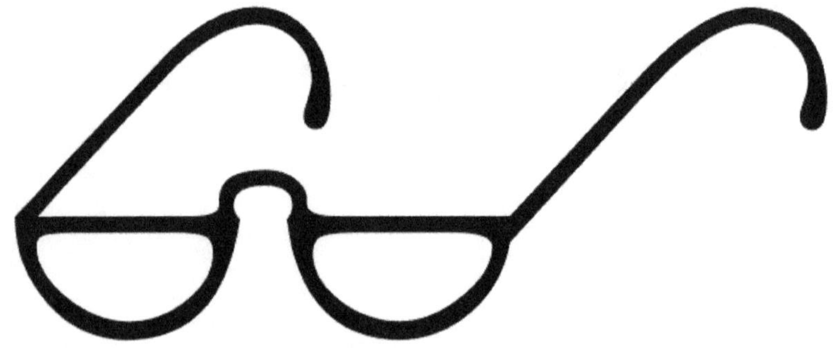

CHAPTER SIXTEEN

Blueprint for Success: Drafting Your Business Plan

"Writing a business plan forces you into disciplined thinking if you do an intellectually honest job. An idea may sound great in your mind, but when you put down the details and numbers, it may fall apart."— JEFF BEZOS, FOUNDER OF AMAZON

Roll out the blueprint paper and sharpen your pencils—it's time to architect your future with the most crucial tool in any entrepreneur's belt: the business plan. This isn't just about dotting your i's and crossing your t's; it's about laying the foundation of a skyscraper while everyone else is playing in the sandbox.

In this chapter, we'll guide you through each line and curve of your business plan, from the executive summary to the financial forecasts. Think of it as crafting a road map where X marks the spot of your future successes. We'll show you how to articulate your vision with the clarity of a seasoned CEO and the precision of a Swiss watchmaker. You'll learn how to convincingly outline your business objectives, market strategies, and competitive advantages that will make investors and stakeholders want to come aboard your venture.

Let's transform that brilliant idea flickering in your mind into a shining beacon on paper. By the end of this chapter, you'll not only have a document that guides your business but one that can open doors to funding, partnerships, and exponential growth. Ready to plot the course of your business destiny? Let's start drafting a plan that's as ambitious as your dreams!

Executive Summary

The executive summary is arguably the most critical section of your business plan. It serves as the gateway to enticing readers—whether they are potential investors, partners, or other stakeholders—to delve deeper into the document. This section provides guidance on crafting an executive summary that is both compelling and informative.

Purpose of the Executive Summary

- **Overview**: Introduce the executive summary as a concise encapsulation of your business plan. It should highlight the key points of the plan, including your business concept, fundamental financial information, and what sets your business apart from the competition.
- **First Impression**: Emphasize that the executive summary is often the first (and sometimes the only) part of your business plan that people will read, making it crucial for capturing the interest of your audience quickly.

Components of a Strong Executive Summary

- **Business Description**: Briefly describe what your business does and the market needs it addresses. Include your business model, what products or services you offer, and your target market.
- **Mission Statement**: Articulate your business's mission and the objectives that guide your operations. This should resonate with your business's core values and long-term vision.

- **Main Achievements and Milestones**: Highlight key milestones already achieved, such as patent approvals, key contracts secured, partnerships formed, or capital already raised.
- **Financial Information**: Summarize the financial outlook of your business, including past earnings if applicable and projected profitability. Clearly state any funding requirements, specifying how much is needed and how it will be used.
- **Competitive Advantage**: Clearly articulate what gives your business a competitive edge. This could be innovation, location, expertise, or superior products/services.

Tips for Writing an Effective Executive Summary

- **Keep It Concise**: Limit the executive summary to one or two pages. It should be a snapshot that entices readers to review the detailed plan.
- **Use Clear and Compelling Language**: Write in a clear, persuasive manner without jargon. Your aim is to communicate the business opportunity compellingly and succinctly.
- **Tailor the Content**: Adapt the summary to suit the interests of different readers. Highlight elements of the business plan that are particularly relevant to the audience you are addressing.
- **Focus on the Opportunity**: Ensure the summary conveys the business opportunity clearly. What problem are you solving, and why will your solution succeed?

Final Touches

- **Review and Refine**: After drafting the summary, review it to ensure it aligns with the contents of the full business plan. It should reflect the same predictions and aspirations outlined in more detail in the later sections.
- **External Feedback**: Consider getting feedback from trusted mentors or colleagues. They can provide insights on whether the summary captures the essence of your business plan effectively.

The executive summary is your chance to make a strong first impression. By crafting this section with clarity and focus, you set the stage for stakeholders to understand and be excited about your business vision and goals.

Business Description

The business description section of your business plan provides a comprehensive overview of the essential aspects of your company. It serves as a detailed introduction to the nature of your business, its background, and the market needs it addresses. This section outlines how to effectively describe your business to inform and engage your plan's readers.

Purpose of the Business Description

- **Foundational Overview**: Explain that the business description offers a foundational look at what your business does, including its legal structure, history, and primary activities.
- **Context and Clarity**: Provide context for the rest of the business plan, ensuring that readers understand the background against which your strategies and plans have been developed.

Key Elements of a Business Description

- **Nature of the Business**: Describe what your business does, the industry it operates in, and the consumer needs it addresses. Include information on the core products or services offered.
- **Company History and Background**: Provide a brief history of your business, including when and why it was founded, major milestones achieved, and any evolutionary changes that have influenced its current focus.
- **Business Model**: Clearly articulate your business model. Explain how your company makes money, detailing your revenue streams and any significant partnerships or customer segments.

- **Legal Structure**: Outline the legal structure of your business (e.g., sole proprietorship, partnership, corporation, LLC) and discuss why this structure is optimal for your operations.
- **Location and Facilities**: Describe the physical location of your business, including details about manufacturing facilities, retail spaces, or office buildings. Explain how these locations support the operational needs of your business.
- **Vision and Mission Statements**: Present your company's vision and mission statements. These should reflect your long-term aspirations and the immediate objectives that guide your business operations and culture.

Writing an Effective Business Description

- **Be Specific**: Provide specific details that give a clear and precise picture of your business. Avoid vague descriptions that could apply to any company in your industry.
- **Highlight Unique Factors**: Emphasize any aspects of your business that set you apart from competitors. This could include specialized expertise, proprietary technologies, or unique business processes.
- **Connect with Your Audience**: Write in a way that resonates with potential investors, partners, and other stakeholders. Tailor the description to highlight elements that are most likely to interest them.

Challenges and Opportunities

- **Identify Challenges**: Briefly discuss the primary challenges your business faces, providing context for the strategies you will detail later in the plan.
- **Outline Opportunities**: Convey the opportunities you see for your business, setting the stage for the marketing and operational strategies that will exploit these opportunities.

Review and Refinement

- **Consistency Check**: Ensure that the information provided in the business description aligns with the details and projections in other sections of the business plan.
- **Feedback and Revisions**: Seek feedback on this section from trusted advisors or stakeholders and be prepared to revise it to improve clarity and impact.

By thoroughly detailing the nature and scope of your business, the business description section helps set the foundation for the rest of your business plan, providing essential background that informs the strategies and objectives discussed in subsequent sections.

Market Analysis

A thorough market analysis is a cornerstone of a robust business plan, providing critical insights into your industry, target markets, competitors, and customer behaviors. This section outlines how to conduct a comprehensive market analysis to demonstrate a deep understanding of the environment in which your business operates.

Purpose of Market Analysis

- **Informed Strategy Development**: Stress that a well-executed market analysis informs strategic decisions, helping to tailor products, marketing efforts, and business models to the demands of the market.
- **Investor Confidence**: Highlight how a detailed analysis can boost investor confidence by showcasing your knowledge of the market and your preparedness to navigate its challenges and opportunities.

Components of a Market Analysis

- **Industry Description**: Begin with a broad overview of your industry, including its size, growth rate, and trends. Explain the industry's lifecycle stage (e.g., emerging, mature, declining) and the implications for your business.

- **Target Market**: Define your target market with as much precision as possible, detailing demographics, psychographics, purchasing habits, and the size of the target market. Discuss how you segment the market and identify your primary audience.
- **Market Needs and Trends**: Analyze the needs and trends driving consumer behavior in your target market. Discuss how these needs and trends have evolved and how they are expected to change in the future, considering factors like technological advancements, economic shifts, and cultural influences.
- **Competitive Analysis**: Conduct a detailed competitive analysis, identifying key competitors, their market share, strengths, and weaknesses. Use tools like SWOT analysis to compare your business to competitors and identify opportunities for differentiation.
- **Regulatory Environment**: Address any regulatory factors affecting your industry, such as licensing requirements, health and safety regulations, or environmental laws. Explain how these regulations impact your operations and competitive landscape.

Conducting the Market Analysis

- **Data Sources**: List credible sources of information for your market analysis, such as industry reports, market research firms, government publications, and academic studies. Mention any primary research you conducted, such as surveys or focus groups.
- **Analytical Tools**: Describe the tools and frameworks used to analyze the market data, such as Porter's Five Forces, PESTEL analysis, or other relevant analytical models.
- **Customer Feedback**: Incorporate feedback from current or potential customers to validate assumptions about market needs and preferences.

Using Market Analysis to Support Business Decisions

- **Strategic Alignment**: Use the insights gained from your market analysis to align your business strategy with market demands. This includes product development, pricing strategies, and marketing campaigns.

- **Risk Management**: Identify potential risks discovered during your market analysis, such as competitive threats or market saturation, and discuss strategies to mitigate these risks.

Presenting Market Analysis Findings

- **Clarity and Conciseness**: Present your findings in a clear and concise manner. Use visual aids like charts, graphs, and tables to help illustrate data points and trends.
- **Actionable Insights**: Ensure that the insights from your market analysis are actionable. Tie these insights directly to the strategic actions you plan to take, demonstrating how your business will capitalize on opportunities and navigate challenges.

A comprehensive market analysis not only demonstrates your understanding of the broader market environment but also reinforces the viability of your business strategy to stakeholders. By effectively assessing and articulating the dynamics of your market, you set the stage for presenting a well-informed, strategically sound business plan.

Operations and Management Plan

The Operations and Management Plan is a crucial component of your business plan, detailing how the day-to-day activities are handled and who is responsible for managing these tasks. This section outlines the operational workflow and organizational structure, offering a clear view of the internal workings of your business.

Purpose of the Operations and Management Plan

- **Operational Efficiency**: Illustrate how your business will operate on a daily basis, showing the efficiency and logic behind processes that support the delivery of products or services.
- **Leadership and Management Team**: Showcase the strength and competence of your management team, underscoring their roles in driving the business's success.

Components of the Operations Plan

- **Operational Workflow**: Describe the production or service delivery process, from the sourcing of raw materials to the final delivery of the product or service to the customer. Include information on suppliers, manufacturing processes, and logistics.
- **Facilities and Location**: Discuss the physical requirements of your business, including facilities, location, and equipment. Explain why each location or facility was chosen and how it fits into your operational needs.
- **Technology Utilization**: Highlight the technology and systems that will be used in operations, such as inventory management software, customer relationship management (CRM) systems, or advanced manufacturing technologies.

Management Team Structure

- **Organizational Structure**: Provide an organizational chart that outlines the structure of your management team and staff. Clarify the lines of authority and responsibility.
- **Key Personnel**: Introduce key members of the management team, providing their backgrounds, areas of expertise, and specific roles within the company. Discuss how their experience and skills benefit the business.
- **Staffing Requirements**: Discuss your plans for staffing, including the number of employees needed, the recruitment process, and any training programs.

Roles and Responsibilities

- **Detailed Roles**: For each key member of the management team, describe in detail their responsibilities. Include how these responsibilities align with the overall business objectives.

- **Performance Monitoring**: Explain the metrics or performance indicators that will be used to evaluate the effectiveness of the management team and operational processes.

Operational Challenges and Solutions

- **Identifying Potential Bottlenecks**: Identify potential operational bottlenecks or challenges and how you plan to address them. This could include scaling production, logistical issues, or supplier reliability.
- **Quality Assurance**: Detail your strategies for maintaining quality control and meeting regulatory standards within your operations.

Legal and Regulatory Considerations

- **Compliance**: Outline any regulatory requirements affecting your operations, including environmental regulations, health and safety standards, and labor laws. Discuss how you will comply with these regulations.

Sustainability and Innovation

- **Sustainable Practices**: If applicable, describe any environmentally sustainable practices your business will implement in its operations, such as recycling, waste management, or energy-efficient technologies.
- **Continuous Improvement**: Discuss how your business will stay innovative and competitive, detailing any strategies for continuous process improvement or technology upgrades.

By providing a comprehensive view of how your business functions on a daily basis and who manages these processes, the Operations and Management Plan not only reassures investors of your business's operational viability but also showcases the strategic organization behind your business goals. This plan serves as a roadmap for how your business intends to achieve its objectives efficiently and effectively.

Financial Projections and Needs

Creating robust financial projections is essential for any business plan, as these figures demonstrate the financial viability and growth potential of your business to investors and stakeholders. This section outlines how to develop accurate financial forecasts and articulate funding requirements clearly.

Purpose of Financial Projections

- **Demonstrating Viability**: Explain that detailed financial projections help to demonstrate the financial viability of your business over the coming years. They are crucial for securing funding and managing business finances effectively.
- **Setting Expectations**: Financial forecasts set benchmarks for business performance and provide a basis for measuring progress against financial goals.

Components of Financial Projections

- **Profit and Loss Statement**: Provide a projected profit and loss statement that includes revenue, costs of goods sold, gross margin, and net profit over time. Explain the assumptions behind your revenue projections and cost estimates.
- **Cash Flow Forecast**: Outline a cash flow forecast that shows the inflow and outflow of cash within the business. This will help demonstrate the business's ability to manage cash effectively and sustain operations.
- **Balance Sheet**: Include a projected balance sheet that offers a snapshot of the business's financial position at specific intervals. It should detail assets, liabilities, and equity.
- **Break-even Analysis**: Perform a break-even analysis to determine when the business is expected to start generating a profit. This analysis is critical for understanding the financial health of the business.

Detailing Funding Requirements

- **Capital Needs**: Clearly articulate the amount of funding needed to start or expand the business. Specify what these funds will be used for, such as capital expenditures, working capital, or debt repayment.
- **Sources of Funds**: Identify potential sources of funds, whether through equity financing, debt financing, or other means like grants or crowdfunding.
- **Use of Funds**: Provide a detailed account of how the funds raised will be used. Break down the allocation toward different areas such as product development, marketing, staffing, and operational expenses.

Assumptions and Risk Management

- **Financial Assumptions**: Document all assumptions made during the financial planning process, such as growth rates, pricing strategies, and market penetration. Assumptions should be realistic and based on industry data or market analysis.
- **Risk Analysis**: Include a risk analysis in relation to financial projections. Discuss potential risks that could impact your financial forecasts, such as market fluctuations or changes in supply chain costs, and how these risks will be managed.

Presentation and Review

- **Clear and Professional Presentation**: Ensure that financial data is presented clearly and professionally, making it easy for stakeholders to understand your business's financial prospects.
- **Regular Review and Update**: Financial projections should be reviewed and updated regularly to reflect actual business performance and changing market conditions. This ensures that they remain relevant and accurate.

Seeking Expert Advice

- **Consulting Financial Experts**: Consider consulting with financial experts or accountants when preparing your financial projections. Their expertise can help ensure accuracy and enhance the credibility of your financial plan.

By providing comprehensive and realistic financial projections, you demonstrate a deep understanding of your business's financial dynamics and its potential for success. This clarity and foresight are crucial for attracting investment, securing loans, and guiding your business strategy.

Quick Tips and Recap

- **Craft a Compelling Executive Summary**: Ensure your executive summary is clear, concise, and compelling to grab attention and summarize key aspects of your business plan effectively.
- **Detail Your Business Description**: Provide a thorough description of your business, including its history, structure, and the unique value it offers to the market.
- **Conduct a Comprehensive Market Analysis**: Perform detailed research to understand your industry, target market, competitive landscape, and market trends.
- **Outline Your Operations and Management Plan**: Clearly describe your business operations, logistical details, and management hierarchy to illustrate how your business functions on a daily basis.
- **Develop Robust Financial Projections**: Include detailed financial statements such as profit and loss, cash flow forecasts, and a balance sheet to demonstrate the financial viability and growth potential of your business.
- **Clearly State Funding Requirements**: Explicitly articulate how much funding you need, what it will be used for, and the potential sources of these funds.
- **Use Clear and Accessible Language**: Avoid jargon and overly complex language to ensure that your business plan is accessible to all readers, including those who may not have a financial background.

- **Consistently Review and Update Your Plan**: Regularly update your business plan to reflect any significant changes in your business or market conditions to keep it relevant and accurate.
- **Seek Feedback Before Finalizing**: Get feedback on your draft plan from trusted business advisors, mentors, or financial experts to refine your arguments and ensure clarity.
- **Present Data Visually Where Possible**: Use charts, graphs, and tables to present statistical information and financial data for easier comprehension and impact.

These tips will help you craft a comprehensive and persuasive business plan that effectively communicates your business vision, operational strategy, and financial needs to stakeholders.

CHAPTER SEVENTEEN

From Paper to Reality: Navigating the Incorporation Process

"Getting through the incorporation process is like setting the cornerstone of a building. It's your first real commitment on paper, legally speaking, that you're in it to win it."— ELON MUSK, CEO OF TESLA AND SPACEX

Welcome to the bureaucratic ballet, where every step in the incorporation process is a dance with paperwork and protocols. But fear not! This chapter is your backstage pass to mastering the moves that turn your business blueprint into a living, breathing entity.

Think of incorporation not as mundane form-filling, but as the grand opening of your business's debut on the world stage. We'll demystify the jargon, untangle the red tape, and streamline the steps so you can glide through with grace and efficiency. From choosing the right type of corporation to understanding the nuances of state and federal requirements, you're in for a practical guide that packs a punch.

You'll learn how to register your business without getting lost in a sea of legal lingo, how to seal the deal with the state, and how to set the stage for your company's future growth. So, capes on, entrepreneurs—let's turn those paper dreams into corporate reality with a flair that would make even the sternest bureaucrat crack a smile!

Choosing the Right Business Structure

Selecting the appropriate business structure is a foundational decision that will significantly impact your company's legal obligations, tax liabilities, and ability to attract investment. This section explores the various business entities available and helps you determine the best fit for your business goals and needs.

Overview of Business Structures

- **Sole Proprietorship**: Explain that this is the simplest form of business structure, ideal for a single owner. Highlight its ease of setup and total control aspects but note the personal liability for all debts and obligations.

- **Partnership**: Discuss the two common types of partnerships—general and limited. Detail how profits are shared and the differences in liability, with general partners having unlimited liability and limited partners typically only liable up to their investment.

- **Limited Liability Company (LLC)**: Describe the LLC as a flexible structure that offers the liability protection of a corporation with the tax benefits of a partnership. Explain the ease of operation with fewer formalities compared to a corporation.

- **Corporation (C-Corp and S-Corp)**: Differentiate between C-Corps and S-Corps, discussing the independent legal and tax identities of corporations, their ability to raise capital through the sale of stock, and the more complex regulatory requirements. Emphasize the limited liability for owners but note the potential for double taxation in C-Corps and the eligibility requirements for S-Corps.

Factors to Consider When Choosing a Structure

- **Liability**: Stress the importance of understanding the liability implications of each structure. Encourage readers to consider how much personal risk they are willing to assume in their business operations.
- **Taxation**: Discuss how each business structure is taxed. For instance, sole proprietors and partnerships face taxation on personal income levels, while corporations are taxed as separate entities. Mention the pass-through taxation benefits of S-Corps and LLCs.
- **Investment Needs**: Analyze the capacity of each structure to attract investment. Corporations are often more suited to raising capital through the sale of equity.
- **Future Growth and Scalability**: Consider how the business might grow in the future and whether the structure allows for easy scaling. Corporations offer more flexibility for growth through the issuance of stock.
- **Cost and Complexity of Formation and Maintenance**: Review the initial and ongoing administrative responsibilities and costs associated with each business structure, noting that corporations generally require more extensive record-keeping and reporting.

Decision-Making Guidance

- **Consultation with Professionals**: Advise on the importance of consulting with legal and financial professionals to choose the best structure based on specific business needs and goals.
- **Adaptability Over Time**: Remind readers that the initial choice of business structure is not final and can change as the business evolves. Discuss the process and implications of restructuring a business.

By carefully considering each of these factors, entrepreneurs can select a business structure that not only meets their current needs but also supports their long-term business vision and objectives. This critical decision lays the groundwork for future operations, growth, and success.

Understanding State and Federal Requirements

Incorporating a business involves navigating a complex landscape of state and federal regulations. This section provides a comprehensive overview of these requirements, helping entrepreneurs understand the legal framework within which they must operate and how to strategically choose the best state for incorporation.

Overview of Regulatory Differences

- **State-Specific Regulations**: Explain that each state has its own set of rules regarding the incorporation process, operational requirements, taxation, and annual reporting. Highlight the importance of understanding these differences when choosing where to incorporate.
- **Federal Compliance**: Outline the federal regulations that affect all businesses regardless of location, such as tax obligations, securities laws (if applicable), and employment laws.

Choosing the Right State for Incorporation

- **Popular States for Incorporation**: Discuss why some states, like Delaware, Nevada, and Wyoming, are popular choices for incorporation due to business-friendly laws, tax policies, and well-established legal precedents that protect businesses.
- **Local vs. Foreign Incorporation**: Contrast the advantages and disadvantages of incorporating in your home state versus a state known for favorable incorporation conditions. Consider factors like physical presence, nature of business activities, and potential foreign qualification requirements.

Key State Requirements

- **Articles of Incorporation**: Detail the process of filing Articles of Incorporation, which is the primary document needed to register your business with the state. Include common requirements like naming the business, appointing directors, and specifying share structure.
- **Registered Agent**: Explain the requirement for a registered agent who is authorized to receive legal papers on behalf of the company within the state of incorporation.
- **Annual Reports and Fees**: Discuss the necessity of filing annual reports and paying associated fees to keep the corporation in good standing. Note that requirements vary by state.

Federal Requirements

- **Employer Identification Number (EIN)**: Guide readers through the process of obtaining an EIN from the IRS, which is necessary for tax purposes, opening bank accounts, and hiring employees.
- **Securities and Exchange Commission (SEC) Regulations**: For businesses planning to issue stock, explain the need to comply with SEC regulations, including the filing of registration statements and ongoing disclosures.

Navigating Compliance

- **Legal and Accounting Assistance**: Recommend consulting with legal and accounting professionals to ensure compliance with both state and federal regulations. This is crucial for navigating complex tax laws and regulatory filings.
- **Ongoing Compliance Monitoring**: Emphasize the importance of ongoing compliance monitoring to adapt to changes in laws and regulations. Suggest setting up compliance calendars and regular legal audits.

Strategic Considerations

- **Cost-Benefit Analysis**: Encourage entrepreneurs to perform a cost-benefit analysis when choosing a state for incorporation, considering both short-term and long-term implications on taxes, privacy, legal exposure, and operational flexibility.
- **Future Business Needs**: Urge consideration of future business needs, including potential expansion, which might influence the choice of state due to scalability and resource accessibility.

By understanding and carefully considering state and federal requirements, entrepreneurs can make informed decisions that align with their business objectives and legal obligations, setting a solid foundation for their company's future.

Filing the Necessary Documents

Properly filing the necessary incorporation documents is a critical step in formalizing your business's legal structure. This section provides a detailed guide on how to prepare and submit these documents, ensuring compliance with state requirements and a successful registration process.

Understanding Incorporation Documents

- **Articles of Incorporation**: Outline the primary purpose of the Articles of Incorporation, which is to register the business as a legal entity with the state. Discuss the typical information required, such as the company name, principal address, purpose of the business, stock details, and information about incorporators and registered agents.
- **Operating Agreement or Bylaws**: Explain the importance of an operating agreement for LLCs or bylaws for corporations. These documents govern the internal operations of the company, outlining rules for meetings, member or shareholder rights, and management structure.

Preparation of Documents

- **Gathering Information**: List the necessary information needed to complete the incorporation documents, such as the business name, contact details, business purpose, and details about the ownership structure.
- **Choosing a Business Name**: Provide guidelines on selecting a business name, including state-specific naming requirements, trademark considerations, and the process for checking name availability.
- **Appointing a Registered Agent**: Discuss the role of the registered agent, who must be available during business hours to receive legal and tax documents. Emphasize the option to hire professional registered agent services if needed.

Filing Process

- **Where to File**: Describe the options for filing incorporation documents, which can typically be done online, by mail, or in person at the relevant state office.
- **Filing Fees**: Provide information on the filing fees associated with incorporation, noting that fees vary by state and the type of incorporation.
- **Review and Approval Process**: Explain what happens after the documents are filed, including how long it typically takes for the state to review and approve the incorporation, and how the business will be notified of the decision.

Common Mistakes to Avoid

- **Inaccurate or Incomplete Forms**: Warn against the common pitfalls of submitting forms that are incorrect or incomplete, which can delay the process or lead to rejection.
- **Misunderstanding Legal Requirements**: Highlight the importance of understanding all legal requirements to ensure that all aspects of the incorporation documents comply with state laws.

Post-Filing Considerations

- **Obtaining Certificates of Incorporation**: Once the documents are approved, the state will issue a certificate of incorporation, officially recognizing the business as a legal entity.
- **Public Record**: Note that incorporation documents are public records. Discuss the implications of this transparency, particularly concerning the privacy of business information.

Next Steps

- **Tax Registrations**: Guide new corporations to apply for an Employer Identification Number (EIN) from the IRS and register for state and local taxes where applicable.
- **Licenses and Permits**: Remind businesses to obtain any necessary licenses and permits to operate legally in their location and industry.
- **Opening Business Accounts**: Suggest setting up business banking accounts using the corporation's name and EIN to clearly separate personal and business finances.

By meticulously preparing and properly filing incorporation documents, entrepreneurs can ensure a smooth transition from a conceptual business to a legally recognized entity, setting the stage for operational and financial activities under the protection of corporate status.

Obtaining Licenses and Permits

Securing the necessary licenses and permits is a critical step to ensure that your newly incorporated business can operate legally and in compliance with local, state, and federal regulations. This section guides you through the process of identifying and obtaining the required licenses and permits for your business.

Importance of Licenses and Permits

- **Legal Compliance**: Emphasize the importance of obtaining all necessary licenses and permits as a fundamental aspect of legal compliance. Operating without these can lead to fines, penalties, or even the forced closure of your business.

- **Building Trust**: Explain how properly licensed and permitted businesses are more trusted by customers, suppliers, and financial institutions.

Types of Business Licenses and Permits

- **General Business License**: Describe the general business license, which is typically required for the operation of any business within a certain locality.
- **Specialized Permits**: Detail various specialized permits that may be required depending on the nature of the business. For example, health permits for restaurants, manufacturing permits for factories, or environmental permits for construction.
- **Professional Licenses**: Discuss professional licenses required for individuals in certain fields, such as healthcare, legal, real estate, or accounting.

Steps to Obtain Licenses and Permits

- **Identify Requirements**: Guide businesses on how to identify the specific licenses and permits required for their operations. This may involve consulting local, state, and federal government websites, or hiring a professional service or attorney.
- **Application Process**: Outline the typical application process for licenses and permits, including where to apply, what documents are needed, and the associated fees.
- **Inspections and Approvals**: Note that some permits might require an inspection of the business premises or an assessment of the business operations before approval is granted.

Common Challenges

- **Navigating Local Regulations**: Highlight the challenge of differing requirements across localities and provide tips on how to effectively navigate these complexities.
- **Time for Processing**: Alert businesses to the potential delays in the processing of licenses and permits. Encourage them to apply well in advance of their planned start date to avoid any disruptions to their business operations.

Maintaining Compliance

- **Renewals**: Remind businesses that many licenses and permits require regular renewals. Failure to renew on time can result in the same penalties as operating without a license.
- **Record-Keeping**: Advise on maintaining detailed records of all licenses and permits, including copies of applications and renewal dates, as part of ongoing compliance efforts.

Utilizing Resources

- **Local Business Resources**: Recommend utilizing resources such as local chambers of commerce, small business development centers, or online government portals that provide consolidated information on business licensing requirements.
- **Professional Assistance**: For businesses facing complex regulatory environments, suggest considering professional assistance from lawyers or specialized consultants who can provide expertise and simplify the process.

By thoroughly understanding and adhering to the licensing and permitting requirements applicable to their business, entrepreneurs can ensure that their operations are compliant, thus protecting their investments and building a foundation for successful and uninterrupted business activity.

Setting Up for Future Success

After navigating the initial stages of incorporation, obtaining necessary licenses, and ensuring compliance with relevant regulations, it's crucial to set your business up for ongoing success. This final section provides strategic advice on post-incorporation activities that solidify your business's operational foundation and position it for growth and scalability.

Establishing Fundamental Business Operations

- **Bank Accounts**: Stress the importance of opening a business bank account to separate personal and business finances, which is crucial for financial management and legal reasons.
- **Accounting Systems**: Advise on setting up an accounting system to track revenues, expenses, and profits accurately. Consider whether in-house software or outsourced services are best suited to your business needs.
- **Insurance Coverage**: Beyond the initial policies discussed earlier, evaluate additional insurance needs that may arise as your business grows, such as employee liability, product liability, or business interruption insurance.

Building a Strong Corporate Governance Framework

- **Board of Directors**: If applicable, establish a board of directors. Outline the roles and responsibilities of the board in providing oversight, strategic direction, and governance for the business.
- **Corporate Policies and Procedures**: Develop comprehensive policies and procedures that govern daily operations and employee behavior. These should cover areas such as HR policies, ethical guidelines, and operational procedures.

Strategic Planning and Goal Setting

- **Long-term Strategic Planning**: Engage in strategic planning sessions to set long-term goals for the business. This includes identifying key performance indicators (KPIs) that will help measure success.

- **Business Plan Updates**: Regularly update your business plan to reflect the evolving goals, market conditions, and financial status of your company.

Regulatory Compliance and Legal Check-Ups

- **Ongoing Legal Compliance**: Establish routines for regularly reviewing and updating your legal compliance in line with changing laws and industry standards. Consider annual check-ups with a legal professional.
- **Intellectual Property Management**: If your business relies on intellectual property (IP), implement strategies to protect and manage it effectively, including registering trademarks, patents, or copyrights.

Human Resources Management

- **Recruitment and Training**: Develop robust recruitment strategies to attract skilled employees. Implement training programs that ensure employees are well-equipped to perform their roles effectively.
- **Employee Retention Strategies**: Focus on creating a positive workplace culture that encourages retention through employee engagement, competitive compensation packages, and career development opportunities.

Marketing and Customer Engagement

- **Marketing Strategies**: Develop and execute marketing strategies that effectively promote your products or services. Utilize digital marketing, social media, and traditional advertising as appropriate.
- **Customer Relationship Management (CRM)**: Implement a CRM system to enhance customer interactions and satisfaction, which is crucial for customer retention and word-of-mouth referrals.

Leveraging Technology for Efficiency

- **Adopting Technology Solutions**: Invest in technology solutions that enhance operational efficiency, improve customer service, and reduce costs. This may include ERP systems, e-commerce platforms, or remote collaboration tools.

By carefully implementing these strategies, newly incorporated businesses can ensure they are well-positioned for future growth and success. This solid foundation not only supports day-to-day operations but also facilitates scalability as the business evolves and market demands change.

Quick Tips and Recap

- **Choose the Right Business Structure**: Evaluate your business needs and goals to select the most appropriate legal structure, considering liability, taxation, and investment needs.
- **Understand and Comply with State and Federal Requirements**: Familiarize yourself with the specific incorporation requirements of the state where you plan to incorporate and ensure compliance with all relevant federal regulations.
- **Prepare and File Necessary Documents Accurately**: Ensure all incorporation documents, like Articles of Incorporation and operating agreements, are accurately completed and filed with the appropriate state agency.
- **Obtain Necessary Licenses and Permits**: Identify and secure all required licenses and permits to operate legally and avoid penalties or business interruptions.
- **Set Up Essential Business Operations**: Establish fundamental operations such as bank accounts, accounting systems, and initial insurance coverage immediately after incorporation.
- **Establish Strong Corporate Governance**: Implement a robust governance framework, including forming a board of directors and developing corporate policies.
- **Engage in Strategic Planning**: Regularly update your business plan and engage in long-term strategic planning to align with your evolving business objectives.

- **Ensure Ongoing Legal and Regulatory Compliance**: Schedule regular legal check-ups to adapt to changes in laws and industry standards and protect intellectual property vigorously.
- **Develop Human Resources Management**: Invest in recruitment and training to build a skilled workforce and foster a positive workplace culture for employee retention.
- **Implement Effective Marketing and CRM**: Develop comprehensive marketing strategies and use CRM systems to enhance customer relationships and support business growth.
- **Leverage Technology for Business Efficiency**: Adopt technology solutions that improve operational efficiency and enable scalability.

By following these tips, you can effectively navigate the incorporation process and set a strong foundation for your business's future growth and success.

CHAPTER EIGHTEEN

Legal Toolkit: Utilizing Sample Agreements and Forms

"Having a robust legal toolkit, complete with sample agreements and forms, isn't just about compliance—it's about building a foundation of trust and clarity in every business relationship." — RUTH BADER GINSBURG, ASSOCIATE JUSTICE OF THE U. S. SUPREME COURT

Dive into the legal jungle with a machete of sample agreements and forms in hand—because why start from scratch when you can build on the groundwork laid by legal eagles? This chapter is like having a Swiss Army knife in your entrepreneurial toolkit, each blade a ready-to-use template that slices through the red tape and carves out clear, concise agreements.

We'll show you how to wield these tools with the precision of a legal maestro, ensuring that every contract, from partnerships to NDAs, is as watertight as a submarine hatch. Learn the art of adapting templates to suit your specific business needs without getting tangled in legal jargon. Think of it as legal origami—folding standard forms into the unique shape of your business requirements.

So, gear up to arm yourself with a robust arsenal of forms that not only protect your venture but also propel it by establishing clear expectations and boundaries. It's time to turn potential legal landmines into solid stepping stones for your business's journey forward. Ready to legally safeguard your enterprise with the ease of a pro? Let's dive in!

Understanding Common Business Agreements

Navigating the world of business requires a solid understanding of various legal agreements that define and protect relationships between parties, including owners, partners, vendors, and customers. This section provides an overview of common business agreements, explaining their purpose, typical content, and the crucial elements that should be included to ensure they are legally robust.

Types of Common Business Agreements

- **Partnership Agreements**: Essential for businesses operated by more than one individual, these agreements outline the roles, responsibilities, profit sharing, and conflict resolution methods among partners. They serve to prevent disputes by clarifying what each partner brings to the table and their entitlements.
- **Service Contracts**: Used when hiring service providers or when providing services to clients, these contracts specify the scope of work, timelines, payment terms, and standards expected for the services provided. They help in managing expectations and define recourse in case of non-performance.
- **Lease Agreements**: For businesses that operate in leased spaces, lease agreements detail the terms of the lease, including rent, duration, usage policies, and maintenance responsibilities, protecting both the landlord and the tenant.

Purpose of Business Agreements

- **Clear Expectations**: Agreements are vital for setting clear expectations between parties, detailing rights and responsibilities to avoid misunderstandings.
- **Legal Protection**: Well-crafted agreements provide legal protection by outlining the terms of engagement and what happens if these terms are not met. They serve as legally binding documents that can be enforced in court if necessary.
- **Flexibility and Structure**: While providing a structured relationship, agreements also offer flexibility by allowing parties to negotiate terms that best suit their needs before signing.

Fundamental Elements of Business Agreements

- **Parties Involved**: Clearly identify all parties involved with legal names and addresses to avoid any ambiguity about who is bound by the agreement.
- **Terms and Conditions**: Specify the terms of the agreement, including any deadlines, financial arrangements, and other obligations. This section forms the core of the agreement and must be detailed and precise.
- **Confidentiality Clauses**: When necessary, include confidentiality clauses to protect sensitive information shared between parties during the course of business.
- **Dispute Resolution**: Outline mechanisms for resolving disputes should they arise, including mediation, arbitration, or legal actions. This clause helps manage conflicts efficiently without damaging business relations.
- **Termination Conditions**: Specify conditions under which the agreement can be terminated by either party. This includes detailing any notice periods and what constitutes a breach of the agreement.
- **Signatures**: Ensure that all parties sign the agreement, as a signed contract is essential to its enforceability. Digital signatures are also legally binding in many jurisdictions.

Reviewing and Updating Agreements

- **Regular Reviews**: Business agreements should be reviewed periodically to ensure they remain relevant and reflective of the current business relationship and legal environment.
- **Legal Consultation**: It is advisable to have all agreements reviewed by a legal professional before they are signed to ensure they are comprehensive and legally sound.

Understanding these fundamental aspects of business agreements arms entrepreneurs with the knowledge to develop contracts that not only meet their business needs but also provide essential legal protections. This foundation is critical for building stable and secure business relationships.

Using Non-Disclosure Agreements (NDAs)

Non-disclosure agreements (NDAs) are essential legal tools for protecting sensitive information within a business context. Whether dealing with potential partners, investors, or employees, NDAs ensure that confidential information stays secure. This section explains the importance of NDAs, when to use them, and key terms to include for effective protection.

Purpose of NDAs

- **Protection of Confidential Information**: NDAs are designed to safeguard any non-public business information from being disclosed to unauthorized parties. This includes trade secrets, business plans, customer lists, and other proprietary data.
- **Foundation for Trust**: By establishing a legal framework for confidentiality, NDAs help create a foundation of trust between parties engaging in business discussions or collaborations.

COMPANY NAME
MUTUAL NON-DISCLOSURE AGREEMENT

THIS CONFIDENTIAL INFORMATION NON-DISCLOSURE AGREEMENT is made and entered into this date ____________________, by and between ____, a ____________________ corporation, having its principal place of business at __________________ ____ , and Company Name, a [insert state] business, having its principal place of business at [address].

In consideration of the mutual promises and covenants contained in this Agreement and the disclosure of Confidential Information to each other, the parties to this Agreement agree as follows:

1. The parties agree that all Confidential Information (as defined below) shall be and remain the sole property of the party ("Transmitting Party") transmitting such Confidential Information to the other party ("Receiving Party"), that Transmitting Party shall be the sole owner of all patents, copyrights and other proprietary rights in connection therewith and that no license is granted to Receiving Party hereby. As used herein, "Confidential Information" means confidential and proprietary information which provides either party to this Agreement with a competitive advantage, including but not limited to trade secrets, ideas, processes, formulas, computer software, circuit designs, schematics, data and know-how, copyrightable material, improvements, inventions (whether patentable or not), techniques, marketing plans, strategies, business and product development plans, timetables, forecasts and customer lists as related to the products and services (current and prospective) of each of the parties.

Without limiting the foregoing, the Confidential Information to be disclosed under this Agreement is described as follows:____

____

2. The Receiving Party may use the Confidential Information solely for the purpose of:

____

____

____

3. The Receiving Party agrees to hold in confidence and trust and to maintain as confidential all Confidential Information of Transmitting Party. The Receiving Party shall not disclose the Confidential Information, or any information derived therefrom, to any third person, and shall use the same degree of care to avoid publication or dissemination of such information as Receiving Party employs with respect to its own information which it does not desire to have published or disseminated, including any affiliates, fiduciaries and employees of Receiving Party to whom disclosure is necessary in order to permit Receiving Party to evaluate the Confidential Information of Transmitting Party for the

purpose(s) set forth in paragraph 2 above, and who have agreed in writing to hold such Confidential Information in confidence and not to use it for their own purposes.

4. The provision of paragraph 3 shall not apply to any information (a) which is in the public domain at the time of disclosure to Receiving Party or which thereafter enters the public domain through no action or inaction by Receiving Party or its employees; or (b) which Receiving Party can establish and document was in the possession of or known by Receiving Party prior to its receipt from Transmitting Party; (c) which is rightfully disclosed to Receiving Party by another person not in violation of the proprietary or other rights of Transmitting Party or any other person or entity; (d) which Receiving Party can establish was independently developed by Receiving Party; or (e) is approved for release by written authorization of Transmitting Party.

5. Immediately upon the accomplishment of purpose(s) set forth in paragraph 2, or upon Transmitting Party's request, Receiving Party shall (i) cease using the Confidential Information, (ii) return the Confidential Information and all copies, notes or extracts thereof to Disclosing Party within seven (7) days from accomplishment of the purpose(s) set forth in paragraph 2 above, or receipt of demand (whichever is earlier), and (iii) upon request of the Disclosing Party, certify in writing that the Receiving Party has complied with the obligations set forth in this paragraph.

6. The Receiving Party shall not reverse-engineer, decompile, or disassemble any software disclosed to it and shall not remove, overprint or deface any notice of copyright, trademark, logo, legend, or other notices of ownership from any originals or copies of Confidential Information it obtains from the Disclosing Party.

7. Neither party shall transmit, directly or indirectly, the Confidential Information or any technical data received from the other party, nor any subset or portion thereof, outside the United States without the Disclosing Party's prior written consent and in accordance with all export laws and regulations of the United States.

8. Each party acknowledges that monetary remedies may be inadequate to protect Confidential Information and that injunctive relief may be appropriate to protect such Confidential Information.

9. All Confidential Information is provided by each party and accepted by the other party "AS IS," and nothing contained herein, nor any information or material furnished relating to such Confidential Information, shall constitute any representation or warranty by either party with respect to (a) the non-infringement of patent, copyright or other rights of third parties by such data or its use, or (b) the accuracy, completeness or usefulness of any such data, or (c) any commitment by either party to the other regarding any future business transactions between the parties.

10. Except for actions arising out of or related to either party's breach of the obligations herein, in no event shall either party be liable to the other in connection with said Confidential Information including, without limitation, any indirect, incidental, special or consequential damages, including loss of revenue or profits.

11. This Agreement supersedes all prior discussions and writings and constitutes the entire Agreement between the parties with respect to the information transmitted hereunder. No waiver or modification of this Agreement shall be binding upon either party unless made in writing and signed by a duly authorized representative of such party. The failure of either party to enforce at any time or for any period of time the provisions hereof shall not be construed to be a waiver of such provisions or of the right of such party to enforce each and every such provision.

12. This Agreement shall remain in effect for a period of three (3) years from the date hereof, unless earlier terminated by either party upon a thirty (30) day written notice to the other. Notwithstanding the termination or expiration of the Agreement, the obligations of the Receiving Party not to disclose any Confidential Information to third parties pursuant to this Agreement shall remain in effect for a period of three (3) years following the date of its disclosure by Transmitting Party to Receiving Party.

13. This Agreement shall be construed in accordance with the laws of the State of _________, and subject to the exclusive jurisdiction of its courts in ___________ County, [state].

IN WITNESS WHEREOF, the parties have caused this Agreement to be entered into within the State of [insert state] as of the date first set forth above.

Company: ________________________	Company: ______________________
By:______________________________	By:____________________________
Name:____________________________	Name:__________________________
Title:_____________________________	Title:__________________________
Date:_____________________________	Date:__________________________

▶ If you are interested in receiving an electronic copy of this document, please email us at documents@AuthorsDoor.com with the subject line "Request for Mutual Non-Disclosure Agreement." Upon receiving your email, we will promptly send you a Microsoft Word copy of the document. **Disclaimer:** Please note that all agreements are provided for informational purposes only and should not be construed as legal advice. We recommend consulting with a qualified attorney to ensure that any legal documents or decisions are tailored to your specific circumstances.

When to Use NDAs

- **New Business Partnerships or Ventures**: Whenever discussing potential business relationships or joint ventures where sensitive information will be exchanged, an NDA should be in place before any detailed meetings occur.
- **Product Development and Innovation**: Protect any innovative processes, designs, or products that give your business a competitive edge, especially when collaborating with external parties like manufacturers or designers.
- **Employee Relations**: Use NDAs with employees who have access to critical business information to prevent leaks that could benefit competitors.

Key Elements of an Effective NDA

- **Identification of Parties**: Clearly specify who is involved in the agreement. This includes the discloser (the party sharing the information) and the recipient (the party receiving the information).
- **Definition of Confidential Information**: Clearly define what constitutes confidential information in the context of the agreement. Be specific about what is included and, if necessary, what is excluded.
- **Obligations of the Receiving Party**: Outline the duties of the receiving party, including how they should handle the confidential information, the standards of care to apply, and how to dispose of the information once the relationship or the agreement concludes.
- **Duration**: State how long the NDA will be in effect. This includes both the duration of the obligation to keep the information confidential and the term during which information may be disclosed between parties.
- **Permitted Disclosure**: Specify any circumstances under which the confidential information can be disclosed, such as legal requirements to release information through a court order or governmental regulation.

- **Consequences of Breach**: Define the penalties or legal actions that may be taken if the agreement is violated. This could include financial compensation or other remedies.

Drafting and Implementing NDAs

- **Customization to Fit the Situation**: Tailor NDAs to fit specific interactions. The level of detail and strictness might vary depending on whether you're dealing with an employee, a contractor, or a potential business partner.
- **Legal Review**: Have NDAs reviewed by a legal professional to ensure they are enforceable and compliant with local laws and regulations.
- **Regular Updates**: As business operations and relationships evolve, regularly review and update the terms of NDAs to adapt to new circumstances or legal requirements.

NDAs are a crucial component of legal protection for businesses, especially those that depend heavily on proprietary information for their competitive advantage. By understanding how to effectively use NDAs, businesses can secure their operations and foster safer, more productive collaborations.

Employment Contracts and Policies

Creating clear and comprehensive employment contracts and workplace policies is essential for defining the terms of employment and setting expectations between the employer and employees. This section explores the importance of these documents and outlines how to craft them to ensure legal compliance and promote a healthy workplace culture.

Purpose of Employment Contracts

- **Clarify Employment Terms**: Employment contracts specify the terms of the employment relationship, including job responsibilities, salary, benefits, work hours, and other employment conditions.

- **Protect Both Parties**: These contracts protect both the employer and the employee by clearly stating what each can expect from the other. They provide a reference that can be consulted in case of disputes.

Essential Elements of Employment Contracts

- **Job Description**: Clearly define the role and responsibilities of the employee. This should include the title of the position, key duties, and performance expectations.
- **Compensation and Benefits**: Detail the salary structure, bonus potential, and benefits such as health insurance, retirement plans, and paid leave. Explain the criteria for salary increments and promotions.
- **Work Hours and Conditions**: Specify the working hours, workplace location, and remote work policies if applicable. Include expectations for overtime work and compensation.
- **Duration of Employment**: Clarify whether the employment is at-will, temporary, or for a fixed term. If it's for a fixed term, state the start and end dates.
- **Confidentiality and Non-compete Clauses**: Incorporate clauses that protect the company's confidential information and restrict employees from joining competitors or starting similar businesses within a certain period after leaving the company.
- **Termination Conditions**: Outline the conditions under which the employment can be terminated by either party, including notice periods and any severance packages.

Developing Effective Workplace Policies

- **Scope and Purpose**: Workplace policies should cover all critical areas of employment, including equal opportunity employment, workplace safety, harassment, and grievance handling procedures.
- **Compliance with Laws**: Ensure that all policies comply with local, state, and federal employment laws. Regular updates are necessary to accommodate changes in legislation.

- **Accessibility and Understanding**: Policies should be written in clear, accessible language. Employees must acknowledge that they understand and agree to these policies.

Implementation and Enforcement

- **Orientation and Training**: Introduce new employees to these contracts and policies during their orientation. Provide training sessions to explain the policies in detail.
- **Consistent Enforcement**: Apply the policies consistently across the organization to maintain fairness and prevent legal challenges.
- **Regular Reviews and Updates**: Regularly review and update the employment contracts and workplace policies to reflect changes in the company's operations and legal requirements.

Engaging Legal Expertise

- **Legal Review**: Have employment contracts and workplace policies reviewed by a labor law attorney to ensure they are legally sound and enforceable.
- **Customization to Business Needs**: Customize these documents to reflect the specific needs and culture of your business. Generic contracts and policies might not address specific challenges or opportunities in your business environment.

Employment contracts and workplace policies are not just formalities; they are foundational tools for managing human resources effectively and legally. By carefully crafting these documents, businesses can protect themselves from potential disputes and create a supportive and clear work environment for all employees.

▶ A Contract for Services Agreement can be found in the **Appendix**. If you are interested in receiving an electronic copy of this document, please email us at documents@AuthorsDoor.com with the subject line "Request for Contract for Services Agreement." Upon receiving your email, we will promptly send you a Microsoft Word copy of the document. **Disclaimer:** Please note that all agreements are provided for informational purposes only and should not be construed as legal advice. We recommend consulting with a qualified attorney to ensure that any legal documents or decisions are tailored to your specific circumstances.

Sales Contracts and Customer Agreements

Sales contracts and customer agreements are crucial for defining the terms of commerce between a business and its customers. This section explains how to draft these agreements to ensure clarity, enforceability, and customer satisfaction, thus safeguarding the business's interests while fostering positive customer relationships.

Purpose of Sales Contracts and Customer Agreements

- **Define the Terms of Sale**: These agreements specify the conditions under which products or services are sold, detailing what the customer can expect and what obligations the seller must fulfill.
- **Legal Protection**: By clearly outlining terms and conditions, these documents protect both parties legally, reducing the likelihood of misunderstandings and disputes.

Key Elements of Effective Sales Contracts

- **Product or Service Descriptions**: Clearly describe the products or services being offered, including any specifications or quality standards that define their suitability for use.
- **Pricing and Payment Terms**: Detail the pricing structure, including any taxes, shipping costs, and available payment methods. Clearly state payment terms, such as deposits required, payment schedules, and penalties for late payments.
- **Delivery Terms**: Specify delivery commitments, including timelines, delivery methods, and any shipping fees. Clarify who bears the risk of loss or damage during shipping.

- **Warranties and Guarantees**: Outline any warranties or guarantees offered with the product or service. Specify what protections these cover, any exclusions, and the duration of the warranty.
- **Dispute Resolution**: Include terms for resolving disputes arising from the contract, specifying any arbitration or mediation processes and the jurisdiction under which disputes will be settled.
- **Return and Refund Policies**: Clearly define the conditions under which returns and refunds are accepted, including time limits, the state of the product, and the process for claiming refunds.

Drafting Customer Agreements for Services

- **Scope of Services**: Define precisely what services will be provided, including any deliverables, deadlines, and performance criteria.
- **Cancellation Policies**: State terms for contract cancellation, including any notice required and penalties or fees for early termination.
- **Confidentiality Clauses**: If applicable, include clauses that protect any confidential information that may be shared during the provision of services.
- **Renewal Terms**: Specify how the agreement can be renewed, including any changes to terms that apply upon renewal.

Implementing Sales Contracts and Customer Agreements

- **Accessibility**: Ensure that contracts and agreements are easy to understand and accessible to customers before purchase decisions are made.
- **Signature and Acknowledgment**: Use processes that ensure customers acknowledge and agree to these terms, whether through digital signatures or signed physical copies.
- **Customer Service Training**: Train customer service teams to understand these agreements thoroughly so they can explain terms to customers and handle issues that arise.

Legal Review and Compliance

- **Regular Legal Review**: Have all sales contracts and customer agreements reviewed by legal professionals to ensure they comply with current laws and regulations.
- **Adaptation to New Regulations**: Update these documents as necessary to adapt to new consumer protection laws, commercial regulations, or changes in business operations.

By meticulously crafting sales contracts and customer agreements, businesses not only protect their operational interests but also build trust with their customers by providing clear, fair terms that enhance customer satisfaction and loyalty.

Customizing Templates for Your Business

While sample agreements and forms provide a strong foundation, customizing these documents to fit the specific needs of your business is crucial. This section offers guidance on how to adapt legal templates to your unique situation, ensuring they remain relevant, compliant, and effective in protecting your business interests.

Advantages of Customization

- **Tailored to Specific Needs**: Customizing templates ensures that the contracts or agreements specifically address the unique aspects and needs of your business operations, industry standards, and customer interactions.
- **Enhanced Legal Protection**: By tailoring agreements to reflect the precise nature of your business, you enhance the legal protections by including specific clauses relevant to your sector's risks and regulatory environment.

Steps for Customizing Legal Templates

- **Review Standard Templates**: Start with a reliable template that covers the general essentials applicable to the type of agreement you need.

Ensure the template is sourced from a credible provider to guarantee it includes all necessary legal provisions.

- **Identify Business-Specific Requirements**: Analyze your business operations to identify any special conditions, obligations, or provisions that need to be explicitly included in the contract. This could relate to intellectual property, liability issues, or specific regulatory compliance needs.
- **Consult with Stakeholders**: Engage with key stakeholders, including management, financial advisors, and department heads, to gather input on what needs to be covered in the agreement to protect all facets of the business.
- **Incorporate Specific Clauses**: Modify the template by adding or altering clauses that specifically relate to your business. This might include payment terms, delivery conditions, confidentiality requirements, or dispute resolution mechanisms tailored to your business model and industry practices.

Legal Considerations in Customization

- **Ensure Compliance**: Ensure that the customized agreement complies with local, state, and federal laws. Pay special attention to any regulations that govern your specific industry.
- **Maintain Clarity and Concision**: While customizing, keep the language clear and concise to avoid potential ambiguities that could lead to legal disputes. Ensure that any additions or changes are as straightforward as the original template.
- **Legal Review**: Once customized, have the document reviewed by a legal professional. This step is crucial to ensure that the modifications are legally sound and enforceable.

Implementing Customized Agreements

- **Employee Training**: Train employees who handle contracts about the specifics of the customized agreements to ensure they understand the terms and can manage contracts effectively.

- **Monitor and Update**: Regularly review and update customized agreements to adapt to changes in your business environment, such as new products, services, or changes in the legal landscape.
- **Digital Management**: Use digital contract management tools to store, track, and manage your customized agreements efficiently. These tools can also help in monitoring deadlines, renewal dates, and compliance checks.

Feedback and Continuous Improvement

- **Solicit Feedback**: After using the customized agreements, solicit feedback from users and stakeholders to identify any areas for improvement.
- **Continuous Improvement**: Treat contract customization as an ongoing process. Regularly refine and update the documents as you gather more insights from their practical application and as business needs evolve.

Customizing legal templates allows your business to have agreements that are not only legally enforceable but also perfectly aligned with the operational realities and specific challenges of your business. This strategic approach ensures that all contractual relationships are optimally managed, safeguarding your business's interests effectively.

Quick Tips and Recap

- **Start with Reliable Templates**: Use proven templates as a base to ensure all foundational legal elements are covered.
- **Customize for Your Business**: Tailor templates to address the specific needs, risks, and operations of your business to enhance relevance and protection.
- **Consult Legal Experts**: Always have customized agreements reviewed by legal professionals to ensure compliance and enforceability.

- **Keep Language Clear and Simple**: Use straightforward and clear language in agreements to avoid misunderstandings and legal ambiguities.
- **Update Regularly**: Regularly review and update your agreements to reflect changes in your business operations and legal requirements.
- **Educate Your Team**: Ensure that employees who handle contracts are trained on the specific terms and legal implications of your business agreements.
- **Use Digital Tools**: Implement contract management software to organize, track, and maintain your legal documents efficiently.
- **Monitor Legal Changes**: Stay informed about changes in laws that affect your business sector and adjust your documents accordingly.
- **Gather Feedback**: Solicit and incorporate feedback from stakeholders to continually improve the relevance and effectiveness of your agreements.
- **Include Necessary Clauses**: Make sure to include specific clauses such as confidentiality, dispute resolution, and termination to protect your business adequately.
- **Clarify Roles and Responsibilities**: Clearly define the obligations and rights of all parties involved to prevent potential conflicts and ensure smooth business operations.

These tips will help you effectively utilize and customize legal templates, ensuring your business agreements are not only comprehensive and compliant but also tailored to support your specific business objectives and challenges.

CHAPTER NINETEEN

Startup Checklists: Your Guide to Getting Off the Ground

"Checklists turn overwhelming challenges into practical actions. They provide a visible path to success and a measure of how far you've come and what's left to tackle."— TIM COOK, CEO OF APPLE

Welcome to the ultimate checklist challenge, where ticking boxes isn't just satisfying—it's a strategic move that propels your startup from concept to launchpad. This isn't your average grocery list; it's the entrepreneur's flight checklist ensuring every system is go before liftoff.

In this chapter, we'll arm you with the ultimate startup checklists, covering everything from securing your intellectual property to setting up your accounting systems. Think of it as your personal co-pilot, guiding you through the pre-launch turbulence with the precision of a seasoned aviator. We'll help you navigate the essential tasks that lay the groundwork for a successful takeoff, ensuring no bolt is loose and no stone unturned.

Prepare to tick your way through preparations with the efficiency of a conductor leading an orchestra—each check a note in the symphony of your impending success. By the end of this chapter, you'll be ready to not just start up, but soar. Buckle up, entrepreneurs; it's time to transform those startup dreams into actionable, checked-off realities!

Legal and Regulatory Checklist

Launching a startup involves navigating a complex legal and regulatory landscape. This checklist provides a comprehensive guide to ensure you meet all necessary legal and regulatory requirements, setting a solid foundation for your business's future growth and compliance.

1. Choose the Right Business Structure

- Evaluate the pros and cons of different business structures (e.g., sole proprietorship, partnership, LLC, corporation) based on liability, taxation, and investment needs.
- Consult with a legal advisor to select the structure that best suits your business goals and legal requirements.

2. Register Your Business

- File the necessary paperwork with state and local authorities to legally establish your business.
- Obtain a federal Employer Identification Number (EIN) from the IRS for tax purposes.

3. Obtain Necessary Licenses and Permits

- Research and secure all required local, state, and federal licenses and permits based on your business activities.
- Regularly review and renew these documents to remain compliant with changes in regulations.

4. Protect Intellectual Property

- Identify all intellectual property (IP) that needs protection, such as trademarks, patents, copyrights, and trade secrets.
- File for appropriate protections with relevant authorities to safeguard your business ideas and products.

5. Draft Foundational Agreements

- Create and formalize key business agreements including partnership agreements, founder agreements, and any other contracts necessary for your business operations.
- Ensure that all agreements clearly define roles, responsibilities, and dispute resolution mechanisms.

6. Comply with Employment Laws

- Understand and implement all required employment laws and regulations if you plan to hire employees.
- Develop employment contracts, employee handbooks, and policies that comply with labor laws.

7. Setup for Data Protection Compliance

- If your business will collect, store, or use personal data, ensure compliance with data protection regulations such as GDPR or CCPA.
- Implement necessary policies and technologies to protect customer and employee data.

8. Prepare for Industry-Specific Regulations

- Identify any industry-specific regulations that apply to your business (e.g., health and safety for manufacturing, confidentiality in consulting).
- Implement compliance measures to meet these specific regulatory requirements.

9. Review Insurance Needs

- Assess the types of business insurance needed to protect against potential risks (e.g., general liability insurance, professional liability insurance, product liability insurance).
- Obtain adequate insurance coverage to mitigate identified risks.

10. Keep Legal Documents Organized

- Maintain a well-organized system for all your legal and regulatory documentation.
- Consider using digital tools or services to manage documents, track deadlines for renewals, and ensure easy access when needed.

By meticulously following this legal and regulatory checklist, you ensure that your startup not only complies with all necessary legal requirements but also secures a strong legal foundation to support future business activities and growth.

Financial Setup Checklist

Setting up the financial backbone of your startup is crucial for managing cash flow, securing funding, and ensuring compliance with tax laws. This checklist will guide you through the essential financial tasks you need to address as you establish and grow your new business.

1. Establish Business Banking Accounts

- Open a dedicated business bank account to separate personal finances from business transactions, which is crucial for financial clarity and tax purposes.
- Consider opening both checking and savings accounts to manage operational expenses and allocate funds for future growth.

2. Set Up an Accounting System

- Choose an accounting software that fits the scale and needs of your business, allowing for scalability as your business grows.

- Ensure your system can handle invoicing, expense tracking, payroll, and financial reporting.

3. Develop a Budget and Financial Projections

- Create a detailed budget that outlines expected revenues, costs, and profits for at least the first year of operations.
- Develop financial projections for the next three to five years to guide business decisions and to present to potential investors.

4. Plan Initial Funding

- Assess your startup costs and determine how much capital you need to launch and operate your business until it becomes profitable.
- Identify potential sources of funding, including personal savings, loans, angel investors, venture capital, or crowdfunding.

5. Establish Credit

- Apply for a business credit card to help manage cash flow and build your business's credit history.
- Consider establishing lines of credit with banks or vendors to ensure liquidity in case of unforeseen expenses.

6. Setup Payroll Systems

- If hiring employees, set up a payroll system compliant with federal and state tax requirements.
- Register for employer taxes, including federal income tax withholding, Social Security, and Medicare.

7. Understand and Manage Taxes

- Register for the appropriate federal, state, and local taxes, which may include income tax, sales tax, and employment taxes.
- Familiarize yourself with tax deadlines and requirements to avoid penalties.

8. Secure Financial Advisory Services

- Engage a financial advisor or accountant who can provide expert advice on financial management, tax planning, and compliance.
- Regularly consult with your advisor to ensure financial health and to strategize for growth.

9. Implement Internal Controls

- Develop internal controls to manage and monitor finances. This includes checks and balances to prevent errors or fraud.
- Ensure proper authorization processes for financial transactions and establish audit trails.

10. Financial Documentation and Record Keeping

- Maintain thorough records of all financial transactions, agreements, and obligations.
- Keep financial documents organized and readily accessible for auditing purposes and financial analysis.

By diligently following this financial setup checklist, you will lay a robust financial foundation for your startup. Effective financial management not only facilitates smoother daily operations but also positions your business for successful growth and expansion.

Market and Customer Research Checklist

Thorough market and customer research is pivotal for understanding the competitive landscape, identifying your target market, and tailoring your products or services to meet customer needs. This checklist guides you through the essential steps to gather and analyze critical market data to ensure your startup's offerings are well-positioned and appealing to potential customers.

1. Define Your Target Market

- Clearly define who your ideal customers are based on demographic, psychographic, and behavioral criteria.

- Use data from market reports, surveys, and industry trends to support your definitions.

2. Conduct Competitive Analysis

- Identify direct and indirect competitors in your market. Gather information about their products, pricing, marketing strategies, and market share.
- Analyze their strengths and weaknesses to find opportunities where your startup can differentiate itself.

3. Understand Market Trends

- Stay informed about the latest trends affecting your industry, including technological advancements, consumer behavior changes, and regulatory shifts.
- Analyze how these trends can impact your business now and in the future, and plan how to leverage or mitigate them.

4. Evaluate Market Size and Potential

- Estimate the size of the market you are entering, including potential customer base, predicted growth rates, and total possible revenue.
- Determine the market potential for your specific products or services to ensure sufficient demand exists.

5. Collect Customer Feedback

- Gather input from potential customers through interviews, focus groups, or surveys to understand their needs, preferences, and pain points.
- Use this feedback to refine your product or service offerings and to tailor your marketing messages.

6. Test Market Your Product or Service

- Conduct a pilot launch or soft launch in a controlled environment to gather real-world data on how your product or service performs.

- Use the insights gained to make any necessary adjustments before a full-scale launch.

7. Develop Pricing Strategies

- Based on your competitive analysis and customer feedback, develop pricing strategies that position your product competitively and appeal to your target market.
- Consider different pricing models (e.g., subscription, one-time purchase, freemium) to find what works best for your market and margins.

8. Plan Marketing and Distribution Strategies

- Develop a detailed marketing plan that outlines how you will reach your target audience, including specific channels, campaigns, and promotional tactics.
- Determine the most effective distribution channels for your products or services, considering both online and offline options.

9. Monitor and Adapt Based on Feedback

- Establish processes for continually monitoring market conditions and customer feedback.
- Be prepared to adapt your strategies in response to new information or changes in the market to stay relevant and competitive.

10. Document and Review Your Findings

- Keep thorough records of all research findings, including sources, methodologies, and results.
- Regularly review this data with your team to ensure strategies and decisions are data-driven and align with current market conditions.

By completing these tasks, you will have a solid understanding of your market and target customers, which is crucial for making informed decisions and increasing the likelihood of your startup's success.

Operational Setup Checklist

Efficiently setting up your operations is key to ensuring that your startup can deliver products or services effectively upon launch. This checklist will guide you through the critical steps required to establish and streamline your startup's operations.

1. Secure a Business Location

- Decide whether your business needs a physical location, like a retail space, office, or warehouse, or if it can operate remotely.
- Consider factors such as cost, accessibility, space requirements, and proximity to suppliers and customers when choosing a location.

2. Purchase Necessary Equipment and Technology

- List all the essential equipment and technology needed for your business operations, including computers, manufacturing equipment, or software.
- Research and compare suppliers to find the best quality and prices. Consider leasing options for high-cost items to reduce upfront expenses.

3. Set Up Production or Service Delivery Processes

- Develop efficient processes for producing your product or delivering your service. Document these processes in detailed operational manuals.
- Test these processes to ensure they are efficient and scalable, making adjustments as needed based on trial runs.

4. Implement Inventory Management Systems

- Choose and set up inventory management software that suits your business size and complexity.
- Establish procedures for tracking inventory levels, ordering supplies, and handling storage to minimize costs and maximize efficiency.

5. Establish Supply Chain and Vendor Relationships

- Identify and vet suppliers and vendors who can provide the raw materials or services necessary for your operations.

- Negotiate contracts that secure favorable terms and build strong, reliable supply chain partnerships.

6. Hire and Train Staff

- Determine staffing needs and create job descriptions that clearly outline roles and responsibilities.
- Develop a hiring plan, conduct interviews, and select candidates who fit your company culture and possess the necessary skills.
- Create training programs to ensure all employees are competent in their roles and understand your business processes and goals.

7. Develop Quality Control Systems

- Implement systems to monitor and maintain the quality of your products or services.
- Set up regular reviews and audits of your products or services to ensure they meet industry standards and customer expectations.

8. Plan Logistics for Distribution

- If applicable, plan the logistics for distributing your products. This includes selecting delivery methods, packaging solutions, and logistics partners.
- Ensure that your distribution network is capable of delivering products efficiently and cost-effectively to your target markets.

9. Set Up Communication Systems

- Establish internal communication tools and protocols to ensure smooth information flow among team members.
- Choose customer communication platforms that align with your service standards and customer preferences.

10. Prepare for Operational Risks

- Identify potential operational risks, such as supply chain disruptions or equipment failures.

- Develop contingency plans to mitigate these risks, ensuring that your business can continue operations under various scenarios.

By diligently following this operational setup checklist, you'll ensure that your startup's foundational activities are robust and capable of supporting successful business operations from day one. This preparation is crucial for smoothing out potential kinks that could impact your business's ability to deliver to its customers efficiently.

Launch Preparation Checklist

The final stages before launching your startup are crucial for ensuring a smooth and successful entry into the market. This checklist will guide you through the key activities needed to prepare your business for launch, setting the stage for initial and sustained success.

1. Finalize Product or Service Offerings

- Ensure that all products or services are fully developed, tested, and ready to meet customer needs.
- Make any necessary adjustments based on feedback from your test marketing or pilot programs.

2. Develop a Comprehensive Marketing Plan

- Create a detailed marketing plan that outlines your branding, key messages, target audiences, and the channels you will use to reach them.
- Prepare all marketing materials, including digital content, brochures, and advertisements.

3. Build an Online Presence

- Develop a professional website that reflects your brand and provides essential information about your products or services.
- Set up social media profiles on platforms relevant to your target audience to build engagement and awareness.

4. Set Up Sales Channels

- Establish and prepare your sales channels, whether they are online platforms, physical stores, or through third-party distributors.
- Ensure that all sales platforms are integrated and functioning smoothly to handle customer transactions.

5. Implement Customer Service Systems

- Develop customer service policies and set up support channels, such as email, phone, or live chat.
- Train your customer service team on how to handle inquiries, complaints, and feedback efficiently and professionally.

6. Organize a Launch Event

- Plan a launch event or campaign to generate excitement and attract initial customers. Consider how to make your launch memorable and impactful.
- Coordinate with public relations and media to maximize exposure and reach a wider audience.

7. Establish Partnerships and Alliances

- Identify and secure partnerships with other businesses or influencers that can help promote your launch and extend your market reach.
- Leverage these relationships to create buzz around your startup and drive early traffic and sales.

8. Ensure Legal and Regulatory Compliance

- Double-check that all legal and regulatory requirements are met, including licenses, permits, and intellectual property protections.
- Ensure compliance with industry standards and practices to avoid any legal issues post-launch.

9. Conduct a Final Review

- Review all aspects of your business operations, marketing, and sales strategies to ensure they are fully aligned and integrated.

- Make final adjustments based on a comprehensive assessment of readiness and potential challenges.

10. Engage Your Network

- Notify your network, including friends, family, professional contacts, and early supporters, about your launch date.
- Encourage them to help spread the word and support your initial business activities.

By completing these steps, you'll position your startup not only to launch successfully but also to maintain momentum in its critical early days. This checklist ensures that every element of your business is aligned and optimized for public reception, operational functionality, and market impact.

Quick Tips and Recap

- **Finalize Your Offerings**: Ensure your products or services are thoroughly tested and ready for the market.
- **Develop a Robust Marketing Plan**: Have a detailed marketing strategy in place that targets your audience effectively across the right channels.
- **Establish a Strong Online Presence**: Create a professional website and active social media profiles to build engagement and visibility.
- **Prepare Sales Channels**: Set up and integrate all sales platforms to ensure they are ready for transactions.
- **Implement Customer Service Systems**: Develop efficient customer service protocols and train your team to handle queries and issues.
- **Plan a Memorable Launch Event**: Organize a launch event to generate excitement and attract initial customers.
- **Secure Strategic Partnerships**: Form alliances with other businesses or influencers to extend your reach and enhance credibility.
- **Ensure Legal Compliance**: Double-check all legal and regulatory requirements are met to avoid future complications.

- **Conduct a Comprehensive Final Review**: Assess all business aspects one last time to ensure readiness and cohesion.
- **Engage Your Network**: Leverage personal and professional networks to support and promote your launch.

Following these tips will help ensure that you cover all critical bases, allowing your startup to not only successfully launch but also sustain and grow in its initial phase.

CHAPTER TWENTY

Beyond the Launch: Strategies for Sustaining Growth

"Long-term growth requires more than initial success; it demands persistent innovation and strategic planning to adapt and thrive in an evolving market." — SUNDAR PICHAI, CEO OF ALPHABET INC. AND GOOGLE

Congratulations! Your business has successfully blasted off. But what about the journey beyond the launch? This chapter isn't just about keeping your business in orbit; it's about propelling it into uncharted territories of growth and innovation.

We'll explore the galaxy of post-launch strategies that ensure your business doesn't just survive but thrives. From refining your service offerings to exploring new market frontiers, this is your guide to avoiding the black holes of business stagnation. We'll dive into the art of iterative improvement—because your business is a living entity that deserves to evolve.

Think of this as your map to the stars, where each strategy boosts your trajectory, keeping your business vibrant and visible in a crowded marketplace. Ready to turn that initial spark into a sustained blaze? Let's fuel up and chart a course for continuous expansion, ensuring your business legacy shines brighter than a supernova!

Continuous Improvement and Innovation

In the ever-evolving business landscape, continuous improvement and innovation are not just advantageous—they are essential for sustained growth and competitiveness. This section explores how to embed these principles into your business operations to ensure your offerings remain relevant and appealing.

Embracing a Culture of Continuous Improvement

- **Feedback Loops**: Establish robust mechanisms to collect and analyze feedback from customers, employees, and partners. Use this feedback to make informed decisions about product enhancements, service improvements, and process optimizations.
- **Kaizen Approach**: Adopt the Kaizen philosophy of continuous improvement, focusing on small, incremental changes that cumulatively lead to significant enhancements over time.
- **Employee Involvement**: Encourage employees at all levels to contribute ideas for improvement. This not only fosters a sense of ownership and engagement but also pools a wider range of insights into the innovation process.

Innovation as a Core Business Strategy

- **Dedicated Innovation Teams**: Consider establishing a team dedicated to innovation, tasked with exploring new ideas and technologies that could benefit the business.

- **R&D Investment**: Allocate resources towards research and development (R&D) to stay ahead of industry trends and develop groundbreaking products or services.
- **Innovation Challenges and Hackathons**: Regularly organize challenges or hackathons to stimulate creativity within your team and solve business problems in novel ways.

Integrating Technology for Innovation

- **Leverage Emerging Technologies**: Stay abreast of technological advancements that can disrupt or enhance your industry. Evaluate and integrate technologies such as AI, IoT, or blockchain where they can add value to your business operations or customer experiences.
- **Digital Transformation**: Continuously assess and upgrade your digital tools and platforms to enhance productivity, improve customer interactions, and streamline operations.

Prototyping and Market Testing

- **Rapid Prototyping**: Utilize rapid prototyping tools to quickly turn new ideas into testable products, allowing for immediate feedback and iteration.
- **Pilot Programs**: Launch new concepts in controlled environments to test their viability before a full-scale rollout. This minimizes risk and allows for refinements based on actual user interactions.

Learning from Failures

- **Foster a Safe-to-Fail Environment**: Cultivate a company culture where calculated risks are encouraged, and failures are viewed as learning opportunities.
- **Post-Mortem Analysis**: When projects do not yield the expected results, conduct thorough analyses to extract lessons and apply these learnings to future initiatives.

By integrating continuous improvement and innovation into every aspect of your business, you ensure that your offerings evolve with changing customer demands and market conditions. This ongoing commitment to excellence and adaptation not only enhances your current market position but also secures long-term growth and success.

Customer Retention Strategies

Securing a customer's business for the first time is just the beginning. Developing strategies to keep these customers over the long term is crucial for sustainable growth and profitability. This section outlines effective customer retention strategies that can help transform one-time buyers into loyal patrons.

Understanding Customer Retention

- **Significance of Retention**: Highlight the importance of customer retention in enhancing lifetime customer value and reducing churn. Retaining customers is generally more cost-effective than acquiring new ones due to lower marketing and sales costs.
- **Metrics to Monitor**: Identify key metrics to monitor customer retention, such as repeat purchase rates, customer lifetime value (CLV), and net promoter score (NPS).

Developing a Customer-Centric Culture

- **Employee Training**: Train employees across all levels and departments on the importance of customer service and retention. Equip them with the skills and knowledge needed to enhance the customer experience.
- **Customer Feedback Systems**: Implement systems to regularly collect and analyze customer feedback. Use this data to make informed decisions about product improvements, service enhancements, and policy changes.

Enhancing Customer Engagement

- **Regular Communication**: Keep in touch with customers through regular updates via email newsletters, social media posts, or personalized communications about new products, special offers, and company news.

- **Loyalty Programs**: Develop loyalty programs that reward repeat customers with discounts, special offers, or exclusive access to new products or services. Make sure these programs are easy to understand and genuinely valuable to customers.

Personalization Tactics

- **Tailored Experiences**: Utilize customer data to personalize interactions and product offerings. This can range from personalized emails addressing the customer by name to recommendations based on past purchases.
- **Customer Segmentation**: Segment your customer base by behaviors, preferences, or demographics to tailor marketing strategies and communications more effectively.

Quality Assurance and Consistency

- **Maintain Product/Service Quality**: Consistently deliver high-quality products and services to maintain customer trust and satisfaction.
- **Consistent Service Delivery**: Ensure that all customer service interactions are consistently positive. Train customer service teams thoroughly and provide them with the tools and authority needed to solve customer issues effectively.

Building Community and Trust

- **Engage on Social Media**: Actively engage with customers on social media platforms by responding to comments, sharing relevant content, and participating in conversations.
- **Transparency**: Foster trust by being transparent about your business practices, including pricing, product sourcing, and handling of customer data.

Recovery Strategies for At-Risk Customers

- **Identify At-Risk Customers**: Use analytics to identify customers who may be at risk of churning. Look for indicators such as reduced purchase frequency or negative feedback.

- **Win-Back Campaigns**: Implement targeted win-back campaigns offering special incentives, personalized messages, or direct outreach to re-engage these customers.

By prioritizing customer retention and implementing these strategies, businesses can not only increase the profitability of existing customer relationships but also create a strong base of advocates who contribute to new customer acquisition through positive word-of-mouth.

Exploring New Markets

Expanding into new markets is a pivotal strategy for sustaining growth after the initial launch of your business. This section discusses how to identify potential new markets, evaluate their viability, and strategically enter them to maximize success and minimize risk.

Identifying Potential New Markets

- **Geographic Expansion**: Consider expanding geographically, either domestically or internationally, based on where demand for your products or services might exist beyond your current market.
- **Demographic Diversification**: Explore opportunities in different demographic segments that may not have been your initial target. Analyze demographic data to identify potential new customer groups with similar needs or interests.
- **New Industry Sectors**: Evaluate the feasibility of entering new industry sectors where your offerings could be adapted or repurposed to meet different needs.

Market Research for Expansion

- **In-depth Market Analysis**: Conduct comprehensive market research to understand the competitive landscape, customer preferences, legal and regulatory requirements, and economic conditions of the new market.

- **Customer Needs Assessment**: Utilize surveys, focus groups, and market trials to gather information about the specific needs and expectations of customers in the potential new market.

Strategic Market Entry

- **Pilot Projects**: Test your product or service in a small segment of the new market to gauge reception and refine your approach before a full-scale rollout.
- **Partnerships and Collaborations**: Form alliances with local businesses or distributors that have established networks and understand the local market dynamics. This can facilitate smoother entry and faster growth.
- **Localized Marketing Strategies**: Develop marketing campaigns tailored to the cultural, economic, and social nuances of the new market. Localization can significantly enhance acceptance and brand recognition.

Adapting Products and Services

- **Customization for Local Needs**: Modify your offerings to meet the specific needs or preferences of the new market, which may involve changes in product features, pricing strategies, or service models.
- **Compliance with Local Regulations**: Ensure your products and services comply with local regulations and standards, which may differ significantly from those in your original market.

Risk Management and Mitigation

- **Assess Market Risks**: Clearly identify and assess potential risks associated with market expansion, including political risks, economic instability, or cultural barriers.
- **Contingency Planning**: Develop contingency plans to address possible challenges during market entry. This could involve setting aside budget reserves, considering exit strategies, or having flexible business operations that can adapt to changing conditions.

Monitoring and Evaluation

- **Set Clear Metrics for Success**: Define what success looks like in the new market, including sales targets, market share goals, and customer satisfaction levels.
- **Ongoing Evaluation**: Continuously monitor performance in the new market against these metrics. Be prepared to make adjustments to your strategies based on what is or isn't working.

By carefully planning and executing a strategy to explore new markets, your business can continue to grow by tapping into new customer bases and diversifying its revenue streams. This proactive approach not only mitigates the risk of stagnation but also strengthens the business's overall market position.

Leveraging Data and Technology

In today's digital age, harnessing the power of data and technology can significantly amplify your business's ability to sustain growth and remain competitive. This section outlines strategies to effectively utilize technological tools and data insights to drive innovation, enhance customer experiences, and optimize operations.

Implementing Advanced Data Analytics

- **Data Collection**: Systematically collect data across various points of your business operations, from customer interactions and sales transactions to supply chain logistics.
- **Analytics Tools**: Invest in advanced analytics tools that can help you analyze large datasets to uncover patterns, predict trends, and make informed decisions.
- **Data-Driven Decisions**: Use insights gained from data analytics to refine marketing strategies, enhance product development, optimize operations, and improve customer service.

Enhancing Customer Experiences with Technology

- **CRM Systems**: Implement a robust Customer Relationship Management (CRM) system to manage customer data, track interactions, and personalize customer communications.
- **E-commerce Platforms**: Optimize or introduce e-commerce solutions that provide seamless shopping experiences, integrating advanced features like AI-driven recommendations, virtual try-ons, or one-click checkouts.
- **Mobile Solutions**: Develop mobile applications or optimize websites for mobile use to meet customers where they are increasingly active.

Streamlining Operations with Digital Tools

- **Automation**: Automate routine tasks such as inventory management, billing, and customer inquiries through software solutions to reduce errors, save time, and lower costs.
- **Cloud Computing**: Utilize cloud services for scalable storage solutions, enhanced collaboration, and better data security. This allows for flexibility and accessibility of business resources from anywhere.
- **Internet of Things (IoT)**: For businesses involved in manufacturing or products, integrating IoT devices can help monitor equipment performance, track product conditions, and optimize supply chain management.

Securing Your Business

- **Cybersecurity Measures**: As you integrate more technology into your operations, invest in strong cybersecurity measures to protect your business and customer data from breaches.
- **Regular Updates and Maintenance**: Ensure all your technology systems are regularly updated and maintained to guard against vulnerabilities and keep the systems running efficiently.

Innovating with Emerging Technologies

- **Exploring New Technologies**: Stay informed about emerging technologies such as blockchain, augmented reality, or machine learning, and evaluate their applicability to your business.
- **Pilot Innovative Projects**: Run pilot projects to test new technologies on a small scale before fully integrating them into your business operations.

Building a Tech-Savvy Workforce

- **Training and Development**: Provide training for your employees to upgrade their tech skills and understand how to leverage new tools for better performance.
- **Hiring Talent**: Invest in hiring tech-savvy talent who can bring fresh perspectives and expertise in cutting-edge technologies to your team.

By strategically integrating data and technology into every aspect of your business, you can enhance operational efficiencies, create richer customer experiences, and open new avenues for growth. These technologies not only support your current business processes but also pave the way for future innovations and market expansions.

Strategic Partnerships and Collaborations

Building strategic partnerships and engaging in collaborations can be transformative for a business seeking sustained growth and expanded market reach. This section discusses how to identify, secure, and manage partnerships that can leverage mutual strengths and drive collective success.

Identifying Potential Partnerships

- **Complementary Businesses**: Look for companies whose products or services complement your own, offering a broader range of solutions to shared customer bases.

- **Industry Leaders**: Consider partnerships with established leaders in your industry or adjacent industries to gain credibility, access to a larger customer base, and shared expertise.
- **Innovative Startups**: Keep an eye out for emerging startups with innovative offerings or technologies that could enhance your business operations or product lines.

Evaluating Partnership Opportunities

- **Alignment of Goals**: Ensure that potential partners share similar business goals, values, and visions for growth. Alignment in these areas is crucial for the longevity and effectiveness of the partnership.
- **Strengths and Capabilities**: Assess the strengths and resources each partner brings to the table. Effective partnerships should result in mutual benefits where each party can leverage the other's capabilities to overcome their own weaknesses.
- **Cultural Fit**: Consider the corporate culture of potential partners. A good cultural fit can facilitate smoother collaborations and synergistic relationships.

Establishing Partnership Agreements

- **Clear Roles and Responsibilities**: Define clear roles, responsibilities, and expectations for each partner to prevent conflicts and misunderstandings.
- **Revenue Sharing Models**: Agree on financial arrangements, including how revenues and costs will be shared. Ensure these terms are equitable and reflect the value contributed by each partner.
- **Intellectual Property Rights**: Address the ownership and usage rights of any intellectual property created during the partnership. Clear agreements will prevent disputes over IP rights.

Managing and Maintaining Partnerships

- **Regular Communication**: Establish regular intervals for communication to discuss ongoing projects, resolve issues, and share feedback. Effective communication is key to maintaining a healthy partnership.

- **Joint Marketing Efforts**: Collaborate on marketing campaigns to maximize reach and impact. Joint efforts could include co-branded marketing materials, shared event sponsorships, or collaborative social media campaigns.
- **Performance Review and Adaptation**: Regularly review the performance of the partnership against predefined metrics or goals. Be open to adapting the terms of the partnership as needed to address changing market conditions or opportunities.

Leveraging Partnerships for Growth

- **Expand Market Access**: Use partnerships to access new geographical markets or customer segments that would be difficult to reach independently.
- **Innovate Faster**: Collaborate on research and development efforts to innovate more quickly and cost-effectively than working alone.
- **Increase Supply Chain Efficiency**: Work with partners to streamline supply chain processes, reduce costs, and improve speed to market.

Strategic partnerships and collaborations can significantly enhance your business's ability to innovate, compete, and grow. By carefully selecting partners, crafting thoughtful agreements, and actively managing relationships, your business can unlock new opportunities and achieve greater success.

Quick Tips and Recap

- **Continuously Innovate**: Always seek ways to improve and innovate your products and services based on customer feedback and market trends.
- **Prioritize Customer Retention**: Implement strategies that enhance customer loyalty and satisfaction to boost retention rates.

- **Explore New Markets**: Regularly assess potential new markets for expansion opportunities, considering geographic, demographic, and industry dimensions.
- **Harness Data and Technology**: Utilize advanced data analytics and embrace digital transformation to enhance operational efficiency and customer engagement.
- **Forge Strategic Partnerships**: Build alliances with businesses that complement or enhance your offerings to expand your market reach and access new resources.
- **Maintain Flexibility**: Stay adaptable in your strategies to swiftly respond to market changes or challenges.
- **Monitor Performance**: Continually assess the effectiveness of your growth strategies and make data-driven adjustments.
- **Cultivate a Strong Network**: Maintain a robust professional network to support business growth and development.
- **Invest in Your Team**: Ensure your team has the skills and resources needed to implement growth strategies effectively.
- **Commit to Continuous Learning**: Stay informed about industry trends and new business strategies to keep your business relevant and competitive.

These tips are designed to keep your business on a trajectory of growth and innovation, ensuring you not only sustain but also enhance your market position post-launch.

Conclusion

Wrap-Up: Where Do We Go from Here?

Congratulations on reaching the end of this comprehensive journey through the intricacies of launching and growing a successful business. From the initial steps of conceptualizing and structuring your startup to navigating complex legal landscapes, establishing robust financial foundations, and propelling your venture beyond the launch, this guide has equipped you with the essential tools and knowledge needed to start strong and sustain growth.

The Entrepreneur's Journey

Launching a business is akin to setting out on a grand adventure. It requires courage, resilience, and an unyielding commitment to your vision. The chapters of this book have served as your roadmap, guiding you through each critical phase of your entrepreneurial journey. You've learned to not only address the immediate challenges of starting a business but also to anticipate future obstacles and opportunities.

The Importance of a Solid Foundation

We began by establishing the legal and operational frameworks that form the backbone of any successful enterprise. Understanding and implementing these foundational aspects are crucial, as they provide the stability and structure needed to support all future growth and innovation. As you have seen, skipping these steps can lead to vulnerabilities that might jeopardize the long-term viability of your business.

Growth Through Innovation and Adaptation

As your business evolves, continual innovation and adaptation are key. This book has emphasized the importance of staying agile, allowing you to pivot and adapt in response to market feedback and changing conditions. Sustaining growth in a business requires an ongoing commitment to learning and evolving—a dynamic process that challenges you to perpetually refine and expand your offerings.

Building Lasting Relationships

Strategic relationships and partnerships have been highlighted as vital elements in scaling your business and extending your reach. These alliances not only open new avenues for growth but also enhance your capabilities and provide essential market insights. Nurturing these relationships will continue to be a critical part of your strategy as your business matures.

Harnessing Technology and Data

In an age dominated by digital transformation, leveraging technology and data analytics stands out as a fundamental strategy to drive efficiency, enhance customer experiences, and create value. Your ability to integrate these tools into your business operations can be a significant differentiator, setting you apart from competitors.

Looking Ahead

As you move forward, keep in mind that the landscape of business is ever-changing. New challenges and opportunities will emerge, but with the foundation you've built and the strategies you've learned, you are well-prepared to navigate them. Remember, the ultimate goal is not just to survive but to thrive—to create a business that not only meets the needs of today but also anticipates the demands of tomorrow.

Final Thoughts

The journey of an entrepreneur is one of perpetual learning and growth. Let the lessons contained within these pages be a starting point, not an endpoint. Continue to seek knowledge, embrace change, and challenge yourself to think innovatively. With determination and resilience, the path you chart from here can lead to extraordinary achievements.

Thank you for trusting this book to guide you through the early stages of your business venture. Here's to your continued success—may your business soar to new heights and your entrepreneurial spirit continue to thrive.

Where Do We Go From Here?

Having laid a solid foundation with "Brick by Brick: The Entrepreneur's Guide to Constructing a Company," the first book in the Empire Builders Series, you are now well-equipped with the strategies and insights needed to start and grow your business. But the journey doesn't end here. The road to business mastery is continuous, requiring ongoing education and adaptation to navigate the ever-evolving marketplace successfully.

Introducing the Next Step

As you continue to build and refine your business, it's essential to deepen your understanding of specific aspects that can further safeguard and propel your enterprise. That's why the next book in the Empire Builders Series, "Mark Your Territory: Navigating Trademarks in the Modern Marketplace," is an indispensable resource.

Focus of the Next Book

"Mark Your Territory" will explore the critical role of trademarks in establishing and protecting your brand identity in a competitive business landscape. This masterclass will guide you through:

- The intricacies of trademark law,
- Strategic branding insights,
- Steps to register and maintain trademarks,
- Handling potential infringements,
- Leveraging your intellectual property for business growth.

Why Trademarks Matter

In today's global market, where branding can significantly impact your business's visibility and profitability, understanding how to effectively navigate trademarks is more crucial than ever. This next installment will equip you with the tools to assert your presence confidently and creatively in the marketplace.

Continuing Your Educational Journey

Each book in the Empire Builders Series builds on the last, offering specialized knowledge that is crucial for specific areas of business and law. By continuing your journey with "Mark Your Territory," you'll not only reinforce your business's market position but also ensure its intellectual assets are well-protected and strategically employed.

Looking Forward

Stay engaged, continue to educate yourself, and be ready to adapt. The landscape of business is dynamic, and with each new book in the Empire Builders Series, you'll gain valuable expertise to navigate these changes effectively. Whether you're solidifying your brand's legal foundations or exploring new growth strategies, our series is here to guide you every step of the way.

Prepare to deepen your understanding and expand your empire. Your next step starts with "Mark Your Territory," where you'll learn to protect and maximize the value of your business's most crucial assets. Let's continue building your empire, one strategic step at a time.

READ ON for a bonus chapter!

BONUS CHAPTER

The Future of Entrepreneurship: Emerging Trends and How to Prepare

"Looking ahead, the frontiers of entrepreneurship will be driven by a blend of artificial intelligence, sustainability, and hyper-connectivity, challenging today's entrepreneurs to think globally and act ethically."
— JACK MA, FOUNDER OF ALIBABA GROUP

Welcome to the crystal ball of entrepreneurship, where we peek into the future without the need for a time machine. This chapter isn't just about predictions; it's about preparation. We're diving into the emerging trends that are reshaping the landscape of business, and more importantly, how you can gear up to ride these waves of change rather than get swept away.

From the rise of AI and machine learning to the growing importance of sustainability and social responsibility, the business world is evolving at warp speed. We'll explore how these trends are not just buzzwords but pivotal elements that could define your entrepreneurial success or failure in the coming years.

Think of this as your training montage in a futuristic movie, where you, the protagonist, are gearing up with gadgets and wisdom to face the new world. Whether it's adapting to the gig economy or harnessing the power of blockchain, this chapter will help you tool up with the knowledge and strategies to not just survive but thrive. So, strap in and let's prepare to meet the future head-on—after all, tomorrow's business moguls are made today!

Artificial Intelligence and Machine Learning

Artificial intelligence (AI) and machine learning are not just futuristic concepts but active drivers of today's business innovation. This section explores how these technologies are reshaping industries and how entrepreneurs can harness their power to enhance operations, innovate products, and personalize customer experiences.

Understanding AI and Machine Learning

- **Basics of AI and Machine Learning**: Define AI and machine learning, explaining how they differ and their relevance to modern business applications.
- **Current Applications**: Highlight current uses of AI and machine learning across various sectors such as finance, healthcare, customer service, and marketing.

Integrating AI into Business Operations

- **Automation of Routine Tasks**: Discuss how AI can automate administrative tasks like scheduling, data entry, and customer queries to increase efficiency and reduce costs.
- **Enhanced Data Analytics**: Explain how machine learning algorithms can analyze vast amounts of data to identify patterns, predict customer behavior, and inform business decisions.

- **Customization and Personalization**: Showcase examples of AI-driven personalization, such as customized marketing messages and product recommendations, which enhance customer engagement and satisfaction.

Innovating with AI

- **Product Development**: Describe how AI can be used in product development, from initial design to testing, by simulating customer reactions and improving product features.
- **Operational Improvements**: Detail how AI can optimize business operations, including inventory management, logistics, and supply chain efficiencies.

Challenges and Considerations

- **Ethical Implications**: Address the ethical considerations of using AI, including privacy concerns and the potential for bias in algorithmic decision-making.
- **Skill Requirements**: Discuss the skills needed to implement and manage AI technologies and how businesses can acquire these competencies through hiring or training.

Preparing for AI Integration

- **Strategic Planning**: Encourage businesses to develop a clear strategy for AI integration, identifying key areas where AI can add the most value.
- **Technology Partnerships**: Suggest forming partnerships with AI technology providers or participating in industry consortia to stay abreast of the latest developments and gain access to cutting-edge technology.
- **Continuous Learning and Adaptation**: Emphasize the importance of staying informed about AI trends and continuously adapting business practices to leverage new AI capabilities as they emerge.

By understanding and integrating AI and machine learning, entrepreneurs can not only streamline their operations but also provide enhanced, personalized services to their customers. This section equips them with the knowledge to start implementing these technologies thoughtfully and effectively, ensuring they remain competitive in an increasingly tech-driven market landscape.

Sustainability and Social Responsibility

As consumer awareness and regulatory requirements increase, sustainability and social responsibility have moved from optional to essential elements of business strategy. This section explains how entrepreneurs can integrate these concepts into their operations to not only meet ethical and environmental standards but also enhance brand loyalty and open new market opportunities.

Understanding Sustainability and Social Responsibility

- **Definitions and Importance**: Define what sustainability and social responsibility mean in a business context, emphasizing their growing importance in consumer choices and corporate governance.
- **Benefits to Business**: Discuss the tangible benefits these practices can bring, such as improved brand image, customer loyalty, reduced operational costs through energy savings, and potential tax incentives.

Developing a Sustainable Business Model

- **Sustainable Sourcing**: Outline strategies for sourcing materials and products responsibly, including choosing local suppliers, prioritizing renewable resources, and ensuring suppliers adhere to ethical standards.
- **Eco-friendly Operations**: Suggest methods to reduce the environmental impact of business operations, such as minimizing waste, using energy-efficient appliances and machinery, and implementing recycling programs.
- **Product Lifecycle Management**: Discuss the importance of considering the environmental impact of products throughout their lifecycle, from design and manufacturing to usage and disposal.

Corporate Social Responsibility (CSR) Initiatives

- **Community Engagement**: Explore ways businesses can engage with and give back to their communities, such as through volunteering, sponsorships, and partnerships with local organizations.
- **Employee Welfare**: Highlight the importance of ensuring employee welfare, including fair wages, safe working conditions, and opportunities for training and advancement.
- **Transparency and Reporting**: Explain the role of transparency in CSR, such as publishing sustainability reports and openly communicating CSR efforts and outcomes to stakeholders.

Challenges and Risk Management

- **Managing Costs**: Address the perception that implementing sustainable practices can be cost-prohibitive, offering strategies for managing costs and achieving long-term financial benefits.
- **Regulatory Compliance**: Discuss the need to stay informed about and comply with increasing environmental regulations and standards.

Implementing Sustainability and CSR

- **Step-by-Step Implementation**: Provide a phased approach to implementing sustainability and CSR practices, starting with quick wins to gain momentum.
- **Stakeholder Involvement**: Emphasize the importance of involving stakeholders, including employees, customers, and suppliers, in sustainability efforts to ensure broad support and shared benefits.
- **Monitoring and Adjustment**: Recommend establishing monitoring systems to measure the effectiveness of sustainability initiatives and making necessary adjustments based on performance data.

By adopting sustainable and socially responsible practices, businesses not only contribute to environmental and societal well-being but also position themselves competitively in a marketplace where consumers increasingly favor companies that do good. This section guides entrepreneurs on starting this transition, ensuring they understand the steps, benefits, and considerations involved in building a conscientious business.

The Rise of the Gig Economy

The gig economy has revolutionized the way people work, offering flexibility and autonomy that traditional jobs often do not. For entrepreneurs, this shift presents unique opportunities and challenges. This section explores how startups can adapt to and thrive in the gig economy, leveraging its benefits to scale operations effectively while managing a fluid workforce.

Understanding the Gig Economy

- **Definition and Growth**: Define the gig economy and discuss its rapid growth, driven by the increasing demand for flexible work arrangements and the proliferation of platforms that facilitate gig work.
- **Characteristics of Gig Workers**: Describe typical characteristics of gig workers, including their desire for flexibility, varied skill sets, and independence.

Benefits of the Gig Economy for Startups

- **Scalability**: Explain how the gig economy allows startups to scale labor up or down as needed without the commitments and overhead associated with full-time employees.
- **Access to Diverse Skills**: Highlight how startups can access a broad pool of talent with diverse skills and expertise for short-term projects or specialized tasks.

Integrating Gig Workers into Your Business Model

- **Identifying Needs**: Assist entrepreneurs in identifying aspects of their operations that are well-suited to gig workers, such as marketing campaigns, project-based assignments, or IT support.
- **Recruitment and Management**: Provide strategies for effectively recruiting and managing gig workers, including choosing the right

platforms for hiring, setting clear expectations, and ensuring quality control.

Challenges and Considerations

- **Regulatory Landscape**: Discuss the evolving regulatory landscape surrounding gig work, including worker classification laws and implications for benefits and labor protections.
- **Building Loyalty and Culture**: Explore ways to foster a sense of loyalty and inclusion among gig workers, despite their temporary or peripheral role, to enhance productivity and integration.

Best Practices for Leveraging Gig Economy

- **Use of Technology**: Recommend technologies and tools that facilitate the efficient management of gig workers, such as freelancer management systems, communication tools, and project management software.
- **Creating a Win-Win Environment**: Suggest creating mutually beneficial arrangements that offer gig workers flexibility and fair compensation while ensuring they meet business needs.
- **Legal and Ethical Considerations**: Advise on navigating the legal and ethical aspects of employing gig workers, ensuring fair treatment and compliance with applicable laws.

Future Trends in the Gig Economy

- **Increasing Professionalization**: Predict the potential for increased professionalization within the gig economy, as more skilled professionals choose freelancing over traditional employment.
- **Integration with Traditional Employment Models**: Discuss how the gig economy might integrate more seamlessly with traditional employment models, offering hybrid solutions that blend flexibility with job security.

By understanding and strategically integrating gig economy principles into their operations, startups can enjoy increased flexibility and access to talent while managing costs effectively. This section provides entrepreneurs with the knowledge and tools to make the most of the gig economy, preparing them for a dynamic and adaptable business operation.

Blockchain Technology

Blockchain technology, known for its role in cryptocurrencies, offers much more, particularly in enhancing transparency, security, and efficiency in various business operations. This section explores how startups can leverage blockchain to innovate processes, build trust, and open new business opportunities beyond traditional financial applications.

Understanding Blockchain Technology

- **Basics of Blockchain**: Define blockchain as a decentralized digital ledger that records transactions across multiple computers securely and transparently.
- **Key Features**: Highlight key features of blockchain, such as immutability, transparency, and the elimination of intermediaries, which can provide significant advantages in various business contexts.

Applications of Blockchain in Business

- **Supply Chain Management**: Discuss how blockchain can enhance supply chain transparency and traceability, allowing businesses to track product provenance, reduce fraud, and improve compliance.
- **Smart Contracts**: Explain smart contracts, self-executing contracts with the terms directly written into code, which can automate processes, ensure contract adherence, and reduce disputes.
- **Data Security and Privacy**: Explore blockchain's potential to enhance data security and privacy through its encryption and decentralized nature, making it ideal for managing sensitive or personal data in compliance with regulations like GDPR.

Implementing Blockchain in Your Startup

- **Assessment of Needs and Feasibility**: Guide startups in assessing whether blockchain is suitable for their specific business needs and the feasibility of integration given their current technology infrastructure.
- **Partnerships and Collaborations**: Encourage forming partnerships with blockchain technology providers or participating in blockchain consortia to leverage shared expertise and reduce development costs.
- **Pilot Projects**: Suggest starting with pilot projects to test the impact and effectiveness of blockchain in small, controlled scenarios before full-scale implementation.

Challenges and Considerations

- **Technical Complexity**: Acknowledge the technical complexity and resource requirements of developing blockchain solutions, which may necessitate specialized knowledge or outsourcing.
- **Scalability Issues**: Address potential scalability issues, as some blockchain solutions, particularly those that are public and permissionless, can face challenges in handling large volumes of transactions efficiently.
- **Regulatory Uncertainty**: Discuss the rapidly evolving regulatory landscape regarding blockchain and the need for startups to stay informed about legal implications, particularly in sectors heavily regulated like finance and healthcare.

Looking Ahead: The Future of Blockchain in Business

- **Emerging Trends**: Forecast emerging trends in blockchain technology, such as the growth of decentralized finance (DeFi), increased use of blockchain for environmental sustainability efforts, and the expansion of blockchain into mainstream business applications.
- **Strategic Adoption**: Advise on strategic adoption, recommending that startups focus not only on the technology itself but also on how it can

fundamentally improve business models, enhance customer value, and provide a competitive edge.

By integrating blockchain technology, startups can not only solve traditional business problems more efficiently but also innovate and position themselves as leaders in the adoption of cutting-edge technology. This section helps entrepreneurs understand the potential of blockchain and provides a roadmap for thoughtful and strategic implementation.

Adapting to Changing Consumer Behaviors

The rapidly evolving market landscape necessitates that businesses remain agile and responsive to shifts in consumer behavior. This section delves into the importance of staying attuned to these changes and outlines strategies to adapt effectively, ensuring your business continues to meet and exceed customer expectations.

Understanding Consumer Behavior Trends

- **Continuous Monitoring**: Emphasize the importance of continuous market research to detect shifts in consumer preferences, values, and buying habits. Utilize tools like social media listening, customer surveys, and market analysis reports to gather actionable insights.
- **Influence of Technology**: Discuss how advancements in technology, especially mobile and digital media, have transformed consumer expectations, leading to demands for greater convenience, faster service, and more personalized experiences.

Strategies for Adapting to Consumer Changes

- **Agility in Product Development**: Encourage a flexible approach to product development that allows quick adjustments based on consumer feedback and emerging trends. Implement lean methodology to prototype, test, and refine products or services rapidly.
- **Personalization**: Utilize data analytics to create personalized experiences for customers. Tailor marketing messages, product

recommendations, and services to individual preferences and previous interactions.

- **Enhanced Customer Engagement**: Develop dynamic engagement strategies that use multiple channels — social media, email, mobile apps — to communicate with and listen to customers. Foster community through interactive content, user-generated content, and participatory events.

Leveraging Technology for Responsiveness

- **AI and Machine Learning**: Leverage AI tools to predict customer behavior more accurately and provide scalable customization. Use chatbots and virtual assistants to enhance customer service with instant responses and 24/7 availability.
- **Real-time Data Utilization**: Implement systems that utilize real-time data to offer immediate insights into consumer behavior, allowing for swift business decisions and better resource allocation.

Building a Consumer-Centric Culture

- **Employee Training**: Train employees across the organization on the importance of customer focus and empower them to make decisions that enhance customer satisfaction.
- **Feedback Loops**: Create efficient feedback loops within the company, ensuring that insights from customer interactions are quickly communicated back to decision-makers and relevant departments.

Challenges of Adapting to Consumer Behavior

- **Balancing Cost and Benefits**: Address the challenge of balancing the costs of adaptation strategies, like technology investment and training, with the anticipated benefits in customer loyalty and increased sales.
- **Over-Adaptation Risks**: Warn against over-adaptation which might lead to losing sight of the core business values or alienating existing customers while trying to attract new ones.

Future Outlook

- **Anticipating Future Trends**: Encourage proactive strategies that not only respond to current consumer behavior changes but also anticipate future trends. This can involve scenario planning and investing in emerging technologies that have the potential to disrupt consumer behavior further.
- **Sustainability and Ethical Considerations**: Highlight how growing consumer awareness around sustainability and ethics could shape future buying patterns, advising businesses to integrate these considerations into their long-term strategy.

By actively adapting to changing consumer behaviors, businesses can not only survive but thrive in a competitive marketplace. This section provides a comprehensive guide to understanding, anticipating, and responding to these changes, ensuring that your business remains relevant and preferred by consumers.

Quick Tips and Recap

- **Stay Informed on AI Advancements**: Regularly update your knowledge on AI and machine learning to leverage these technologies for business efficiency and innovation.
- **Integrate Sustainability**: Embed sustainability and social responsibility into your core business strategy to meet consumer expectations and regulatory requirements.
- **Utilize the Gig Economy**: Tap into the flexibility and diverse skills of gig workers to scale operations efficiently and cost-effectively.
- **Explore Blockchain Applications**: Consider blockchain for enhancing transparency and security beyond financial transactions, particularly in supply chain management and contract enforcement.
- **Adapt to Consumer Behavior Changes**: Continuously monitor and adapt to changing consumer behaviors to maintain relevance and competitiveness in your market.

- **Leverage Data for Personalization**: Use consumer data to personalize experiences, enhancing customer satisfaction and loyalty.
- **Foster a Culture of Innovation**: Cultivate an environment that encourages creativity and continuous improvement across all levels of your organization.
- **Engage with Consumers Across Multiple Channels**: Maintain active and engaging communication with consumers across various platforms to build a loyal community.
- **Plan for Long-term Trends**: Anticipate and prepare for long-term consumer and technological trends to stay ahead of the curve.
- **Maintain Flexibility**: Keep your business model flexible to swiftly adapt to market changes and consumer demands.

By following these tips, you can ensure that your business not only keeps pace with current trends but is also well-prepared to capitalize on future opportunities.

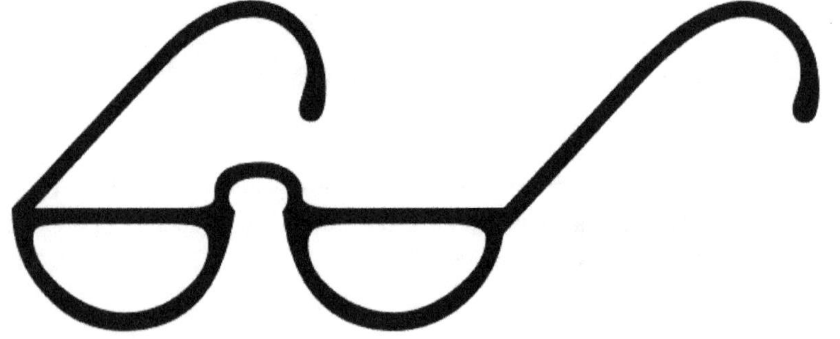

Appendix

Essential Agreements and Documents

This Appendix serves as a comprehensive resource, providing you with key legal documents and agreements that are fundamental to structuring and managing a business. Each document included here has been carefully selected to offer practical, real-world applicability, supporting a variety of business arrangements and corporate structures. Below is a list of the agreements and documents available in this section:

1. **Limited Partnership Agreement** – Outlines the terms and conditions between partners, defining roles, responsibilities, and profit-sharing.
2. **LLC Operating Agreement** – Specifies the operational and financial relationships among business owners and the LLC itself.
3. **Management Agreement** – Details the obligations and rights of managers in the operations of a business.
4. **Articles of Incorporation** – A legal document used to define the primary governing rules of a corporation.

5. **Bylaws** – Establishes the internal rules required to run a corporation, guiding the board's operations and management decisions.
6. **Indemnity Agreement** – Provides a contract for one party to compensate another for potential losses or damages.
7. **Employment Agreement** – Defines the bounds of the relationship between an employer and an employee, including compensation, duties, and duration.
8. **Annual Meeting Documents** – Necessary paperwork and protocols for conducting annual meetings of shareholders and directors.
9. **Stock Purchase Agreement** – Governs the sale and purchase of company shares.
10. **Contract for Services Agreement** – Specifies the terms of service between a service provider and a client, detailing the work to be performed and the compensation involved.

Each document is provided to give you a foundational framework that can be customized according to your specific needs. These templates are intended for informational purposes only and should be used with the advice of legal counsel to ensure they meet your individual business requirements and comply with relevant laws.

Disclaimer: Please note that all agreements are provided for informational purposes only and should not be construed as legal advice. We recommend consulting with a qualified attorney to ensure that any legal documents or decisions are tailored to your specific circumstances.

▶ If you are interested in receiving an electronic copy of any of the following documents, please email us at documents@AuthorsDoor.com with the subject line "Request for [fill in the blank]." Upon receiving your email, we will promptly send you a Microsoft Word copy of the document. **Disclaimer:** Please note that all agreements are provided for informational purposes only and should not be construed as legal advice. We recommend consulting with a qualified attorney to ensure that any legal documents or decisions are tailored to your specific circumstances.

1. Limited Partnership Agreement

[ACRONYM OF SUCCESS] VENTURES, L.P.
LIMITED PARTNERSHIP AGREEMENT

This Agreement is made and entered into as of the ___ day of _____, 20__, by and among **ANC Management, L.L.C.**, a Delaware limited liability company (the "***General Partner***"), and each of the entities identified as a limited partner on Exhibit A (the "***Limited Partners***"), who hereby form **[Acronym of Success] Ventures, L.P.** (the "***Partnership***"), pursuant to the provisions of the Delaware Revised Uniform Limited Partnership Act (the "Act"), as follows:

ARTICLE 1
NAME, PURPOSE AND OFFICES OF PARTNERSHIP

1.1 Name. The name of the Partnership is [Acronym of Success] Ventures, L.P. The affairs of the Partnership shall be conducted under the Partnership name.

1.2 Purpose. The primary purpose of the Partnership is to make venture capital type investments principally by investing in equity or equity-oriented securities of privately-held corporations in information technology, Internet, software, communications, new media, multi-media, entertainment, telecommunications infrastructure, wireless applications and related industries. The general purposes of the Partnership are to buy, sell, hold, and otherwise invest in securities of every kind and nature and rights and options with respect thereto, including, without limitation, stock, notes, bonds and debentures; to exercise all rights, powers, privileges, and other incidents of ownership or possession with respect to securities held or owned by the Partnership; to enter into, make, and perform all contracts and other undertakings; and to engage in all activities and transactions as may be necessary, advisable, or desirable to carry out the foregoing.

1.3 Principal Office. The principal office of the Partnership shall be ________________________, or such other place or places as the General Partner may from time to time designate. The General Partner shall provide the Limited Partners with prompt written notice of any change in the location of the Partnership's principal office.

1.4 Registered Agent and Office. The name of the registered agent for service of process of the Partnership and the address of the Partnership's registered office in the State of Delaware shall be ________________________, or such other agent or office in the State of Delaware as the General Partner may from time to time designate.

ARTICLE 2
TERM OF PARTNERSHIP

2.1 Term. The term of the Partnership shall commence upon the date of the filing of the Certificate of Limited Partnership of the Partnership with the office of the Secretary of the State of the State of Delaware and shall continue until _______, 20__, unless extended pursuant to paragraph 10.1 or sooner dissolved as provided in paragraph 10.2.

2.2 Events Affecting a Member of the General Partner. Except as specifically provided in paragraph 10.2, the bankruptcy, liquidation, dissolution, reorganization, merger, sale of all or substantially all the stock or assets of, or other change in ownership or nature of the General Partner shall not dissolve the Partnership.

2.3 Events Affecting a Limited Partner of the Partnership. The bankruptcy, liquidation, dissolution, reorganization, merger, sale of all or substantially all the stock or assets of, or other change in the ownership or nature of a Limited Partner shall not dissolve the Partnership.

2.4 Events Affecting the General Partner. Except as specifically provided in paragraph 10.2, the bankruptcy, liquidation, dissolution, reorganization, merger, sale of all or substantially all the stock or assets of, or other change in ownership or nature of the General Partner shall not dissolve the Partnership.

ARTICLE 3
NAME AND ADMISSION OF PARTNERS

3.1 Name and Address. The name and address of the General Partner and each Limited Partner (hereinafter the General Partner and the Limited Partners shall be referred to collectively as the "***Partners***" and each individually as a "***Partner***"), the amount of such Partner's Capital Commitment to the Partnership, and such Partner's Partnership Percentage are set form on Exhibit A hereto. The General Partners shall cause Exhibit A to be amended from time to time to reflect the admission of any new Partner, the withdrawal or substitution of a Partner, the transfer of interests among Partners, receipt by the Partnership of notice of any change of address of a Partner, or the change in the Partner's Capital Commitment or Partnership Percentage. An amended Exhibit A shall supersede any prior Exhibit A and become a part of this Agreement. A copy of the most recent amended Exhibit A shall be kept on file at the principal office of the Partnership.

3.2 Admission of Additional Partners.

(a) Except as provided in paragraphs 3.2(b), 4.5(b)(ii)(2), 4.5(f) and 9.6, an additional person may be admitted as a Partner only with the consent of the General Partner and a Majority in Interest of the Limited Partners.

(b) Notwithstanding subparagraph (a) above, additional persons may be admitted as Limited Partners with the consent of only the General Partner prior to the date six (6) months after the commencement of the Partnership, *provided* that, after such admission, the aggregate amount of capital committed for contribution by the Limited Partners, when combined with the capital commitments of any investors in any Sid by Side Fund, does not exceed _____________ ($_____).

(c) Each additional person admitted as a Partner shall (i) execute and deliver to the Partnership a counterpart of this Agreement or otherwise take such actions as the General Partner shall deem appropriate in order for such additional Partner to become bound by the terms of this Agreement, and (ii) contribute that portion of its Capital Commitment which is equal to the portion of their respective Capital Commitments contributed to date by the Partnership's previously admitted Partners.

ARTICLE 4
CAPITAL ACCOUNTS, CAPITAL CONTRIBUTIONS, AND NONCONTRIBUTING PARTNERS

4.1 Capital Accounts. An individual Capital Account shall be maintained for each Partner.

4.2 Capital Contributions of the Limited Partners.

(a) Each Limited Partner shall contribute capital to the Partnership upon fifteen (15) days' prior written notice; *provided* that: (a) each capital contribution shall be in accordance with Partnership Percentages, and (b) no Limited Partner shall be required to contribute any capital following the date six (6) years after the commencement of the Partnership except as may be necessary for (i) operational purposes, including payment of the management fee pursuant to Article 6, (ii) completion of transactions in process on such date, and (iii) follow-on investments in the Securities of issuers in which the Partnership already holds an interest as of the date of such proposed follow-on investment. Each capital contribution by any Limited Partner shall be made in cash.

(b) Notwithstanding paragraph 4.2(a), no ERISA Partner (as defined in paragraph 13.1) or Governmental Plan Partner (as defined in paragraph 13.2) shall be required to contribute capital pursuant to this Agreement until such time as the Partnership shall have delivered a written notice ("***VCOC Notice***") reasonably satisfactory to each such Partner to the effect that either (i) the Partnership's first portfolio company investment qualifies, or will qualify upon its closing, as a "***venture capital investment***" within the meaning of the U.S. Department of Labor regulations ("***DOL Regulations***") such that the Partnership qualifies, as a "***venture capital operating company***" under applicable DOL Regulations, or (ii) less than twenty-five percent (25%) of the Partnership's limited partnership interests are held in the aggregate by "***benefit plan investors,***" as that term is defined in the DOL Regulations. In the event that an ERISA Partner or Governmental Plan Partner has not received the VCOC Notice prior to the date on which any capital contribution would otherwise be due under paragraph 4.2(a), such Partner shall pay such capital contribution into an interest-bearing escrow account designated by the General Partner which meets the requirements for such accounts as set forth in the DOL Regulations. Upon delivery of the VCOC Notice, all amounts in such escrow account shall be delivered to the Partnership in fulfillment of the ERISA Partner's or Governmental Plan Partner's obligation under paragraph 4.2(a).

4.3 Capital Contributions of the General Partner. The General Partner shall contribute capital to the Partnership in an amount equal to one and one ninety-ninth percent (1 1/99%) of the amount contributed by the Limited Partners on each date on which any Limited Partner makes a contribution. Each capital contribution made by the General Partner shall be made in cash.

4.4 Acquisition of an Additional Interest by the General Partner. In the event that the General Partner acquires a Limited Partner's interest pursuant to the terms of this Agreement, the General Partner shall have two Partnership Percentages and two Capital Account balances for purposes of making Partnership allocations, as if such subsequently acquired interest were held by a separate entity which is a Limited Partner, although for all other purposes the General Partner shall have only one Capital Account.

4.5 Noncontributing Partners.

(a) The Partnership shall be entitled to enforce the obligations of each Limited Partner to make the contributions to capital set forth in paragraph 4.2, and the Partnership shall have all remedies available at law or in equity in the event any such contribution is not so made. If any legal proceedings relating to the failure of a Limited Partner to make such a contribution are commenced, such Limited Partner shall pay all costs and expenses incurred by the Partnership, including attorneys' fees, in connection with such proceedings.

(b) Additionally, should any Limited Partner fail to make any of the capital contributions required of it under paragraph 4.2 of this Agreement, such Partner shall be in default, and the General Partner may, in its sole discretion, elect to enforce the provisions of paragraphs 4.5(b)(i) and (ii) in connection with such a default.

(i) Should the General Partner, in its sole discretion, elect to exercise the provisions of this paragraph 4.5(b)(i), such defaulting Limited Partner shall pay the interest on the amount of the contribution to the Partnership then due at an interest rate equal to the floating commercial rate of interest publicly announced by Citibank (or its successors) as its prime rate (the "***Prime Rate***") plus four percent (4%) per annum, such interest to accrue from the date the contribution to the Partnership was required to be made pursuant to paragraph 4.2 hereof until the date the contribution is made by such defaulting Limited Partner. The accrued interest shall be paid by the defaulting Limited Partner to the partnership upon payment of such contribution. The accrued interest so paid shall not be treated as an additional contribution to the capital of the Partnership, but shall be deemed to be income to the Partnership. Until such time as the unpaid contribution and accrued interest thereon shall have been paid by the defaulting Limited Partner, the General Partner may elect to withhold any or all distributions to be made to such defaulting Limited Partner pursuant to Article 7 or Article 10.

(ii) Should the General Partner, in its sole discretion, elect to exercise the provisions of this paragraph 4.5(b)(ii), and the default of such Limited Partner shall have continued for ten (10) or more days after notice by the General Partner to such Limited Partner of the default, the nondefaulting Limited Partners and the General Partner (the "***Optionees***") shall have the right and the option, but not the obligation, to acquire the Partnership interest of the defaulting Limited Partner (the "***Optionor***"), as follows:

(1) If the default continues for ten (10) or more days after notice of the default, the General Partner shall notify the Optionees of the default within twenty (20) days of the expiration of the aforesaid ten (10) day notice period. Such notice shall advise each Optionee of the portion and the price of the Optionor's interest available to it. The portion available to each Optionee shall be that portion of the Optionor's interest that bears the same ratio to the Optionor's entire interest as each Optionee's Partnership Percentage bears to the aggregate Partnership Percentages of all the Optionees. The aggregate price for the Optionor's interest shall be the lesser of (A) the amount of the Optionor's Capital Account calculated as of the due date of the additional contribution and adjusted to reflect the allocation of the appropriate proportion of the Partnership's unrealized gains and losses as of the due date of such defaulted contribution, and (B) the aggregate amount of the Optionor's capital contributions actually made less any distributions (valued at their fair market value on the date of distribution in accordance with paragraph 12.1) on or prior to such due date. The option granted hereunder shall be exercisable at any time after the date thirty (30 days following the date of the initial notice of default from the General Partner to the Optionor by delivery to the Optionor of a notice of exercise of option together with a nonrecourse promissory note for the purchase price and a security agreement in accordance with subparagraph (3) below.

(2) Should any Optionee not exercise in entirety its option pursuant to subparagraph (1) above (such unexercised portion, the "***Remaining Portion***"), the General Partner may, if it deems it in the best interest of the Partnership, sell the Remaining Portion to any other investor (including without limitation any nondefaulting Limited Partner) of quality, net worth and standing comparable to the other Limited Partners, on terms not more favorable to any such investor than those applicable to the Optionees' option, and upon the consent of the General Partner, any such third party investor may become a Limited Partner to the extent of the interest purchased hereunder.

(3) The price due from any Optionee or any third party investor shall be payable by a noninterest bearing, nonrecourse promissory note (in such form as the General Partner shall designate) due upon final liquidation of the Partnership. Each such note shall be secured by the portion of the Optionor's Partnership interest so purchased by its maker pursuant to a security agreement in a form designed by the General Partner and shall be enforceable by the Optionor only against such security.

(4) Upon exercise of any option hereunder, the Optionee or any third party investor, as applicable, shall be obligated (A) to contribute to the Partnership that portion of any additional capital then due from the Optionor equal to the percentage of the Optionor's interest purchased by such person and (B) to pay the same percentage of any further contributions otherwise due from such Optionor on the date such contributions are otherwise due. Each such person who purchases a portion of the Optionor's Partnership interest shall be deemed to have acquired such portion as of the due date of the additional capital contribution with respect to which the Optionor defaulted, and any distributions made after the due date on account of the Optionor's interest shall be distributed among such purchasers (and, unless the entire interest was purchased, the Optionor) in accordance with their respective interests in the Optionor's interest. Distributions otherwise allocable to the Optionor under the preceding sentence shall first be used to offset any defaulted contribution of the Optionor still due to the Partnership. Upon completion of any transaction pursuant to this paragraph 4.5(b), the General Partner shall cause Exhibit A to be amended to reflect all necessary changes resulting therefrom including, without limitation, admission as a third party investor as a Limited Partner and adjustment of Capital Account balances, Capital Commitment amounts and partnership Percentages as of the date of Optionor's default to reflect the acquisition from Optionor of the appropriate pro rata portion of each such item. The purchase and transfer of the Partnership interest of the Optionor shall occur automatically upon exercise by any Optionee or any third party investor of its option hereunder, without any action by Optionor. Notwithstanding the foregoing, each Limited Partner agrees that in the event it fails to make any capital contribution required of it under this Agreement, it will execute any instruments or perform any other acts that are or may be necessary to effectuate and carry out the transactions contemplated by this paragraph 4.5.

(c) Notwithstanding any provision of this Agreement, if at any time before a date on which any unpaid capital contribution is payable hereunder, any ERISA Partner or Governmental Plan Partner shall obtain and deliver to the General Partner an opinion of independent legal counsel, which opinion is reasonably acceptable to the General Partner, to the effect that, as a result of applicable statutes, regulations, case law, administrative interpretations, or similar authority, the payment by such ERISA Partner or Governmental Plan Partner of such unpaid capital contribution would result, or there is a material likelihood that such payment would result, in a material violation of ERISA or any comparable state statute or in the fiduciaries of such ERISA Partner or Governmental Plan Partner being deemed under ERISA or any comparable state statute, to have delegated investment discretion over plan assets (as determined by or under ERISA or any comparable state statute) to any person or entity which is not an "investment manager" (as determined by or under ERISA or any comparable state statute), then such ERISA Partner or Governmental Plan Partner shall be released from any further obligation to make further capital contributions under paragraph 4.2, and thereafter for purposes of this Agreement such ERISA Partner's or Governmental Plan Partner's obligation to make capital contributions to the Partnership shall be deemed to be equal to the total capital contributions theretofore made by such Partner. The General Partner shall cause Exhibit A to be amended to reflect all necessary changes resulting from this subparagraph (c) including, without limitation, adjustments to such ERISA Partner's or Governmental Plan Partner's Capital Commitment and Partnership Percentage.

(d) Notwithstanding any other provision of this Agreement, if at any time before a date on which any unpaid capital contribution is payable hereunder, any Private Foundation Partner (as defined in paragraph 13.3) shall obtain and deliver to the General Partner an opinion of independent legal counsel, which opinion is reasonably acceptable to the General Partner, to the effect that, as a result of applicable statutes, regulations, case law, administrative interpretations, or similar authority, the payment by such Private Foundation Partner of such unpaid capital contribution would result, or there is a material likelihood that such payment would result, in (i) payment by the Private Foundation Partner of excise taxes imposed by Subchapter A of Chapter 42 of the Code (other than Sections 4940 and 4942 thereof), or (ii) a material breach of the fiduciary duties of its trustees under any federal or state law applicable to private foundations or any rule or regulation adopted thereunder by any agency, commission, or authority having jurisdiction, then such Private Foundation Partner shall be released from any further obligation to make further capital contributions under paragraph 4.2, and thereafter for purposes of this Agreement such Private Foundation Partner's obligation to make capital contributions to the Partnership shall be deemed to be equal to the total capital contributions theretofore made by such Partner. The General Partner shall cause Exhibit A to be amended to reflect all necessary changes resulting from this subparagraph (d) including, without limitation, adjustments to such Private Foundation Partner's Capital Commitment and Partnership Percentage.

(e) Notwithstanding any other provision of this Agreement, if at any time before a date on which any unpaid capital contribution is payable hereunder, any BHC Partner (and defined in paragraph 13.4) shall obtain and deliver to the General Partner (as defined in paragraph 13.4) shall obtain and deliver to the General Partner an opinion of independent legal counsel, which opinion is reasonably acceptable to the General Partner, to the effect that the payment by such BHC Partner of such unpaid capital contribution would result in the violation by the BHC Partner of any provision of the Bank Holding Company Act of 1956, as amended (the "***BHC Act***"), including any regulation, written interpretation or directive of any governmental authority having regulatory authority over the BHC Partner, enacted or promulgated after the date of formation of the Partnership, then such BHC Partner shall be released from any further obligation to make further capital contributions under paragraph 4.2, and thereafter for purposes of this Agreement such BHC Partner's obligation to make capital contributions to the Partnership shall be deemed to be equal to the total capital contributions theretofore made by such Partner. The General Partner shall cause Schedule A to be amended to reflect all necessary changes resulting from this subparagraph (e) including, without limitation, adjustments to such BHC Partner's Capital Commitment and Partnership Percentage.

(f) Following any release pursuant to paragraphs 4.5 (c), (d) or (e) above of any ERISA Partner, Governmental Plan Partner, Private Foundation Partner or BHC Partner, respectively, from the obligation to make any additional capital contributions to the Partnership, the General Partner may, in its sole discretion, provide notice to all Limited Partners that additional contributions to the Partnership may be requested on account of such shortfall. No Limited Partner shall be required to make any additional capital contributions as a result of such notice. If any Limited Partner makes, in its sole discretion, any additional capital contribution to the Partnership as a result of such notice, the General Partner shall cause Exhibit A to be amended to reflect all necessary changes resulting from such contribution, including, without limitation, adjustments to any such contributing Partner's Capital Commitment and Partnership Percentage.

4.6 Suspension Period.

(a) Notwithstanding any other provision of this Agreement, no Limited Partner shall be required to contribute capital to the Partnership in respect of its Capital Commitment during any Suspension Period (as defined in subparagraph (b)) except for:

(i) Partnership expenses, including payment of any management fee due to the General Partner;

(ii) follow-on investments in portfolio companies in which the Partnership had invested prior to commencement of the Suspension Period; and

(iii) investments which the Partnership had committed to make prior to commencement of the Suspension Period.

(b) A "***Suspension Period***" shall be deemed to commence immediately in the event that both ____________ and ____________, each an Original manager, cease to be Managers of the General Partner or otherwise active in the affairs of the General Partner.

(c) A Suspension Period may be terminated at any time upon the affirmative vote of a Majority in Interest of the Limited Partners, regardless of whether an additional individual or entity has been approved as a new manager of the General Partner.

ARTICLE 5
PARTNERSHIP ALLOCATIONS

5.1 Allocation of Profit or Loss. Except as otherwise provided in this Article 5:

(a) Profit of the Partnership for each Accounting Period shall be allocated as follows:

(i) Twenty-five percent (25%) of the Partnership's Profit shall be allocated to the Capital Accounts of all of the Partners to the extent that such accounts were previously allocated a Contingent Loss that has not been restored by previous allocations pursuant to this paragraph 5.1(a)(i) or paragraph 7.5(f). Such Profit shall be allocated to a Partner's Capital Account on the basis of the proportion that the unrestored Contingent Losses contained in such Partner's Capital Account bear to the aggregate unrestored Contingent Losses contained in all Partners' Capital Accounts. Any balance of such twenty-five percent (25%) of the Partnership's Profit shall be allocated to the Capital Account of the General Partner.

(ii) Seventy-five percent (75%) of the Partnership's Profit shall be allocated to the Capital Accounts of all of the Partners in proportion to their respective Partnership Percentages.

(b) Loss of the Partnership for each Accounting Period shall be allocated as follows:

(i) Twenty-five percent (25%) of the Partnership's Loss shall be allocated to the Capital Account of the General Partner.

(ii) Seventy-five percent (75%) of the Partnership's Loss shall be allocated to the Capital Accounts of all of the Partners in proportion to their respective Partnership Percentages.

(c) All Ordinary Income and all management fees and other expenses of the Partnership for each Accounting Period shall be allocated to the Capital Accounts of all of the Partners in proportion to their respective Partnership Percentages.

5.2 Reallocation of Contingent Losses.

(a) Except as provided in paragraph 5.2(b), if, for any Accounting Period, after the allocations provided in this Article 5 (including any allocation required by reference to paragraph 7.5(f)) have been made, the balance of the Capital Account of the General Partner has been reduced to less than one percent (1%) of the sum of the balances of the Capital Accounts of all Partners, an amount (the "***Contingent Loss***") shall be reallocated from the General Partner's Capital Account to all of the Partner's Capital Accounts (in proportion to each Partner's respective Partnership Percentage) so that the General Partner's Capital Account balance is equal to one percent (1%) of the sum of the balances of the Capital Accounts of all Partners. For purposes of this paragraph 5.2, the General Partner's Capital Account shall not be deemed to include any amounts attributable to a Limited Partner's interest held by the General Partner, but shall be deemed to include any outstanding obligations by the General Partner to contribute capital to the Partnership.

(b) The amount of Contingent Loss that would otherwise be reallocated from the General Partner's Capital Account under paragraph 5.2(a) shall instead be allocated to the General Partner's Capital Account until allocations of Loss to the General Partner's Capital Account pursuant to this paragraph 5.2(b) equal the amount of distributions, if any, that the General Partner would have to return to the Partnership under paragraph 10.5 if the Partnership were then in liquidation.

5.3 Special Allocations.

(a) To the extent the Partnership has taxable interest income or expense with respect to any promissory note between any Partner and the Partnership as holder and maker or maker and holder pursuant to Section 483, Sections 1271 through 1288, or Section 7872 of the Code, such interest income or expense shall be specially allocated to the Partner to whom such promissory note relates, and such Partner's Capital Account adjusted if appropriate.

(b) If additional persons are admitted to the Partnership as Limited Partners subsequent to the date of its formation and prior to the date six (6) months after commencement of the Partnership pursuant to paragraph 3.2(b) ("***Additional Limited Partners***"), then organizational costs, fees (including the management fee set forth in paragraph 6.1), and expense of the Partnership that are allocated to the Partners on or after the effective date of such admission shall be allocated first to such new Partners to the extent necessary to cause such persons to be treated with respect to such items as if they had been Partners from the commencement of the Partnership's term.

5.4 Regulatory Allocations.

(a) This Agreement is intended to comply with the safe harbor provisions set forth in Treasury Regulation 1.704-1(b) and the allocations set forth in paragraph 5.4(b) (the "***Regulatory Allocations***") are intended to comply with certain requirements of Treasury Regulation Section 1.704-1(b). In the event the Regulatory Allocations result in allocations being made that are inconsistent with the manner in which the Partners intend to divide Partnership Profit and Loss as reflected in paragraphs 5.1, 5.2 and 5.3, the General Partner shall use its best efforts to adjust subsequent allocations of any items of profit, gain, loss, income or expense such that the net amount of the Regulatory Allocations and such subsequent special adjustments to each Partner is zero.

(b) The allocations provided in this Article 5 shall be subject to the following exceptions:

(i) Any loss or expense otherwise allocable to a Limited Partner which exceeds the positive balance in such Limited Partner's Capital Account shall instead be allocated first to all Partners who have positive balances in their Capital Accounts in proportion to their respective Partnership Percentages, and when all Partners' Capital Accounts have been reduced to zero, then to the General Partner; income shall first be allocated to reverse any loss allocated under this paragraph 5.4(b)(i), in reverse order of such loss allocations, until all such prior loss allocations have been reversed.

(ii) In the event any Limited Partner unexpectedly receives any adjustments, allocations, or distributions described in Treasury Regulation Section 1.704-1(b)(2)(ii)(d)(4) through (d)(6), which causes or increases a deficit balance in such Limited Partner's Capital Account, items of Partnership income and gain shall be specially allocated such Limited Partner in an amount and manner sufficient to eliminate the deficit balance in its Capital Account created by such adjustments, allocations, or distributions as quickly as possible.

(iii) For purposes of this paragraph 5.4(b), the balance in a Partner's Capital Account shall take into account the adjustments provided in Treasury Regulation Section 1.704-1(b)(2)(ii)(d)(4) through (d)(6).

5.5 Income Tax Allocations.

(a) Except as otherwise provided in this paragraph or as otherwise required by the Code and the rules and Treasury Regulations promulgated thereunder, a Partner's distributive share of Partnership income, gain, loss, deduction, or credit for income tax purposes shall be the same as is entered in the Partner's Capital Account pursuant to this Agreement.

(b) In accordance with Code Section 704(c) and the Treasury Regulations thereunder, income, gain, loss and deduction with respect to any asset contributed to the capital of the Partnership shall, solely for tax purposes, be allocated among the Partners so as to take account of any variation between the adjusted basis of such property to the Partnership for federal income tax purposes and its initial Adjusted Asset Value.

(c) In the event the Adjusted Asset Value of the Partnership asset is adjusted pursuant to the terms of this Agreement, subsequent allocations of income, gain, loss and deduction with respect to such asset shall take account of any variation between the adjusted basis of such asset for federal income tax purposes and its Adjusted Asset Value in the same manner as under Code Section 704(c) and the Treasury Regulations thereunder.

ARTICLE 6
MANAGEMENT FEE; PARTNERSHIP EXPENSES

6.1 Management Fee.

(a) The General Partner or an entity or entities designated by the General Partner shall be compensated on a quarterly basis for services rendered during the term of the Partnership by the payment by the Partnership in cash to the General Partner (or its designee) on the first day of each fiscal quarter (or portion thereof) of a management fee.

(b) The management fee for each fiscal quarter shall be an amount equal to the aggregate Capital Commitments of al Partners as of the first day of each such quarter multiplied by one-half of one percent (0.50%) (the "***Base Rate***"); *provided, however*, that (1) the Base Rate used in computing the management fee for each fiscal quarter beginning on or after ____________, 20__ shall be reduced by five one-hundredths of a percent (0.05%) per fiscal quarter, an (2) thereafter, the Base Rate used in computing the quarterly management fee shall be further reduced annually by increments of five one-hundredths of one percent (0.05%); and *provided further*, that (i) the management fee for each of the Partnership's first and last fiscal quarters shall be proportionately reduced based upon the ratio the number of days in each such period bears to ninety (90), and (ii) an additional management fee shall be payable upon the date of admission of any Additional Partner to reflect the increased Capital Commitments calculated as if such Partner had been admitted to the Partnership as of the date the first Limited Partner was admitted. Notwithstanding the foregoing, in the event the term of the Partnership is extended pursuant to paragraph 10.1, then the quarterly management fee shall be an amount equal to one-quarter of one percent (0.25%) multiplied by the lower of (A) the cost basis of the assets of the Partnership, and (B) the fair market value of all assets of the Partnership, as of the first day of each fiscal quarter during such extension period.

(c) One hundred percent (100%) of the amount of any compensation paid as transaction, break-up, board or consulting fees to the General Partner or to any member or manager of the General partner from any entity in which the Partnership has an interest in connection with the General Partner's activities as General Partner (net of any unreimbursed expenses of the General Partner or any of its members or managers, and as adjusted for any similar reductions with respect to any Side by Side Fund to prevent double counting), shall be deducted in full from the management fee otherwise payable by the Partnership in the calendar quarter following the date of receipt of such fees. In the event such reduction exceeds the management fee payable for any given period, subsequent period management fees shall be reduced by such excess amount until there has been a full reduction of management fees with respect to amounts described in the foregoing sentence.

6.2 Expenses.

(a) From the management fee, the General Partner shall bear all normal operating expenses incurred in connection with the management of the Partnership, except for those expenses borne directly by the Partnership as set forth in subparagraphs (b), (c) and (d) below and elsewhere herein. Such normal operating expenses to be borne by the General Partner shall include, without limitation, expenditures on account of salaries, wages, travel, entertainment, and other expenses of the Partnership's employees and of the General Partner's managers and employees, rentals payable for space used by the General Partner or the Partnership, bookkeeping services and equipment, and expenses incurred in investigating and evaluating investment opportunities and in managing investments of the Partnership.

(b) The Partnership shall bear all costs and expenses incurred in the holding, purchase, sale or exchange of Securities (whether or not ultimately consummated), including, but not by way of limitation, private placement fees, finder's fees, interest on borrowed money, real property or personal property taxes on investments, brokerage fees, legal fees, audit and accounting fees, consulting fees relating to investments or proposed investments, taxes applicable to the Partnership on account of its operations, fees incurred in connection with the maintenance of bank or custodian accounts, and all expenses incurred in connection with the registration of the Partnership's Securities under applicable securities laws and regulations. The Partnership shall also bear expenses incurred by the General Partner in serving as the tax matters partner (as described in paragraph 11.6), the cost of liability and other insurance premiums, all out-of-pocket expenses of preparing and distributing reports to Partners, out-of-pocket costs associated with Partnership meetings or Advisory Committee matters, all legal and accounting fees relating to the Partnership and its activities, all costs and expense arising out of the Partnership's indemnification obligation pursuant to this Agreement, and all expenses that are not normal operating expenses.

(c) The Partnership shall bear all organization and syndication costs, fees, and expenses incurred by or on behalf of the General Partner in connection with the formation and organization of the Partnership and the General Partner, including legal and accounting fees and expense incident thereto, up to a maximum of _________________ ($_______); *provided, however*, that the Partnership shall not be responsible for any private placement fee or finder's fee incurred in connection with the formation and organization of the Partnership or the General Partner.

(d) The Partnership shall bear all liquidation costs, fees, and expenses incurred by the General Partner (or its designee) in connection with the liquidation of the Partnership at the end of the Partnership's term, specifically including but not limited to legal and accounting fees and expenses.

(e) Each of the Partnership and the General Partner agree to reimburse the other as appropriate to give effect to the provisions of this paragraph 6.2 in the event that either such party pays an obligation which is properly the responsibility of the other.

ARTICLE 7
WITHDRAWALS BY AND DISTRIBUTIONS TO THE PARTNERS

7.1 Interest. No interest shall be paid to any Partner on account of its interest in the capital of or on account of its investment in the Partnership.

7.2 Withdrawals by the Partners. No Partner may withdraw any amount from its Capital Account unless such withdrawal is made pursuant to this Article 7 or Article 10.

7.3 Partners' Obligation to Repay or Restore. Except as required by law or the terms of this Agreement, no Limited Partner shall be obligated at any time to repay or restore to the Partnership all or any part of any distribution made to it from the Partnership in accordance with the terms of this Article 7.

7.4 Mandatory Distributions.

(a) Each Partner shall be paid in cash within ninety (90) days after the end of each fiscal year during the original term of the Partnership an amount equal to the excess, if any, of (a) thirty percent (30%) of the net taxable income (net of taxable losses) allocated to such Partner as a result of such Partner's ownership of an interest in the Partnership for all prior fiscal years, over (b) all cash prior distributions made pursuant to this paragraph 7.4(a) or paragraph 7.5; *provided* that the General Partner shall not be required to make any such distribution if the total amount to be distributed to all Partners is less than _______________ ($_________). The provisions of this paragraph 7.4(a) shall apply equally to all Partners, without regard to their tax-exempt status under the Code.

(b) The General Partner shall distribute all Marketable Securities acquired and held by the Partnership within three (3) years after the date that such Securities become Marketable, or, in the case of Securities Marketable at the time of their acquisition by the Partnership, within three (3) years of such acquisition; *provided, however*, that with the prior consent of the Advisory Committee, such Marketable Securities may be distributed at such later date as the Advisory Committee and the General Partner shall mutually agree. All distributions of Securities pursuant to this paragraph 7.4(b) shall be subject to the applicable provisions of paragraph 7.5.

7.5 Discretionary Distributions. In addition to any distributions made pursuant to paragraph 7.4 above:

(a) The General Partner may make distributions of cash or Marketable Securities from time to time in its discretion in the following proportions: seventy-five percent (75%) to all Partners in accordance with their respective Partnership Percentages and twenty-five percent (25%) to the General Partner; *provided, however*, the General Partner shall distribute the cost basis of Securities sold to all Partners in accordance with their respective Partnership Percentages.

(b) Notwithstanding paragraph 7.5(a), the General Partner may at any time make distributions of cash or Marketable Securities one hundred percent (100%) to all Partners in accordance with their respective Partnership Percentages.

(c) In order to maintain its proportionate interest in the Partnership in the event of a distribution in kind pursuant to paragraph 7.5(a) above, the General Partner shall (i) make a contribution to the Partnership in cash concurrently with such distribution in an amount equal to twenty-five percent (25%) of the cost basis of the Securities distributed to all Partners in such distribution, or (ii) be obligated to contribute to the Partnership an amount equal to the amount of cash described in the foregoing clause (i), which contribution obligation shall be secured by the Securities so distributed and shall be payable upon the earlier of (A) the date two (2) years from the date of the in kind distributions giving rise to the payment obligation under this clause (ii), (B) four (4) years from the date the Securities distributed in kind became Marketable Securities, (C) the disposition of such Securities by the General Partner, or (D) the date of the Partnership's final dissolution.

(d) Securities distributed in kind shall be subject to such conditions and restrictions as the General Partner determines are legally required or appropriate. Whenever types of classes of Securities are distributed in kind, each Partner shall receive its ratable portion of each type or class of Securities distributed in kind;

provided, however, if any Limited Partner would receive an amount of any Security that would cause such Limited Partner to own or control in excess of the amount of such Security that it may lawfully own or control, then, upon receipt of notice to such effect from such Limited Partner, the General Partner shall vary the method of distribution, in an equitable manner, so as to avoid such excessive ownership or control.

(e) Notwithstanding any other provision of this paragraph 7.5, prior to the dissolution of the Partnership, the Partnership shall not, without the prior approval of the Advisory Committee, make a distribution of Marketable Securities which are subject to any material restrictions on transfer as a result of applicable contractual provisions or the Securities Act (other than volume and method of sale restrictions of Rule 144 promulgated thereunder or any successor thereto).

(f) Immediately prior to any distribution in kind, the Deemed Gain or Deemed Loss of any Securities distributed shall be allocated to the Capital Accounts of all Partners as Profit or Loss pursuant to Article 5.

(g) Notwithstanding any other provision of this paragraph 7.5, prior to dissolution of the Partnership, the Partnership shall not make a distribution of Nonmarketable Securities.

7.6 Withholding Obligations.

(a) If and to the extent the Partnership is required by law (as determined in good faith by the General Partner) to make payments ("***Tax Payments***") with respect to any Partner in amounts required to discharge any legal obligation of the Partnership or the General Partner to make payments to any governmental authority with respect to any federal, state or local tax liability of such Partner arising as a result of such Partner's interest in the Partnership, then the amount of any such Tax Payments shall be deemed to be a loan by the Partnership to such Partner, which loan shall: (i) be secured by such Partner's interest in the Partnership, (ii) bear interest at the Prime Rate (as defined in paragraph 4.5(b)(i)), and (iii) be payable upon demand.

(b) If and to the extent the Partnership is required to make any Tax Payments with respect to any distribution to a Partner, either (i) such Partner's proportionate share of such distribution shall be reduced by the amount of such Tax Payments (*provided* that such Partner's Capital Account shall be adjusted pursuant to paragraph 14.4 for such Partner's full proportionate share of the distribution), or (ii) such partner shall pay to the Partnership prior to such distribution an amount of cash equal to such Tax Payments. In the event a portion of a distribution in kind is retained by the Partnership pursuant to clause (i), such retained Securities may, in the discretion of the General Partner, either (A) be distributed to the Partners in accordance with the terms of this Article 7 including this paragraph 7.6(b), or (B) be sold by the Partnership to generate the cash necessary to satisfy such Tax Payments. If the Securities are sold, then for purposes of income tax allocations only under this Agreement, any gain or loss on such sale or exchange shall be allocated to the Partner to whom the Tax Payments relate.

ARTICLE 8
MANAGEMENT DUTIES AND RESTRICTIONS

8.1 Management. The General Partner shall have the sole and exclusive right to manage, control, and conduct the affairs of the Partnership and to do any and all acts on behalf of the Partnership, including exercise of rights to elect to adjust the tax basis of Partnership assets and to revoke such elections and to make such other tax elections as the General Partner shall deem appropriate.

8.2 No Control by the Limited Partners; No Withdrawal.

(a) No Limited Partner shall take part in the control or management of the affairs of the Partnership nor shall any Limited Partner have any authority to act for or on behalf of the Partnership or to vote on any matter relative to the Partnership and its affairs except as is specifically permitted by this Agreement. Except as specifically set forth in this Agreement, no Limited Partner shall withdraw or be required to withdraw from the Partnership.

(b) Any interest in the Partnership held for its own account by a BHC Partner that is determined at the time of admission of such BHC Partner to be in excess of 4.99% (or such greater percentage as may be permitted under the BHC Act), of the cumulative interests of all of the Limited Partners, excluding for purposes of calculating such percentage portions of any other interest that are non-voting interests pursuant to this paragraph 8.2(b) (collectively, the "***Non-Voting Interests***"), shall be a Non-Voting Interest (whether or not subsequently transferred in whole or in part to any other party except as provided in the following sentence), and shall not be entitled to vote or consent with respect to such interests, and shall be deemed to have waived any rights to vote or consent with respect to such Non-Voting Interests under the Act, which interest would otherwise be identical in all material respects with other limited partnership interests in the Partnership. Upon the admission of each additional Limited Partner to the Partnership, recalculation of the interests in the Partnership held by all BHC Partners shall be made, and only that portion of the total interest in the Partnership held by each BHC Partner that is determined as of the date of such admission to be in excess of 4.99% (or such greater percentage as may be permitted under the BHC Act) of the interests in the Limited Partners, excluding Non-Voting Interests as of such date, shall be a Non-Voting Interest. Non-Voting Interests shall not be counted as interests of Limited Partners for purposes of determining under this Agreement whether any vote required hereunder has been approved by the requisite Percentage in Interest of the Limited Partners.

8.3 Existing Funds; Follow On funds; Side by Side Funds.

(a) Except as provided below, each of the Original Managers of the General Partner shall, so long as each shall remain a manager of the General Partner, devote substantially all of his business time to the affairs of the Partnership, ABC Ventures, L.P. (the "***Prior Fund***") and those entities formed for the purpose of managing each of the foregoing. The foregoing notwithstanding, the Original Managers of the General Partner may (i) continue to carry out certain duties at companies where the Original Managers of the General Partner have relationships as of the commencement of the Partnership, (ii) form one or more Side by Side Funds (as defined in paragraph 8.3(b)), and (iii) form successor private equity funds on or after the earlier of (a) ____________, 20__ and (b) such time as at least seventy percent (70%) of the Partnership's Committed Capital has been invested, committed or reserved for investment in portfolio companies, or applied, committed or reserved for Partnership working capital or expenses.

(b) Pursuant to paragraph 8.3(a)(ii), the General Partner and the Original Managers may form and serve as general partner (or in a similar management role) of (i) one or more entities organized to accommodate the capital investment of the members of the General Partner and its employees and their respective families, (ii) one or more investment partnerships or similar entities comprised of entities and persons having strategic or other important relationships with the Partnership and (iii) one or more investment partnerships or similar entities to accommodate the tax, regulatory or other special needs of investors who otherwise would invest as Limited Partners of the Partnership (collectively, the "***Side by Side Funds***"). In the event that any Side by Side Fund is formed, upon each purchase of Securities (other than short term obligations such as money market instruments) by the Partnership, each Side by Side Fund will simultaneously invest on the same terms as the Partnership; *provided, however* that a Side by Side Fund shall not be required to make any such investment in a Security if the General Partner receive from the issuer thereof a written notice to the effect that the issuer will not permit such Side by Side Fund to invest on the same terms as the Partnership. Each Side by Side Fund will invest a fixed percentage of each investment by the Partnership.

8.4 Investment Opportunities and Restrictions.

(a) Each Limited Partner hereby agrees that the General Partner may offer the right to participate in investment opportunities of the Partnership to other private investors, groups, partnerships or corporations whenever the General Partner, in its discretion, so determines, including, without limitation, subsequent funds managed by some or all of the managers of the General Partner; *provided, however*, that neither the General Partner nor its members nor their respective Affiliates shall invest personally in Securities of portfolio companies in which the Partnership holds an investment except (i) through a Side by Side Fund or (ii) where the Securities of such portfolio company are at the time of such investment Marketable Securities. Except upon the prior consent of the Advisory Committee, for so long as the Partnership may call capital pursuant to paragraph 4.2 for purposes of investing in Securities of issuers in which it does not yet hold an investment, neither the General Partner nor its members nor their respective Affiliates shall invest in any Securities of any private company in which the Partnership does not hold an investment (A) where such Securities would be within the Partnership's investment criteria or (B) where such private company directly competes with any company in which the Partnership then holds an interest, except through a Side by Side Fund.

(b) Neither the General Partner nor any of its managers nor any of their respective Affiliates may (i) buy from or sell to the Partnership any Securities without the prior approval of the Advisory Committee or (ii) lend money to the Partnership.

(c) Except as approved by the Advisory Committee, not more than ten percent (10%) of the Partnership's Committed Capital shall be invested in any single portfolio company (determined on a cost basis at the time of the investment, including follow-up costs resulting from investments in such portfolio company); *provided, however*, that such approval shall be deemed to have been given if the Advisory Committee has not notified the General Partner in writing within ten (10) days of notice of such proposed transaction. Guarantees of the indebtedness of a portfolio company by the Partnership shall be deemed to have been "***invested***" in such portfolio company for purposes of calculations under this paragraph 8.4(c).

(d) Subject to paragraph 8.4(e), the General Partner shall not borrow money or otherwise incur indebtedness on behalf of the Partnership, or guaranty indebtedness of companies in which the Partnership has invested, in an aggregate amount exceeding five percent (5%) of the Partnership's Committed Capital.

(e) The General Partner shall use reasonable efforts to operate the Partnership in a manner that will not cause any Partner subject to Section 511 of the Code to recognize unrelated business taxable income under Section 512 of the Code or unrelated debt-financing income under Section 514 of the Code ("***UBTI***"). The Partnership shall not invest in any other partnership or other non-corporate entity unless such entity is subject to similar restrictions regarding UBTI.

(f) The General Partner shall use reasonable efforts to ensure that the Partnership not enter into any transaction that would constitute participation by the Partnership or the Limited Partner in a "***prohibited transaction***" under Section 4975 of the Code.

(g) The Partnership may not carry out portfolio company investments the cost basis of which in the aggregate exceeds one hundred percent (100%) of all Capital Commitments.

(h) The prior consent of the Advisory Committee shall be required in connection with the purchase by the Partnership of the Securities of any issuer of the Securities of which are then held by the Prior Fund.

8.5 Media Companies.

(a) In the event that the Partnership invests in one or more companies that, directly or indirectly, own, control or operate a broadcast radio or television station, a cable or wireless cable television system, a daily newspaper or other similar enterprise subject to FCC Ownership Rules (as defined below) (collectively, "***Media Companies***"), the Partners agree that, notwithstanding any other provision of this Agreement conferring rights on the Limited Partners, the following additional limitations shall apply to any Limited Partner (the "***Exempt Limited Partners***") seeking exemption from attribution of ownership interests in such Media Companies under the attribution rules and the media multiple and cross-ownership rules of the Federal Communications Commission ("***FCC***") set forth in 47 C.F.R. paragraphs 21.912, 73.3555, 74.931(h) and 76.501 (collectively, the "***Ownership Rules***"), as the same may be modified from time to time. Such an Exempt Limited Partner shall be prohibited from:

(i) acting as an employee of the Partnership if such employee's functions, directly or indirectly, relate to media enterprises of the Partnership or any Media Company in which the Partnership has invested;

(ii) serving, in any material capacity, as an independent contractor or agent with respect to the media enterprises of the Partnership or any Media Company in which the Partnership has invested;

(iii) communicating on matters pertaining to the day-to-day media operations of the Partnership or a Media Company in which the Partnership has invested with (A) an officer, director, partner, agent, representative or employee of such Media Company, or (B) the General Partner;

(iv) performing any services for the Partnership materially relating to the media activities of the Partnership or any Media Company in which the Partnership has invested;

(v) becoming actively involved in the management or operation of the Partnership's media businesses; or

(vi) voting an admission of new or additional general partners to the Partnership unless such admission may be rejected by the General Partner. The foregoing limitations are intended to insulate an Exempt Limited Partner from attribution of ownership interests in Media Companies under the Ownership Rules.

(b) An Exempt Limited Partner may, upon five (5) business days' prior written notice to the General Partner, elect to be excluded from the limitations set forth in paragraph 8.5(a)(i)-(vi) and shall thereafter be denominated a "***Non-Exempt***

Limited Partner"; *provided*, that upon such election the General Partner shall review the Partnership's compliance with the Ownership Rules and take such steps as are reasonably necessary to comply therewith, and the electing Limited Partner shall cooperate in providing reasonably available information to the General Partner in such regard. A Limited partner (including a Non-Exempt Limited Partner) may, upon five (5) business days' prior written notice to the General Partner, elect to become an Exempt Limited Partner.

8.6 Venture Capital Operating Company. The General Partner shall use its reasonable best efforts to operate the Partnership so that it will remain at all times a "venture capital operating company" ("***VCOC***") as that term is defined in the DOL Regulations. The General Partner shall notify the Limited Partners as soon as reasonably practicable in the event the General Partner determines that the Partnership has ceased to meet the requirements to be a VCOC.

ARTICLE 9
INVESTMENT REPRESENTATION AND TRANSFER OF PARTNERSHIP INTERESTS

9.1 Investment Representation of the Limited Partners. This Agreement is made with each of the Limited Partners in reliance upon each Limited Partner's representation to the Partnership, which by executing this Agreement each Limited Partner hereby confirms, that its interest in the Partnership is to be acquired for investment, and not with a view to the sale or distribution of any part thereof, and that it has no present intention of selling, granting participation in, or otherwise distributing the same, and each Limited Partner understands that its interest in the Partnership has not been registered under the Securities Act and that any transfer or other disposition of the interest may not be made without registration under the Securities Act or pursuant to an applicable exemption therefrom. Each Limited Partner further represents that it does not have any contract, undertaking, agreement, or arrangement with any person to sell, transfer, or grant participations to such person, or to any third person, with respect to its interest in the Partnership.

9.2 Qualifications of the Limited Partners. Each Limited partner represents that it is an "***accredited investor***" within the meaning of that term as defined in Regulation D promulgated under the Securities Act.

9.3 Transfer by General Partner. The General Partner shall not sell, assign, mortgage, pledge or otherwise dispose of its interest in the Partnership or in its capital assets or property without the prior written consent of a Majority in Interest of the Limited Partners. Admissions of new members of the General Partner or the transfer of interests in the General Partner by its members shall not be deemed to be a sale or other disposition of the General Partner's interest in the Partnership. Notwithstanding the foregoing, in no event shall the General Partner make any transfer of an interest in the Partnership prohibited by the events described in paragraphs 9.5(a) through 9.5(h).

9.4 Transfer by Limited Partner. No Limited Partner shall sell, assign, pledge, mortgage, or otherwise dispose of or transfer its interest in the partnership without the prior written consent of the General Partner; *provided, however*, that the General Partner agrees that such consent will not be unreasonably withheld. Notwithstanding the foregoing, after delivery of the opinion of counsel hereinafter required by this Article 9, a Limited Partner may sell, assign, pledge, mortgage, or otherwise dispose of or transfer its interest in the Partnership without such consent (a) to any entity directly or indirectly holding eighty percent (80%) or more of the interests of the Limited Partner or any entity of which eighty percent (80%) or more of the beneficial ownership are held directly or indirectly, eighty percent (80%) or more of the beneficial ownership, (b) pursuant to a merger, plan of reorganization, sale or pledge of, or other general encumbrance on all or substantially all of the Limited Partner's assets, (c) as may be required by any law or regulation, (d) by testamentary disposition or intestate succession, or (e) to a trust, profit sharing plan or other entity controlled by, or for the benefit of, such Limited Partner or one or more family members. A change in any trustee or fiduciary of the Limited Partner shall not be considered to be a transfer, sale, assignment, mortgage, pledge or other disposition under this paragraph 9.4, *provided* (i) any replacement trustee or fiduciary of an ERISA Partner or a Governmental Plan Partner is also a fiduciary under ERISA (or under the state law applicable to the Governmental Plan Partner), and (ii) written notice of such change is given to the General Partner within a reasonable period of time after the effective date thereof.

9.5 Requirements for Transfer. No transfer or other disposition of the interest of the Limited Partner shall be permitted until the General Partner shall have received an opinion of counsel satisfactory to it that the effect of such transfer or disposition would not:

(a) result in the Partnership's assets being considered, in the opinion of counsel for the Partnership, as "***plan assets***" within the meaning of the Employment Retirement Income Security Act of 1974, as amended ("ERISA"), or any regulations proposed or promulgated thereunder;

(b) result in the termination of the Partnership's tax year under Section 708(b)(1)(B) of the Code;

(c) result in violation of the Securities Act or any comparable state law;

(d) require the Partnership to register as an investment company under the Investment Company Act of 1940, as amended;

(e) require the Partnership, the General Partner, or any member of the General Partner to register as an investment adviser under the Investment Advisers Act of 1940, as amended;

(f) result in a termination of the Partnership's status as a partnership for tax purposes;

(g) result in a violation of any law, rule, or regulation by the Limited Partner, the Partnership, the General Partner, or any member of the General Partner; or

(h) cause the Partnership to be deemed to be a "***publicly traded partnership***" as such term is defined in Section 7704(b) of the Code.

Such legal opinion shall be provided to the General Partner by the transferring Limited Partner or the proposed transferee. Any costs associated with such opinion shall be borne by the transferring Limited Partner or the proposed transferee. Upon request the General Partner will use its good faith diligent efforts to provide any information possessed by the Partnership and reasonably requested by a transferring Limited Partner to enable it to render the foregoing opinion.

9.6 Substitution as a Limited Partner. A transferee of a Limited Partner's interest pursuant to this Article 9 shall become a substituted Limited Partner only if the underlying transfer is permitted by paragraph 9.4 hereof and only if such transferee

(a) elects to become a substituted Limited Partner and (b) executes, acknowledges and delivers to the Partnership such other instruments as the General Partner may deem necessary or advisable to effect the admission of such transferee as a substituted Limited Partner, including, without limitation, the written acceptance and adoption by such transferee of the provisions of this Agreement. No assignment by the Limited Partner of its interest in the Partnership shall release the assignor from its liability to the Partnership pursuant to paragraph 4.2; *provided* that if the assignee becomes a Limited Partner as provided in this paragraph 9.6, the assignor shall thereupon so be released (in the case of a partial assignment, to the extent of such assignment).

ARTICLE 10
DISSOLUTION AND LIQUIDATION OF THE PARTNERSHIP

10.1 Extension of Partnership Term. Upon __________, 20__, or such subsequent dates to which the Partnership term has previously been extended pursuant to this paragraph 10.1, the General Partner may extend the Partnership term from an additional one (1) year period; *provided* that in no event shall there be more than two (2) such one year extensions without the approval of a Majority in Interest of the Limited Partners. During such one (1) year extensions periods, the General Partner shall use its best efforts to convert the Partnership's Nonmarketable Securities into Marketable Securities or cash, and all Securities that become Marketable Securities during such period or periods, and all cash in excess of working capital requirements shall be promptly distributed to the Partners. The General Partner shall not purchase the Securities of any new portfolio company during such period; *provided, however*, that the General Partner may (a) purchase additional Securities of an existing portfolio company if it deems such a purchase to be in the best interests of the Partnership, and (b) exchange the Securities of an existing portfolio company for other Securities. This management fee during any extension period shall be as set forth in Article 6; *provided, however*, that no management fee shall be payable for any period commencing more than twelve (12) years from the commencement of the Partnership.

10.2 Early Termination of the Partnership.

(a) The Partnership shall dissolve, and the affairs of the Partnership shall be wound up prior to ____________, 20__ (or such subsequent dates to which the Partnership term has previously been extended pursuant to paragraph 10.1):

(i) Ninety (90) days after the withdrawal, bankruptcy, or dissolution of the sole remaining general partner of the Partnership, unless a Majority in Interest of the Limited Partners within ninety (90) days of such event elect to continue the Partnership and appoint a new general partner effective as of the date of such event; or

(ii) Upon the affirmative vote of Eighty Percent (80%) in Interest of the Limited Partners in the event that a Suspension Period has commenced and remained uncured for one hundred eighty (180) days.

(b) In the event that the Partnership is dissolved pursuant to the provisions of this paragraph, the Partnership shall elect one or more liquidators to manage the liquidation of the Partnership in the manner described in this Article 10.

10.3 Winding Up Procedures.

(a) Promptly upon dissolution of the Partnership (unless the Partnership is continued in accordance with this Agreement or the provisions of the Act), the affairs of the Partnership shall be wound up and the Partnership liquidated. The closing Capital Accounts of all the Partners shall be computed as of the date of dissolution as if the date of dissolution were the last day of an Accounting Period in accordance with Article 5, and then adjusted in the following manner:

(i) All assets and liabilities of the Partnership shall be valued as of the date of dissolution.

(ii) The Partnership's assets as of the date of dissolution shall be deemed to have been sold at their fair market values and the resulting Profit or Loss shall be allocated to the Partner's Capital Accounts in accordance with the provisions of Article 5.

The result of reach Partner shall be its closing Capital Account. The amount of each Partner's closing Capital Account divided by the sum of the closing Capital Accounts for all of the Partners as of such date shall be such Partner's "***Final Partnership Percentage***."

(b) Distributions during the winding up period may be made in cash or in kind or partly in cash and partly in kind. The General Partner or the liquidator shall use its best judgment as to the most advantageous time for the Partnership to sell Securities or to make distributions in kind. All cash and each Security distributed in kind after the date of dissolution of the Partnership shall be distributed ratably in accordance with the General Partner and the Limited Partners' Final Partnership Percentages, unless such distribution would result in a violation of a law or regulation applicable to a Limited Partner, in which event, upon receipt by the General Partner of notice to such effect, such Limited Partner may designate a different entity to receive the distribution, or designate, subject to the approval of the General Partner, an alternative distribution procedure (*provided* such alternative distribution procedure does not prejudice any of the other Partners). Each Security so distributed shall be subject to reasonable conditions and restrictions necessary or advisable in order to preserve the value of such Security or for legal reasons.

10.4 Payments in Liquidation. The assets of the Partnership shall be distributed in final liquidation of the Partnership in the following order:

(a) to the creditors of the Partnership, other than Partners, in the order of priority established by law, either by payment or by establishment of reserves;

(b) to the Partners, in repayment of any loans made to, or other debts owed by, the Partnership to such Partners; and

(c) the balance, if any, to the General Partner and the Limited Partners in respect of the positive balances in their Capital Accounts in compliance with Treasury Regulation Section 1.704-1(b)(2)(ii) (b)(2); and the General Partner shall contribute to the capital of the Partnership the amount, if any, described in paragraph 10.5.

10.5 Return of Excess Distributions. Notwithstanding paragraphs 7.3 and 10.4, upon liquidation of the Partnership pursuant to this Article 10, the General Partner shall be required to pay back to the Partnership the amount by which the cumulative net profit distributions received by the General Partner over the life the Partnership (excluding amounts received by the General Partner in respect of its one percent (1%) Capital Commitment) exceeds twenty-five percent (25%) of the amount by which the Partnership's (a) cumulative Profits exceed (b) its cumulative Losses (the "***Excess Amount***"); *provided, however*, that the amount of repayment described in this paragraph 10.5 shall be reduced by the federal and state income taxes payable on the Excess Amount by the members of the General Partner (assuming for this purpose a combined federal and state tax rate of thirty percent (30%)). In the event that the assets of the General Partner are insufficient to satisfy the obligation described in the preceding sentence, each Original Manager agrees to contribute capital to the General Partner in the amount not to exceed his pro rata share of the General Partner's remaining obligation to the Partnership under this paragraph 10.5, which amounts shall be promptly contributed to the Partnership. The sum of the pro rata shares described in the preceding sentence shall be based on relative distributions received by each Original Manager from the General Partner and shall collectively equal one hundred percent (100%) of the amount to be contributed to the General Partner.

ARTICLE 11
FINANCIAL ACCOUNTING, REPORTS, MEETINGS AND VOTING

11.1 Financial Accounting; Fiscal Year. The books and records of the Partnership shall be kept in accordance with the provisions of this Agreement and otherwise in accordance with generally accepted accounting principles consistently applied, and shall be audited at the end of each fiscal year by an independent public accountant of recognized national standing selected by the General Partner. The Partnership's fiscal year shall be the calendar year.

11.2 Supervision; Inspection of Books. Proper and complete books of account of the Partnership, copies of the Partnership's federal, state and local tax returns for each fiscal year, the Schedule of Partners set forth in Exhibit A, this Agreement and the Partnership's Certificate of Limited Partnership shall be kept under the supervision of the General Partner at the principle office of the Partnership. Such books and records shall be open to inspection by the Limited Partners, or their accredited representatives, at any reasonable time during normal business hours after reasonable advance notice. Such books and records shall be maintained by the General Partner or its designee for a period of three (3) years following final dissolution of the Partnership.

11.3 Quarterly Reports. The General Partner shall transmit to the Limited Partners within forty five (45) days after the close of each of the first three quarters of each fiscal year, a summary of acquisitions and dispositions of investments made by the Partnership during such quarter, and a list of investments then held, together with a valuation of the investments then held.

11.4 Annual Report; Financial Statements of the Partnership. The General Partner shall transmit to the Limited Partners within ninety (90) days after the close of the Partnership's fiscal year audited financial statements of the Partnership prepared in accordance with the terms of this Agreement and otherwise in accordance with generally accepted accounting principles, including an income statement for the year then ended and a balance sheet as of the end of such year, a statement of changes in the Partners' Capital Accounts, and a list of investments then held. The financial statements shall be accompanied by a report from the General Partner to the Limited Partners, which shall include a status report on investments then held, a summary of acquisitions and dispositions of investments made by the Partnership during the preceding quarter and a valuation of each such investment.

11.5 Tax Returns. The General Partner shall cause the Partnership's federal, state and local tax returns and IRS Form 1065, Schedule K-1, to be prepared and delivered to the Limited Partners within ninety (90) days after the close of the Partnership's fiscal year.

11.6 Tax Matters Partner. The General Partner shall be the Partnership's tax matters partner under the Code and under any comparable provision of state law. The General Partner shall have the right to resign as tax matters partner by giving thirty (30) days' written notice to each Partner. Upon such resignation a successor tax matters partner shall be selected by the Partnership. The tax matters partner shall employ experienced tax counsel to represent the Partnership in connection with any audit or investigation of the Partnership by the Internal Revenue Service and in connection with all subsequent administrative and judicial proceedings arising out of such audit. If the tax matters partner is required by law or regulation to incur fees and expenses in connection with tax matters not affecting all the Partners, then the Partnership shall be entitled to reimbursement from those Partners on whose behalf such fees and expenses were incurred. The tax matters partner shall keep the Partners informed of all administrative and judicial proceedings, as required by Section 6223(g) of the Code, and shall furnish to each Partner, if such Partner so requests in writing, a copy of each notice or other communication received by the tax matters partner from the Internal Revenue Service, except such notices or communications are sent directly to such requesting Partner by the Internal Revenue Service. The relationship of the tax matters partner to the Limited Partners is that of a fiduciary, and the tax matters partner has fiduciary obligations to perform its duties as tax matters partner in such manner as will service the best interests of the Partnership and all of the Partnership's Partners. To the fullest extent permitted by law, but subject to the limitations and exclusions of paragraph 15.4, the Partnership agrees to indemnify the tax matters partner and its agents and save and hold them harmless, from and in respect to all (a) fees, costs and expenses in connection with or resulting from any claim, action, or demand against the tax matters partner, the General Partner or the Partnership that arise out of or in any way relate to the tax matters partner's status as tax matters partner for the Partnership, and (b) all such claims, actions, and demands and any losses or damages therefrom, including amounts paid in settlement or compromise of any such claim, action, or demand.

ARTICLE 12
VALUATION

12.1 Valuation. Subject to the specific standards set forth below, the valuation of Securities and other assets and liabilities under this Agreement shall be at fair market value. Except as may be required under applicable Treasury Regulations, no value shall be placed on the goodwill or the name of the Partnership in determining the value of the interest of any Partner or in any accounting among the Partners.

(a) The following criteria shall be used for determining the fair market value of Securities:

(i) If traded on one or more securities exchanges or the NASDAQ National Market System, the value shall be deemed to be the average of the Securities' closing price on the principal of such exchanges during the period which includes the valuation date and the two trading days immediately preceding the valuation date.

(ii) If actively traded over the counter (other than on the NASDAQ National Market System), the value shall be deemed to be the average of the average closing bid and ask prices of such Securities during the period which includes the valuation date and the two trading days immediately preceding the valuation date.

(iii) If there is no active public market, the value shall be the fair market value thereof, as determined by the General Partner, taking into consideration the purchase price of the Securities, developments concerning the investee company subsequent to the acquisition of the Securities, any financial data and projections of the investee company provided to the General Partner, and such other factor or factors as the General Partner may deem relevant.

(b) If the General Partner in good faith determines that, because of special circumstances, the valuation methods set forth in this Article 12 do not fairly determine the value of a Security, the General Partner shall make such adjustments or use such alternative valuation method as it deems appropriate.

(c) The General Partner shall have the power at any time to determine, for all purposes of this Agreement, the fair market value of any assets and liabilities of the Partnership, subject to paragraph 12.1(d).

(d) In the event that any Limited Partner shall disagree with any valuation made by the General Partner under this Article 12, such Limited Partner shall deliver written notice to the General Partner, briefly summarizing the basis for such disagreement. The General Partner and such Limited Partner shall then meet and confer and use their good faith efforts to reach a mutually acceptable valuation. In the event that the General Partner and such Limited Partner cannot agree, then a mutually acceptable professional appraiser shall be selected to determine the valuation. The fees and expenses of any expert or experts retained in accordance with this paragraph 12.1(d) shall be borne by the Partnership.

12.2 Advisory Committee. The General Partner will appoint an Advisory Committee of up to five (5) members, who shall be representatives of Limited Partners of the Partnership (or of any Side by Side Fund organized pursuant to paragraph 8.3(b)(iii)) selected by the General Partner from time to time in its discretion. The duties of the Advisory Committee will include (a) consideration of any approvals sought by the General Partner pursuant to the terms of this Agreement, (b) advice regarding all matters pertaining to conflicts of interest by the Partnership, the General Partner or any of the managers of the General Partner, and (c) such advice and counsel as is requested by the General Partner in connection with the Partnership's investments and other Partnership matters. However, the General Partner will retain ultimate responsibility for asset valuations and for making all investment decisions. Any Limited Partner that has elected to be an Exempt Limited Partner pursuant to paragraph 8.5(a) shall be prohibited from participating on the Advisory Committee if and to the extent that such participation would violate or be inconsistent with any of the limitations on Exempt Limited Partners set forth in paragraph 8.5(a). The Partnership will reimburse each member for his or her reasonable out-of-pocket expenses. All actions, consents or approvals of the Advisory Committee shall require a majority of its members serving at the time such action, consent or approval is taken, which actions, consents or approvals may be carried out by telephone, facsimile or electronic mail or other means reasonably acceptable to the General Partner.

ARTICLE 13
PARTNERS SUBJECT TO SPECIAL REGULATION

13.1 ERISA Partners.

(a) Each Limited Partner that is, or whose equity interests are at least partially owned by, an "***employee benefit plan***" (an "***ERISA Partner***") within the meaning of, and subject to the provisions of, ERISA hereby (i) acknowledges that it is its understanding that neither the Partnership, the General Partner, nor any of the Affiliates of the General Partner, are "***fiduciaries***" of such Limited Partner within the meaning of ERISA by reason of the Limited Partner investing its assets in, and being a Limited Partner of, the Partnership; (ii) acknowledges that it has been informed of and understands the investment objectives and policies of, and the investment strategies that may be pursued by, the Partnership; (iii) acknowledges that it is aware of the provisions of Section 404 of

ERISA relating to the requirements for investment and diversification of the assets of employee benefit plans and trusts subject to ERISA; (iv) represents that it has given appropriate consideration to the facts and circumstances relevant to the investment by that ERISA Partner's plan in the Partnership and has determined that such investment is reasonably designed, as part of such portfolio, to further the purposes of such plan, (v) represents that, taking into account the other investments made with the assets of such plan, and the diversification thereof, such plan's investment in the Partnership is consistent with the requirements of Section 404 and other provisions of ERISA: (vi) acknowledges that it understands that current income will not be a primary objective of the Partnership; and (vii) represents that, taking into account the other investments made with the assets of such plan, the investment of assets of such plan in the Partnership is consistent with the cash flow requirements and funding objectives of such plan.

(b) Notwithstanding any provision of this Agreement to the contrary, each ERISA Partner may elect to withdraw from the Partnership, or upon demand by the General Partner shall withdraw from the Partnership, at the time and in the manner hereinafter provided, if either the ERISA Partner or the General Partner shall obtain on opinion of counsel (which counsel shall be reasonably acceptable to both the ERISA Partner and the General Partner) to the effect that, as a result of applicable statutes, regulations, case law, administrative interpretations, or similar authority (i) the continuation of the ERISA Partner as a Limited Partner of the Partnership or the conduct of the Partnership will result, or there is a material likelihood the same will result, in a material violation of ERISA, or (ii) all or any portion of the assets of the Partnership constitutes assets of the ERISA Partner for the purposes of ERISA and are subject to the provisions of ERISA to substantially the same extent as if owned directly by the ERISA Partner. In the event of the issuance of such opinion of counsel, a copy of such opinion shall be given to all the Partners, together with the written notice of the election of the ERISA Partner to withdraw or the written demand of the General Partner for withdrawal, whichever the case may be. Thereupon, unless within one hundred twenty (120) days after receipt of such written notice and opinion the General Partner is able to eliminate the necessity for such withdrawal to the reasonable satisfaction of the ERISA Partner and the General Partner, whether by correction of the condition giving rise to the necessity of such Limited Partner's withdrawal, or the amendment of this Agreement, or otherwise, such Limited Partner shall withdraw its entire interest in the Partnership, such withdrawal to be effective upon the last day of the fiscal quarter during which such one hundred twenty (120) day period expired.

(c) In the event the General Partner receives from its counsel the legal opinion described in paragraph 13.1(b), it shall promptly give notice of such receipt to all ERISA Partners and Governmental Plan Partners. In the event any ERISA Partner or Governmental Plan Partner receives from its counsel the legal opinion described in paragraph 13.1(b), such ERISA or Governmental Plan Partner shall promptly give notice of such receipt to the General Partner.

(d) The withdrawing Limited Partner shall be entitled to receive within one hundred twenty (120) days after the date of such withdrawal an amount equal to the fair value of such Partner's interest as of the effective date of such withdrawal (calculated by treating all Partnership assets as though sold at fair market value as determined under paragraph 12.1 with any resulting net Profit or Loss allocated in accordance with Article 5.

(e) Any distribution or payment to a withdrawing Limited Partner pursuant to this paragraph may, in the sole discretion of the General Partner, be made in cash, in Securities, in the form of a promissory note, or any combination thereof. The terms of any such promissory note shall be mutually agreed upon the General Partner and the withdrawing Limited Partner.

13.2 Governmental Plan Partners. Notwithstanding any provision of the Agreement to the contrary, any Limited Partner that is either (i) a "***governmental plan***" as defined in Title 29, Section 1002(32) of the United States Code, (ii) an employee benefit plan subject to regulation under applicable state laws that are similar in purpose and intent to ERISA, or (iii) whose equity interests are at least partially owned by any party described in the foregoing clauses (i) or (ii) (a "***Governmental Plan Partner***"), may elect to withdraw from the Partnership, or upon demand by the General Partner shall withdraw from the Partnership, if either the Governmental Plan Partner or the General Partner shall obtain an opinion of counsel (which counsel shall be reasonably acceptable to both the Governmental Plan Partner and the General Partner) to the effect that the Governmental Plan Partner, the Partnership, or the General Partner (including its Affiliates) would be in violation, or there is a material likelihood the same would result, of any statute or regulation of the state of residence of the Governmental Plan Partner or any political subdivision of such state, enacted or promulgated after the date of formation of the Partnership, as a result of the Governmental Plan Partner continuing as a Limited Partner. In the event of the issuance of the opinion of counsel referred to in the preceding sentence, the withdrawal of and disposition of the Governmental Plan Partner's interest in the Partnership shall be governed by paragraph 13.1, as if the Governmental Plan Partner were an ERISA Partner.

13.3 Private Foundation Partners. Notwithstanding any provision of the Agreement to the contrary, any Limited Partner that is, or whose equity interests are at least partially owned by, a "***private foundation***" as described in Section 509 of the Code (a "***Private Foundation Partner***"), may elect to withdraw from the Partnership, or upon demand by the General Partner shall withdraw from the Partnership, if either the Private Foundation Partner or the General Partner shall obtain an opinion of counsel (which counsel shall be reasonably acceptable to both the Private Foundation Partner and the General Partner) to the effect that such withdrawal is necessary in order for the Private Foundation Partner to avoid (a) excise taxes imposed by Subchapter A of Chapter 42 of the Code (other than Securities 4940 and 4942 thereof), or (b) a material breach of the fiduciary duties of its trustees under any federal or state law applicable to private foundations or any rule or regulation adopted thereunder by any agency, commission, or authority having jurisdiction. In the event of the issuance of the opinion of counsel referred to in the preceding sentence, the withdrawal of and disposition of the Private Foundation Partner's interest in the Partnership shall be governed by paragraph 13.1, as if the Private Foundation Partner were an ERISA Partner.

13.4 Bank Holding Company Act Partners. Notwithstanding any provision of the Agreement to the contrary, any Limited Partner that is subject to the BHC Act (a "***BHC Partner***") may elect to withdraw from the partnership if the BHC Partner shall obtain an opinion of counsel (which counsel shall be reasonably acceptable to the General Partner) to the effect that the BHC Partner would be in violation of any provision of the BHC Act, including any regulation, written interpretation or directive of any governmental authority having regulatory authority over the BHC Partner, enacted or promulgated after the date of formation of the Partnership, as a result of the BHC Partner continuing as a Limited Partner. In the event of the issuance of the opinion of counsel referred to in the preceding sentence, the withdrawal of the disposition of the BHC Partner's interest in the Partnership shall be governed by paragraph 13.1 of the Agreement, as if the BHC Partner were an ERISA Partner.

ARTICLE 14
CERTAIN DEFINITIONS

14.1 Accounting Period. An Accounting Period shall be (a) a calendar year if there are no changes in the Partners' respective interests in the Profits or Losses of the Partnership during such calendar year except on the first day thereof, or (b) any other period beginning on the first day of a calendar year, or any other day during a calendar year upon which occurs a change in such respective interests, and ending on the last day of a calendar year, or on the day preceding an earlier day upon which any change in such respective interests shall occur.

14.2 Adjusted Asset Value. The Adjusted Asset Value with respect to any asset shall be the asset's adjusted basis for federal income tax purposes, except as follows:

(a) The initial Adjusted Asset Value of any asset contributed by a Partner to the Partnership shall be the gross fair market value of such asset at the time of contribution, as determined by the contributing Partner and the Partnership.

(b) In the discretion of the General Partner, the Adjusted Asset Values of all Partnership assets may be adjusted to equal their respective gross fair market values, as determined by the General Partner, and the resulting unrealized profit or loss allocated to the Capital Accounts of the Partners pursuant to Article 5, upon distribution by the Partnership to a Partner of more than a *de minimis* amount of Partnership assets, unless all Partners receive simultaneous distributions of either undivided interests in the distributed property or identical Partnership assets in proportion to their interests in Partnership distributions as provided in paragraphs 7.4, 7.5 and 7.6.

(c) The Adjusted Asset Values of all Partnership assets shall be adjusted to equal their respective gross fair market values, as determined by the General Partner, and the resulting unrealized profit or loss allocated to the Capital Accounts of the Partners pursuant to Article 5, as of the termination of the Partnership either by expiration of the Partnership's term or the occurrence of an event described in paragraph 10.2.

14.3 Affiliate. An Affiliate of any person shall mean (a) any person that directly, or indirectly through one or more intermediaries, controls, or is controlled by or is under common control with the person specified or (b) such person's immediate family members (excluding family members who do not reside in the same household).

14.4 Capital Account. The Capital Account of each Partner shall consist of its original capital contribution, (a) increased by any additional capital contributions, its share of income or gain that is allocated to it pursuant to this Agreement, and the amount of any Partnership liabilities that are assumed by it or that are secured by any Partnership property distributed to it, and (b) decreased by the amount of any distributions to or withdrawals by it, its share of expense or loss that is allocated to it pursuant to this Agreement, and the amount of any of its liabilities that are summed by the Partnership or that are secured by any property contributed by it to the Partnership. The foregoing provision and the other provisions of this Agreement relating to the maintenance of Capital Accounts are intended to comply with Treasury Regulation Section 1.704-1(b)(2)(iv), and shall be interpreted and applied in the manner consistent with such Regulations. In the event the General Partner shall determine that it is prudent to modify the manner in which the Capital Accounts, or any debits or credits thereto, are computed in order to comply with such Regulations, the General Partner may make such modification, *provided* that it is not likely to have more than an insignificant effect on the total amounts distributable to any Partner pursuant to Article 7 and Article 10.

14.5 Capital Commitment. A Partner's Capital Commitment shall mean the amount that such Partner has agreed to contribute to the capital of the Partnership as set forth opposite such Partner's name on Exhibit A hereto. The Partnership's Committed Capital shall equal the sum of the aggregate Capital Commitments of all Partners.

14.6 Code. The Code is the Internal Revenue Code of 1986, as amended from time to time (or any corresponding provisions of succeeding law).

14.7 Deemed Gain or Deemed Loss. The Deemed Gain from any in kind distribution of Securities shall be equal to the excess, if any, of the fair market value of the Securities distributed (valued as of the date of distribution in accordance with paragraph 12.1), over the aggregate Adjusted Asset Value of the Securities distributed. The Deemed Loss from any in kind distribution of Securities shall be equal to the excess, if any, of the aggregate Adjusted Asset Value of the Securities distributed over the fair market value of the Securities distributed (valued as of the date of distribution in accordance with paragraph 12.1).

14.8 Marketable; Marketable Securities; Marketability. These terms shall refer to Securities that are (a) traded on a national securities exchange or over the counter or (b) currently the subject of an effective Securities Act registration statement. Notwithstanding the foregoing, a Security shall not be deemed to be a Marketable Security if, in the good faith judgment of the General Partner, the market on which such Security trades is not adequate to permit an orderly sale of all shares of such Security held by the Partnership within a reasonable time period.

14.9 Nonmarketable Securities. Nonmarketable Securities are all Securities other than Marketable Securities.

14.10 Ordinary Income. Ordinary Income shall mean all income received by the Partnership from commercial paper, certificates of deposit, treasury bills, and other money market investments with maturities of less than twelve (12) months, and all interest income and dividends, or other non-liquidating corporate distributions which are not a return of capital for federal income tax purposes.

14.11 Original Managers. Original Managers shall refer to _______, _______ and _______.

14.12 Partnership Percentage. The Partnership Percentage for each Partner shall be the percentage set forth opposite each Partner's name on Exhibit A hereto.

14.13 Percentage in Interest; Majority in Interest. A specified fraction or percentage in interest of the Partners or of the Limited Partners shall mean Partners or Limited Partners of the Partnership, and of any Side by Side Fund organized pursuant to paragraph 8.3(b)(iii), whose capital commitments, stated as a percentage of the aggregate capital commitments of the Partnership and of any such Side by Side Fund, equal to exceed the required fraction or percentage in interest of all such Partners or Limited Partners; *provided, however*, that where expressly stated, a specified fraction or percentage in interest of the Partners or of the Limited Partners shall mean Partners or Limited Partners whose Partnership Percentages equal or exceed the required fraction or percentage of the Partnership Percentages of all such Partners or Limited Partners of this Partnership. A Majority in Interest shall mean more than fifty percent (50%) in interest. Any limited partnership interest owned or controlled by the General Partner shall be deemed not to be outstanding for purposes of any determination under this Agreement of a particular percentage in interest of the Limited Partners.

14.14 Profit or Loss. Profit or Loss shall be an amount computed for each Accounting Period as of the last day thereof that is equal to the Partnership's taxable income or loss for such Accounting Period, determined in accordance with Section 703(a) of the Code (for this purpose, all items of income, gain, loss, or deduction required to be stated separately pursuant to Code Section 703(a)(1) shall be included in taxable income or loss), with the following adjustments:

(a) Any income of the Partnership that is exempt from federal income tax and not otherwise taken into account in computing Profit or Loss pursuant to this paragraph shall be added to such taxable income or loss;

(b) Any expenditures of the Partnership described in Code Section 705(a)(2)(B) or treated as Code Section 705(a)(2)(B) expenditures pursuant to Treasury Regulation Section 1.704-1(b)(2)(iv)(i) and not otherwise taken into account in computing Profit or Loss pursuant to this paragraph shall be subtracted from such taxable income or loss;

(c) Gain or loss resulting from any disposition of a Partnership asset with respect to which gain or loss is recognized for federal income tax purposes shall be computed by reference to the Adjusted Asset Value of the asset disposed of rather than its adjusted tax basis;

(d) The difference between the gross fair market value of all Partnership assets and their respective Adjusted Asset Values shall be added to such taxable income or loss in the circumstances described in paragraph 14.2;

(e) Items which are specially allocated pursuant to paragraphs 5.1(c) and 5.3 shall not be taken into account in computing Profit or Loss; and

(f) The amount of any Deemed Gain or Deemed Loss on any Securities distributed in kind shall be added to or subtracted from (as the case may be) such taxable income or loss.

14.15 Securities. Securities shall mean securities of every kind and nature and rights and options with respect thereto, including stock, notes, bonds, debentures, evidences of indebtedness and other business interests of every type, including partnerships, joint ventures, proprietorships and other business entities.

14.16 Securities Act. Securities Act shall mean the Securities Act of 1933, as amended.

14.17. Treasury Regulations. Treasury Regulations shall mean the Income Tax Regulations promulgated under the Code, as such Regulations may be amended from time to time (including corresponding provisions of succeeding Regulations).

ARTICLE 15
OTHER PROVISIONS

15.1 Governing Law. This Agreement shall be governed by and construed under the laws of the State of Delaware as applied to agreements among the residents of such state made and to be performed entirely within such state in accordance with the provisions of the Act.

15.2 Limitation of Liability of the Limited Partners. Except as required by law, no Limited Partner shall be bound by, nor be personally liable for, the expenses, liabilities, or obligations of the Partnership in excess of its capital commitment to the Partnership.

15.3 Exculpation. Neither the tax matters partner, the General Partner, the members of the General Partner, the members of the Advisory Committee nor their respective agents or Affiliates shall be liable to the Limited Partners or the Partnership for honest mistakes of judgment, or for action or inaction, taken in good faith for a purpose that was reasonably believed to be in the best interests of the Partnership, or for losses due to such mistakes, action, or inaction, or to the negligence, dishonesty, or bad faith of any employee, broker, or other agent of the Partnership, *provided* that such employee, broker, or agent was selected, engaged, or retained with reasonable care. The General Partner and such persons may consult with counsel and accountants in respect of Partnership affairs and be fully protected and justified in any action or inaction that is taken in accordance with the advice or opinion of such counsel or accountants, *provided* that they shall have been selected with reasonable care. Notwithstanding any of the foregoing to the contrary, the provisions of this paragraph and the immediately following paragraph shall not be construed so as to relieve (or attempt to relieve) any person of any liability by reason of willful misconduct, recklessness or gross negligence or to the extent (but only to the extent) that such liability may not be waived, modified, or limited under applicable law, but shall be construed so as to effectuate the provisions of such paragraphs to the fullest extent permitted by law.

15.4 Indemnification. The Partnership agrees to indemnify, out of the assets of the Partnership only, the General Partner, the members of the General Partner, the members of the Advisory Committee, the tax matters partner and their agents and Affiliates to the fullest extent permitted by law and to save and hold them harmless from and in respect of all (a) reasonable fees, costs, and expenses, including legal fees, paid in connection with or resulting from any claim, action, or demand against the General Partner, the members of the General Partner, the tax matters partner, the Partnership and their agents that arise out of or in any way relate to the Partnership, its properties, business, or affairs and (b) such claims, actions, and demands and any losses or damages resulting from such claims, actions, and demands, including amounts paid in settlement or compromise (if recommended by attorneys for the Partnership) of any such claim, action or demand; *provided, however*, that this indemnity shall not extend to conduct not undertaken in good faith to promote the best interests of the Partnership or the portfolio companies of the Partnership, nor to any conduct which constitutes recklessness, willful misconduct or gross negligence. Expenses incurred by any indemnified person in defending a claim or proceeding covered by this paragraph shall be paid by the Partnership in advance of the final disposition of such claim or proceeding, *provided* the indemnified person undertakes to repay such amount if it is ultimately determined that such person was not entitled to be indemnified. The provisions of this paragraph 15.4 shall remain in effect as to each indemnified person whether or not such indemnified person continues to serve in the capacity that entitled such person to be indemnified. Without limiting the generality of this paragraph 15.4, each indemnified person shall use reasonable efforts to pursue indemnification, insurance or other similar rights from portfolio companies of the partnership and to permit the Partnership to be subrogated to the indemnified person's rights with respect to any such portfolio company indemnification, insurance or other similar rights.

15.5 Arbitration. Any controversy or claim arising out of or relating to this Agreement, or the breach thereof, except with respect to the valuation of Partnership assets, shall be settled by arbitration in ________________, ________________ in accordance with the rules, then obtaining, of the American Arbitration Association, and judgment upon the award rendered may be entered in any court having jurisdiction thereof.

15.6 Execution and Filing of Documents. This Agreement may be executed in two or more counterparts, each of which shall be deemed an original but all of which together shall constitute one and the same instrument.

15.7 Other Instruments and Acts. The Partners agree to execute any other instruments or perform any other acts that are or may be reasonably necessary to effectuate and carry on the partnership created by this Agreement.

15.8 Binding Agreement. This Agreement shall be binding upon the transferees, successors, assigns, and legal representatives of the Partners.

15.9 Notices. Any notice or other communication that one Partner desires to give to another Partner shall be in writing, and shall be deemed effectively given upon personal delivery or three (3) days after deposit in any United States mail box, by registered or certified mail, postage prepaid, upon confirmed transmission by facsimile, or upon confirmed delivery by overnight commercial courier service, addressed to the other Partner at the address shown on Exhibit A or at such other address as a Partner may designate by ten (10) days' advance written notice to the other Partners.

15.10 Power of Attorney. By signing this Agreement, each Limited Partner designates and appoints the General Partner its true and lawful attorney, in its name, place, and stead to make, execute, sign, and file the Certificate of Limited Partnership and any amendment thereto and such other instruments, documents, or certificates that may from time to time be required of the Partnership by the laws of the United States of America, the laws of the state of the Partnership's formation, or any other state in which the Partnership shall conduct its affairs in order to qualify or otherwise enable the Partnership to conduct its affairs in such jurisdictions. Such attorney is not hereby granted any authority on behalf of the Limited Partners to amend this Agreement except that as attorney for each of the Limited Partners, the General Partner shall have the authority to amend this Agreement and the Certificate of Limited Partnership (and to execute any amendment to the Agreement or the Certificate of Limited Partnership on behalf of itself and as attorney in fact for each of the Limited Partners) as may be required to effect:

(a) Admission of additional Partners pursuant to Article 3;

(b) Transfers of Limited Partnership interests pursuant to Article 9;

(c) Extensions of the Partnership term pursuant to Article 10; and

(d) Withdrawal of Partners pursuant to Article 13.

This power of attorney granted by each Limited Partner shall expire as to such Partner immediately after the dissolution of the Partnership or the amendment of the Partnership's Exhibit A to reflect the complete withdrawal of such Partner as a Partner of the Partnership.

15.11 Amendment.

(a) Except as provided by the immediately preceding paragraph and subject to paragraph 15.11(b), this Agreement may be amended only with the written consent of the General Partner and a Majority in Interest of the Limited Partners.

(b) Notwithstanding paragraph 15.11(a), (i) no amendment to the provisions of paragraphs 4.5(c), 4.5(d), 4.5(e) or Article 13 may be made without the consent of each ERISA Partner, Governmental Plan Partner, Private Foundation Partner and BHC Partner who may be adversely affected by such amendment, and (ii) no amendment to paragraph 8.4(e) may be made without the consent of a Majority in Interest of those Limited Partners who are tax exempt under the Code (including those Limited Partners whose interests are at least partially owned by any tax exempt person).

(c) Notwithstanding paragraphs 15.11(a) and (b), no amendment of this Agreement may (i) modify an provision requiring the consent of more than a majority in Interest o the Limited Partners without the consent of such higher Percentage in Interest, or (ii) modify the method of making Partnership allocations or distributions, modify the method of determining the Partnership Percentage of any Partner, reduce any Partner's Capital Account, modify any provision of this Agreement pertaining to limitations on liability of the Limited Partners, or (iii) change the restrictions contained in this paragraph 15.11(c), unless each Partner materially adversely affected thereby in a manner different than the other Partners has expressly consented in writing to such amendment.

(d) The Partnership's or General Partner's (or its managers', members' or employees') noncompliance with any provision hereof in any single transaction or event may be waived in writing by a Majority in Interest of Limited Partners to the extent such consent would be required to amend such provision pursuant to paragraph 15.11(a). No waiver shall be deemed a waiver of any subsequent event of noncompliance.

15.12 Entire Agreement. This Agreement constitutes the full, complete, and final agreement of the Partners and supersedes all prior written or oral agreements between the Partners with respect to the Partnership.

15.13 Titles; Subtitles. The titles and subtitles used in this Agreement are used for convenience only and shall not be considered in the interpretation of this Agreement.

15.14 Partnership Name. The Partnership shall have the exclusive right to use the Partnership name as long as the Partnership continues. Upon termination of the Partnership, the Partnership shall assign whatever rights it may have in such name to the General Partner. No value shall be placed upon the name or the goodwill attached to it for the purpose of determining the value of any Partner's Capital Account or interest in the Partnership.

IN WITNESS WHEREOF, the Partners have executed this Agreement as of the date first written above.

GENERAL PARTNER: **ANC MANAGEMENT, L.L.C.**	**LIMITED PARTNER:**
	____________________________ (Print name of investing entity)
By: ____________________________ Managing Partner	By: ____________________________ Name: __________________________ Title: ___________________________

"THE SECURITIES EVIDENCED BY THIS PARTNERSHIP AGREEMENT HAVE NOT BEEN REGISTERED UNDER THE SECURITIES ACT OF 1933, AS AMENDED, AND MAY NOT BE SOLD, TRANSFERRED, ASSIGNED OR HYPOTHECATED

UNLESS THERE IS AN EFFECTIVE REGISTRATION STATEMENT UNDER THE 1933 ACT COVERING SUCH SECURITIES OR THE GENERAL PARTNER RECEIVES AN OPINION OF COUNSEL FOR THE HOLDER OF THESE SECURITIES REASONABLY SATISFACTOR TO THE GENERAL PARTNER, STATING THAT SUCH SALE, TRANSFER, ASSIGNMENT OR HYPOTHECATION IS EXEMPT FROM THE REGISTRATION AND PROSPECTUS DELIVERY REQUIREMENTS OF THE 1933 ACT."

Each of the undersigned acknowledges his respective obligations under paragraph 10.5 of this Agreement.

____

____

____

2. LLC Operating Agreement

OPERATING AGREEMENT
OF
SMITH VENTURES, LLC
A CALIFORNIA LIMITED LIABILITY COMPANY

THE SECURITES REPRESENTED BY THIS AGREEMENT HAVE NOT BEEN REGISTERED UNDER THE SECURITIES ACT OF 1933 NOR REGISTERED NOR QUALIFED UNDER ANY STATE SECURITEIS LAWS. SUCH SECURITIES MAY NOT BE OFFERED FOR SALE, SOLD, DELIVERED AFTER SALE, TRANSFERRED, PLEDGED, OR HYPOTHECATED UNLESS QUALIFED AND REGISTERED UNDER APPLICABLE STATE AND FEDERAL SECURITIES LAWS OR UNLESS, IN THE OPINION OF COUNSEL SATISFACTORY TO THE COMPANY, SUCH QUALIFICATION AND REGISTRATION IS NOT REQUIRED. ANY TRANSFER OF THE SECURITIES REPRESENTED BY THIS AGREEMENT IS FUTHER SUBJECT TO OTHER RESTRICTIONS, TERMS AND CONDITONS WHICH ARE SET FORTH HEREIN.

OPERATING AGREEMENT
OF
SMITH VENTURES, LLC
A CALIFORNIA LIMITED LIABILITY COMPANY

This Operating Agreement is made and entered into as of the ____ day of ________, 20__, by and between John Smith and Jane Smith. John Smith and Jane Smith are hereinafter sometimes collectively referred to as the "Members" and individually as the "Member").

RECITALS

A. On __________, 20__, the Articles of Organization for SMITH VENTURES, LLC, a California limited liability company ("Company"), were filed with the California Secretary of State.

B. The Members desire to adopt this Operating Agreement.

Appendix

AGREEMENT
ARTICLE 1
DEFINITIONS

When used in this Agreement, the following terms shall have the meanings set forth below (all terms used in this Agreement that are not defined in this Article shall have the meanings set forth elsewhere in this Agreement):

1.1 "Act" shall mean the Beverly-Killea Limited Liability Company Act, codified in the California Corporations Code, Section 17000 et seq., as the same may be amended from time to time.

1.2 "Affiliate" shall mean any individual, partnership, corporation, trust or other entity or association, directly or indirectly, through one or more intermediaries, controlling, controlled by, or under common control with the Member. The term "control," as used in the immediately preceding sentence, means, with respect to a corporation or limited liability company the right to exercise, directly or indirectly, more than fifty percent (50%) of the voting rights attributable to the controlled corporation or limited liability company, and, with respect to any individual, partnership, trust, other entity or association, the possession, directly or indirectly, of the power to direct or cause the direction of the management or policies of the controlled entity.

1.3 "Agreement" shall mean this Operating Agreement, as originally executed and as amended from time to time.

1.4 "Articles" shall mean the Articles of Organization for the Company originally filed with the California Secretary of State and as amended from time to time.

1.5 "Bankruptcy" shall mean: (i) the filing of an application by a Member for his, her, or its consent to, the appointment of a trustee, receiver, or custodian of his, her, or its other assets; (ii) the entry of an order for relief with respect to a Member in proceedings under the United States Bankruptcy Code, as amended or superseded from time to time; (iii) the making by a Member of a general assignment for the benefit of creditors; (iv) the entry of an order, judgment, or decree by any court of competent jurisdiction appointing a trustee, receiver, or custodian of the assets of a Member unless the proceedings and the person appointed are dismissed within ninety (90) days; or (v) the failure by a Member generally to pay his, her, or its debts as the debts become due within the meaning of Section 303(h)(1) of the United States Bankruptcy Code, as determined by the Bankruptcy Court, or the admission in writing of his, her, or its inability to pay his, her, or its debts as they become due.

1.6 "Capital Account" shall mean with respect to any Member the Capital Account which the Company establishes and maintains for such Member pursuant to Section 3.

1.7 "Capital Contribution" shall mean the total value of cash and fair market value of property (including promissory notes or other obligation to contribute cash or property) contributed and/or services rendered, or to be rendered to the Company by Members.

1.8 "Code" shall mean the Internal Revenue Code of 1986, as amended from time to time, the provisions of succeeding law, and to the extent applicable, the Regulations.

1.9 "Company" shall mean the SMITH VENTURES, LLC, a California limited liability company.

1.10 "Company Minimum Gain" shall have the meaning ascribed to the term "Partnership Minimum Gain" in the Regulations Section 1.704-2(d).

1.11 "Corporations Code" shall mean the California Corporation Code, as amended from time to time, and the provisions of succeeding law.

1.12 "Dissociation Event" shall mean with respect to any Member one or more of the following: the withdrawal, death, bankruptcy or dissolution of the Member.

1.13 "Distributable Cash" shall mean the amount of cash which the Manager reasonably deems available for distribution, taking into account all Company debts, liabilities, and obligations of the Company then due, amounts which the Manager deems necessary to place into reserves for customary and usual expenses with respect to the Company's business, and anticipated repairs and maintenance to Company assets.

1.14 "Economic Interest" shall mean a Member's or Economic Interest Owner's share of one or more of the Company's Net Profits, Net Losses, and distributions of the Company's assets pursuant to this Agreement and the Act, but shall not include any other rights of a Member, including, without limitation, the right to vote or participate in the management, or any right to information concerning the business and affairs of Company. Unless otherwise provided in this Agreement, a Member's or Economic Interest Owner's Economic Interest in the Company's Net Profits, Net Losses, and distributions shall be such Member's or Economic Interest Owner's Percentage Interest as defined in Section 1.

1.15 "Economic Interest Owner" shall mean the owner of an Economic Interest who is not a Member.

1.16 "Fiscal Year" shall mean the Company's Fiscal Year, which shall be the calendar year.

1.17 "Former Member" shall mean a Member who withdraws from the Company in accordance with Section 4. For purposes of Sections 9 through 9, a "Former Member" is any Member who is obligated to sell his or her interest in the Company to the Remaining Members and/or the Company.

1.18 "Former Member's Interest" shall mean a Former Member's Membership Interest in the Company.

1.19 "Majority Interest" shall mean one or more Members who own Percentage Interests which taken together exceed fifty percent (50%) of the aggregate of all Percentage Interests.

1.20 "Management Agreement" shall mean the agreement between the Company and Jane Smith, whereby Jane Smith shall be compensated for performance of her duties as Manager.

1.21 "Manager" shall mean one or more Managers. Specifically, "Manager" shall mean Jane Smith, or any other Person that succeeds her in that capacity.

1.22 "Member" shall mean each Person who (i) is an initial signatory to this Agreement, has been admitted to the Company as a Member in accordance with the Articles or this Agreement or is an assignee who has become a Member in accordance with Article 8, and (ii) has not withdrawn or, if other than an individual, dissolved.

1.23 "Member Nonrecourse Debt" shall have the meaning ascribed to the term "Partner Nonrecourse Debt" in Regulations Section 1.704-2(b)(4).

1.24 "Member Nonrecourse Deductions" shall mean items of Company loss, deduction, or Code Section 705(a)(2)(B) expenditures which are attributable to Member Nonrecourse Debt.

1.25 "Membership Interest" shall mean a Member's entire interest in the Company including the Member's Economic Interest, the right to vote on or participate in the management, and the right to receive information concerning the business and affairs, of the Company. Unless otherwise provided in this Agreement, the Percentage Interest of a Member's Membership Interest shall be such Member's Percentage Interest as defined in Section 1.

1.26 "Net Profits" and "Net Losses" shall mean, for each taxable year of the Company (or other period for which Net Profits or Net Losses must be computed), the Company's taxable income or loss determined in accordance with Code Section 703(a), with the following adjustments: (a) All items of income, gain, loss, deduction, or credit required to be stated separately pursuant to Code Section 703(a)(1) shall be included in computing taxable income or loss; (b) Any tax-exempt income of the Company, not otherwise taken into account in computing taxable income or loss, shall be included in computing Net Profits or Net Losses; (c) Any expenditures of the Company described in Code Section 705(a)(2)(B) (or treated as such pursuant to Regulations Section 1.704-1(b)(2)(iv)(i)) and not otherwise taken into account in computing Net Profits or Net Losses, shall be subtracted from taxable income or loss; (d) Gain or loss resulting from any taxable disposition of Company property shall be computed by reference to the book value as adjusted under Regulations Section 1.704-1(b) (for purposes of this Section 1 "adjusted book value") of the property disposed of, notwithstanding the fact that the adjusted book value differs from the adjusted basis of the property for federal income tax purposes; (e) In lieu of the depreciation, amortization or cost recovery deductions allowable in computing taxable income or loss, there shall be taken into account the depreciation computed based upon the adjusted book value of the asset; and (f) Notwithstanding any other provision of this definition, any items which are specially allocated pursuant to Section 6 shall not be taken into account in computing Net Profits or Net Losses.

1.27 "Nonrecourse Liability" shall have the meaning set forth in Regulations Section 1.752-1(a)(2).

1.28 "Percentage Interest" shall mean the percentage of a Member set forth opposite the name of such Member under the column "Percentage Interest" in **Exhibit A** hereto, as such percentage may be adjusted from time to time pursuant to the terms of this Agreement.

1.29 "Person" shall mean an individual, general partnership, limited partnership, limited liability company, corporation, trust, estate, real estate investment trust association or any other association or business entity.

1.30 "Regulations" shall, unless the context clearly indicates otherwise, mean the regulations currently in force as final or temporary that have been issued by the United States Department of Treasury pursuant to its authority under the Code.

1.31 "Remaining Members" shall, upon the occurrence of a Dissociation Event as defined in Section 1, mean all the Members except the Member subject to the Dissociation Event.

1.32 "Secretary of State" shall mean the Secretary of State for the State of California and its delegates responsible for the administration of the Act.

1.33 "Tax Matters Partner" shall be Jane Smith or her successor as designated below.

ARTICLE 2

ORGANIZATIONAL MATTERS

2.1 Formation. Pursuant to the Act, the Members have formed a California limited liability company under the laws of the State of California by filing the Articles of Organization with the Secretary of State and entering into this Agreement. The rights and liabilities of the Members shall be determined pursuant to the Act and this Agreement. To the extent that the rights or obligations of any Member are different by reason of any provision of this Agreement than they would be in the absence of such provisions, this Agreement shall, to the extent permitted by the Act, control.

2.2 Name. The name of the Company shall be "SMITH VENTURES, LLC." The business of the Company may be conducted under that name or, upon compliance with applicable laws, any other name that the Manager deems appropriate or advisable. The Manager shall file any fictitious name certificates and similar filings, and any amendments thereto, that the Manager considers appropriate or advisable.

2.3 Term. The term of this Company commenced on the date the Articles of Organization were filed with the Secretary of State and shall continue until the Company is dissolved as provided herein, or ____________, 20__, whichever shall first occur, provided, however, the term may be extended beyond such date by the unanimous agreement of the Members.

2.4 Office and Agent. The Company shall continuously maintain an office and registered agent in the State of California as required by the Act. The principal office of the Company shall be as the Manager may determine. The Company also may have such offices, anywhere within and without the State of California, as the Manager from time to time may determine, or the business of the Company may require. The initial registered office and agent of the Company shall be stated in the Articles or as otherwise determined by the Manager.

2.5 Addresses of the Members and Manager. The respective addresses of the Members and the Manager are set forth on **Exhibit A**.

2.6 Purpose of Company. The purpose of the Company is to engage in any lawful business for which a limited liability company may be organized under the Act.

ARTICLE 3

CAPITAL CONTRIBUTIONS

3.1 Initial Capital Contributions. Upon execution of this Agreement, each of the Original Members shall have contributed to the Company as such Member's initial Capital Contribution cash in the amounts set forth in **Exhibit A**, attached hereto and incorporated herein by reference. In exchange for each Member's initial Capital Contribution, the Member received (i) a Membership Interest in the Company as set forth opposite such Member's name in **Exhibit A**, and (ii) a credit to such Member's Capital Account equal to the sum of the cash and the fair market value of the property contributed.

3.2 Additional Capital Contributions. No Member shall be required to make any additional Capital Contributions. Upon a determination by the Manager that additional Capital Contributions are necessary or appropriate for the conduct of the Company's business, including without limitation, expansion or diversification, the Members may be permitted to make additional Capital Contributions if and to the extent they so desire. In that event, the Members shall have the opportunity, but not the obligation, to participate in such additional Capital Contributions on a pro rata basis in accordance with their Membership Interests. Each Member shall receive a credit to such Member's Capital Account in the amount of any additional capital which the Member contributes to the Company, and such Member shall receive an additional Membership Interest determined by the value of the Additional Capital Contribution in relation to the value of the Company as a whole. The value of the Company as a whole shall be determined at the time the Additional Capital Contribution is made pursuant to the appraisal mechanism stated in Section 9 below. Immediately following such Capital Contributions, the Manager shall amend this Agreement to adjust the Membership Interests and Economic Interests to reflect the new relative proportions of the Capital Accounts of the Members and Economic Interest Owners. Notwithstanding anything to the contrary, such an amendment shall not require the vote or approval of the Members.

3.3 Capital Accounts. The Company shall establish an individual Capital Account for each Member and Economic Interest Owner. The Company shall determine and maintain each Capital Account in accordance with Regulations Section 1.704-1(b)(2)(iv). If a Member or an Economic Interest Owner transfers all or a part of his, her, or its Economic Interest in accordance with this Agreement, such Member's or Economic Interest Owner's Capital Account attributable to the transferred Economic Interest shall carry over to the new owner of such Economic Interest pursuant to Regulations Section 1.704-1(b)(2)(iv)(1).

3.4 No Interest. No Member or Economic Interest Owner shall be entitled to receive any interest on his, her, or its Capital Contributions.

3.5 Valuation of Company Assets. The book values of all Company assets shall be adjusted to equal their respective fair market values (taking Code Section 7701(g) into account), as reasonably determined by the Manager, upon the occurrence of any of the following events: (i) a contribution of money or property (other than a de minimis amount) to the Company by a new or existing Member as consideration for a Membership Interest; (ii) a distribution of money or property (other than a de minimis amount) by the Company to a Member as consideration for a Membership Interest; and (iii) the liquidation of the Company within the meaning of Regulations Section 1.704-1(b)(2)(ii)(g). Any such adjustments shall be reflected by corresponding adjustments to the Capital Accounts which reflect the manner in which the unrealized income, gain, loss, or deduction inherent in such property (that has not been reflected in the Capital Accounts previously) would be allocated among the Members if there were a taxable disposition of such assets for such fair market values.

ARTICLE 4

MEMBERS

4.1 Limited Liability. Except as set forth in this Agreement, no Member shall be personally liable for any debt, obligation, or liability of the Company, whether that liability or obligation arises in contract, tort, or otherwise.

4.2 Admission of Additional Members. The Manager may admit to the Company additional Members, from time to time, subject to the following: (a) The Manager consents to the admission; (b) The additional Member shall make a Capital Contribution in such amount and on such terms as the Manager determines to be appropriate based upon the needs of the Company, the net value of the Company's assets, the Company's financial condition, and the benefits anticipated to be realized by the additional Member; and (c) No additional Member shall be admitted if the effect of such admission would be to terminate the Company within the meaning of Code Section 708(b).

Notwithstanding the foregoing, substitute Members may only be admitted in accordance with Article 8. The Manager shall amend this Agreement to reflect the admission of additional Members and such amendment shall not require the vote or approval of the Members.

4.3 Withdrawals. No Member may withdraw from the Company without the consent of the Manager. If a withdrawal is consented to, such Member's Membership Interest shall be subject to purchase and sale as provided in Section 9.

4.4 Termination of Membership Interest. Upon (i) the transfer of all or a portion of a Member's Membership Interest in violation of this Agreement, (ii) the occurrence of a Dissociation Event of a Member which does not result in the admission of a substitute Member pursuant to Section 8 as to such Member's Membership Interest, or (iii) the withdrawal of a Member in accordance with Section 4, the Membership Interest of such Member may be purchased by the Company or Remaining Members as provided herein, or, if not so purchased, such Membership Interest shall become an Economic Interest and the balance of the rights associated with the Membership Interest (including without limitation, the right of the Member to vote or participate in the management of the business, property and affairs of the Company) may, in the sole discretion of the Manager, be purchased by the Company pursuant to Section 8.

4.5 Transactions With The Company. Subject to any limitations set forth in this Agreement and with the prior approval of the Manager after full disclosure of the Member's involvement, a Member may engage in any transaction (including, without limitation, the purchase, sale, lease or exchange of any property, or the lending of funds, or the rendering of any service, or the establishment of any salary, other compensation or other terms of employment) with the Company. Subject to other applicable law, such Member has the same rights and obligations with respect thereto as a Person who is not a Member.

4.6 Remuneration To Members. Except as otherwise authorized in, or pursuant to, this Agreement, no Member is entitled to remuneration for acting in the Company business, subject to the entitlement of Members winding up the affairs of the Company to reasonable compensation pursuant to Section 11. Notwithstanding the prior sentence and subject to the provisions of Section 4, the Company shall pay the Members for services rendered to the Company to the extent that the Members are not required to render such services themselves without charge to the Company.

4.7 Members Are Not Agents. Pursuant to Section 5 and the Articles, the management of the Company is vested in the Manager. No Member, acting solely in the capacity of a Member, is an agent of the Company nor can any Member in such capacity bind nor execute any instrument on behalf of the Company.

This Section supersedes any authority granted to the Members pursuant to Section 17157 of the Act. Any Member who takes any action or binds the Company in violation of this Section shall be solely responsible for any loss and expense incurred by the Company as a result of the unauthorized action and shall indemnify and hold the Company harmless with respect to the loss or expense.

4.8. Voting Rights. Except as expressly provided in this Agreement or the Articles, Members shall have no voting, approval or consent rights. Members who are not the subject of a Dissociation Event or who have not assigned their Membership Interests shall have the right to approve or disapprove matters as specifically stated in this Agreement, including the following: (a) Those matters specified in Section 5; (b) Any other matter expressly set forth in this Agreement; and (c) Such other matters as the Manager may from time to time elect to submit to the vote of the Members, provided however, that the Manager shall not be obligated to submit any matter to the vote of the Members except as otherwise provided in this Agreement.

4.9 Meetings of Members. No annual or regular meetings of Members are required.

ARTICLE 5

MANAGEMENT AND CONTROL OF THE COMPANY

5.1 Management of the Company by Manager.

(a) Exclusive Management by Manager. The business, property and affairs of the Company shall be managed exclusively by the Manager, who may, but need not, be Members. Except for situations in which the approval of the Members is expressly required by the Act, the Articles or this Agreement, the Manager shall have full, complete and exclusive authority, power, and discretion to manage, and control the business, property and affairs of the Company, to make all decisions regarding those matters and to perform any and all other acts or activities customary or incident to the management of the Company's business, property and affairs.

(b) Agency Authority of Manager. Subject to Section 5, the Manager (if only one) or each Manager (if there are more than one Managers), acting alone, is authorized to (i) endorse checks, drafts, and other evidence of indebtedness made payable to the order of the Company, but only for the purpose of deposit into the Company's accounts, (ii) sign all checks, drafts, and other instruments obligating the Company to pay money, and (iii) sign all contracts obligations, or any other instrument or document on behalf of the Company. Notwithstanding anything to the contrary, the Manager may, subject to any limitations that the Manager deems necessary or appropriate, authorize one or more agents of the Company, which may or may not be employees or Members of the Company, to (i) endorse checks, drafts, and other evidence of indebtedness made payable to the order of the Company, but only for the purpose of deposit into the Company's accounts, and (ii) sign checks, drafts, and other instruments obligating the Company to pay money.

(c) Meetings of Managers. Meetings of Managers, if there are more than one Manager, are not required.

5.2 Election of Managers.

(a) Number, Term, and Qualifications. The Company shall initially have one (1) Manager. Jane Smith shall be and is hereby appointed the initial Manager. Upon the death, resignation or removal of Jane Smith, John Smith shall be the successor Manager. If John Smith predeceases Jane Smith or is unable to perform his duties as successor Manager upon the death, resignation or removal of Jane Smith for some other reason, then the successor Manager shall be elected pursuant to subsection (d) of this Section.

The number of Managers of the Company shall be fixed from time to time by the affirmative vote or written consent of Members holding a Majority Interest, provided that if the number of Managers is increased from one (1) to more than one (1), the Articles shall be amended to delete the statement that the Company has only one (1)

Manager. At no time shall there be less than one (1) Manager. Unless a Manager resigns or is removed, each Manager shall hold office until a successor shall have been elected and qualified. Successor Managers shall be elected by the affirmative vote or written consent of Members holding a Majority Interest. A Manager need not be a Member, an individual, a resident of the State of California, or a citizen of the United States.

(b) Resignation. Any Manager may resign at any time by giving written notice to the Members and the remaining Managers, if any. Any such resignation shall be without prejudice to the rights, if any, of the Company under any contract to which the resigning Manager is a party. The resignation of any Manager shall take effect upon receipt of that notice or at such later time as shall be specified in the notice; and, unless otherwise specified in the notice, the acceptance of the resignation shall not be necessary to make it effective. The resignation of a Manager who is also a Member shall not affect the Manager's rights as a Member and shall not constitute a withdrawal of a Member.

(c) Removal.

(i) Except as set forth in this Section, the Members shall have no power to remove or expel a Manager. A Manager may only be removed by the vote of Members holding a majority of the Percentage Interest (including the Percentage Interest of such Manager in her capacity as a Member) upon default in the performance of her obligations as a Manager. The following acts and/or omissions shall constitute a default by a Manager: the failure to perform any duty or act required of the Manager by this Agreement or the Act, or the performance of any act prohibited by this Agreement or the Act, provided that the Manager (1) shall have received written notice from the remaining Members of such default, and (2) shall not have cured such default, if it is a monetary default, within thirty (30) days thereafter, or (3) shall not have commenced to cure or remedy such default, if it is a non-monetary default, within thirty (30) days thereafter, and (4) shall not have thereafter pursued any such correction to completion with diligence and continuity and corrected such default within a reasonable time.

(ii) Upon the occurrence of an event of default of a Manager as specified above, the Remaining Members may remove the Manager by giving said Manager written notice of removal. Notice of removal shall be served on the Manager either by certified or registered mail, return receipt requested, or by personal service, and shall set forth the effective date of the removal.

(iii) Any removal shall be without prejudice to the rights, if any, of the Manager under any employment or management contract and, if the Manager is also a Member, shall not affect the Manager's rights as a Member or constitute a withdrawal of a Member.

(d) Vacancies. Any vacancy occurring for any reason in the number of Managers may be filled by the affirmative vote or written consent of a Majority Interest of Members.

5.3 Powers of Manager. Without limiting the generality of Section 5, but subject to Section 5 and to the express limitations set forth elsewhere in this Agreement, the Manager shall have all necessary powers to manage and carry out the purposes, business, property, and affairs of the Company and to make all decisions affecting such business and affairs, including, without limitation, the power to exercise on behalf of the Company all powers described in Corporations Code Section 17003, including without limitation, the power to: (a) Acquire, purchase, renovate, improve, alter, rebuild, demolish, replace, and own property or assets that the Manager determines is necessary or appropriate or in the interest of the business of the Company, and to acquire options for the purchase of any such property; (b) Sell, exchange, lease, or otherwise dispose of the property and assets owned by the Company, or any part thereof, or any interest therein; (c) Guarantee the payment of money or the performance of any contract or obligation of any Person; (d) Sue on, defend, or compromise any and all claims or liabilities in favor of or against the Company; and/or submit any or all such claims or liabilities to arbitration; (e) Make contracts and guarantees, incur liabilities, act as surety, and borrow money; (f) Issue notes, bonds, and other obligations and secure any of them by mortgage or deed of trust or security interest of any or all of the Company's assets; (g) Retain legal counsel, auditors, and other professionals in connection with the Company business and to pay therefore such remuneration as the Manager may determine; (h) Care for and distribute funds to the Members by way of cash flow, income, return of capital, or otherwise, all in accordance with the provisions of this Agreement, and perform all matters in furtherance of the objectives of the Company or this Agreement; (i) Employ from time to time, at the expense of the Company, on such terms and for such compensation as the Manager may determine, but subject to this Agreement, Persons to render services to the Company; (j) Pay or cause to be paid all expenses, fees, charges, taxes, and liabilities incurred or arising in connection with the Company, or in connection with the management thereof, including without limitation, such expenses and charges for the services of the Company employees, accountants, attorneys, and other agents or independent contractors, and such other expenses and charges as the Manager deems is necessary or advisable to incur; and (k) Make elections for federal, state and local tax purposes, including without limitation, any election permitted by applicable law to (i) adjust the basis of the Company property pursuant to Code Sections 754, 734(b), and/or 743(b), and/or comparable provisions of state or local law in connection with the transfer of Membership Interests; and (ii) extend the statute of limitations for assessment of tax deficiencies against Members with respect to adjustments to the Company's federal, state or local tax returns.

The expression of any power or authority of the Manager in this Agreement shall not in any way limit or exclude any other power or authority which is not specifically or expressly set forth in this Agreement. If there is more than one (1) Manager, the rights and powers of the Manager hereunder shall be exercised by such Manager in such manner as they may agree, including without limitation by delegating responsibility for conduct of Company business or any portion thereof to any one (1) or more of the Managers. Any such delegation of responsibility or authority to one (1) or more Managers may be revoked at any time by the Remaining Managers. In the absence of any agreement among such persons, no Manager may exercise any of such rights and powers without the consent of a majority (in number) of the Managers. Furthermore, any provision in this Agreement requiring the consent of the Managing Manager shall mean the consent of a majority (in number) of the Managers unless otherwise expressly stated.

5.4 Limitations on Power of Manager. Notwithstanding any other provisions of this Agreement, the Manager shall have no authority hereunder to cause the Company to engage in the following transactions without first obtaining the affirmative vote or written consent of a Majority Interest (or such greater Percentage Interests set forth below) of the Members: (a) The merger of the Company with another limited liability company, limited partnership, general partnership or other Person (provided (i) in no event shall a Member be required to become a general partner in a merger with a limited partnership without his, her, or its express consent or unless the agreement of merger provides each Member with dissenter's rights described in the Act, and (ii) in a merger of the Company with a general partnership, if the Members become personally liable for any obligations as a result of the merger, the principal terms of the agreement of merger must be approved by all of the Members unless the agreement of merger provides that all Members will have dissenter's rights provided in the Act); (b) An alteration of the primary purpose of the Company as set forth in Section 2; (c) Any act which would make it impossible to carry on the ordinary business of the Company; (d) Any other transaction described in this Agreement as requiring the vote, consent, or approval of the Members; or (e) Entering into any amendment of the Articles or this Agreement (except as otherwise provided in this Agreement) shall require the unanimous vote, consent, or approval of the Members.

5.5 Members Have No Managerial Authority. The Members shall have no power to participate in the management of the Company except as expressly authorized by this Agreement or the Articles and except as expressly required by the Act. Unless expressly and duly authorized in writing to do so by the Manager, no Member shall have any power or authority to bind or act on behalf of the Company in any way, to pledge its credit, or to render it liable for any purpose.

5.6 Performance of Duties; Liability of Manager. A Manager shall not be liable to the Company or to any Member for any loss or damage sustained by the Company or any Member, unless the loss or damage shall have been the result of fraud, deceit, gross negligence, reckless or intentional misconduct, or a knowing violation of law by the Manager.

5.7 Devotion of Time. The Manager is not obligated to devote all of her time or business efforts to the affairs of the Company. The Manager shall devote whatever time, effort, and skill as she deems appropriate for the operation of the Company.

5.8 Competing Activities. The Manager and her Affiliates may engage or invest in any business activity of any type or description, including without limitations those that might be the same as or similar to the Company's business and that might be in director or indirect competition with the Company. Any such activity may be engaged in independently or with others, and may include without limitation the conduct of the same business as that of the Company for the account of any one or all of such Persons. Neither the Company nor any Member shall have any right in or to such other ventures or activities, or to the income or proceeds derived there from. The Manager shall not be obligated to present any investment opportunity or prospective economic advantage to the Company, even if the opportunity is of the character that, if presented to the Company, could be taken by the Company. The Manager shall have the right to hold any investment opportunity or prospective economic advantage for their own account or to recommend such opportunity to Persons other than the Company. The Members acknowledge that the Manager and her Affiliates own and/or manage other businesses, including businesses that may compete with the Company and for the Manager's time. The Members hereby waive any and all rights and claims which they may otherwise have against the Manager and her Affiliates as a result of any such activities.

5.9 Transactions between the Company and a Manager. Notwithstanding that it may constitute a conflict of interest, the Manager may, and may cause her Affiliates to, engage in any transaction (including, without limitation, the purchase, sale, lease, or exchange of any property, or the lending of funds, or the rendering of any service, or the establishment of any salary, other compensation, or other terms of employment) with the

Company so long as such transaction is not expressly prohibited by this Agreement and so long as the terms and conditions of such transaction on an overall basis, are fair and reasonable to the Company and are at least as favorable to the Company as those that are generally available from Persons capable of similarly performing them and in similar transactions between parties operating at arm's length.

A transaction between a Manager and/or his, her, or its Affiliates, on the one hand, and the Company, on the other hand, shall be conclusively determined to constitute a transaction on terms and conditions, on an overall basis, fair and reasonable to the Company and at least as favorable to the Company as those generally available in a similar transaction between parties operating at arm's length if Members holding a majority of the Percentage Interests of Members having no interest in such transaction (other than their interest as Members) affirmatively vote or consent in writing to approve the transaction. Notwithstanding the foregoing, the Manager shall not have any obligation in connection with any such transaction between the Company and the Manager or an Affiliate of the Manager, to seek the consent of the Members having no interest in such transaction.

5.10 Payments to Manager. Except as otherwise authorized in, or pursuant to, this Section, this Agreement or the Management Agreement, neither the Manager nor her Affiliates are entitled to remuneration for services rendered or goods provided to the Company. The Manager and her Affiliates shall receive only the following payments: (a) Services Performed by Manager or Affiliates. The Company shall pay a Manager and/or her Affiliates for services rendered or goods provided to the Company pursuant to the Management Agreement. (b) Expenses. The Company shall reimburse the Manager and Affiliates for the actual cost of goods and materials used for or by the Company.

5.11 Limited Liability of Manager. No person who is a Manager of the Company shall be personally liable under any judgment of a court, or in any other manner, for any debt, obligation, or liability of the Company, whether that liability or obligation arises in contract, tort, or otherwise, solely by reason being a Manager of the Company.

ARTICLE 6

ALLOCATIONS OF NET PROFITS AND NET LOSSES AND DISTRIBUTIONS

6.1 Allocations of Net Profit and Net Loss.

(a) Net Loss. Subject to the limitation set forth in Section 6, Net Loss for each Fiscal Year shall be allocated to the Members and Economic Interest Owners in accordance with their Economic Interests.

(b) Loss Limitation. Notwithstanding Section 6, loss allocations to a Member or Economic Interest Owner shall be made only to the extent that such loss allocations will not create a deficit Capital Account balance for that Member or Economic Interest Owner in excess of an amount, if any, equal to such Member's or Economic Interest Owner's share of Company Minimum Gain that would be realized on a foreclosure of the Company's property. Any loss not allocated to a Member or Economic Interest Owner because of the foregoing provision shall be allocated to the other Members and Economic Interest Owners (to the extent the other Members and Economic Interest Owners are not limited in respect of the allocation of losses under this Section). Any loss reallocated under this Section shall be taken into account in computing subsequent allocations of income and losses pursuant to this Article, so that the net amount of any item so allocated and the income and losses allocated to each Member or Economic Interest Owner pursuant to this Article, to the extent possible, shall be equal to the net amount that would have been allocated to each such Member or Economic Interest Owner pursuant to this Article if no reallocation of losses had occurred under this Section.

(c) Net Profit. Subject to allocations under Section 6 and 6, Net Profit shall be allocated to the Members and Economic Interest Owners in accordance with their Economic Interests.

6.2 Special Allocations.

(a) Minimum Gain Chargeback. Notwithstanding Section 6, if there is a net decrease in Company Minimum Gain during any Fiscal Year, each Member and Economic Interest Owner shall be specially allocated items of Company income and gain for such Fiscal Year (and, if necessary, in subsequent Fiscal Years) in an amount equal to the portion of such Member's or Economic Interest Owner's share of the net decrease in Company Minimum Gain that is allocable to the disposition of Company property subject to a Nonrecourse Liability which share of such net decrease shall be determined in accordance with Regulations Section 1.704-2(g)(2). Allocations pursuant to this Section shall be made in proportion to the amounts required to be allocated to each Member and Economic Interest Owner under this Section. The items to be so allocated shall be determined in accordance with Regulations Section 1.704-2(f). This Section is intended to comply with the minimum gain chargeback requirement contained in Regulations Section 1.704-2(f) and shall be interpreted consistently therewith.

(b) Chargeback of Minimum Gain Attributable to Member Nonrecourse Debt. Notwithstanding Section 6 of this Agreement, if there is a net decrease in Company Minimum Gain attributable to a Member Nonrecourse Debt, during any Fiscal Year, each Member and Economic Interest Owner who has a share of the Company Minimum Gain attributable to such Member Nonrecourse Debt (which share shall be determined in accordance with Regulations Section 1.704-2(i)(5)) shall be specially allocated items of Company income and gain for such Fiscal Year (and, if necessary, in subsequent Fiscal Years) in an amount equal to that portion of such Member's or Economic Interest Owner's share of the net decrease in Company Minimum Gain attributable to such Member Nonrecourse Debt that is allocable to the disposition of Company property subject to such Member Nonrecourse Debt (which share of such net decrease shall be determined in accordance with Regulations Section 1.704-2(i)(5)). Allocations pursuant to this Section shall be made in proportion to the amounts required to be allocated to each Member and Economic Interest Owner under this Section. The items to be so allocated shall be determined in accordance with Regulations Section 1.704-2(i)(4). This Section is intended to comply with the Minimum Gain Chargeback requirement contained in Regulations Section 1.704-2(i)(4) and shall be interpreted consistently therewith.

(c) Nonrecourse Deductions. Notwithstanding Section 6, any Nonrecourse Deductions (as defined Regulations Section 1.704-2(b)(1)) for any Fiscal Year or other period shall be specially allocated to the Members and Economic Interest Owners in proportion to their Economic Interests.

(d) Member Nonrecourse Deductions. Notwithstanding Section 6, those items of Company loss, deduction, or Code Section 705(a)(2)(B) expenditures which are attributable to Member Nonrecourse Debt for any Fiscal Year or other period shall be specially allocated to the Member or Economic Interest Owner who bears the economic risk of loss with respect to the Member Nonrecourse Debt to which such items are attributable in accordance with Regulations Section 1.704-1(i).

(e) Qualified Income Offset. Notwithstanding Section 6, if a Member or Economic Interest Owner unexpectedly receives any adjustments, allocations, or distributions described in Regulations Section 1.704-1(b)(2)(ii)(d)(4), (5) or (6), or any other event creates a deficit balance in such Member's Capital Account in excess of such Member's or Economic Interest Owner's share of Company Minimum Gain, items of Company income and gain shall be specially allocated to such Member or Economic Interest Owner in an amount and manner sufficient to eliminate such excess deficit balance as quickly as possible. Any special allocations of items of income and gain pursuant to this Section shall be taken into account in computing subsequent allocations of income and gain pursuant to this Article so that the net amount of any item so allocated and the income, gain, and losses allocated to each Member and Economic Interest Owner pursuant to this Article to the extent possible, shall be equal to the net amount that would have been allocated to each such Member and Economic Interest Owner pursuant to the provisions of this Section if such unexpected adjustments, allocations, or distributions had not occurred.

6.3 Tax Allocations.

(a) General Tax Allocations. Except as otherwise provided in this Agreement, every item of income, gain, loss, deduction, or credit of the Company shall be allocated for income tax purposes to each Member and Economic Interest Owner insofar as possible in accordance with the allocation of Net Profits and Net Losses for book accounting purposes.

(b) Contributed Property. In accordance with Code Section 704(c) and the Regulations thereunder, income, gain, loss and deduction with respect to any property contributed to the capital of the Company shall, solely for tax purposes, be allocated among the Members and Economic Interest Owners so as to take account of any variation between the adjusted basis of such property to the Company for federal income tax purposes and its fair market value on the date of contribution.

(c) Method of Allocations. The Manager shall make any elections or other decisions relating to tax allocations in a manner that reasonably reflects the intention of this Agreement. Allocations pursuant to this Section are solely for purposes of federal, state, and local taxes and shall not affect, or in any way be taken into account in computing, any Person's Capital Account or share of Net Profits, Net Losses, other items or distributions pursuant to any provision of this Agreement.

6.4 Allocation of Net Profits and Losses and Distributions in Respect of a Transferred Interest. If any Economic Interest is transferred, or is increased or decreased by reason of the admission of a new Member or otherwise, during any Fiscal Year of the Company, each item of income, gain, loss, deduction, or credit of the Company for such Fiscal Year shall be assigned pro rata to each day in the particular period of such fiscal year to which such item is attributable (i.e., the day on or during which it is accrued or otherwise incurred) and the amount of each such item so assigned to any such day shall be allocated to the Member or Economic Interest Owner based upon his, her or its respective Economic Interest at the close of such day.

However, for the purpose of accounting convenience and simplicity, the Company shall treat a transfer of, or an increase or decrease in, an Economic Interest which occurs at any time during a calendar month as having been consummated on the last day of such calendar month, regardless of when during the month such transfer, increase, or decrease actually occurs.

Notwithstanding any provision above to the contrary, gain or loss of the Company realized in connection with a sale or other disposition of any of the assets of the Company shall be allocated solely to the parties owning Economic Interests as of the date of such sale or other disposition occurs.

6.5 Obligations of Members to Report Allocations. The Members are aware of the income tax consequences of the allocations made by this Article and hereby agree to be bound by the provisions of this Article in reporting their shares of Company income and loss for income tax purposes.

ARTICLE 7

DISTRIBUTIONS

7.1 Distribution of Cash by the Company. Subject to applicable law and any limitations contained elsewhere in this Agreement, the Manager shall from time to time, at her own discretion, distribute Distributable Cash to the Members and Economic Interest Owners, which distributions shall to the Members and Economic Interest Owners in proportion to their Economic Interests.

All such distributions shall be made only to the Persons who, according to the books and records of the Company, are the holders of record of the Economic Interests in respect of which such distributions are made on the actual date of distribution. Neither the Company nor any Manager shall incur any liability for making distributions in accordance with this Section.

7.2 Form of Distribution. A Member or Economic Interest Owner, regardless of the nature of the Member or Economic Interest Owner's Capital Contribution, has no right to demand and receive any distribution from the Company in any form other than money. No Member or Economic Interest Owner may be compelled to accept from the Company a distribution of any asset in kind in lieu of a proportionate distribution of money being made to other Members and Economic Interest Owners. Except upon a dissolution and the winding up of the Company, no Member or Economic Interest Owner may be compelled to accept a distribution of any asset in kind.

7.3 Return of Distributions. Except for distributions made in violation of the Act or this Agreement, no Member or Economic Interest Owner shall be obligated to return any distribution to the Company or pay the amount of any distribution for the account of the Company or to any creditor of the Company. The amount of any distribution returned to the Company by a Member or Economic Interest Owner or paid by a Member or Economic Interest Owner for the account of the Company or to a creditor of the Company shall be added to the account or accounts from which it was subtracted when it was distributed to the Member or Economic Interest Owner.

ARTICLE 8

TRANSFER AND ASSIGNMENT OF INTERESTS

8.1 Transfer and Assignment of Interests. Except as otherwise provided in this Article, a Member may not transfer, assign, convey, sell, or encumber all or any part of such Member's Membership Interest without the consent of the Manager. Until the transferee of the Membership Interest or any portion thereof is admitted as a substitute Member pursuant to Section 8.3, the transferee shall have no right to vote or participate in the management of the business, property and affairs of the Company or to exercise any rights of a Member. Such transferee shall only be entitled to become an Economic Interest Owner and thereafter shall only receive the share of one or more of the Company's Net

Profits, Net Losses and distributions of the Company's assets to which the transferor of such Economic Interest would otherwise be entitled. After the consummation of any transfer of any part of a Membership Interest, the Membership Interest so transferred shall continue to be subject to the terms and provisions of this Agreement and any further transfers shall be required to comply with all the terms and provisions of this Agreement.

8.2 Restrictions on Transfer of Interests. In addition to other restrictions found in this Agreement, no Member shall transfer, assign, convey, sell, encumber or in any way alienate all or any part of his, her, or its Membership Interest: (i) without compliance with the Securities Act of 1933, as amended, the California Corporate Securities Law of 1968, as amended, or any other applicable securities laws, and (ii) if the Membership Interest to be transferred, assigned, sold or exchanged, when added to the total of all other Membership Interests sold or exchanged in the preceding twelve (12) consecutive months prior thereto, would cause the termination of the Company under the Code, as determined by the Manager. Any transfer in violation of this Section shall be null and void and the purported transferee shall not become either a Member or an Economic Interest Holder.

8.3 Substitution of Members. A transferee of a Membership Interest shall have the right to become a substitute Member only if: (i) the requirements of Section 8 relating to securities and tax requirements hereof are met; (ii) such Person executes an instrument satisfactory to the Manager accepting and adopting the terms and provisions of this Agreement; (iii) such Person executes or causes to be executed such additional documents that the Manager deems necessary or appropriate including, without limitation, a Consent of Spouse; (iv) such Person pays any reasonable expenses in connection with his, her, or its admission as a new Member, as determined by the Manager; and (v) the Manager consents to the substitution of the Member. The admission of a substitute Member shall not result in the release of the Member who assigned the Membership Interest from any liability that such Member may have to the Company. The Manager shall amend this Agreement to reflect the admission of a substitute Member pursuant to this Section and such amendment shall not require the vote or approval of the Members.

8.4 Transfers to Certain Family Members and Affiliates. Notwithstanding Section 8, the Membership Interest of any Member may be transferred subject to compliance with Section 8, by the Member by (i) gift, sale, or inheritance to any Member, or to the parent, children, grandchildren, sibling, or other issue of a Member or to a trust for any of aforementioned group, or to a trust to provide income to a spouse so long as the remainder interest is to pass to any of the aforementioned group, or (ii) to any Affiliate of the Member; it being agreed that in executing this Agreement, each Member has consented to such transfer. A transferee pursuant to this Section shall be an Economic Owner until and unless such transferee becomes a substitute Member pursuant to Section 8. Notwithstanding anything to the contrary in this Section and Section 8, a transferee of a Membership Interest who is already a Member, an Affiliate of a Member, or a trust for the benefit of a Member shall automatically become a substitute Member with respect to the transferred Membership Interest.

8.5 Effective Date of Transfer. The transfer of all or any portion of a Membership Interest shall be effective as of the date provided in Section 6 following the date upon which the requirements of Sections 8 and 8 have been met. Any transferee of a Membership Interest shall take subject to the restrictions on transfer imposed by this Agreement.

8.6 Rights of Legal Representative. If a Member who is an individual dies or is adjudged by a court of competent jurisdiction to be incompetent to manage the Member's person or property, the Member's executor, administrator, guardian, conservator, or other legal representative may exercise all of the Member's rights for the purpose of settling the Member's estate or administering the Member's property, including any power the Member has under the Articles or this Agreement to give an assignee the right to become a Member. If a Member is a corporation, trust, or other entity and is dissolved or terminated, the powers of that Member may be exercised by his, her, or its legal representative or successor.

8.7 Option to Purchase Membership Rights. Upon and contemporaneously with any transfer, assignment, conveyance or sale (whether arising out of an attempted charge upon that Member's Economic Interest by judicial process, a foreclosure by a creditor of the Member or otherwise) of a Member's Economic Interest (or portion thereof) which does not at the same time transfer the balance of the rights associated with the Membership Interest transferred by the Member (including, without limitation, the rights of the Member to vote or participate in the management of the business, property and affairs of the Company), the Company, in the sole discretion of the Manager, shall have the option to purchase from the Member, and if exercised, the Member shall sell to Company for a purchase price of ____________ ($_______), all remaining rights and interest retained by the Member that immediately before the transfer, assignment, conveyance or sale were associated with the transferred Economic Interest. The Manager, in her sole discretion, may assign the Company's option rights hereunder to any Member. Such purchase and sale shall not, however, result in the release of the Member from any liability to the Company as a Member nor a forfeiture of his, her, or its Economic Interest.

Each Member hereby acknowledges and agrees that the option granted to the Company to purchase all remaining rights and interests retained by a Member who transfers his, her, or its Economic Interest (or portion thereof) which does not at the same time transfer the balance of the rights associated with the Membership Interest is not unreasonable under the circumstances existing as of the date hereof.

8.8 Right of First Refusal. Each time a Member or Economic Interest Owner ("Transferor") proposes to transfer, assign, convey, sell, encumber or in any way alienate all or any part of his, her, or its Membership or Economic Interest ("Interest") (or as required by operation of law or other involuntary transfer to do so), other than pursuant to Section 8, such Transferor shall first offer such Interest to the Company and the non-transferring Members in accordance with the following provisions: (a) Transferor shall deliver a written notice to the Company and the non-transferring Members stating (i) Transferor's bona fide intention to transfer such Interest, (ii) the name and address of the proposed transferee, (iii) the Interest to be transferred, and (iv) the purchase price in terms of payment for which the Transferor proposes to transfer such Interest. (b) Within thirty (30) days after receipt of the notice described above, or, if the transfer is by gift or inheritance, within thirty (30) days after the determination of the purchase price, each non-transferring Member shall notify the Manager in writing of his, her, or its desire to purchase a portion of the Interest being so transferred. The failure of any Member to submit a notice within the applicable period shall constitute an election on the part of that Member not to purchase any of the Interest which may be so transferred. Each Member so electing to purchase shall be entitled to purchase a portion of such Membership Interest in the same proportion that the Percentage Interest of such Member bears to the aggregate of the Percentage Interests of all of the Members electing to so purchase the Interest being transferred. In the event any Member elects to purchase none or less than all of his or her pro rata share of such Interest, then the other Members can elect to purchase more than their pro rata share. (c) If the Members fail to purchase the entire Interest being transferred, the Company may purchase any remaining share of such Interest. (d) Within ninety (90) days after receipt of the notice described above or the determination of the purchase price if a transfer by gift or inheritance, the Company and the Members electing to purchase such Interest shall have the first right to purchase or obtain such Interest upon the price and terms of payment designated in such notice. If such notice provides for the payment of non-cash consideration, the Company and such purchasing Members each may elect to pay the consideration in cash equal to the good faith estimate of the present fair market value of the non-cash consideration offered as determined by the Manager. (e) If the Transferor proposes to transfer the Interest by gift or inheritance to Persons other than those set forth in Section 8 and the Company and/or the non-transferring Members elect to purchase the Interest as set forth in this Section, then the purchase price and the terms shall be determined pursuant to purchase terms set forth in Sections 9 and 9 through 9. (f) If the Company or the non-transferring Members elect not to purchase or obtain all of the Interest designated in such notice, then the Transferor may transfer the Interest described in the notice to the proposed transferee, providing such transfer (i) is completed within thirty (30) days after the expiration of the Company's and the non-transferring Members' right to purchase such Interest, (ii) is made on terms no less favorable to the Transferor than as designated in the notice, and (iii) the requirements of Sections 8 and 8 relating to unanimous consent of non-transferring Members, securities and tax requirements hereof are met. If such Membership Interest is not so transferred, the Transferor must give notice in accordance with this Section prior to any other or subsequent transfer of such Membership Interest.

8.9 Dissolution of Marriage. In the event of any dissolution of marriage of any married Member decreed by a court of competent jurisdiction, the Membership Interest shall be allocated and distributed between such Member ("Divorced Member") and his or her spouse pursuant to a court order or agreement, assignment, stipulation or otherwise ("Event of Divorce"); provided, however, that (i) no spouse shall become a Member of the Company by virtue of an Event of Divorce; (ii) any such spouse shall only be an Economic Owner; (iii) as between the Divorced Member and his or her spouse, if such Divorced Member retains a Membership Interest in the Company following such transfer of Economic Interest to his or her spouse, such Divorced Member shall, pursuant to Corporations Code Section 17301(a)(4), continue to have the exclusive right and authority to act as a Member with respect to the Economic Interest allocated or distributed to such Divorced Member's spouse; (iv) if the Divorced Member transfers his or her entire Membership Interest in the Company to the spouse, then neither the Divorced Member nor the spouse shall have any rights or authority to act as a Member and the Company shall have an option to purchase pursuant to Section 8 the balance of the rights associated with the Membership Interest not transferred to the spouse (including, without limitation, the rights of a Member to vote or participate in the management of the business, property and affairs of the Company); and (v) any action, consent or approval taken or given or any document or instrument executed by such Member on his or her own behalf (and on behalf of the spouse as an Economic Owner hereunder) shall be binding upon such Member and his or her spouse, and the other Members and any third party shall be entitled to rely on any action so taken by such Member in accordance herewith.

Notwithstanding anything to the contrary, an Event of Divorce shall be a transfer for purposes of Section 8 of that portion of the Divorced Member's Membership Interest allocated and distributed to his or her spouse. The Company and the non-transferring Members shall have the right to purchase such Membership Interest and all terms and conditions of Section 8 shall apply, except that (i) the purchase price shall be the value of the Membership Interest stipulated, agreed to or established in the settlement agreement, court order, or consent, whichever is applicable, or if none, determined in accordance with Section 9, and (ii) the purchase price shall be paid in cash.

ARTICLE 9

CONSEQUENCES OF WITHDRAWAL, DEATH, DISSOLUTION, OR BANKRUPTCY OF MEMBER

9.1 Dissociation. The occurrence of a Dissociation Event shall not dissolve the Company.

9.2 Withdrawal. Upon the withdrawal of a Member in accordance with Section 4, the Company may elect to purchase the withdrawing Member's Membership Interest pursuant to the terms set forth in this Article or may allow the Remaining Members to do so pursuant to Section 9. If the Company elects to purchase the withdrawing Member's Membership Interest, the Manager shall give the withdrawing Member notice of the Company's election to purchase such withdrawing Member's Membership Interest within thirty (30) days following affirmative vote or written consent of the remaining Members consenting to the withdraw pursuant to Section 4.

9.3 Purchase Price. If the Company and/or the remaining Members elect to purchase the Former Member's Interest, the Company and the Former Member or the Former Member's legal representative shall set the purchase price ("Purchase Price") for the Former Member's Interest by mutual agreement. If the parties cannot agree within thirty (30) days of the event triggering the obligation to purchase and/or sale, then the Purchase Price of the Former Member's Interest shall be determined by appraisal.

Within fifteen (15) days following the expiration of the thirty (30) day period, the Company and the Former Member or the Former Member's legal representative each shall appoint an independent appraiser to give an opinion as to the value of the Former Member's Interest. If either party fails to so designate an appraiser, the appraisal of the one (1) appraiser appointed shall be conclusive. Each appraiser shall deliver such written opinion to the Manager and to the Former Member or the Former Member's legal representative within thirty (30) days after his or her appointment.

If the two opinions of value differ by not more than ten percent (10%) of the higher opinion of value, then the value of the Former Member's Interest shall be deemed to be the average of the two opinions of value. If the two opinions of value differ by more than ten percent (10%) of the higher opinion of value, then the appraisers shall, within ten (10) days after delivery of their opinions of value, jointly select a third qualified appraiser who shall review the previous two appraisals, perform his or her own independent appraisal, and then select a value for the Former Member's Interest that is not higher than the higher nor lower than the lower of the first two opinions of value. The third appraiser shall deliver his or her written opinion of value to the Company and the Former Member or the Former Member's legal representative within thirty (30) days after appointment, and it shall be binding on the parties as the value of the Former Member's Interest.

The decision of the appraisers as provided hereinabove shall be final, conclusive and binding on all parties. The Manager shall notify all the remaining Members of the Purchase Price within ten (10) days after the Purchase Price is determined pursuant to this Section. Each of the parties shall pay one-half of all reasonable and proper costs and expenses of the appraisals; provided however, that each party shall bear his, her or its respective attorneys' fees incurred in connection with the appraisal procedure. The Members intend and hereby agree that all of the appraisers acting hereunder, however appointed shall be qualified by profession and/or experience to make the evaluation required hereunder. Also, the Members intend and hereby agree that any appraisal of a Former Member's Interest in the Company shall take into consideration all appropriate discounts.

9.4 Notice of Intent to Purchase. Within thirty (30) days after the remaining Members have been notified as to the Purchase Price of the Former Member's Interest determined in accordance with Section 9, each Remaining Member shall notify the Manager in writing of his, her, or its desire to purchase a portion of the Former Member's Interest. The failure of any Remaining Member to submit a notice within the applicable period shall constitute an election on the part of the Member not to purchase any of the Former Member's Interest. Each Remaining Member so electing to purchase shall be entitled to purchase a portion of the Former Member's Interest in the same proportion that the Percentage Interest of the Remaining Member bears to the aggregate of the Percentage Interests of all of the Remaining Members electing to purchase the Former Member's Interest. If any Remaining Member elects to purchase none or less than all of his, her, or its pro rata share of the Former Member's Interest, then the Remaining Members can elect to purchase more than their pro rata share. If the Remaining Members fail to purchase the entire interest of the Former Member, the Company shall purchase any remaining share of the Former Member's Interest.

9.5 Payment of Purchase Price. The Purchase Price shall be paid by the Company or the Remaining Members, as the case may be, by either of the following methods, each of which may be selected separately by the Company or the Remaining Members: (a) The Company or the Remaining Members shall at the closing pay in cash the total Purchase Price for the Former Member's Interest; or (b) The Company or the Remaining Members shall pay at the closing one-fifth (1/5) of the Purchase Price in which case the balance of the Purchase Price shall then be paid in four equal annual principal installments, plus accrued interest, and be payable each year on the anniversary date of the closing. The unpaid principal balance shall accrue interest at the current applicable federal rate as provided in the Code for the month in which the initial payment is made, but the Company and the Remaining Members shall have the right to prepay in full or in part at any time without penalty. The obligation to pay the balance due shall be evidenced by a promissory note, and if purchased by a Remaining Member, secured by a pledge of the Membership Interest being purchased.

9.6 Closing of Purchase of Former Member's Interest. The closing for the sale of a Former Member's Interest pursuant to this Article shall be held at the principal office of Company no later than sixty (60) days after the determination of the Purchase Price, except that if the closing date falls on a Saturday, Sunday, or California legal holiday, then the closing shall be held on the next succeeding business day. At the closing, the

Former Member or such Former Member's legal representative shall deliver to the Company or the Remaining Members an instrument of transfer (containing warranties of title and no encumbrances) conveying the Former Member's Interest. The Former Member or such Former Member's legal representative, the Company and the Remaining Members shall do all things and execute and deliver all papers as may be necessary to fully consummate such sale and purchase in accordance with the terms and provisions of this Agreement.

9.7 Purchase Terms Varied by Agreement. Nothing contained herein is intended to prohibit Members from agreeing upon other terms and conditions for the purchase by the Company or any Member of the Membership Interest of any Member in the Company desiring to retire, withdraw or resign, in whole or in part, as a Member.

ARTICLE 10

ACCOUNTING, RECORDS, REPORTING BY MEMBERS

10.1 Books and Records. The books and records of the Company shall be kept, and the financial position and the results of its operations recorded, in accordance with the accounting methods followed for federal income tax purposes. The books and records of the Company shall reflect all the Company transactions and shall be appropriate and adequate for the Company's business. The Company shall maintain at its principal office in California all of the following: (a) A current and past list of the full name and last known business or residence address of each Member and Economic Interest Owner set forth in alphabetical order, together with the Capital Contributions, Capital Account and Percentage Interest of each Member and Economic Interest Owner; (b) A current list of the full name and business or residence address of each Manager; (c) A copy of the Articles and any and all amendments thereto together with executed copies of any powers of attorney pursuant to which the Articles or any amendments thereto have been executed; (d) Copies of the Company's federal, state, and local income tax or information returns and reports, if any, for the six (6) most recent taxable years; (e) A copy of this Agreement and any and all amendments thereto together with executed copies of any powers of attorney pursuant to which this Agreement or any amendments thereto have executed; (f) Copies of the financial statements of the Company, if any, for the six (6) most recent Fiscal Years; and (g) The Company's books and records as they relate to the internal affairs of the Company for at least the current and past four (4) Fiscal Years.

10.2 Delivery to Members and Inspection.

(a) Upon the request of any Member for purposes reasonably related to the interest of that Person as a Member, the Manager shall promptly deliver to the requesting Member, at the expense of the Company, a copy of the information required to be maintained by Sections 10, 10 and 10.

(b) Each Member has the right, upon reasonable request for purposes reasonably related to the interest of the Person as a Member, to: (i) inspect and copy during normal business hours any of the Company records described in Sections 10 through 10; and (ii) obtain from the Company, promptly after their becoming available, a copy of the Company's federal, state, and local income tax or information returns for each Fiscal Year.

(c) Any request, inspection or copying by a Member under this Section may be made by that Person or that Person's agent or attorney.

(d) The Manager shall promptly furnish to a Member a copy of any amendment to the Articles or this Agreement executed by the Manager pursuant to a power of attorney from the Member.

10.3 Annual Statements.

(a) The Manager shall cause to be prepared at least annually, at Company expense, information necessary for the preparation of the Members' and Economic Interest Owners' federal and state income tax returns. The Manager shall send or cause to be sent to each Member or Economic Interest Owner within ninety (90) days after the end of each taxable year such information as is necessary to complete federal and state income tax or information returns, and a copy of the Company's federal, state, and local income tax or information returns for that year.

(b) The Manager shall cause to be filed at least annually with the California Secretary of State the statement required under Corporations Code Section 17060.

10.4 Filings. The Manager, at Company expense, shall cause the income tax returns for the Company to be prepared and timely filed with the appropriate authorities. The Manager, at Company expense, shall also cause to be prepared and timely filed, with appropriate federal and state regulatory and administrative bodies, amendments to, or restatements of, the Articles and all reports required to be filed by the Company with those entities under the Act or other then current applicable laws, rules, and regulations. If a Manager required by the Act to execute or file any document fails, after demand, to do so within a reasonable period of time or refuses to do so, any other Manager or Member may prepare, execute and file that document with the Secretary of the State.

10.5 Bank Accounts. The Manager shall maintain the funds of the Company in one or more separate bank accounts in the name of the Company, and shall not permit the funds of the Company to be commingled in any fashion with the funds of any other Person.

10.6 Accounting Decisions and Reliance on Others. All decisions as to accounting matters, except as otherwise specifically set forth herein, shall be made by the Manager. The Manager may rely upon the advice of the Company's accountants as to whether such decisions are in accordance with accounting methods followed for federal income tax purposes.

10.7 Tax Matters for the Company Handled by Manager and Tax Matters Partner. The Manager shall from time to time cause the Company to make such tax elections as they deem to be in the best interests of the Company and the Members. The Tax Matters Partner, as defined in Code Section 6231, shall represent the Company (at the Company's expense) in connection with all examinations of the Company's affairs by tax authorities, including resulting judicial and administrative proceedings, and shall expend the Company funds for professional services and costs associated therewith. The Tax Matters Partner shall oversee the Company tax affairs in the overall best interest of the Company. If for any reason the Tax Matters Partner can no longer serve in that capacity or ceases to be a Member or Manager, as the case may be, Members holding a Majority Interest may designate another to be Tax Matters Partner.

ARTICLE 11
DISSOLUTION AND WINDING UP

11.1 Dissolution. The Company shall be dissolved, its assets shall be disposed of, and its affairs wound up on the first to occur of the following: (a) Upon the happening of any event of dissolution specified in the Articles; (b) Upon the entry of a decree of judicial dissolution pursuant to Section 17351 of the Corporations Code; or (c) Upon the vote of Members holding a Majority Interest and the consent of all the Managers.

11.2 Certificate of Dissolution. As soon as possible following the occurrence of any of the events specified in Section 11, the Managers who have not wrongfully dissolved the Company, or, if none, a Member shall execute a Certificate of Dissolution in such form as shall be prescribed by the California Secretary of State and file the Certificate as required by the Act.

11.3 Winding Up. Upon the occurrence of any event specified in Section 11, the Company shall continue solely for the purpose of winding up its affairs in an orderly manner, liquidating its assets, and satisfying the claims of its creditors. The Managers who have not wrongfully dissolved the Company, or, if none, the Members shall (i) be responsible for overseeing the winding up and liquidation of Company, (ii) take full account of the liabilities of Company and assets, (iii) either cause its assets to be sold or distributed, and if sold as promptly as is consistent with obtaining the fair market value thereof, and (iv) cause the sale proceeds and/or the assets, to the extent sufficient therefore, to be applied and distributed as provided in Section 11. The Persons winding up the affairs of the Company shall give written notice of the commencement of winding up by mail to all known creditors and claimants whose addresses appear on the records of the Company. The Manager or Members winding up the affairs of the Company shall be entitled to reasonable compensation for such services.

11.4 Distributions in Kind. Except as provided in Section 7, any non-cash asset distributed to one or more Members shall first be valued at its fair market value to determine the Net Profit or Net Loss that would have resulted if such asset were sold for such value, such Net Profit or Net Loss shall then be allocated pursuant to Article 6, and the Members' Capital Accounts shall be adjusted to reflect such allocations. The amount distributed and charged to the Capital Account of each Member receiving an interest in such distributed asset shall be the fair market value of such interest (net of any liability secured by such asset that such Member assumes or takes subject to). The fair market value of such asset shall be determined by the Manager or by the Members or if any Member objects by an independent appraiser (any such appraiser must be recognized as an expert in valuing the type of asset involved) selected by the Manager or liquidating trustee and approved by the Members.

11.5 Order of Payment of Liabilities Upon Dissolution.

(a) After determining that all known debts and liabilities of the Company in the process of winding up, including, without limitation, debts and liabilities to Members who are creditors of the Company, have been paid or adequately provided for, the remaining assets shall be distributed to the Members in accordance with their positive Capital Account balances, after taking into account income and loss allocations for the Company's taxable year during which liquidation occurs. Such liquidating distributions shall be made by the end of the Company's taxable year in which the Company is liquidated, or, if later, within ninety (90) days after the date of such liquidation.

(b) The payment of a debt or liability, whether the whereabouts of the creditor is known or unknown, has been adequately provided for if payment thereof has been assumed or guaranteed in good faith by one or more financially responsible persons or by the United States government or any agency thereof, and the provision, including the financial responsibility of the Person, was determined in good faith and with reasonable care by the Manager or Members to be adequate at the time of any distribution of the assets pursuant to this Section. This Section shall not prescribe the exclusive means of making adequate provision for debts and liabilities.

11.6 Compliance with Regulations. All payments to the Members upon the winding-up and dissolution of Company shall be made strictly in accordance with the positive Capital Account balance limitation and other requirements of Regulations Section 1.704-1(b)(2)(ii)(d).

11.7 Limitations on Payments Made in Dissolution. Except as otherwise specifically provided in this Agreement, each Member shall only be entitled to look solely at the assets of Company for the return of his, her, or its positive Capital Account balance and shall have no recourse for his, her, or its Capital Contribution and/or share of Net Profits (upon dissolution or otherwise) against the Manager or any other Member except as provided in Article 12.

11.8 Certificate of Cancellation. Upon the completion of the winding up of the affairs and distribution of all of the assets of the Company as provided in this Article or when a domestic limited liability company is not the surviving entity, the Manager or Members who filed the Certificate of Dissolution shall cause to be filed in the office of, and on a form prescribed by, the Secretary of State, a certificate of cancellation of the Articles.

11.9 No Action Causing Dissociation. Except as expressly permitted in this Agreement, a Member shall not take any action that directly causes a Dissociation Event.

ARTICLE 12

INDEMNIFICATION AND INSURANCE

12.1 Indemnification of Any Agents. The Company shall indemnify any Member or Manager and may indemnify any other Person who was or is a party or is threatened to be made a party to any threatened, pending or completed action, suit or proceeding by reason of the fact that he, she, or it is or was a Member, Manager, officer, employee or other agent of the Company or that, being or having been such a Member, Manager, officer, employee or agent, he, she, or it is or was serving at the request of the Company as a manager, director, officer, employee or other agent of another limited liability company, corporation, partnership, joint venture, trust or other enterprise (all such persons being referred to hereinafter as an “agent”), to the fullest extent permitted by applicable law in effect on the date hereof and to such greater extent as applicable law may hereafter from time to time permit.

12.2 Insurance. The Company shall have the power to purchase and maintain insurance on behalf of any Person who is or was an agent of the Company against any liability asserted against such Person and incurred by such Person in any such capacity, or arising out of such Person’s status a an agent, whether or not the Company would have the power to indemnify such Person against such liability under the provisions of Section 12 or under applicable law.

ARTICLE 13
INVESTMENT REPRESENTATIONS

Each Member hereby represents and warrants to, and agrees with, the Manager, the other Members, and the Company as follows:

13.1 Preexisting Relationship or Experience.

(a) Such Member has a preexisting personal or business relationship with the Company, the Manager or control persons; or

(b) By reason of such Member's business or financial experience, or by reason of the business or financial experience of his, her, or its financial advisor who is unaffiliated with and who is not compensated, directly or indirectly, by the Company or any Affiliate or selling agent of the Company, he, she, or it is capable of evaluating the risks and merits of an investment in the Membership Interest and of protecting his, her, or its own interests in connection with this investment.

13.2 No Advertising. Such Member has not seen, received, been presented with, or been solicited by any leaflet, public promotional meeting, newspaper or magazine article or advertisement, radio or television advertisement, or any other form of advertising or general solicitation with respect to the sale of the Membership Interest.

13.3 Investment Intent. Such Member is acquiring the Membership Interest for investment purposes for his, her, or its own account only and not with a view to or for sale in connection with any distribution of all or any part of the Membership Interest. No other person will have any direct or indirect beneficial interest in or right to the Membership Interest.

13.4 Purpose of Entity. If the Member is a corporation, partnership, limited liability company, trust, or other entity, it was not organized for the specific purpose of acquiring the Membership Interest.

13.5 Residency. Such Member is a resident of the State of California.

13.6 Economic Risk. Such Member is financially able to bear the economic risk of an investment in the Membership Interest, including the total loss thereof.

13.7 No Registration of Membership Interest. Such Member acknowledges that the Membership Interest has not been registered under the Securities Act of 1933, as amended (the "Securities Act"), or qualified under the California Corporate Securities Law of 1968, as amended, or any other applicable securities laws in reliance, in part, on such Member's representations, warranties, and agreements herein.

13.8 Membership Interest in Restricted Security. Such Member understands that the Membership Interest is a "restricted security" under the Securities Act in that the Membership Interest will be acquired from the Company in a transaction not involving a public offering, and that the Membership Interest may be resold without registration under the Securities Act only in certain limited circumstances and that otherwise the Membership Interest must be held indefinitely.

13.9 No Obligation to Register. Such Member represents, warrants, and agrees that the Company and the Manager are under no obligation to register or qualify the Membership Interest under the Securities Act or under any state securities law, or to assist such Member in complying with any exemption from registration and qualification.

13.10 No Disposition in Violation of Law. Without limiting the representation set forth above, and without limiting Article 8 of this Agreement, such Member will not make any disposition of all or any part of the Membership Interest which will result in the violation by such Member or by the Company of the Securities Act, the

California Corporate Securities Law of 1968, or any other applicable securities laws. Without limiting the foregoing, such Member agrees not to make any disposition of all or any part of the Membership Interest unless and until: (a) There is then in effect a registration statement under the Securities Act covering such proposed disposition and such disposition is made in accordance with such registration statement and any applicable requirements of state securities laws; or (b) Such Member has notified the Company of the proposed disposition and has furnished the Company with a detailed statement of the circumstances surrounding the proposed disposition, and if reasonably requested by the Manager, such Member has furnished the Company with a written opinion of counsel, reasonably satisfactory to the Company, that such disposition will not require registration of any securities under the Securities Act or the consent of or a permit from appropriate authorities under any applicable state securities law.

13.11 Legends. Such Member understands that the certificates (if any) evidencing the Membership Interest may bear one or all of the following legends: (a) "THE SECURITIES REPRESENTED BY THIS AGREEMENT HAVE NOT BEEN REGISTERED UNDER THE SECURITIES ACT OF 1933 NOR REGISTERED NOR QUALIFED UNDER ANY STATE SECURITIES LAWS. SUCH SECURITES MAY NOT BE OFFERED FOR SALE, SOLD, DELIVERED AFTER SALE, TRANSFERRED, PLEDGED, OR HYPOTHECATED UNLESS QUALIFED AND REGISTERED UNDER APPLICABLE STATE AND FEDERAL SECURITIES LAWS OR UNLESS, IN THE OPINION OF COUNSEL SATISFACTORY TO THE COMPANY, SUCH QUALIFICATION AND REGISTRATION IS NOT REQUIRED. ANY TRANSFER OF THE SECURITIES REPRESENTAED BY THIS AGREEMENT IS FURTHER SUBJECT TO OTHER RESTRICTIONS, TERMS, AND CONDITIONS WHICH ARE SET FORTH HEREIN." (b) Any legend required by applicable state securities laws.

13.12 Investment Risk. Such Member acknowledges that the Membership Interest is a speculative investment which involves a substantial degree of risk or loss by the Member of such Member's entire investment in the Company, that such Member understands and takes full cognizance of the risk factors related to the purchase of the Membership Interest, and that the Company is newly organized.

13.13 Investment Experience. Such Member is an experienced investor in unregistered and restricted securities of speculative and high-risk ventures.

13.14 Restrictions on Transferability. Such Member acknowledges that there are substantial restrictions on the transferability of the Membership Interest pursuant to this Agreement, that there is no public market for the Membership Interest and none is expected to develop, and that, accordingly, it may not be possible for the Member to liquidate such Member's investment in the Company.

13.15 Information Reviewed. Such Member has received and reviewed all information the Member considers necessary or appropriate for deciding whether to purchase the Membership Interest. Such Member has had an opportunity to ask questions and receive answers from the Company and its officers, Manager and employees regarding the terms and conditions of purchase of the Membership Interest and regarding the business, financial affairs, and other aspects of the Company and has further had the opportunity to obtain all information (to the extent the Company possesses or can acquire such information without unreasonable effort or expense) which such Member deems necessary to evaluate the investment and to verify the accuracy of information otherwise provided to such Member.

13.16 No Representations By Company. Neither any Manager, any agent or employee of the Company or of any Manager, nor any other Person has at any time expressly or implicitly represented, guaranteed, or warranted to such Member that the Member may freely transfer the Membership Interest, that a percentage of profit and/or amount or type of consideration will be realized as a result of an investment in the Membership Interest, that past performance or experience on the part of the Manager or his Affiliates or any other person in any way indicates the predictable results of the ownership of the Membership Interest or of the overall Company business, that any cash distributions from Company operations or otherwise will be made to the Members by any specific date or will be made at all, or that any specific tax benefits will accrue as a result of an investment in the Company.

13.17 Consultation with Attorney. Such Member has been advised to consult with such Member's own attorney regarding all legal matters concerning an investment in the Company and the tax consequences of participating in the Company, and has done so, to the extent such Member considers necessary.

13.18 Tax Consequences. Such Member acknowledges that the tax consequences to the Member's investment in the Company will depend on the Member's particular circumstances, and neither the Company, the Manager, the Members, nor the partners, shareholders, agents, officers, directors, employees, Affiliates, or consultants of any of them will be responsible or liable for the tax consequences to him, her, or it of an investment in the Company. Such Member will look solely to, and rely upon, such Member's own advisers with respect to the tax consequences of this investment.

13.19 No Assurance of Tax Benefits. Such Member acknowledges that there can be no assurance that the Code or the Regulations will not be amended or interpreted in the future in such a manner so as to deprive the Company and the Members of some or all of the tax benefits they might now receive, nor that some of the deductions claimed by the Company or the allocations of items of income, gain, loss, deduction, or credit among the Members may not be challenged by the Internal Revenue Service.

13.20 Indemnity. Such Member shall indemnify and hold harmless the Company, each and every Manager, each and every other Member, and any officers, directors, shareholders, employees, partners, agents, attorneys, registered representatives, and control persons of any such entity who was or is a party or is threatened to be made a party to any threatened, pending, or completed action, suit, or proceeding, whether, civil, criminal, administrative, or investigative, by reason of or arising from any misrepresentation or misstatement of facts or omission to represent or state facts made by such Member including, without limitation, the information in this Agreement, against losses, liabilities, and expenses of the Company, each and every Manager, each and every other Member, and any officers, directors, shareholders, employees, partners, attorneys, accountants, agents, registered representatives, and control persons of any such Person (including attorneys' fees, judgments, fines, and amounts paid in settlement, payable as incurred) incurred by such Person in connection with such action, suit, proceeding, or the like.

ARTICLE 14

MISCELLANEOUS

14.1 Complete Agreement. This Agreement and the Articles constitute the complete and exclusive statement of agreement among the Members and Manager with respect to the subject matter herein and therein and replace and supersede all prior written and oral agreements or statements by and among the Members and Manager or any of them. No representation, statement, condition or warranty not contained in this Agreement or the Articles will be binding on the Members or Manager or have any force or affect whatsoever. To the extent that any provision of the Articles conflict with any provision of this Agreement, the Articles shall control.

14.2 Binding Effect. Subject to the provisions of this Agreement relating to transferability, this Agreement will be binding upon and inure to the benefit of the Members, and their respective successors and assigns.

14.3 Parties in Interest. Except as expressly provided in the Act, nothing in this Agreement shall confer any rights or remedies under or by reason of this Agreement on any Persons other than the Members and Manager and their respective successors and assigns, nor shall anything in this Agreement relieve or discharge the obligation or liability of any third person to any party to this Agreement, nor shall any provision give any third person any right of subrogation or action over or against any party to this Agreement.

14.4 Pronouns; Statutory References. All pronouns and all variations thereof shall be deemed to refer to the masculine, feminine, or neuter, singular or plural, as the context in which they are used may require. Any reference to the Code, the Regulations, the Act, Corporations Code or other statutes or laws will include all amendments, modifications, or replacements of the specific sections and provisions concerned.

14.5 Headings. All headings herein are inserted only for convenience and ease of reference and are not to be considered in the construction or interpretation of any provision of this Agreement.

14.6 Interpretation. In the event any claim is made by any Member relating to any conflict, omission or ambiguity in this Agreement, no presumption or burden of proof or persuasion shall be implied by virtue of the fact that this Agreement was prepared by or at the request of a particular Member or his, her, or its counsel.

14.7 References to this Agreement. Numbered or lettered articles, sections and subsections herein contained refer to articles, sections and subsections of this Agreement unless otherwise expressly stated.

14.8 Jurisdiction. Each Member hereby consents and acknowledges that this Agreement is executed and intended to be performed in the State of California, and the laws of that state shall govern its interpretation and effect. Any disputes between or among the then Members concerning enforcement of the terms of this Agreement shall be tried in the United States District Court for the Northern District Court of California in San Jose or the Santa Clara County Superior or Municipal Court. Each Member further agrees that personal jurisdiction over him, her, or it may be effected by service of process by certified mail addressed as provided in Section 14 of this Agreement, and when so made shall be as if served upon him, her, or it personally within the State of California.

14.9 Exhibits. All Exhibits attached to this Agreement are incorporated and shall be treated as if set forth herein.

14.10 Severability. If any provision of this Agreement or the application of such provision to any Person or circumstance shall be held invalid, the remainder of this Agreement or the application of such provision to Persons or circumstances other than those to which it is held invalid shall not be affected thereby.

14.11 Additional Documents and Acts. Each Member agrees to execute and deliver such additional documents and instruments and to perform such additional acts as may be necessary or appropriate to effectuate, carry out and perform all of the terms, provisions, and conditions of this Agreement and the transactions contemplated hereby.

14.12 Notices. Any notice to be given or to be served upon the Company or any party hereto in connection with this Agreement must be in writing (which may include facsimile), and will be deemed to have been given and received when delivered to the address specified by the party to receive the notice. Such notices will be given to a Member or Manager at the address specified in **Exhibit A** hereto. Any party may, at any time by giving five (5) days prior written notice to the other parties, designate any other address in substitution of the foregoing address to which such notice will be given.

14.13 Amendments. Except as specifically provided in Sections 4, 8 and elsewhere in this Agreement, all amendments to this Agreement will be in writing and signed by all the Members. All amendments to the Articles shall require the vote, approval or consent of all the Members.

14.14 Covenant of Capacity to Sign. All Members covenant that they possess all necessary capacity and authority to sign and enter this Agreement. All individuals signing this Agreement for a Member which is a corporation, a partnership, or other legal entity, or signing under a power of attorney or as a trustee, guardian, conservator, or in any other legal capacity, covenant that they have the necessary capacity and authority to act for, sign, and bind the respective entity or principal on whose behalf they are signing. If a Member is not a natural person, neither the Company nor any Member will (i) be required to determine the authority of the individual signing this Agreement to make any commitment or undertaking on behalf of such entity or to determine any fact or circumstance bearing upon the existence of the authority of such individual, or (ii) be responsible for the application or distribution of proceeds paid or credited to individuals signing this Agreement on behalf of such entity.

14.15 No Interest in Company Property; Waiver of Action for Partition. No Member or Economic Interest Owner has any interest in specific property of the Company. Without limiting the foregoing, each Member and Economic Interest Owner irrevocably waives during the term of the Company any right that he, she, or it may have to maintain any action for partition with respect to the property of the Company.

14.16 Multiple Counterparts. This Agreement may be executed in two or more counterparts, each of which shall be deemed an original, but all of which shall constitute one and the same instrument.

14.17 Attorneys' Fees. In the event that any dispute between the Company and the Members or among the Members should result in litigation or arbitration, the prevailing party in such dispute shall be entitled to recover from the other party all reasonable fees, costs and expenses of enforcing any right of the prevailing party, including without limitation, reasonable attorneys' fees and expenses. In addition to the foregoing award for attorneys' fees, the prevailing party shall be entitled to its attorneys' fees incurred in any post-judgment proceedings to enforce any such judgment. The provisions set forth in this section shall survive the merger of these provisions into any judgment.

14.18 Time is of the Essence. All dates and times in this Agreement are of the essence.

14.19 Remedies Cumulative. The remedies under this Agreement are cumulative and shall not exclude any other remedies to which any person may be lawfully entitled.

14.20 Special Power of Attorney.

(a) Attorney In Fact. Each Member hereby grants the Manager a special power of attorney irrevocably making, constituting, and appointing the Manager as the Member's attorney in fact, with all power and authority to act in the Member's name and on the Member's behalf to execute, acknowledge and deliver and swear to in the execution, acknowledgment, delivery and filing of the following documents: (i) Promissory notes, security agreements, and/or UCC-1 financing statements (and all amendments thereto) to be delivered in connection of such Member's failure to make a capital contribution if required; (ii) Assignments of Membership Interest or other documents of transfer to be delivered in connection with the purchase or other transfer of a Membership Interest pursuant to Section 8, 8, 8 or 9; or (iii) Any other instrument or document that may be reasonably required by the Manager in connection with any of the foregoing or to reflect any reduction in the Member's Capital Account, Percentage Interest, Economic Interest or Membership Interest.

(b) Irrevocable Power. The special power of attorney granted pursuant to this Section (i) is irrevocable, (ii) is coupled with an interest, and (iii) shall survive a Member's death, incapacity or dissolution.

(c) Signatures. The Manager may exercise the special power of attorney granted in this Section by a facsimile signature of any Manager or by the signature of any Manager.

IN WITNESS WHEREOF, all of the Members of SMITH VENTURES, LLC, a California limited liability company, have executed this Agreement, effective as of the date written above.

MEMBERS:

Jane Smith **John Smith**

Exhibit A

MEMBER INFORMATION

Member Names	**Member Addresses**	**Capital Account**	**Percentage Interest**
John Smith	1234 Street Address City, State and Zip code	$	50%
Jane Smith	1234 Street Address City, State and Zip code	$	50%
		$	100%

MANAGER INFORMATION

Manager Name	**Manager Address**
Jane Smith	1234 Street Address City, State and Zip code

3. Management Agreement

SMITH VENTURES, LLC
AND
JANE SMITH
MANAGEMENT AGREEMENT

THIS MANAGEMENT AGREEMENT (this "Agreement") is made on ______, 20__ **BETWEEN**:

A. **SMITH VENTURES, LLC**, a California limited liability company, whose registered office is at ________________________ (the "SVLLC"); and

B. Jane Smith of **SMITH VENTURES, LLC**, a California limited liability company, whose registered office is at ____________________ (the "Manager").

WHEREAS the SVLLC wishes to appoint the Manager, and the Manager has agreed to act as the manager of the SVLLC and its Investments (as defined below) upon the following terms and conditions.

IT IS AGREED as follows:

ARTICLE I

DEFINITION OF TERMS

1.1 In this Agreement the following words and expressions shall have the following meanings respectively:

1.1.1 "**Affiliate**" shall mean, with respect to any Person, any other Person with regard to which the Person is controlling, controlled or commonly controlled. For purposes of the preceding sentence, "control" shall mean the power to direct the principal business management and activities of a Person, whether through ownership of voting securities, by agreement, or otherwise.

1.1.2 "**Articles**" means the articles of organization of the SVLLC as amended from time to time and any reference herein to an Article shall be taken to refer to the Articles unless otherwise specified.

1.1.3 "**Bank**" shall mean ______________.

1.1.4 "**Bankruptcy**" shall mean, with respect to a Person: (i) an assignment of all or substantially all of the assets of such Person for the benefit of its creditors generally; (ii) the commencement of any bankruptcy or insolvency case or proceeding against such Person which shall continue and remain unsuspended and in effect for a period of sixty (60) days; (iii) the filing by such Person of a petition, answer or consent seeking relief under any bankruptcy, insolvency or similar law; or (iv) the occurrence of any other event that is deemed to constitute bankruptcy for purposes of any applicable laws.

1.1.5 "**Board of Directors**" shall mean the Board of Directors of the SVLLC.

1.1.6 "**Business Day**" shall mean any day (other than a Saturday, Sunday or any statutory public holiday) when banks in the United States are open for normal business.

1.1.7 "**Cause**" shall mean any act that both (i) constitutes fraud, a felony relating to the Manager's role as a Member or Manager or involving moral turpitude, gross negligence in the management of the SVLLC, or a willful breach of a fiduciary duty arising under this Agreement and (ii) in the reasonable judgment of eighty percent (80%) in interest of the Members of the SVLLC, clearly reflects an unfitness to serve in a management capacity with regard to the SVLLC.

1.1.8 "**Close of Business**" shall mean 5:00 p.m., local time, in California.

1.1.9 "**Custodial Account**" shall mean that certain custodial account held by the Bank and opened by the SVLLC in accordance with the Custodial Agreement.

1.1.10 "**Custodial Agreement**" shall mean that certain Agreement on Custody of Venture Capital Account made by and among the SVLLC, the Manager, and the Bank.

1.1.11 "**Deposit Assets**" shall mean the assets that the SVLLC entrusts to the Bank's safeguarding according to the Custodial Agreement and other forms of assets derived from the operation or increment of the value of such assets, including all kinds of properties, creditors' rights and interests that also include the increment of SVLLC.

1.1.12 "**Fair Market Value**" shall have the meaning set forth on **Exhibit A**.

1.1.13 "**Fiscal Year**" shall mean the period beginning from January 1 to December 31.

1.1.14 "**Investment**" shall mean each and every investment that SVLLC makes from time to time and the assets and rights acquired by SVLLC, which are analogous to investment by nature, including Portfolio Securities.

1.1.15 "**Manager**" shall mean one or more Managers. Specifically, "Manager" shall mean Jane Smith, or any other Person that succeeds her in that capacity.

1.1.16 "**Managers Committee**" shall mean the committee of SVLLC managers that is set up pursuant to Clause 3.6 of this Agreement.

1.1.17 "**Person**" shall mean any individual or legal entity including but not limited to a partnership, corporation, limited liability company, non-corporate entity, trust, joint venture, government organ, or other domestic and overseas entities.

1.1.18 "**Portfolio Company**" shall mean any corporation or other business entity which is an issuer of securities held by SVLLC.

1.1.19 "**Portfolio Securities**" shall mean securities (including any interest in any non-publicly traded securities and promissory notes) issued by Portfolio Companies and held by SVLLC.

1.1.20 "**SVLLC Agreement**" shall mean that certain Joint Venture Agreement signed by and among the members of the SVLLC regarding the joint investment into and the establishing of the SVLLC.

1.1.21 "**SVLLC Fund Amount**" shall mean an amount that (as of the time of determination) is equal to the excess of the sum of: (i) the amount of cash (or Fair Market Value of property) released from the Custodial Account and paid to an account controlled by the investors of the SVLLC.

1.1.22 "**Unanimous Approval**" shall mean the approval of all Persons present or represented at a meeting and entitled to vote, provided that in respect of any proposal which was not described in the notice of meeting issued for such meeting, unanimous approval shall mean the approval of all Persons entitled to vote thereon whether or not present at such meeting.

1.2 In this Agreement, a reference to a Clause or Schedule, unless the context otherwise requires, is a reference to a clause of or a schedule to this Agreement.

1.3 The Schedules form part of this Agreement and shall have the same force and effect as if set out in the body of this Agreement and references to this Agreement include the Schedules.

1.4 The headings in this Agreement shall not affect the interpretation of this Agreement.

1.5 Any reference to the Manager includes a reference to its or their duly authorized agents or delegates.

ARTICLE 2

TERM OF AGREEMENT

2.1 The Agreement shall come into force as of the date the Articles were filed with the California Secretary of State, and the term of the Agreement shall be seven (7) years; *provided, however*, the Manager may extend the term of the Agreement for up to three periods of one year each.

ARTICLE 3

APPOINTMENT AND FUNCTIONS OF THE MANAGER

3.1 SVLLC hereby appoints the Manager to manage the day-to-day business and affairs of SVLLC and to manage the Investments on the terms contained in this Agreement.

3.2 Subject to Clause 3.6 hereof, without prejudice to the generality of Clause 3.1 above, the duties to be performed by the Manager on behalf of SVLLC shall include:

3.2.1 sourcing, identifying and evaluating suitable Investments for SVLLC;

3.2.2 introducing, deciding and establishing the Investments on behalf of SVLLC;

3.2.3 managing the investment activities, including but not limited to purchasing (or otherwise acquiring), selling (or otherwise disposing of) and invest in investments, moneys and other assets;

3.2.4 liaising with SVLLC and keeping SVLLC informed on matters relating to the Investments;

3.2.5 withdrawing from the Deposit Assets from time to tome to pay the Manager as contemplated under this Agreement or reimburse the Manager for expenditures incurred by the Manager on SVLLC 's behalf in connection with carrying out the Manager's obligations under this Agreement;

3.2.6 arranging for the payment and disbursements on behalf of SVLLC for (a) fees and taxes and other liabilities that may be imposed on SVLLC by competent governmental authorities, (b) fees and expenses incurred in connection with Clause 5 of this Agreement, and (c) other liabilities of SVLLC incurred in connection with transactions contemplated by this Agreement or in the ordinary course of business;

3.2.7 collecting the interests and dividends and other income and revenues derived from the investment made with the Deposit Assets on behalf of SVLLC;

3.2.8 releasing to SVLLC that portion of the Deposit Assets and Investments to which SVLLC is entitled pursuant to the Custodial Agreement;

3.2.9 supervising the record and maintenance of SVLLC's financial report;

3.2.10 introducing Portfolio Companies to SVLLC which will offer the Portfolio Company directed start-up services, including but not limited to, employee training, technique support, management service, business consultation (as appropriate) and arrange the appointment of the liaising with partners, directors and officers of each such Portfolio Company;

3.2.11 assisting with the winding-up and dissolution of SVLLC in accordance with the Articles following the expiration of the term of SVLLC or the occurrence of the cause(s) for termination as specified in the Articles; and

3.2.12 subject to other provisions of this Agreement, doing all things as may be reasonably requested by the Board (either in writing to the Manager or by a resolution of the Board) in relation to the business of SVLLC.

3.3 Without prejudice to the generality of Clause 4.2, the Manager is hereby granted sole and absolute authority, power and control over the Custodial Account and in the name of SVLLC to perform the following on a fully discretionary basis:

3.3.1 to issue orders and instructions with respect to the acquisition and disposition of investments, moneys and other assets of SVLLC;

3.3.2 to maintain the documents and certificates concerning the ownership of the Investments;

3.3.3 to exercise rights attaching to the investments by SVLLC;

3.3.4 to effect foreign exchange transactions on behalf of and for the Custodial Account of SVLLC in connection with any purchase, other acquisition, sale or other disposal of Investments;

3.3.5 to negotiate, enter into, and perform all contracts, agreements and other undertakings as may in the opinion of the Manager be necessary or advisable or incidental to the carrying out of the objectives of this Agreement (including the entering into of guarantees (exclusive of any financial guarantees) and undertaking in connection with an investment);

3.3.6 to negotiate the borrowing requirements of SVLLC and the provision of any underwriting and guarantees (exclusive of any financial guarantees) by SVLLC;

3.3.7 generally to do all other things as may in the Manager's opinion be reasonably required to manage the Deposit Assets and the Investments; and

3.3.8 to assist with execution of all relevant documentation to be entered into by, or at the request of, SVLLC.

3.4 The Manager is hereby authorized to manage the Custodial Account and the Investments in its sole and absolute discretion and SVLLC shall not interfere with the decisions made by the Manager.

3.5 Manager shall establish a Managers Committee in accordance with Clause 3.6. The Managers Committee's principal responsibility will be to administrate the Manager's fulfillment of its responsibility under Clause 3 of this Agreement, including but not limited to matters related to investment, management, disposal and withdrawal of the Investments. The Managers Committee shall meet regularly as appropriate and shall devote such time and energy as is reasonably necessary to diligently manage SVLLC business and affairs. It is understood that the members of the Managers Committee will fulfill their responsibilities pursuant to this Clause 3 from both within and outside of the United States.

3.6 The Managers Committee shall be comprised of one (2) members, namely John Smith and Jane Smith. All decisions of the Managers Committee shall be adopted by Unanimous Approval of the individual members of the Managers Committee. The individual members of the Managers Committee agree that the exercise of their collective powers and discretion as individual members of Managers Committee conferred under this Agreement shall be made through the Managers Committee.

3.7 SVLLC may appoint representatives to attend the regular meetings of the Managers Committee, to be informed of the investment decisions and operations of SVLLC, to participate in discussions and to table a proposal. However, SVLLC has no voting right and/or veto power with respect to any decision of the Managers Committee. Upon the Manager's request, SVLLC may recommend personnel to be employed by the

Manager as a permanent employee (he or she has to quit the previous job). The ultimate decision whether to employ the recommended person shall, however, be in the sole and absolute discretion of the Manager.

3.8 Any change in the membership or composition of the Managers Committee shall be approved, in writing, by the Board of Directors of the SVLLC.

ARTICLE 4

COMMITMENT AND AUTHORIZATION OF THE SVLLC

4.1 The SVLLC promise it shall deposit into the Custodial Account amounts sufficient to meet its obligations. The SVLLC hereby represents and warrants that it does not have (and will not have): (i) any assets other than the Deposit Assets and Investments held in the Custodial Account; or (ii) any Profits or Losses other than those which are attributable to the assets listed in the immediately preceding clause (i).

4.2 To ensure that the Manager is fully authorized by SVLLC to fulfill its obligation hereunder, unless otherwise regulated by this Agreement, the Manager is hereby fully delegated the sole and absolute authority to manage the Deposit Assets and the Investments and to administrate the daily operation and management of each Investment.

4.3 The SVLLC promises to appoint those directors of each Portfolio Company for which the SVLLC is entitled to appoint directors from among the candidates recommended by the Manager and to require them to exercise their powers as directors as directed by the Manager.

4.4 The SVLLC shall sign and deliver the documents relating to any Investment provided by the Manager, and provide all other required documents and signatures as the Manager may reasonably require.

ARTICLE 5

CONTINUATION AND EXERCISE OF RIGHTS OF MANAGER

5.1 The powers, rights, and authorities of the Manager herein contained are continuing ones and shall remain in full force and effect until revoked by termination of this Agreement and such revocation shall not affect any powers, rights, or authorities of the Manager exercised prior to the Manager's receipt of notice of such revocation.

ARTICLE 6

FEES AND EXPENSES

6.1 In consideration of the services to be performed by the Manager hereunder, SVLLC shall pay to the Manager throughout the term of this Agreement an annual management fee (the "**Management Fee**"). The Management Fee shall be payable quarterly in advance and shall be pro-rated on a daily basis for short fiscal periods, and additionally pro-rated on a daily basis at any time that there is an adjustment of the SVLLC Capital Commitment. The first payment of Management Fee shall be made at the signing of this Agreement. The annual Management Fee shall be equal to three percent (3%) of the SVLLC Capital Commitment. Commencing with the first complete fiscal year following the fifth anniversary after the filing of the Articles, the annual Management Fee rate shall be reduced by one quarter of one percentage (0.25%) point per year, but shall not in any event be reduced to less than one and one half percent (1.5%) of SVLLC's Capital Commitment. In addition, in the event of any increase in SVLLC's Capital Commitment, the SVLLC shall pay the Manager corresponding management fees, expenses and other expenditures in the amount and manner regulated in this article.

6.2 SVLLC shall reimburse or cause to be reimbursed to the Manager without set-off or deduction the following reasonable costs and expenses:

6.2.1 Any expenses which are not generally treated as normal operating expenses of the Manager (including salaries and benefits provided to employees of the Manager or its Affiliates, rent, communications, travel and similar expenses, investment and business consultant fees, and other expenses incurred in investigating, evaluating or monitoring investment opportunities) for fulfilling its obligations under this Agreement; and

6.2.2 Any SVLLC Expenses.

The SVLLC hereby warrants that the Manager has the right to draw the above-mentioned Management Fee, expenses and expenditures from the Deposit Assets and Investments pursuant to the Custodial Agreement.

6.3 The Management Fee and all other sums reimbursable or payable to the Manager under this Clause 6 shall be paid by SVLLC in priority to any other fees, costs and expenses of SVLLC (other than those priorities specifically required by applicable law).

ARTICLE 7

ACCOUNTING, VALUATIONS, RECORDS AND REPORTS

7.1 The Manager shall keep, or cause to be kept, on behalf of SVLLC such books, records, and Custodial Account statements as may be required to give a complete record of all transactions carried out by SVLLC on the recommendation of the Manager in relation to the investment and divestment of the Investments, and as will enable semi-annual progress reports of SVLLC to be prepared.

7.2 The Manager shall prepare and send to SVLLC on a or before September 1 (or if September 1 is not a Business Day, the immediately following Business Day) of each Fiscal Year of SVLLC a semi-annual progress report which includes a statement of Investments and other property and assets of SVLLC, details of Investments purchased, sold and otherwise disposed of during the relevant period and the cost and value of each Investment at the end of June 30 of such Fiscal Year and un-audited Custodial Account statements of SVLLC for the relevant period.

7.3 The Manager shall prepare, or shall assist with the preparation of, the audited Custodial Account statements of SVLLC, which shall be distributed with the report described in Clause 7.4 below.

7.4 On or before March 15 (or if March 15 is not a Business Day, the immediately following Business Day) following each Fiscal year of SVLLC, the Manager shall prepare, or arrange for the preparation of, and send to an annual report which includes a statement of Investments and other property and assets of SVLLC, details of the Investments purchased, sold and otherwise disposed of during the relevant period and the cost and value of each Investment at the end of December 31 of such Fiscal Year.

7.5 SVLLC shall promptly provide all reasonable information and such other reasonable assistance to the Manager as may be reasonably requested by the Manager, in performing its obligations under this Clause 7.

ARTICLE 8

POWER OF DELEGATION

8.1 The Manager may only delegate its powers to members of the Managers Committee.

8.2 Notwithstanding the foregoing, the Manager shall be entitled to retain, at its own expense, the services of investment advisers, to advise it on the Investments of SVLLC.

ARTICLE 9

TERM OF SVLLC

9.1 The term of the SVLLC shall be as set forth in its Articles; *provided* that such term shall expire no earlier than the term of this Agreement.

ARTICLE 10

REGULATORY COMPLIANCE

10.1 The Manager, in performing its obligations hereunder, shall use its reasonable best efforts to comply at all times with all applicable laws and with the terms of all licenses, permissions, authorizations and consents necessary to enable it to perform such obligations.

10.2 The parties shall reasonably co-operate with each other to reduce the imposition of taxes to the maximum extent possible. Notwithstanding the provisions of this Agreement to the contrary, the relationship between the Manager and SVLLC as evidenced by this Agreement shall be treated for federal, state and local income tax purposes in the United States as if SVLLC and its Investments' were a single partnership and all of the equity holders of SVLLC (which, solely for this purpose shall include the Manager) and its Investments' were constituent partners thereof. A Party shall not file (and each party hereby represents that it has not filed) any income tax election or other document in the United States that is inconsistent with the immediately preceding sentence.

ARTICLE 11

EXERCISE OF RIGHTS ATTACHED TO INVESTMENTS

11.1 Any rights conferred by Investments shall be exercised in such manner as the Manager may determine to be appropriate in its sole and absolute discretion. SVLLC shall from time to time upon request from the Manager execute and deliver or cause to be executed and delivered to the Manager or its nominee(s) such powers of attorney or proxies as may reasonably be required authorizing such attorneys or proxies to exercise any rights or otherwise act in respect of all or any part of the investments.

ARTICLE 12

LIABILITY AND INDEMNITY

12.1 None of the members of the Managers Committee, the Manager, or their respective directors, officers, employees or agents shall be liable to SVLLC, any Affiliate of SVLLC or any Shareholders for any action taken or not taken by them or for any action taken or not taken by any other person with respect to SVLLC or in respect of the Investments or Portfolio Companies provided that the Manager shall remain liable for its own respective acts and omissions arising from or in any way related to the fraud, negligence, willful default, willful violation of any applicable law or regulation or bad faith on the part of the Manager or any of its directors, officers, employees or agents acting as such.

12.2 SVLLC hereby indemnifies, and agrees to indemnify, upon demand, each of the members of the Managers Committee, the Manager, and each of their respective directors, officers, employees or agents against any losses, claims, demands, damages, liabilities (including liabilities in contract and in tort), proceedings, costs and expenses (including legal and other expenses reasonably incurred in connection with any of the foregoing) to which such Person may become subject by reason of its actual or alleged management of, or involvement in, the affairs of SVLLC (including such Person's involvement as an officer or director of a Portfolio Company); provided that this indemnity shall not apply in cases of fraud, negligence, willful default, willful violation of any applicable laws or regulation or bad faith on the part of the person seeking indemnification under this Clause 12.2.

ARTICLE 13

TERMINATION

13.1 Except when any of the following events occur, the Agreement shall not be terminated before the expiration of the term set forth in Clause 2: (a) As set forth in a written agreement executed after discussion by both Parties; (b) Bankruptcy, dissolution or liquidation of either Party; or (c) Any incident of force majeure under Clause 19, which materially frustrates the clear purposes of this Agreement.

13.2 On termination of this Agreement the Manager shall be entitled to receive all fees and other moneys accrued due but not yet paid to it up to the date of such termination as provided in this Agreement and shall repay on a pro rata basis fees and other moneys paid to it in respect of any period after the date of such termination. In addition to amounts payable under this Clause 13.2, SVLLC shall also pay to the Manager all such expenses referred to in Clause 6 to the extent to which the Manager is obliged to continue to make such payments beyond the date of termination of this Agreement.

13.3 After termination of this Agreement and subject to Clause 13.2, the Manager shall release to SVLLC the remaining Investments and Deposit Assets.

13.4 Upon termination of this Agreement, the Manager shall promptly deliver to SVLLC or as they shall direct, all books of Custodial Account, records, registers, correspondence and documents relating to the affairs of or belonging to SVLLC in the possession of or under the control of the Manager.

13.5 Clause 3.2.11 shall survive the termination of this Agreement. The termination of this Agreement shall be without prejudice to accrued rights and liabilities and any provisions expressed to survive the termination hereof.

ARTICLE 14

CONFIDENTIALITY

14.1 Each party to this Agreement shall, with respect to the other parties, maintain the full confidentiality, and not to disclose, any confidential information received by it regarding the business and affairs of the others. Each party further undertakes to the other parties not to make use of such confidential information other than for the purposes of this Agreement; *provided, however*, that such party may disclose such information to its employees, partners, directors, officers, advisers, agents or other Persons appointed or retained under Clause 8 to the extent necessary to fulfill the purposes of this Agreement, in which event it shall procure that any such employees, partners, directors, officers, advisers, agents or other persons are made aware of and comply with the obligations of confidentiality under this Agreement.

14.2 Clause 14.1 shall not apply to any information if:

14.2.1 the information is or becomes available to the public (other than through a breach of Clause 14.1);

14.2.2 the information is already known to the recipient, as evidenced by written records maintained in the ordinary course of its business, at the time it is furnished by the other party;

14.2.3 the information becomes known or available to a party from a Person other than the other party and such Person is not under an obligation of confidentiality or such information is independently developed by the recipient;

14.2.4 disclosure is required by law, regulation, a court of competent jurisdiction or any government authority; or

14.2.5 the disclosure of such information to a specified recipient has been agreed upon by the other party in writing provided that such information may only be disclosed subject to obtaining undertakings from such recipient to keep such information confidential.

14.3 The Manager shall be permitted to refer to the appointment made hereunder in its or other corporate literature.

ARTICLE 15

RELIANCE ON DOCUMENTS

15.1 Wherever pursuant to any provision of this Agreement any notice, instruction or other communication is to be given by, or on behalf of, SVLLC to the Manager, the Manager may accept as sufficient evidence thereof:

15.1.1 a document signed or purporting to be signed on behalf of SVLLC by such Person or Persons whose signature the Manager is for the time being authorized by SVLLC to accept; or

15.1.2 a message by telex, electronic mail or facsimile transmitted by, or on behalf of, SVLLC by such Person or Persons whose messages the Manager are for the time being authorized by SVLLC to accept, and the Manager shall not be obligated to accept any document or message signed or transmitted or purporting to be signed or transmitted by any other Person.

ARTICLE 16

NOTICES

16.1 Any and all notices, requests, demands and other communications required or otherwise contemplated to be made under this Agreement shall be in writing, in the English language, and shall be deemed to have been duly given in the absence of evidence of earlier receipt: (i) if delivered personally at the address set out below, when received; (ii) if transmitted by facsimile to the number set out below, upon receipt of an error-free transmittal report by the sender; (iii) if by international courier service, on the fourth (4th) business day (being a day on which banks in the United States are normally open for business) following the date of deposit with such courier service, or such earlier delivery date as may be confirmed to the sender by such courier service; or (iv) if sent by first class prepaid mail (airmail if overseas) on the seventh (7th) day following that on which the letter containing the same is posted, and in providing such service it shall be sufficient to demonstrate that such communication was properly addressed, stamped and posted by first class prepaid mail (airmail if overseas).

16.2 Notices, requests, demands and other communications required or otherwise contemplated to be made under this Agreement shall be delivered or sent as follows:

16.2.1 If to SVLLC:
Address:
Telephone:
Facsimile:
Attention:

16.2.2 If to Jane Smith:]
Address:
Telephone:
Facsimile:
Attention:

ARTICLE 17

CONFLICTS OF INTEREST AND SERVICES TO OTHERS

17.1 SVLLC recognizes and accepts that the functions and duties which the Manager undertakes on behalf of SVLLC shall not be exclusive and the Manager or any Affiliate or shareholder of the Manager may perform similar functions and duties for others.

17.2 SVLLC understands and agrees that the Manager and their Affiliates and shareholders may give advice and take action in the performance of their respective duties owed to any of their respective partners or associates which may differ from the advice given to or the nature of action recommended for SVLLC.

17.3 Notwithstanding any provisions of this Agreement to the contrary, the Manager or its Affiliates may cause one or more affiliated directed start-ups to enter into "Incubation Services Agreements" with one or more Portfolio Companies pursuant to which such incubators will provide office space and equipment as well as a variety of incubation services (collectively, the "Incubation Services") to such Portfolio Companies in exchange for cash and securities issued by such Portfolio Companies; *provided, however*, that, except to the extent the Manager or its beneficial owners have a residual interest in any employee bonus pool of any such incubator formed to hold securities issued by such Portfolio Companies in exchange for such Incubation Services, neither the Manager nor its beneficial owners shall have any beneficial interest in any such securities. For purpose of the preceding sentence, a "residual interest in any employee bonus pool" shall mean an interest in that position of any such pool, if any, which is forfeited by specific employees of such incubator pursuant to vesting arrangements. The SVLLC further acknowledges that the beneficial owners of the Manager: (i) may be involved in the management of the incubators; (ii) may own substantially all of the equity interests of the incubators; and (iii) may receive cash compensation from the incubators.

ARTICLE 18

ASSIGNMENT

18.1 No party hereto shall be entitled to assign or otherwise part with any interest in this Agreement or any of its rights or obligations hereunder in the form of lien, transfer or any other forms and any such lien, transfer or any other forms of transfer shall be null and void. Notwithstanding the above specific provisions and demonstration of intention of both parties, however, if due to implementation of the applicable law there is any result of transferring of any of the rights or interests hereunder then the transferee shall be subject to limitations, obligations and liabilities (including but limited to any obligation to return payments made under this Agreement and any duty to maintain the confidentiality of information) associated with interest transferred hereunder.

ARTICLE 19

FORCE MAJEURE

19.1 No party to this Agreement shall be treated as being in breach of its obligations under this Agreement if its failure to perform any such obligation is due solely to an event of force majeure (including, without limitation, act of God, storm, fire, flood, earthquake and other natural disasters, strike, lock-out, industrial dispute, legislation, governmental regulation or restriction, riot, civil war, civil disturbance, coup d'etat, international hostilities, are or any other cause) outside the reasonable control of that party. The party affected by such event of force majeure shall not later than seven (7) days after the commencement of such event give the other parties' notice of the event and shall use all reasonable means to resume full performance of its obligations under this Agreement as soon as possible.

ARTICLE 20

AMENDMENTS

20.1 Amendments to this Agreement shall be made only by written instrument signed by both parties. If all or part of this Agreement cannot be performed due to change of the laws or regulations or other policies, then the parties hereto shall, on the basis of friendly consultation, amend this Agreement according to the relevant laws and regulations and policies.

ARTICLE 21

SEVERABILITY

21.1 If any provision of this Agreement is found to be invalid or unenforceable, then such provision shall be construed, to the extent feasible, so as to render the provision enforceable and to provide for the consummation of the transactions contemplated hereby on substantially the same terms as originally set forth herein, and if no feasible interpretation would save such provision, it shall be severed from the remainder of this Agreement, which shall remain in full force and effect unless the severed provision is essential to the rights or benefits received by any party. In such event, the parties shall use their best efforts to negotiate, in good faith, a substitute, valid and enforceable provision or agreement which most nearly affects the parties' intent in entering this Agreement.

ARTICLE 22

GOVERNING LAW AND JURISDICTION

22.1 This Agreement is governed by, and shall be construed in accordance with the laws of the State of California.

ARTICLE 23

DISPUTE SETTLEMENT

23.1 Any dispute, controversy or claim arising out of or relating to this Agreement shall be resolved in accordance with the procedures specified in this Clause, which shall be the sole and exclusive procedure for the settlement of any such disputes.

23.2 Negotiation among the Parties:

23.2.1 The parties shall attempt in good faith to resolve any disputes arising out of or relating to this Agreement promptly by negotiation between the appointed representatives of the Manager and SVLLC.

23.2.2 If the dispute has not been resolved by the parties within thirty (30) days from the date of the disputing party's notice, or if the parties fail to meet within fifteen (15) days from the date of such notice, either party may initiate arbitration as provided hereinafter.

23.2.3 All negotiations pursuant to this Clause are on a confidential and without prejudice basis and shall be treated as compromise and settlement negotiations.

23.3 Arbitration:

23.3.1 The parties hereby agree that any dispute, controversy or claim arising out of or relating to this Agreement, or the breach or alleged breach thereof, or affecting this Agreement in any way, shall be resolved exclusively through arbitration held in Santa Clara, California, pursuant to the rules from the American Arbitration Association. The decision of the arbitrators shall be binding upon both parties in accordance with its then-effective arbitration procedural rules. Enforcement of an award arising in connection therewith may be entered in any court having jurisdiction thereof. The parties expressly acknowledge that, under the preceding sentence, they are waiving their right to seek a trial with regard to all matters for which arbitration is required. Any arbitration, mediation, court action, or other adjudicative proceeding arising out of or relating to this Agreement shall be held in the Santa Clara County are or, if such proceeding cannot be lawfully held in such location, as near thereto as applicable law permits. The parties hereby formally subject themselves exclusively to the venue, and personal and subject matter jurisdiction, of the courts located in the California Santa Clara County area for the purpose of: (i) enforcement of an award arising in connection with the arbitration set forth in this Clause 23.3.1; and (ii) the adjudication of any dispute, controversy or claim arising out of or relating to this Agreement for which arbitration is not required.

23.3.2 The provisions under this Clause 23 shall be independent and shall continue to have effect after termination and rescission of this Agreement.

23.4 Continued Performance:

23.4.1 Each party is required to continue to perform its obligations under this Agreement until the final resolution of any dispute arising out of or relating to this Agreement has been worked out.

ARTICLE 24
COUNTERPARTS

24.1 This Agreement may be executed in two or more counterparts, each of which shall be deemed an original, but all of which shall constitute one and the same instrument.

ARTICLE 25
WAIVER

25.1 No waiver of any default or breach hereunder shall be construed to constitute a waiver of such rights and any separate or part exercise of any right hereunder shall not construct any barrier to any future exercise of such rights. No rights of any party hereto will be deemed to be waived unless such waiver is in writing and signed by the authorized representative of the party intending to be bound.

IN WITNESS WHEREOF the parties hereto have caused this Agreement to be executed the day and year first above written.

SVLLC
By:

____

John Smith
Member

JANE SMITH
By:

____

Jane Smith
Managing Member

Exhibit A

"**Fair Market Value**" shall mean, as of the time of determination, the value of the asset in question as determined by the Manager (the "Valuation Party") in its sole and absolute discretion unless otherwise set forth herein. SVLLC shall be notified of such Fair Market Value determination within ninety (90) days of such determination; *provided, however*, a notice stating Fair Market Value shall not be required to be delivered more than once per calendar quarter. If, within thirty (30) days after a notice described in the immediately preceding sentence is mailed or otherwise furnished to SVLLC, a group of SVLLC equity holders whose aggregate capital interests in SVLLC exceed two-thirds (2/3) of the total capital interests in SVLLC held by all SVLLC equity holders (a "Two-Thirds-Interest") notifies the Valuation Party of their objection to the valuation of one or more assets set forth in such notice, the Valuation Partner shall re-determine the value of such assets and shall notify SVLLC of the results of such re-determination. If, within thirty (30) days after such notice, a Two-Thirds-Interest notifies the Valuation Party of their objection to such re-determined value and the Valuation Party thereafter declines to adjust such value in a manner that eliminated continued objection by a Two-Thirds-Interest, the value of the assets in question shall be determined in accordance with the Appraisal Procedure set forth below.

For purposes of this Agreement, "Appraisal Procedure" shall refer to the following steps: (i) The Valuation Party and SVLLC shall each provide the other with notice of their proposed value for the asset(s) in question; (ii) The Valuation Party and SVLLC shall each select an independent appraiser acceptable to the other party (which acceptance shall not be unreasonably withheld); (iii) The two appraisers shall jointly select a third appraiser; (iv) The third appraiser shall determine which of the proposed values is closest to the actual fair market value of the asset(s) in question (as of the time for which such value is to be determined); and (v) Such closest value shall be deemed to be the Fair Market Value of the asset(s) in question (as of the time for which such valuation has been determined) for all purposes under this Agreement.

Special Rules: (a) If there is an adjustment to the valuation of a Security following an objection by SVLLC, SVLLC Amount shall be adjusted accordingly, as determined by the Valuation Party in its reasonable discretion. However, no such valuation adjustment shall give rise to any recall, rescission, or reapportionment of any payment made prior to the time of such adjustment. (b) In determining SVLLC Amount, or in any accounting, no value shall be placed on the goodwill, going concern value, name, records, files, statistical data or similar assets of SVLLC not normally reflected in the accounting records of such fund, but there shall be taken into consideration any items of income earned but not yet received, expenses incurred but not yet paid, liabilities fixed or contingent, and prepaid expenses to the extent not otherwise reflected in the books of account as well as the Fair

Market Value of options or commitments to purchase or sell Securities pursuant to agreements entered into on or prior to the valuation date.

4. Articles of Incorporation

ARTICLES OF INCORPORATION

OF

____

I.

The name of this corporation is ________________.

II.

The purpose of this corporation is to engage in any lawful act or activity for which a corporation may be organized under the General Corporation Law of California other than the banking business, the trust company business or the practice of a profession permitted to be incorporated by the California Corporations Code.

III.

[OPTION 1:

The corporation is authorized to issue only one class of stock, to be designated Common Stock. The total number of shares of Common Stock presently authorized is _______ (___) [par value _______ (____) per share]*

* Companies may wish to state a par value for the shares (although not required under California law) as this may be useful in the foreign qualification process in the future.

OPTION 2:

This corporation is authorized to issue two classes of stock to be designated, respectively, "Common Stock" and "Preferred Stock." The total number of shares which the corporation is authorized to issue is _______ (_____) shares. _______ (_____) shares shall be Common Stock [par value _______ (_____)]* and _______ (_____) shares shall be Preferred Stock [par value _______ (_____) per share]*

* Companies may wish to state a par value for the shares (although not required under California law) as this may be useful in the foreign qualification process in the future.

The Preferred Stock may be issued from time to time in one or more series. The Board of Directors is hereby authorized, to fix or alter the dividend rights, dividend rate, conversion rights, voting rights, rights and terms of redemption (including sinking fund provisions), redemption price or prices, and the liquidation preferences of any wholly unissued series of Preferred Stock, and the number of shares constituting any such series and the designation thereof, or any of them and to increase or decrease the number of shares of any series subsequent to the issuance of shares of that series, but not below the number of shares of such series then outstanding. In case the number of shares of any series shall be so decreased, the shares constituting such decrease shall resume the status that they had prior to the adoption of the resolution originally fixing the number of shares of such series.]

IV.

The liability of the directors of this corporation for monetary damages shall be eliminated to the fullest extent permissible under California law.

(a) This corporation is authorized to provide indemnification of agents (as defined in Section 317 of the California Corporations Code) for breach of duty to the corporation and its shareholders through bylaw provisions or through agreements with the agents, or through shareholder resolutions, or otherwise, in excess of the indemnification otherwise permitted by Section 317 of the Corporations Code, subject to the limits on such excess indemnification set forth in Section 204 of the Corporations Code.

(b) Any repeal or modification of this Article shall only be prospective and shall not affect the rights under this Article in effect at the time of the alleged occurrence of any act or omission to act giving rise to liability or indemnification.

V.

The name and address in the State of California of this corporation's initial agent for service of process is:

____

____

____________________, California _________

IN WITNESS WHEREOF, for the purpose of forming this corporation under the laws of the State of California, the undersigned, as sole incorporator of this corporation, has executed these Articles of Incorporation this __________ day of _____, 20__.

____

[INCORPORATOR'S NAME]

Sole Incorporator

Options

1. For Professional Corporation – Article II should be changed pursuant to Section 202(b)(ii) of the Corporations Code.
2. For "Close Corporation" – Article II should contain the words: "this corporation is a close corporation," and an additional article containing the words: "All of the corporation's issued shares of all classes shall be held of record by not more than _____ persons." (See Section 158 of the Corporations Code.)
3. For Corporations subject to Banking Law or Insurance Code, refer to Section 202(b)(2) and (3), respectively, of the Corporations Code.
4. Permissible but optional provisions for Articles of Incorporation are contained in Section 204 of the Corporations Code.

Action by Written Consent of Sole Incorporator

This action effects the appointment of the initial directors of the corporation by the organizer of the corporation, the sole incorporator, i.e., the incorporator must appoint first Board.

ACTION BY WRITTEN CONSENT OF
SOLE INCORPORATOR OF

____

The undersigned, being the sole incorporator of _________________, a California corporation (the "Company"), pursuant to Section 210 of the California Corporations Code, hereby adopts the following resolution by written consent:

APPOINTMENT OF DIRECTORS

RESOLVED, that, effective as of this date, the following persons be, and they hereby are, appointed as the initial directors of the Company to serve until the first annual meeting of shareholders or until their successors are duly elected and qualified:

____

____

____

IN WITNESS WHEREOF, the undersigned has executed this Action by Written Consent as of the _________ day of _____, 20__.

____

Sole Incorporator

5. Bylaws

BYLAWS
OF

____
(A CALIFORNIA CORPORATION)

ARTICLE I
OFFICES

Section 1. Principal Office. The principal executive office of the corporation shall be located at such place as the Board of Directors may from time to time authorize. If the principal executive office is located outside this state, and the corporation has one or more business offices in this state, the Board of Directors shall fix and designate a principal business office in the State of California.

Section 2. Other Offices. Additional offices of the corporation shall be located at such place or places, within or outside the State of California, as the Board of Directors may from time to time authorize.

ARTICLE II
CORPORATE SEAL

Section 3. Corporate Seal. If the Board of Directors adopts a corporate seal such seal shall have inscribed thereon the name of the corporation and the state and date of its incorporation. If and when a seal is adopted by the Board of Directors, such seal may be engraved, lithographed, printed, stamped, impressed upon, or affixed to any contract, conveyance, certificate for shares, or other instrument executed by the corporation.

ARTICLE III
SHAREHOLDERS' MEETINGS AND VOTING RIGHTS

Section 4. Place of Meetings. Meetings of shareholders shall be held at the principal executive office of the corporation, or at any other place, within or outside the State of California, which may be fixed either by the Board of Directors or by the written consent of all persons entitled to vote at such meeting, given either before or after the meeting and filed with the Secretary of the Corporation.

Section 5. Annual Meeting. The annual meeting of the shareholders of the corporation shall be held on any date and time which may from time to time be designated by the Board of Directors. At such annual meeting, directors shall be elected and any other business may be transacted which may properly come before the meeting.

Section 6. Postponement of Annual Meeting. The Board of Directors and the President shall each have authority to hold at an earlier date and/or time, or to postpone to a later date and/or time, the annual meeting of shareholders.

Section 7. Special Meetings.

(a) Special meetings of the shareholders, for any purpose or purposes, may be called by the Board of Directors, the Chairman of the Board of Directors, the President, or the holders of shares entitled to cast not less than ten percent (10%) of the votes at the meeting.

(b) Upon written request to the Chairman of the Board of Directors, the President, any vice president or the Secretary of the corporation by any person or persons (other than the Board of Directors) entitled to call a special meeting of the shareholders, such officer forthwith shall cause notice to be given to the shareholders entitled to vote, that a meeting will be held at a time requested by the person or persons calling the meeting, such time to be not less than thirty-five (35) nor more than sixty (60) days after receipt of such request. If such notice is not given within twenty (20) days after receipt of such request, the person or persons calling the meeting may give notice thereof in the manner provided by law or in these Bylaws. Nothing contained in this Section 7 shall be construed as limiting, fixing or affecting the time or date when a meeting of shareholders called by action of the Board of Directors may be held.

Section 8. Notice of Meetings. Except as otherwise may be required by law and subject to subsection 7(b) above, written notice of each meeting of shareholders shall be given to each shareholder entitled to vote at that meeting (see Section 15 below), by the Secretary, assistant secretary or other person charged with that duty, not less than ten (10) (or, if sent by third class mail, thirty (30)) nor more than sixty (60) days before such meeting.

Notice of any meeting of shareholders shall state the date, place and hour of the meeting and,

(a) in the case of a special meeting, the general nature of the business to be transacted, and no other business may be transacted at such meeting;

(b) in the case of an annual meeting, the general nature of matters which the Board of Directors, at the time the notice is given, intends to present for action by the shareholders;

(c) in the case of any meeting at which directors are to be elected, the names of the nominees intended at the time of the notice to be presented by management for election; and

(d) in the case of any meeting, if action is to be taken on any of the following proposals, the general nature of such proposal:

(1) a proposal to approve a transaction within the provisions of California Corporations Code, Section 310 (relating to certain transactions in which a director has a direct or indirect financial interest);

(2) a proposal to approve a transaction within the provisions of California Corporations Code, Section 902 (relating to amending the Articles of Incorporation of the corporation);

(3) a proposal to approve a transaction within the provisions of California Corporations Code, Sections 181 and 1201 (relating to reorganization);

(4) a proposal to approve a transaction within the provisions of California Corporations Code, Section 1900 (winding up and dissolution);

(5) a proposal to approve a plan of distribution within the provisions of California Corporations Code, Section 2007 (relating to certain plans providing for distribution not in accordance with the liquidation rights of preferred shares, if any).

At a special meeting, notice of which has been given in accordance with this Section, action may not be taken with respect to business, the general nature of which has not been stated in such notice. At an annual meeting, action may be taken with respect to business stated in the notice of such meeting, given in accordance with this Section, and, subject to subsection 8(d) above, with respect to any other business as may properly come before the meeting.

Section 9. Manner of Giving Notice. Notice of any meeting of shareholders shall be given either personally or by first-class mail, or, if the corporation has outstanding shares held of record by 500 or more persons (determined as provided in California Corporations Code Section 605) on the record date for such meeting, third-class mail, or telegraphic or other written communication, addressed to the shareholder at the address of that shareholder appearing on the books of the corporation or given by the shareholder to the corporation for the purpose of notice. If no such address appears on the corporation's books or is given, notice shall be deemed to have been given if sent to that shareholder by first-class mail or telegraphic or other written communication to the corporation's principal executive office, or if published at least once in a newspaper of general circulation in the county where that office is located. Notice shall be deemed to have been given at the time when delivered personally or deposited in the mail or sent by telegram or other means of written communication.

If any notice addressed to a shareholder at the address of that shareholder appearing on the books of the corporation is returned to the corporation by the United States Postal Service marked to indicate that the United States Postal Service is unable to deliver the notice to the shareholder at that address, all future notices shall be deemed to have been duly given without further mailing if these shall be available to the shareholder on written demand by the shareholder at the principal executive office of the corporation for a period of one (1) year from the date of the giving of the notice.

An affidavit of mailing of any notice or report in accordance with the provisions of this Section 9, executed by the Secretary, Assistant Secretary or any transfer agent, shall be prima facie evidence of the giving of the notice.

Section 10. Quorum and Transaction of Business.

(a) At any meeting of the shareholders, a majority of the shares entitled to vote, represented in person or by proxy, shall constitute a quorum. If a quorum is present, the affirmative vote of the majority of shares represented at the meeting and entitled to vote on any matter shall be the act of the shareholders, unless the vote of a greater number or voting by classes is required by law or by the Articles of Incorporation, and except as provided in subsection (b) below.

(b) The shareholders present at a duly called or held meeting of the shareholders at which a quorum is present may continue to do business until adjournment, notwithstanding the withdrawal of enough shareholders to leave less than a quorum, provided that any action taken (other than adjournment) is approved by at least a majority of the shares required to constitute a quorum.

(c) In the absence of a quorum, no business other than adjournment may be transacted, except as described in subsection (b) above.

Section 11. Adjournment and Notice of Adjourned Meetings. Any meeting of shareholders may be adjourned from time to time, whether or not a quorum is present, by the affirmative vote of a majority of shares represented at such meeting either in person or by proxy and entitled to vote at such meeting.

In the event any meeting is adjourned, it shall not be necessary to give notice of the time and place of such adjourned meeting pursuant to Sections 8 and 9 of these Bylaws; provided that if any of the following three events occur, such notice must be given:

(a) announcement of the adjourned meeting's time and place is not made at the original meeting which it continues or

(b) such meeting is adjourned for more than forty- five (45) days from the date set for the original meeting or

(c) a new record date is fixed for the adjourned meeting.

At the adjourned meeting, the corporation may transact any business which might have been transacted at the original meeting.

Section 12. Waiver of Notice, Consent to Meeting or Approval of Minutes.

(a) Subject to subsection (b) of this Section, the transactions of any meeting of shareholders, however called and noticed, and wherever held, shall be as valid as though made at a meeting duly held after regular call and notice, if a quorum is present either in person or by proxy, and if, either before or after the meeting, each of the persons entitled to vote but not present in person or by proxy signs a written waiver of notice or a consent to holding of the meeting or an approval of the minutes thereof.

(b) A waiver of notice, consent to the holding of a meeting or approval of the minutes thereof need not specify the business to be transacted or transacted at nor the purpose of the meeting; provided that in the case of proposals described in subsection (d) of Section 8 of these Bylaws, the general nature of such proposals must be described in any such waiver of notice and such proposals can only be approved by waiver of notice, not by consent to holding of the meeting or approval of the minutes.

(c) All waivers, consents and approvals shall be filed with the corporate records or made a part of the minutes of the meeting.

(d) A person's attendance at a meeting shall constitute waiver of notice of and presence at such meeting, except when such person objects at the beginning of the meeting to transaction of any business because the meeting is not lawfully called or convened and except that attendance at a meeting is not a waiver of any right to object to the consideration of matters which are required by law or these Bylaws to be in such notice (including those matters described in subsection (d) of Section 8 of these Bylaws), but are not so included if such person expressly objects to consideration of such matter or matters at any time during the meeting.

Section 13. Action by Written Consent Without a Meeting. Any action which may be taken at any meeting of shareholders may be taken without a meeting and without prior notice if written consents setting forth the action so taken are signed by the holders of the outstanding shares having not less than the minimum number of votes that would be necessary to authorize or take such action at a meeting at which all shares entitled to vote thereon were present and voted.

Directors may not be elected by written consent except by unanimous written consent of all shares entitled to vote for the election of directors; provided that any vacancy on the Board of Directors (other than a vacancy created by removal) which has not been filled by the board of directors may be filled by the written consent of a majority of outstanding shares entitled to vote for the election of directors.

Any written consent may be revoked pursuant to California Corporations Code Section 603(c) prior to the time that written consents of the number of shares required to authorize the proposed action have been filed with the Secretary. Such revocation must be in writing and will be effective upon its receipt by the Secretary.

If the consents of all shareholders entitled to vote have not been solicited in writing, and if the unanimous written consent of all such shareholders shall not have been received, the Secretary shall give prompt notice of any corporate action approved by the shareholders without a meeting to those shareholders entitled to vote on such matters who have not consented thereto in writing. This notice shall be given in the manner specified in Section 9 of these Bylaws. In the case of approval of (i) a transaction within the provisions of California Corporations Code, Section 310 (relating to certain transactions in which a director has an interest), (ii) a transaction within the provisions of California Corporations Code, Section 317 (relating to indemnification of agents of the corporation), (iii) a transaction within the provisions of California Corporations Code, Sections 181 and 1201 (relating to reorganization), and (iv) a plan of distribution within the provisions of California Corporations Code, Section 2007 (relating to certain plans providing for distribution not in accordance with the liquidation rights of preferred shares, if any), the notice shall be given at least ten (10) days before the consummation of any action authorized by that approval.

Section 14. Voting. The shareholders entitled to vote at any meeting of shareholders shall be determined in accordance with the provisions of Section 15 of these Bylaws, subject to the provisions of Sections 702 through 704 of the California Corporations Code (relating to voting shares held by a fiduciary, in the name of a corporation, or in joint ownership). Voting at any meeting of shareholders need not be by ballot; *provided, however,* that elections for directors must be by ballot if balloting is demanded by a shareholder at the meeting and before the voting begins.

Every person entitled to vote at an election for directors may cumulate the votes to which such person is entitled, *i.e.,* such person may cast a total number of votes equal to the number of directors to be elected multiplied by the number of votes to which such person's shares are entitled, and may cast said total number of votes for one or more candidates in such proportions as such person thinks fit; *provided, however,* no shareholder shall be entitled to so cumulate such shareholder's votes unless the candidates for which such shareholder is voting have been placed in nomination prior to the voting and a shareholder has given notice at the meeting, prior to the vote, of an intention to cumulate votes. In any election of directors, the candidates receiving the highest number of votes, up to the number of directors to be elected, are elected.

Except as may be otherwise provided in the Articles of Incorporation or by law, and subject to the foregoing provisions regarding the cumulation of votes, each shareholder shall be entitled to one vote for each share held.

Any shareholder may vote part of such shareholder's shares in favor of a proposal and refrain from voting the remaining shares or vote them against the proposal, other than elections to office, but, if the shareholder fails to specify the number of shares such shareholder is voting affirmatively, it will be conclusively presumed that the shareholder's approving vote is with respect to all shares such shareholder is entitled to vote.

No shareholder approval, other than unanimous approval of those entitled to vote, will be valid as to proposals described in subsection 8(d) of these Bylaws unless the general nature of such business was stated in the notice of meeting or in any written waiver of notice.

Section 15. Persons Entitled to Vote or Consent. The Board of Directors may fix a record date pursuant to Section 60 of these Bylaws to determine which shareholders are entitled to notice of and to vote at a meeting or consent to corporate actions, as provided in Sections 13 and 14 of these Bylaws. Only persons in whose name shares otherwise entitled to vote stand on the stock records of the corporation on such date shall be entitled to vote or consent.

If no record date is fixed:

(a) The record date for determining shareholders entitled to notice of or to vote at a meeting of shareholders shall be at the close of business on the business day next preceding the day notice is given or, if notice is waived, at the close of business on the business day next preceding the day on which the meeting is held;

(b) The record date for determining shareholders entitled to give consent to corporate action in writing without a meeting, when no prior action by the Board of Directors has been taken, shall be the day on which the first written consent is given;

(c) The record date for determining shareholders for any other purpose shall be at the close of business on the day on which the Board of Directors adopts the resolution relating thereto, or the sixtieth (60th) day prior to the date of such other action, whichever is later.

A determination of shareholders of record entitled to notice of or to vote at a meeting of shareholders shall apply to any adjournment of the meeting unless the Board of Directors fixes a new record date for the adjourned meeting; *provided, however,* that the Board of Directors shall fix a new record date if the meeting is adjourned for more than forty-five (45) days from the date set for the original meeting.

Shares of the corporation held by its subsidiary or subsidiaries (as defined in California Corporations Code, Section 189(b)) are not entitled to vote in any matter.

Section 16. Proxies. Every person entitled to vote or execute consents may do so either in person or by one or more agents authorized to act by a written proxy executed by the person or such person's duly authorized agent and filed with the Secretary of the corporation; provided that no such proxy shall be valid after the expiration of eleven (11) months from the date of its execution unless otherwise provided in the proxy. The manner of execution, suspension, revocation, exercise and effect of proxies is governed by law.

Section 17. Inspectors of Election. Before any meeting of shareholders, the Board of Directors may appoint any persons, other than nominees for office, to act as inspectors of election at the meeting or its adjournment. If no inspectors of election are so appointed, the chairman of the meeting may, and on the request of any shareholder or a shareholder's proxy shall, appoint inspectors of election at the meeting. The number of inspectors shall be either one (1) or three (3). If inspectors are appointed at a meeting on the request of one or more shareholders or proxies, the majority of shares represented in person or proxy shall determine whether one (1) or three (3) inspectors are to be appointed. If any person appointed as inspector fails to appear or fails or refuses to act, the chairman of the meeting may, and upon the request of any shareholder or a shareholder's proxy shall, appoint a person to fill that vacancy.

These inspectors shall:

(a) Determine the number of shares outstanding and the voting power of each, the shares represented at the meeting, the existence of a quorum, and the authenticity, validity, and effect of proxies;

(b) Receive votes, ballots, or consents;

(c) Hear and determine all challenges and questions in any way arising in connection with the right to vote;

(d) Count and tabulate all votes or consents;

(e) Determine when the polls shall close;

(f) Determine the result; and

(g) Do any other acts that may be proper to conduct the election or vote with fairness to all shareholders.

ARTICLE IV
BOARD OF DIRECTORS

Section 18. Powers. Subject to the provisions of law or any limitations in the Articles of Incorporation or these Bylaws, as to action required to be approved by the shareholders or by the outstanding shares, the business and affairs of the corporation shall be managed and all corporate powers shall be exercised, by or under the direction of the Board of Directors. The Board of Directors may delegate the management of the day-to-day operation of the business of the corporation to a management company or other person, provided that the business and affairs of the corporation shall be managed and all corporate powers shall be exercised under the ultimate direction of the Board of Directors.

Section 19. Number of Directors. The authorized number of directors of the corporation shall be _______ (___), until changed by a duly adopted amendment to these Bylaws approved by the affirmative vote of a majority of the outstanding shares entitled to vote; provided, an amendment reducing the number of directors to less than _______ (___), cannot be adopted if votes cast against its adoption at a meeting or shares not consenting to it in the case of action by written consent are equal to more than 16-2/3 percent of the outstanding shares entitled to vote. No reduction of the authorized number of directors shall remove any director prior to the expiration of such director's term of office.

Section 20. Election of Directors, Term, Qualifications. The directors shall be elected at each annual meeting of shareholders to hold office until the next annual meeting. Each director, including a director elected or appointed to fill a vacancy, shall hold office either until the expiration of the term for which elected or appointed and until a successor has been elected and qualified, or until his death, resignation or removal. Directors need not be shareholders of the corporation.

Section 21. Resignations. Any director of the corporation may resign effective upon giving written notice to the Chairman of the Board, the President, the Secretary or the Board of Directors of the corporation, unless the notice specifies a later time for the effectiveness of such resignation. If the resignation specifies effectiveness at a future time, a successor may be elected pursuant to Section 23 of these Bylaws to take office on the date that the resignation becomes effective.

Section 22. Removal. The Board of Directors may declare vacant the office of a director who has been declared of unsound mind by an order of court or who has been convicted of a felony.

The entire Board of Directors or any individual director may be removed from office without cause by the affirmative vote of a majority of the outstanding shares entitled to vote on such removal; *provided, however,* that unless the entire Board is removed, no individual director may be removed when the votes cast against such director's removal, or not consenting in writing to such removal, would be sufficient to elect that director if voted cumulatively at an election at which the same total number of votes cast were cast (or, if such action is taken by written consent, all shares entitled to vote were voted) and the entire number of directors authorized at the time of such director's most recent election were then being elected.

Section 23. Vacancies. A vacancy or vacancies on the Board of Directors shall be deemed to exist in case of the death, resignation or removal of any director, or upon increase in the authorized number of directors or if shareholders fail to elect the full authorized number of directors at an annual meeting of shareholders or if, for whatever reason, there are fewer directors on the Board of Directors, than the full number authorized.

Such vacancy or vacancies, other than a vacancy created by the removal of a director, may be filled by a majority of the remaining directors, though less than a quorum, or by a sole remaining director. A vacancy created by the removal of a director may be filled only by the affirmative vote of a majority of the shares represented and voting at a duly held meeting at which a quorum is present (which shares voting affirmatively also constitute at least a majority of the required quorum) or by the written consent of shareholders pursuant to Section 13 hereinabove. The shareholders may elect a director at any time to fill any vacancy not filled by the directors. Any such election by written consent, other than to fill a vacancy created by removal, requires the consent of a majority of the outstanding shares entitled to vote. Any such election by written consent to fill a vacancy created by removal requires the consent of all of the outstanding shares entitled to vote.

If, after the filling of any vacancy by the directors, the directors then in office who have been elected by the shareholders constitute less than a majority of the directors then in office, any holder or holders of an aggregate of five percent (5%) or more of the shares outstanding at that time and having the right to vote for such directors may call a special meeting of shareholders to be held to elect the entire Board of Directors. The term of office of any director shall terminate upon such election of a successor.

Section 24. Regular Meetings. Immediately after each annual meeting of shareholders, and at such place fixed by the Board of Directors, or if no such place is fixed at the place of the annual meeting, the Board of Directors shall hold a regular meeting for the purposes of organization, the appointment of officers and the transaction of other business. Other regular meetings of the Board of Directors shall be held at such times, places and dates as fixed in these Bylaws or by the Board of Directors; *provided, however,* that if the date for such a meeting falls on a legal holiday, then the meeting shall be held at the same time on the next succeeding full business day. Regular meetings of the Board of Directors held pursuant to this Section 24 may be held without notice.

Section 25. Electronic Participation. So long as permitted by statute, directors may participate in a meeting through any means of communication, including conference telephone, electronic video screen communication, or other communications equipment. Participating in a meeting pursuant to this section constitutes presence in person at that meeting if each participating director is provided the means to communicate with all of the other directors concurrently and (a) the meeting is held by conference telephone or video conferencing or other communications mode enabling participants to determine, through voice or image recognition, that a participant is or is not a director entitled to participate in the meeting or (b) another communications device (such as a computer modem) is used in conjunction with another method (determined in the discretion of the chairperson of the meeting) enabling participants to determine that a participant is or is not a director entitled to participate in the meeting. Such verification method may include use of passwords or similar codes for gaining access to the meeting or encryption and authentication technology approved in the discretion of the chairperson.

Section 26. Special Meetings. Special meetings of the Board of Directors for any purpose may be called by the Chairman of the Board or the President or any vice president or the Secretary of the corporation or any two (2) directors.

Section 27. Notice of Meetings. Notice of the date, time and place of all meetings of the Board of Directors, other than regular meetings held pursuant to Section 24 above shall be delivered personally, orally or in writing, or by telephone, including a voice messaging system or other system or technology designed to record and communication messages, telegraph, facsimile, electronic mail or other electronic means, to each director, at least forty-eight (48) hours before the meeting, or sent in writing to each director by first-class mail, charges prepaid, at least four (4) days before the meeting. Such notice may be given by the Secretary of the corporation or by the person or persons who called a meeting. Such notice need not specify the purpose of the meeting. Notice of any meeting of the Board of Directors need not be given to any director who signs a waiver of notice of such meeting, or a consent to holding the meeting or an approval of the minutes thereof, either before or after the meeting, or who attends the meeting without protesting prior thereto or at its commencement such director's lack of notice. All such waivers, consents and approvals shall be filed with the corporate records or made a part of the minutes of the meeting.

Section 28. Place of Meetings. Meetings of the Board of Directors may be held at any place within or without the state which has been designated in the notice of the meeting or, if not stated in the notice or there is no notice, designated in the Bylaws or by resolution of the Board of Directors.

Section 29. Action by Written Consent Without a Meeting. Any action required or permitted to be taken by the Board of Directors may be taken without a meeting, if all members of the Board of Directors individually or collectively consent in writing to such action. Such written consent or consents shall be filed with the minutes of the proceedings of the Board of Directors. Such action by written consent shall have the same force and effect as a unanimous vote of such directors.

Section 30. Quorum and Transaction of Business. A majority of the authorized number of directors shall constitute a quorum for the transaction of business. Every act or decision done or made by a majority of the directors present at a meeting duly held at which a quorum is present shall be the act of the Board of Directors, unless the law, the Articles of Incorporation or these Bylaws specifically require a greater number. A meeting at which a quorum is initially present may continue to transact business, notwithstanding withdrawal of directors, if any action taken is approved by at least a majority of the number of directors constituting a quorum for such meeting. In the absence of a quorum at any meeting of the Board of Directors, a majority of the directors present may adjourn the meeting, as provided in Section 31 of these Bylaws.

Section 31. Adjournment. Any meeting of the Board of Directors, whether or not a quorum is present, may be adjourned to another time and place by the affirmative vote of a majority of the directors present. If the meeting is adjourned for more than twenty-four (24) hours, notice of such adjournment to another time or place shall be given prior to the time of the adjourned meeting to the directors who were not present at the time of the adjournment.

Section 32. Organization. The Chairman of the Board shall preside at every meeting of the Board of Directors, if present. If there is no Chairman of the Board or if the Chairman is not present, a Chairman chosen by a majority of the directors present shall act as chairman. The Secretary of the corporation or, in the absence of the Secretary, any person appointed by the Chairman shall act as secretary of the meeting.

Section 33. Compensation. Directors and members of committees may receive such compensation, if any, for their services, and such reimbursement for expenses, as may be fixed or determined by the Board of Directors.

Section 34. Committees. The Board of Directors may, by resolution adopted by a majority of the authorized number of directors, designate one or more committees, each consisting of two (2) or more directors, to serve at the pleasure of the Board of Directors. The Board of Directors, by a vote of the majority of authorized directors, may designate one or more directors as alternate members of any committee, to replace any absent member at any meeting of such committee. Any such committee shall have authority to act in the manner and to the extent provided in the resolution of the Board of Directors, and may have all the authority of the Board of Directors in the management of the business and affairs of the corporation, except with respect to:

(a) the approval of any action for which shareholders' approval or approval of the outstanding shares also is required by the California Corporations Code;

(b) the filling of vacancies on the Board of Directors or any of its committees;

(c) the fixing of compensation of directors for serving on the Board of Directors or any of its committees;

(d) the adoption, amendment or repeal of these Bylaws;

(e) the amendment or repeal of any resolution of the Board of Directors which by its express terms is not so amendable or repealable;

(f) a distribution to shareholders, except at a rate or in a periodic amount or within a price range determined by the Board of Directors; or

(g) the appointment of other committees of the Board of Directors or the members thereof.

Any committee may from time to time provide by resolution for regular meetings at specified times and places. If the date of such a meeting falls on a legal holiday, then the meeting shall be held at the same time on the next succeeding full business day. No notice of such a meeting need be given. Such regular meetings need not be held if the committee shall so determine at any time before or after the time when such meeting would otherwise have taken place. Special meetings may be called at any time in the same manner and by the same persons as stated in Sections 26 and 27 of these Bylaws for meetings of the Board of Directors. The provisions of Sections 25, 28, 29, 30, 31 and 32 of these Bylaws shall apply to committees, committee members and committee meetings as if the words "committee" and "committee member" were substituted for the word "Board of Directors," and "director," respectively, throughout such sections.

ARTICLE V
OFFICERS

Section 35. Officers. The corporation shall have a Chairman of the Board or a President or both, a Secretary, a Chief Financial Officer and such other officers with such titles and duties as the Board of Directors may determine. Any two or more offices may be held by the same person.

Section 36. Appointment. All officers shall be chosen and appointed by the Board of Directors; *provided, however,* the Board of Directors may empower the chief executive officer of the corporation to appoint such officers, other than Chairman of the Board, President, Secretary or Chief Financial Officer, as the business of the corporation may require. All officers shall serve at the pleasure of the Board of Directors, subject to the rights, if any, of an officer under a contract of employment.

Section 37. Inability to Act. In the case of absence or inability to act of any officer of the corporation or of any person authorized by these Bylaws to act in such officer's place, the Board of Directors may from time to time delegate the powers or duties of such officer to any other officer, or any director or other person whom it may select, for such period of time as the Board of Directors deems necessary.

Section 38. Resignations. Any officer may resign at any time upon written notice to the corporation, without prejudice to the rights, if any, of the corporation under any contract to which such officer is a party. Such resignation shall be effective upon its receipt by the Chairman of the Board, the President, the Secretary or the Board of Directors, unless a different time is specified in the notice for effectiveness of such resignation. The acceptance of any such resignation shall not be necessary to make it effective unless otherwise specified in such notice.

Section 39. Removal. Any officer may be removed from office at any time, with or without cause, but subject to the rights, if any, of such officer under any contract of employment, by the Board of Directors or by any committee to whom such power of removal has been duly delegated, or, with regard to any officer who has been appointed by the chief executive officer pursuant to Section 36 above, by the chief executive officer or any other officer upon whom such power of removal may be conferred by the Board of Directors.

Section 40. Vacancies. A vacancy occurring in any office for any cause may be filled by the Board of Directors, in the manner prescribed by this Article of the Bylaws for initial appointment to such office.

Section 41. Chairman of the Board. The Chairman of the Board, if there be such an officer, shall, if present, preside at all meetings of the Board of Directors and shall exercise and perform such other powers and duties as may be assigned from time to time by the Board of Directors or prescribed by these Bylaws. If no President is appointed, the Chairman of the Board is the general manager and chief executive officer of the corporation, and shall exercise all powers of the President described in Section 42 below.

Section 42. President. Subject to such powers, if any, as may be given by the Board of Directors to the Chairman of the Board, if there be such an officer, the President shall be the general manager and chief executive officer of the corporation and shall have general supervision, direction, and control over the business and affairs of the corporation, subject to the control of the Board of Directors. The President may sign and execute, in the name of the corporation, any instrument authorized by the Board of Directors, except when the signing and execution thereof shall have been expressly delegated by the Board of Directors or by these Bylaws to some other officer or agent of the corporation. The President shall have all the general powers and duties of management usually vested in the president of a corporation, and shall have such other powers and duties as may be prescribed from time to time by the Board of Directors or these Bylaws. The President shall have discretion to prescribe the duties of other officers and employees of the corporation in a manner not inconsistent with the provisions of these Bylaws and the directions of the Board of Directors.

Section 43. Vice Presidents. In the absence or disability of the President, in the event of a vacancy in the office of President, or in the event such officer refuses to act, the Vice President shall perform all the duties of the President and, when so acting, shall have all the powers of, and be subject to all the restrictions on, the President. If at any such time the corporation has more than one vice president, the duties and powers of the President shall pass to each vice president in order of such vice president's rank as fixed by the Board of Directors or, if the vice presidents are not so ranked, to the vice president designated by the Board of Directors. The vice presidents shall have such other powers and perform such other duties as may be prescribed for them from time to time by the Board of Directors or pursuant to Sections 35 and 36 of these Bylaws or otherwise pursuant to these Bylaws.

Section 44. Secretary. The Secretary shall:

(a) Keep, or cause to be kept, minutes of all meetings of the corporation's shareholders, Board of Directors, and committees of the Board of Directors, if any. Such minutes shall be kept in written form.

(b) Keep, or cause to be kept, at the principal executive office of the corporation, or at the office of its transfer agent or registrar, if any, a record of the corporation's shareholders, showing the names and addresses of all shareholders, and the number and classes of shares held by each. Such records shall be kept in written form or any other form capable of being converted into written form.

(c) Keep, or cause to be kept, at the principal executive office of the corporation, or if the principal executive office is not in California, at its principal business office in California, an original or copy of these Bylaws, as amended.

(d) Give, or cause to be given, notice of all meetings of shareholders, directors and committees of the Board of Directors, as required by law or by these Bylaws.

(e) Keep the seal of the corporation, if any, in safe custody.

(f) Exercise such powers and perform such duties as are usually vested in the office of secretary of a corporation, and exercise such other powers and perform such other duties as may be prescribed from time to time by the Board of Directors or these Bylaws.

If any assistant secretaries are appointed, the assistant secretary, or one of the assistant secretaries in the order of their rank as fixed by the Board of Directors or, if they are not so ranked, the assistant secretary designated by the Board of Directors, in the absence or disability of the Secretary or in the event of such officer's refusal to act or if a vacancy exists in the office of Secretary, shall perform the duties and exercise the powers of the Secretary and discharge such duties as may be assigned from time to time pursuant to these Bylaws or by the Board of Directors.

Section 45. Chief Financial Officer. The Chief Financial Officer shall:

(a) Be responsible for all functions and duties of the treasurer of the corporation.

(b) Keep and maintain, or cause to be kept and maintained, adequate and correct books and records of account for the corporation.

(c) Receive or be responsible for receipt of all monies due and payable to the corporation from any source whatsoever; have charge and custody of, and be responsible for, all monies and other valuables of the corporation and be responsible for deposit of all such monies in the name and to the credit of the corporation with such depositaries as may be designated by the Board of Directors or a duly appointed and authorized committee of the Board of Directors.

(d) Disburse or be responsible for the disbursement of the funds of the corporation as may be ordered by the Board of Directors or a duly appointed and authorized committee of the Board of Directors.

(e) Render to the chief executive officer and the Board of Directors a statement of the financial condition of the corporation if called upon to do so.

(f) Exercise such powers and perform such duties as are usually vested in the office of chief financial officer of a corporation, and exercise such other powers and perform such other duties as may be prescribed by the Board of Directors or these Bylaws.

If any assistant financial officer is appointed, the assistant financial officer, or one of the assistant financial officers, if there are more than one, in the order of their rank as fixed by the Board of Directors or, if they are not so ranked, the assistant financial officer designated by the Board of Directors, shall, in the absence or disability of the Chief Financial Officer or in the event of such officer's refusal to act, perform the duties and exercise the powers of the Chief Financial Officer, and shall have such powers and discharge such duties as may be assigned from time to time pursuant to these Bylaws or by the Board of Directors.

Section 46. Compensation. The compensation of the officers shall be fixed from time to time by the Board of Directors, and no officer shall be prevented from receiving such compensation by reason of the fact that such officer is also a director of the corporation.

ARTICLE VI
CONTRACTS, LOANS, BANK ACCOUNTS, CHECKS AND DRAFTS

Section 47. Execution of Contracts and Other Instruments. Except as these Bylaws may otherwise provide, the Board of Directors or its duly appointed and authorized committee may authorize any officer or officers, agent or agents, to enter into any contract or execute and deliver any instrument in the name of and on behalf of the corporation, and such authorization may be general or confined to specific instances. Except as so authorized or otherwise expressly provided in these Bylaws, no officer, agent, or employee shall have any power or authority to bind the corporation by any contract or engagement or to pledge its credit or to render it liable for any purpose or in any amount.

Section 48. Loans. No loans shall be contracted on behalf of the corporation and no negotiable paper shall be issued in its name, unless and except as authorized by the Board of Directors or its duly appointed and authorized committee. When so authorized by the Board of Directors or such committee, any officer or agent of the corporation may affect loans and advances at any time for the corporation from any bank, trust company, or other institution, or from any firm, corporation or individual, and for such loans and advances may make, execute and deliver promissory notes, bonds or other evidences of indebtedness of the corporation and, when authorized as aforesaid, may mortgage, pledge, hypothecate or transfer any and all stocks, securities and other property, real or personal, at any time held by the corporation, and to that end endorse, assign and deliver the same as security for the payment of any and all loans, advances, indebtedness, and liabilities of the corporation. Such authorization may be general or confined to specific instances.

Section 49. Bank Accounts. The Board of Directors or its duly appointed and authorized committee from time to time may authorize the opening and keeping of general and/or special bank accounts with such banks, trust companies, or other depositaries as may be selected by the Board of Directors, its duly appointed and authorized committee or by any officer or officers, agent or agents, of the corporation to whom such power may be delegated from time to time by the Board of Directors. The Board of Directors or its duly appointed and authorized committee may make such rules and regulations with respect to said bank accounts, not inconsistent with the provisions of these Bylaws, as are deemed advisable.

Section 50. Checks, Drafts, Etc. All checks, drafts or other orders for the payment of money, notes, acceptances or other evidences of indebtedness issued in the name of the corporation shall be signed by such officer or officers, agent or agents, of the corporation, and in such manner, as shall be determined from time to time by resolution of the Board of Directors or its duly appointed and authorized committee. Endorsements for deposit to the credit of the corporation in any of its duly authorized depositaries may be made, without counter-signature, by the President or any vice president or the Chief Financial Officer or any assistant financial officer or by any other officer or agent of the corporation to whom the Board of Directors or its duly appointed and authorized committee, by resolution, shall have delegated such power or by hand-stamped impression in the name of the corporation.

ARTICLE VII
CERTIFICATES FOR SHARES AND THEIR TRANSFER

Section 51. Certificate for Shares. Every holder of shares in the corporation shall be entitled to have a certificate signed in the name of the corporation by the Chairman or Vice Chairman of the Board or the President or a Vice President and by the Chief Financial Officer or an assistant financial officer or by the Secretary or an assistant secretary, certifying the number of shares and the class or series of shares owned by the shareholder. Any or all of the signatures on the certificate may be facsimile. In case any officer, transfer agent or registrar who has signed or whose facsimile signature has been placed upon a certificate shall have ceased to be such officer, transfer agent or registrar before such certificate is issued, it may be issued by the corporation with the same effect as if such person were an officer, transfer agent or registrar at the date of issue.

In the event that the corporation shall issue any shares as only partly paid, the certificate issued to represent such partly paid shares shall have stated thereon the total consideration to be paid for such shares and the amount paid thereon.

Section 52. Transfer on the Books. Upon surrender to the Secretary or transfer agent (if any) of the corporation of a certificate for shares of the corporation duly endorsed, with reasonable assurance that the endorsement is genuine and effective, or accompanied by proper evidence of succession, assignment or authority to transfer and upon compliance with applicable federal and state securities laws and if the corporation has no statutory duty to inquire into adverse claims or has discharged any such duty and if any applicable law relating to the collection of taxes has been complied with, it shall be the duty of the corporation, by its Secretary or transfer agent, to cancel the old certificate, to issue a new certificate to the person entitled thereto and to record the transaction on the books of the corporation.

Section 53. Lost, Destroyed and Stolen Certificates. The holder of any certificate for shares of the corporation alleged to have been lost, destroyed or stolen shall notify the corporation by making a written affidavit or affirmation of such fact. Upon receipt of said affidavit or affirmation the Board of Directors, or its duly appointed and authorized committee or any officer or officers authorized by the Board so to do, may order the issuance of a new certificate for shares in the place of any certificate previously issued by the corporation and which is alleged to have been lost, destroyed or stolen. However, the Board of Directors or such authorized committee, officer or officers may require the owner of the allegedly lost, destroyed or stolen certificate, or such owner's legal representative, to give the corporation a bond or other adequate security sufficient to indemnify the corporation and its transfer agent and/or registrar, if any, against any claim that may be made against it or them on account of such allegedly lost, destroyed or stolen certificate or the replacement thereof. Said bond or other security shall be in such amount, on such terms and conditions and, in the case of a bond, with such surety or sureties as may be acceptable to the Board of Directors or to its duly appointed and authorized committee or any officer or officers authorized by the Board of Directors to determine the sufficiency thereof. The requirement of a bond or other security may be waived in particular cases at the discretion of the Board of Directors or its duly appointed and authorized committee or any officer or officers authorized by the Board of Directors so to do.

Section 54. Issuance, Transfer and Registration of Shares. The Board of Directors may make such rules and regulations, not inconsistent with law or with these Bylaws, as it may deem advisable concerning the issuance, transfer and registration of certificates for shares of the capital stock of the corporation. The Board of Directors may appoint a transfer agent or registrar of transfers, or both, and may require all certificates for shares of the corporation to bear the signature of either or both.

ARTICLE VIII
INSPECTION OF CORPORATE RECORDS

Section 55. Inspection by Directors. Every director shall have the absolute right at any reasonable time to inspect and copy all books, records, and documents of every kind of the corporation and any of its subsidiaries and to inspect the physical properties of the corporation and any of its subsidiaries. Such inspection may be made by the director in person or by agent or attorney, and the right of inspection includes the right to copy and make extracts.

Section 56. Inspection by Shareholders.

(a) Inspection of Corporate Records.

(1) A shareholder or shareholders holding at least five (5%) percent in the aggregate of the outstanding voting shares of the corporation or who hold at least one percent of such voting shares and have filed a Schedule 14B with the United States Securities and Exchange Commission relating to the election of directors of the corporation shall have an absolute right to do either or both of the following: (i) inspect and copy the record of shareholders' names and addresses and shareholdings during usual business hours upon five (5) business days' prior written demand upon the corporation; or (ii) obtain from the transfer agent, if any, for the corporation, upon five business days' prior written demand and upon the tender of its usual charges for such a list (the amount of which charges shall be stated to the shareholder by the transfer agent upon request), a list of the shareholders' names and addresses who are entitled to vote for the election of directors and their shareholdings, as of the most recent record date for which it has been compiled or as of a date specified by the shareholder subsequent to the date of demand.

(2) The record of shareholders shall also be open to inspection and copying by any shareholder or holder of a voting trust certificate at any time during usual business hours upon written demand on the corporation, for a purpose reasonably related to such holder's interest as a shareholder or holder of a voting trust certificate.

(3) The accounting books and records and minutes of proceedings of the shareholders and the Board of Directors and of any committees of the Board of Directors of the corporation and of each of its subsidiaries shall be open to inspection, copying and making extracts upon written demand on the corporation of any shareholder or holder of a voting trust certificate at any reasonable time during usual business hours, for a purpose reasonably related to such holder's interests as a shareholder or as a holder of such voting trust certificate.

(4) Any inspection, copying, and making of extracts under this subsection (a) may be done in person or by agent or attorney.

(b) Inspection of Bylaws. The original or a copy of these Bylaws shall be kept as provided in Section 44 of these Bylaws and shall be open to inspection by the shareholders at all reasonable times during office hours. If the principal executive office of the corporation is not in California, and the corporation has no principal business office in the state of California, a current copy of these Bylaws shall be furnished to any shareholder upon written request.

Section 57. Written Form. If any record subject to inspection pursuant to Section 56 above is not maintained in written form, a request for inspection is not complied with unless and until the corporation at its expense makes such record available in written form.

ARTICLE IX
MISCELLANEOUS

Section 58. Fiscal Year. Unless otherwise fixed by resolution of the Board of Directors, the fiscal year of the corporation shall end on the 31st day of December in each calendar year.

Section 59. Annual Report.

(a) Subject to the provisions of Section 59(b) below, the Board of Directors shall cause an annual report to be sent to each shareholder of the corporation in the manner provided in Section 9 of these Bylaws not later than one hundred twenty (120) days after the close of the corporation's fiscal year. Such report shall include a balance sheet as of the end of such fiscal year and an income statement and statement of changes in financial position for such fiscal year, accompanied by any report thereon of independent accountants or, if there is no such report, the certificate of an authorized officer of the corporation that such statements were prepared without audit from the books and records of the corporation. When there are more than 100 shareholders of record of the corporation's shares, as determined by Section 605 of the California Corporations Code, additional information as required by Section 1501(b) of the California Corporations Code shall also be contained in such report, provided that if the corporation has a class of securities registered under Section 12 of the United States Securities Exchange Act of 1934, that Act shall take precedence. Such report shall be sent to shareholders at least fifteen (15) (or, if sent by third-class mail, thirty-five (35)) days prior to the next annual meeting of shareholders after the end of the fiscal year to which it relates.

If and so long as there are fewer than 100 shareholders of record of the corporation's shares, the requirement of sending of an annual report to the shareholders of the corporation is hereby expressly waived.

Section 60. Record Date. The Board of Directors may fix a time in the future as a record date for the determination of the shareholders entitled to notice of or to vote at any meeting or entitled to receive payment of any dividend or other distribution or allotment of any rights or entitled to exercise any rights in respect of any change, conversion or exchange of shares or entitled to exercise any rights in respect of any other lawful action. The record date so fixed shall not be more than sixty (60) days nor less than ten (10) days prior to the date of the meeting nor more than sixty (60) days prior to any other action or event for the purpose of which it is fixed. If no record date is fixed, the provisions of Section 15 of these Bylaws shall apply with respect to notice of meetings, votes, and consents and the record date for determining shareholders for any other purpose shall be at the close of business on the day on which the Board of Directors adopts the resolutions relating thereto, or the sixtieth (60th) day prior to the date of such other action or event, whichever is later.

Only shareholders of record at the close of business on the record date shall be entitled to notice and to vote or to receive the dividend, distribution or allotment of rights or to exercise the rights, as the case may be, notwithstanding any transfer of any shares on the books of the corporation after the record date, except as otherwise provided in the Articles of Incorporation, by agreement or by law.

Section 61. Bylaw Amendments. Except as otherwise provided by law or Section 19 of these Bylaws, these Bylaws may be amended or repealed by the Board of Directors or by the affirmative vote of a majority of the outstanding shares entitled to vote, including, if applicable, the affirmative vote of a majority of the outstanding shares of each class or series entitled by law or the Articles of Incorporation to vote as a class or series on the amendment or repeal or adoption of any bylaw or Bylaws; *provided, however,* after issuance of shares, a bylaw specifying or changing a fixed number of directors or the maximum or minimum number or changing from a fixed to a variable board or vice versa may only be adopted by approval of the outstanding shares as provided herein.

Section 62. Construction and Definition. Unless the context requires otherwise, the general provisions, rules of construction, and definitions contained in the California Corporations Code shall govern the construction of these Bylaws.

Without limiting the foregoing, "shall" is mandatory and "may" is permissive.

ARTICLE X
INDEMNIFICATION

Section 63. Indemnification of Directors, Officers, Employees and Other Agents.

(a) Directors and Executive Officers. The corporation shall indemnify its directors and executive officers to the fullest extent not prohibited by the California General Corporation Law; *provided, however,* that the corporation may limit the extent of such indemnification by individual contracts with its directors and executive officers; and, *provided, further,* that the corporation shall not be required to indemnify any director or executive officer in connection with any proceeding (or part thereof) initiated by such person or any proceeding by such person against the corporation or its directors, officers, employees or other agents unless (i) such indemnification is expressly required to be made by law, (ii) the proceeding was authorized by the board of directors of the corporation or (iii) such indemnification is provided by the corporation, in its sole discretion, pursuant to the powers vested in the corporation under the California General Corporation Law.

(b) Other Officers, Employees and Other Agents. The corporation shall have the power to indemnify its other officers, employees and other agents as set forth in the California General Corporation Law.

(c) Determination by the Corporation. Promptly after receipt of a request for indemnification hereunder (and in any event within ninety (90) days thereof) a reasonable, good faith determination as to whether indemnification of the director or executive officer is proper under the circumstances because such director or executive officer has met the applicable standard of care shall be made by:

(1) a majority vote of a quorum consisting of directors who are not parties to such proceeding;

(2) if such quorum is not obtainable, by independent legal counsel in a written opinion; or

(3) approval or ratification by the affirmative vote of a majority of the shares of this corporation represented and voting at a duly held meeting at which a quorum is present (which shares voting affirmatively also constitute at least a majority of the required quorum) or by written consent of a majority of the outstanding shares entitled to vote; where in each case the shares owned by the person to be indemnified shall not be considered entitled to vote thereon.

(d) Good Faith.

(1) For purposes of any determination under this bylaw, a director or executive officer shall be deemed to have acted in good faith and in a manner he reasonably believed to be in the best interests of the corporation and its shareholders, and, with respect to any criminal action or proceeding, to have had no reasonable cause to believe that his conduct was unlawful, if his action is based on information, opinions, reports and statements, including financial statements and other financial data, in each case prepared or presented by: (i) one or more officers or employees of the corporation whom the director or executive officer believed to be reliable and competent in the matters presented; (ii) counsel, independent accountants or other persons as to matters which the director or executive officer believed to be within such person's professional competence; and (iii) with respect to a director, a committee of the Board upon which such director does not serve, as to matters within such committee's designated authority, which committee the director believes to merit confidence; so long as, in each case, the director or executive officer acts without knowledge that would cause such reliance to be unwarranted.

(2) The termination of any proceeding by judgment, order, settlement, conviction or upon a plea of nolo contendere or its equivalent shall not, of itself, create a presumption that the person did not act in good faith and in a manner which he reasonably believed to be in the best interests of the corporation and its shareholders or that he had reasonable cause to believe that his conduct was unlawful.

(3) The provisions of this paragraph (d) shall not be deemed to be exclusive or to limit in any way the circumstances in which a person may be deemed to have met the applicable standard of conduct set forth by the California General Corporation Law.

(e) Expenses. The corporation shall advance, prior to the final disposition of any proceeding, promptly following request therefor, all expenses incurred by any director or executive officer in connection with such proceeding upon receipt of an undertaking by or on behalf of such person to repay said amounts if it shall be determined ultimately that such person is not entitled to be indemnified under this bylaw or otherwise.

Notwithstanding the foregoing, unless otherwise determined pursuant to paragraph (f) of this bylaw, no advance shall be made by the corporation if a determination is reasonably and promptly made by the Board of Directors by a majority vote of a quorum consisting of directors who were not parties to the proceeding (or, if no such quorum exists, by independent legal counsel in a written opinion) that the facts known to the decision making party at the time such determination is made demonstrate clearly and convincingly that such person acted in bad faith or in a manner that such person did not believe to be in the best interests of the corporation and its shareholders.

(f) Enforcement. Without the necessity of entering into an express contract, all rights to indemnification and advances to directors and executive officers under this bylaw shall be deemed to be contractual rights and be effective to the same extent and as if provided for in a contract between the corporation and the director or executive officer. Any right to indemnification or advances granted by this bylaw to a director or executive officer shall be enforceable by or on behalf of the person holding such right in the forum in which the proceeding is or was pending or, if such forum is not available or a determination is made that such forum is not convenient, in any court of competent jurisdiction if (i) the claim for indemnification or advances is denied, in whole or in part, or (ii) no disposition of such claim is made within ninety (90) days of request therefor. The claimant in such enforcement action, if successful in whole or in part, shall be entitled to be paid also the expense of prosecuting his claim. The corporation shall be entitled to raise as a defense to any such action that the claimant has not met the standards of conduct that make it permissible under the California General Corporation Law for the corporation to indemnify the claimant for the amount claimed. Neither the failure of the corporation (including its board of directors, independent legal counsel or its shareholders) to have made a determination prior to the commencement of such action that indemnification of the claimant is proper in the circumstances because he has met the applicable standard of conduct set forth in the California General Corporation Law, nor an actual determination by the corporation (including its board of directors, independent legal counsel or its shareholders) that the claimant has not met such applicable standard of conduct, shall be a defense to the action or create a presumption that claimant has not met the applicable standard of conduct.

(g) Non-Exclusivity of Rights. To the fullest extent permitted by the corporation's Articles of Incorporation and the California General Corporation Law, the rights conferred on any person by this bylaw shall not be exclusive of any other right which such person may have or hereafter acquire under any statute, provision of the Articles of Incorporation, Bylaws, agreement, vote of shareholders or disinterested directors or otherwise, both as to action in his official capacity and as to action in another capacity while holding office. The corporation is specifically authorized to enter into individual contracts with any or all of its directors, officers, employees or agents respecting indemnification and advances, to the fullest extent permitted by the California General Corporation Law and the corporation's Articles of Incorporation.

(h) Survival of Rights. The rights conferred on any person by this bylaw shall continue as to a person who has ceased to be a director or executive officer and shall inure to the benefit of the heirs, executors and administrators of such a person.

(i) Insurance. The corporation, upon approval by the board of directors, may purchase insurance on behalf of any person required or permitted to be indemnified pursuant to this bylaw.

(j) Amendments. Any repeal or modification of this bylaw shall only be prospective and shall not affect the rights under this bylaw in effect at the time of the alleged occurrence of any action or omission to act that is the cause of any proceeding against any agent of the corporation.

(k) Employee Benefit Plans. The corporation shall indemnify the directors and officers of the corporation who serve at the request of the corporation as trustees, investment managers or other fiduciaries of employee benefit plans to the fullest extent permitted by the California General Corporation Law.

(l) Saving Clause. If this bylaw or any portion hereof shall be invalidated on any ground by any court of competent jurisdiction, then the corporation shall nevertheless indemnify each director and executive officer to the fullest extent permitted by any applicable portion of this bylaw that shall not have been invalidated, or by any other applicable law.

(m) Certain Definitions. For the purposes of this bylaw, the following definitions shall apply:

(1) The term **"proceeding"** shall be broadly construed and shall include, without limitation, the investigation, preparation, prosecution, defense, settlement and appeal of any threatened, pending or completed action, suit or proceeding, whether civil, criminal, administrative, arbitrative or investigative.

(2) The term **"expenses"** shall be broadly construed and shall include, without limitation, court costs, attorneys' fees, witness fees, fines, amounts paid in settlement or judgment and any other costs and expenses of any nature or kind incurred in connection with any proceeding, including expenses of establishing a right to indemnification under this bylaw or any applicable law.

(3) The term the **"corporation"** shall include, in addition to the resulting corporation, any constituent corporation (including any constituent of a constituent) absorbed in a consolidation or merger which, if its separate existence had continued, would have had power and authority to indemnify its directors, officers, and employees or agents, so that any person who is or was a director, officer, employee or agent of such constituent corporation, or is or was serving at the request of such constituent corporation as a director, officer, employee or agent of another corporation, partnership, joint venture, trust or other enterprise, shall stand in the same position under the provisions of this bylaw with respect to the resulting or surviving corporation as he would have with respect to such constituent corporation if its separate existence had continued.

(4) References to a **"director," "officer," "employee,"** or **"agent"** of the corporation shall include, without limitation, situations where such person is or was serving at the request of the corporation as a director, officer, employee, trustee or agent of another corporation, partnership, joint venture, trust or other enterprise.

ARTICLE XI
RIGHT OF FIRST REFUSAL

Section 64. Right of First Refusal. No shareholder shall sell, assign, pledge, or in any manner transfer any of the shares of stock of the corporation or any right or interest therein, whether voluntarily or by operation of law, or by gift or otherwise, except by a transfer which meets the requirements hereinafter set forth in this bylaw:

(a) If the shareholder desires to sell or otherwise transfer any of his shares of stock, then the shareholder shall first give written notice thereof to the corporation. The notice shall name the proposed transferee and state the number of shares to be transferred, the proposed consideration, and all other terms and conditions of the proposed transfer.

(b) For thirty (30) days following receipt of such notice, the corporation shall have the option to purchase all (but not less than all) of the shares specified in the notice at the price and upon the terms set forth in such notice; *provided, however,* that, with the consent of the shareholder, the corporation shall have the option to purchase a lesser portion of the shares specified in said notice at the price and upon the terms set forth therein. In the event of a gift, property settlement or other transfer in which the proposed transferee is not paying the full price for the shares, and that is not otherwise exempted from the provisions of this Section 64, the price shall be deemed to be the fair market value of the stock at such time as determined in good faith by the Board of Directors. In the event the corporation elects to purchase all of the shares or, with consent of the shareholder, a lesser portion of the shares, it shall give written notice to the transferring shareholder of its election and settlement for said shares shall be made as provided below in paragraph (d).

(c) The corporation may assign its rights hereunder.

(d) In the event the corporation and/or its assignee(s) elect to acquire any of the shares of the transferring shareholder as specified in said transferring shareholder's notice, the Secretary of the corporation shall so notify the transferring shareholder and settlement thereof shall be made in cash within thirty (30) days after the Secretary of the corporation receives said transferring shareholder's notice; provided that if the terms of payment set forth in said transferring shareholder's notice were other than cash against delivery, the corporation and/or its assignee(s) shall pay for said shares on the same terms and conditions set forth in said transferring shareholder's notice.

(e) In the event the corporation and/or its assignees(s) do not elect to acquire all of the shares specified in the transferring shareholder's notice, said transferring shareholder may, within the sixty-day period following the expiration of the option rights granted to the corporation and/or its assignees(s) herein, transfer the shares specified in said transferring shareholder's notice which were not acquired by the corporation and/or its assignees(s) as specified in said transferring shareholder's notice. All shares so sold by said transferring shareholder shall continue to be subject to the provisions of this bylaw in the same manner as before said transfer.

(f) Anything to the contrary contained herein notwithstanding, the following transactions shall be exempt from the provisions of this bylaw:

(1) A shareholder's transfer of any or all shares held either during such shareholder's lifetime or on death by will or intestacy to such shareholder's immediate family or to any custodian or trustee for the account of such shareholder or such shareholder's immediate family or to any limited partnership of which the shareholder, members of such shareholder's immediate family or any trust for the account of such shareholder or such shareholder's immediate family will be the general of limited partner(s) of such partnership. "Immediate family" as used herein shall mean spouse, lineal descendant, father, mother, brother, or sister of the shareholder making such transfer.

(2) A shareholder's bona fide pledge or mortgage of any shares with a commercial lending institution, provided that any subsequent transfer of said shares by said institution shall be conducted in the manner set forth in this bylaw.

(3) A shareholder's transfer of any or all of such shareholder's shares to the corporation or to any other shareholder of the corporation.

(4) A shareholder's transfer of any or all of such shareholder's shares to a person who, at the time of such transfer, is an officer or director of the corporation.

(5) A corporate shareholder's transfer of any or all of its shares pursuant to and in accordance with the terms of any merger, consolidation, reclassification of shares or capital reorganization of the corporate shareholder, or pursuant to a sale of all or substantially all of the stock or assets of a corporate shareholder.

(6) A corporate shareholder's transfer of any or all of its shares to any or all of its shareholders.

(7) A transfer by a shareholder which is a limited or general partnership to any or all of its partners or former partners.

In any such case, the transferee, assignee, or other recipient shall receive and hold such stock subject to the provisions of this bylaw, and there shall be no further transfer of such stock except in accord with this bylaw.

(g) The provisions of this bylaw may be waived with respect to any transfer either by the corporation, upon duly authorized action of its Board of Directors, or by the shareholders, upon the express written consent of the owners of a majority of the voting power of the corporation (excluding the votes represented by those shares to be transferred by the transferring shareholder). This bylaw may be amended or repealed either by a duly authorized action of the Board of Directors or by the shareholders, upon the express written consent of the owners of a majority of the voting power of the corporation.

(h) Any sale or transfer, or purported sale or transfer, of securities of the corporation shall be null and void unless the terms, conditions, and provisions of this bylaw are strictly observed and followed.

(i) The foregoing right of first refusal shall terminate on either of the following dates, whichever shall first occur:

(1) On _________, 20__; or

(2) Upon the date securities of the corporation are first offered to the public pursuant to a registration statement filed with, and declared effective by, the United States Securities and Exchange Commission under the Securities Act of 1933, as amended.

(j) The certificates representing shares of stock of the corporation shall bear on their face the following legend so long as the foregoing right of first refusal remains in effect:

> "THE SHARES REPRESENTED BY THIS CERTIFICATE ARE SUBJECT TO A RIGHT OF FIRST REFUSAL OPTION IN FAVOR OF THE CORPORATION AND/OR ITS ASSIGNEE(S), AS PROVIDED IN THE BYLAWS OF THE CORPORATION."

ARTICLE XII
LOANS OF OFFICERS AND OTHERS

Section 65. Certain Corporate Loans and Guaranties. If the corporation has outstanding shares held of record by 100 or more persons on the date of approval by the Board of Directors, the corporation may make loans of money or property to, or guarantee the obligations of, any officer of the corporation or its parent or any subsidiary, whether or not a director of the corporation or its parent or any subsidiary, or adopt an employee benefit plan or plans authorizing such loans or guaranties, upon the approval of the Board of Directors alone, by a vote sufficient without counting the vote of any interested director or directors, if the Board of Directors determines that such a loan or guaranty or plan may reasonably be expected to benefit the corporation. Notwithstanding the foregoing, the corporation shall have the power to make loans permitted by the California Corporations Code.

6. Indemnity Agreement

INDEMNITY AGREEMENT

THIS AGREEMENT is made and entered into this ___ day of _______, 20__ by and between **[NAME OF CORPORATION]**, a California corporation (the "***Corporation***"), and _____________________________ ("***Agent***").

RECITALS

WHEREAS, Agent performs a valuable service to the Corporation in his/her capacity as a/an **[director/officer]** of the Corporation;

WHEREAS, the shareholders of the Corporation have adopted Bylaws (the "***Bylaws***") providing for the indemnification of the directors, officers, employees and other agents of the Corporation, including persons serving at the request of the Corporation in such capacities with other corporations or enterprises, as authorized by the California General Corporation Law, as amended (the "***Code***");

WHEREAS, the Bylaws and the Code, by their non-exclusive nature, permit contracts between the Corporation and its agents, officers, employees and other agents with respect to indemnification of such persons; and

WHEREAS, in order to induce Agent to serve as a/an **[director/officer]** of the Corporation, the Corporation has determined and agreed to enter into this Agreement with Agent;

NOW, THEREFORE, in consideration of Agent's service as a/an **[director/officer]** after the date hereof, the parties hereto agree as follows:

AGREEMENT

1. **Services to the Corporation.** Agent will serve, at the will of the Corporation or under separate contract, if any such contract exists, as a/an **[director/officer]** of the Corporation or as a director, officer or other fiduciary of an affiliate of the Corporation (including any employee benefit plan of the Corporation) faithfully and to the best of Agent's ability so long as Agent **[is duly elected and qualified in accordance with the provisions of the Bylaws or other applicable charter documents/is a duly appointed officer]** of the Corporation or such affiliate; *provided, however,* that Agent may at any time and for any reason resign from such position (subject to any contractual obligation that Agent may have assumed apart from this Agreement) and that the Corporation or any affiliate shall have no obligation under this Agreement to continue Agent in any such position.

2. **Indemnity of Agent.** The Corporation hereby agrees to hold harmless and indemnify Agent to the fullest extent authorized or permitted by the provisions of the Bylaws and the Code, as the same may be amended from time to time (but, only to the extent that such amendment permits the Corporation to provide broader indemnification rights than the Bylaws or the Code permitted prior to adoption of such amendment).

3. **Additional Indemnity.** In addition to and not in limitation of the indemnification otherwise provided for herein, and subject only to the exclusions set forth in Section 4 hereof, the Corporation hereby further agrees to hold harmless and indemnify Agent:

(a) against any and all expenses (including attorneys' fees), witness fees, damages, judgments, fines and amounts paid in settlement and any other amounts that Agent becomes legally obligated to pay because of any claim or claims made against or by Agent in connection with any threatened, pending or completed action, suit or proceeding, whether civil, criminal, arbitrational, administrative or investigative (including an action by or in the right of the Corporation) to which Agent is, was or at any time becomes a party, or is threatened to be made a party, by reason of the fact that Agent is, was or at any time becomes a director, officer, employee or other agent of Corporation, or is or was serving or at any time serves at the request of the Corporation as a director, officer, employee or other agent of another corporation, partnership, joint venture, trust, employee benefit plan or other enterprise; and

(b) otherwise to the fullest extent as may be provided to Agent by the Corporation under the non-exclusivity provisions of the Code and Section 43 of the Bylaws.

4. Limitations on Additional Indemnity. No indemnity pursuant to Section 3 hereof shall be paid by the Corporation:

(a) on account of any claim against Agent for an accounting of profits made from the purchase or sale by Agent of securities of the Corporation pursuant to the provisions of Section 16(b) of the Securities Exchange Act of 1934 and amendments thereto or similar provisions of any federal, state or local statutory law;

(b) on account of Agent's conduct that is established by a final judgment as knowingly fraudulent or deliberately dishonest or that constituted willful misconduct;

(c) on account of Agent's conduct that is established by a final judgment as constituting a breach of Agent's duty of loyalty to the Corporation or resulting in any personal profit or advantage to which Agent was not legally entitled;

(d) for which payment is actually made to Agent under a valid and collectible insurance policy or under a valid and enforceable indemnity clause, bylaw or agreement, except in respect of any excess beyond payment under such insurance, clause, bylaw or agreement;

(e) if indemnification is not lawful (and, in this respect, both the Corporation and Agent have been advised that the Securities and Exchange Commission believes that indemnification for liabilities arising under the federal securities laws is against public policy and is, therefore, unenforceable and that claims for indemnification should be submitted to appropriate courts for adjudication); or

(f) in connection with any proceeding (or part thereof) initiated by Agent, or any proceeding by Agent against the Corporation or its directors, officers, employees or other agents, unless (i) such indemnification is expressly required to be made by law, (ii) the proceeding was authorized by the Board of Directors of the Corporation, (iii) such indemnification is provided by the Corporation, in its sole discretion, pursuant to the powers vested in the Corporation under the Code, or (iv) the proceeding is initiated pursuant to Section 9 hereof.

5. Continuation of Indemnity. All agreements and obligations of the Corporation contained herein shall continue during the period Agent is a director, officer, employee or other agent of the Corporation (or is or was serving at the request of the Corporation as a director, officer, employee or other agent of another corporation, partnership, joint venture, trust, employee benefit plan or other enterprise) and shall continue thereafter so long as Agent shall be subject to any possible claim or threatened, pending or completed action, suit or proceeding, whether civil, criminal, arbitrational, administrative or investigative, by reason of the fact that Agent was serving in the capacity referred to herein.

6. Partial Indemnification. Agent shall be entitled under this Agreement to indemnification by the Corporation for a portion of the expenses (including attorneys' fees), witness fees, damages, judgments, fines and amounts paid in settlement and any other amounts that Agent becomes legally obligated to pay in connection with any action, suit or proceeding referred to in Section 3 hereof even if not entitled hereunder to indemnification for the total amount thereof, and the Corporation shall indemnify Agent for the portion thereof to which Agent is entitled.

7. Notification and Defense of Claim. Not later than thirty (30) days after Agent becomes aware, by written or other overt communication, of any pending or threatened litigation, claim or assessment, Agent will, if a claim in respect thereof is to be made against the Corporation under this Agreement, notify the Corporation of such pending or threatened litigation, claim or assessment; but the omission so to notify the Corporation will not relieve it from any liability which it may have to Agent otherwise than under this Agreement. With respect to any such pending or threatened litigation, claim or assessment as to which Agent notifies the Corporation of the commencement thereof:

(a) the Corporation will be entitled to participate therein at its own expense;

(b) except as otherwise provided below, the Corporation may, at its option and jointly with any other indemnifying party similarly notified and electing to assume such defense, assume the defense thereof, with counsel reasonably satisfactory to Agent. After notice from the Corporation to Agent of its election to assume the defense thereof, the Corporation will not be liable to Agent under this Agreement for any legal or other expenses subsequently incurred by Agent in connection with the defense thereof except for reasonable costs of investigation or otherwise as provided below. Agent shall have the right to employ separate counsel in such action, suit or proceeding but the fees and expenses of such counsel incurred after notice from the Corporation of its assumption of the defense thereof shall be at the expense of Agent unless (i) the employment of counsel by Agent has been authorized by the Corporation, (ii) Agent shall have reasonably concluded, and so notified the Corporation, that there is an actual conflict of interest between the Corporation and Agent in the conduct of the defense of such action or (iii) the Corporation shall not in fact have employed counsel to assume the defense of such action, in each of which cases the fees and expenses of Agent's separate counsel shall be at the expense of the Corporation. The Corporation shall not be entitled to assume the defense of any action, suit or proceeding brought by or on behalf of the Corporation or as to which Agent shall have made the conclusion provided for in clause (ii) above; and

(c) the Corporation shall not be liable to indemnify Agent under this Agreement for any amounts paid in settlement of any action or claim effected without its written consent, which shall not be unreasonably withheld. The Corporation shall be permitted to settle any action or claim except that it shall not settle any action or claim in any manner which would impose any penalty or limitation on Agent without Agent's written consent, which may be given or withheld in Agent's sole discretion.

8. Expenses. The Corporation shall advance, prior to the final disposition of any proceeding, promptly following request therefor, all expenses incurred by Agent in connection with such proceeding upon receipt of an undertaking by or on behalf of Agent to repay said amounts if it shall be determined ultimately that Agent is not entitled to be indemnified under the provisions of this Agreement, the Bylaws, the Code or otherwise.

9. Enforcement. Any right to indemnification or advances granted by this Agreement to Agent shall be enforceable by or on behalf of Agent in any court of competent jurisdiction if (i) the claim for indemnification or advances is denied, in whole or in part, or (ii) no disposition of such claim is made within ninety (90) days of request therefor. Agent, in such enforcement action, if successful in whole or in part, shall be entitled to be paid also the expense of prosecuting Agent's claim. It shall be a defense to any action for which a claim for indemnification is made under Section 3 hereof (other than an action brought to enforce a claim for expenses pursuant to Section 8 hereof, *provided that* the required undertaking has been tendered to the Corporation) that Agent is not entitled to indemnification because of the limitations set forth in Section 4 hereof. Neither the failure of the Corporation (including its Board of Directors or its shareholders) to have made a determination prior to the commencement of such enforcement action that indemnification of Agent is proper in the circumstances, nor an actual determination by the Corporation (including its Board of Directors or its shareholders) that such indemnification is improper shall be a defense to the action or create a presumption that Agent is not entitled to indemnification under this Agreement or otherwise.

10. Subrogation. In the event of payment under this Agreement, the Corporation shall be subrogated to the extent of such payment to all of the rights of recovery of Agent, who shall execute all documents required and shall do all acts that may be necessary to secure such rights and to enable the Corporation effectively to bring suit to enforce such rights.

11. Non-Exclusivity of Rights. The rights conferred on Agent by this Agreement shall not be exclusive of any other right which Agent may have or hereafter acquire under any statute, provision of the Corporation's Articles of Incorporation or Bylaws, agreement, vote of stockholders or directors, or otherwise, both as to action in Agent's official capacity and as to action in another capacity while holding office.

12. Survival of Rights.

(a) The rights conferred on Agent by this Agreement shall continue after Agent has ceased to be a director, officer, employee or other agent of the Corporation or to serve at the request of the Corporation as a director, officer, employee or other agent of another corporation, partnership, joint venture, trust, employee benefit plan or other enterprise and shall inure to the benefit of Agent's heirs, executors and administrators.

(b) The Corporation shall require any successor (whether direct or indirect, by purchase, merger, consolidation or otherwise) to all or substantially all of the business or assets of the Corporation, expressly to assume and agree to perform this Agreement in the same manner and to the same extent that the Corporation would be required to perform if no such succession had taken place.

13. Separability. Each of the provisions of this Agreement is a separate and distinct agreement and independent of the others, so that if any provision hereof shall be held to be invalid for any reason, such invalidity or unenforceability shall not affect the validity or enforceability of the other provisions hereof. Furthermore, if this Agreement shall be invalidated in its entirety on any ground, then the Corporation shall nevertheless indemnify Agent to the fullest extent provided by the Bylaws, the Code or any other applicable law.

14. **Governing Law.** This Agreement shall be interpreted and enforced in accordance with the laws of the State of California.

15. **Amendment and Termination.** No amendment, modification, termination or cancellation of this Agreement shall be effective unless in writing signed by both parties hereto.

16. **Identical Counterparts.** This Agreement may be executed in one or more counterparts, each of which shall for all purposes be deemed to be an original but all of which together shall constitute but one and the same Agreement. Only one such counterpart need be produced to evidence the existence of this Agreement.

17. **Headings.** The headings of the sections of this Agreement are inserted for convenience only and shall not be deemed to constitute part of this Agreement or to affect the construction hereof.

18. **Notices.** All notices, requests, demands and other communications hereunder shall be in writing and shall be deemed to have been duly given (i) upon delivery if delivered by hand to the party to whom such communication was directed or (ii) upon the third business day after the date on which such communication was mailed if mailed by certified or registered mail with postage prepaid: (a) if to Agent, at the address indicated on the signature page hereof, and (b) if to the Corporation, to ___________________________, or (c) to such other address as may have been furnished to Agent by the Corporation.

19. **Entire Agreement.** This Agreement constitutes the full and complete agreement of the Corporation and Agent and supersedes all prior written or oral agreements between the parties with respect to the Corporation's indemnification of Agent.

IN WITNESS WHEREOF, the parties hereto have executed this Agreement on and as of the day and year first above written.

[NAME OF CORPORATION]

By: ___________________________

AGENT

____

[Name]

Address:

____

____

7. Employment Agreement

[NAME OF COMPANY]
AT WILL EMPLOYMENT, CONFIDENTIAL INFORMATION, INVENTION ASSIGNMENT, AND ARBITRATION AGREEMENT

As a condition of my employment with [Name of Corporation], its subsidiaries, affiliates, successors or assigns (together the "Company"), and in consideration of my employment with the Company and my receipt of the compensation now and hereafter paid to me by Company, I agree to the following:

1. At-Will Employment.

I UNDERSTAND AND ACKNOWLEDGE THAT MY EMPLOYMENT WITH THE COMPANY IS FOR AN UNSPECIFIED DURATION AND CONSTITUTES "AT-WILL" EMPLOYMENT. I ALSO UNDERSTAND THAT ANY REPRESENTATION TO THE CONTRARY IS UNAUTHORIZED AND NOT VALID UNLESS OBTAINED IN WRITING AND SIGNED BY THE PRESIDENT OF THE COMPANY. I ACKNOWLEDGE THAT THIS EMPLOYMENT RELATIONSHIP MAY BE TERMINATED AT ANY TIME, WITH OR WITHOUT GOOD CAUSE OR FOR ANY OR NO CAUSE, AT THE OPTION EITHER OF THE COMPANY OR MYSELF, WITH OR WITHOUT NOTICE.

2. Confidential Information.

A. Company Information. I agree at all times during the term of my employment and thereafter, to hold in strictest confidence, and not to use, except for the benefit of the Company, or to disclose to any person, firm or corporation without written authorization of the Board of Directors of the Company, any Confidential Information of the Company, except under a non-disclosure agreement duly authorized and executed by the Company. I understand that "Confidential Information" means any non-public information that relates to the actual or anticipated business or research and development of the Company, technical data, trade secrets or know-how, including, but not limited to, research, product plans or other information regarding Company's products or services and markets therefor, customer lists and customers (including, but not limited to, customers of the Company on whom I called or with whom I became acquainted during the term of my employment), software, developments, inventions, processes, formulas, technology, designs, drawings, engineering, hardware configuration information, marketing, finances or other business information. I further understand that Confidential Information does not include any of the foregoing items which have become publicly known and made generally available through no wrongful act of mine or of others who were under confidentiality obligations as to the item or items involved or improvements or new versions thereof.

B. Former Employer Information. I agree that I will not, during my employment with the Company, improperly use or disclose any proprietary information or trade secrets of any former or concurrent employer or other person or entity and that I will not bring onto the premises of the Company any unpublished document or proprietary information belonging to any such employer, person or entity unless consented to in writing by such employer, person or entity.

C. Third Party Information. I recognize that the Company has received and in the future will receive from third parties their confidential or proprietary information subject to a duty on the Company's part to maintain the confidentiality of such information and to use it only for certain limited purposes. I agree to hold all such confidential or proprietary information in the strictest confidence and not to disclose it to any person, firm or corporation or to use it except as necessary in carrying out my work for the Company consistent with the Company's agreement with such third party.

3. Inventions.

A. Inventions Retained and Licensed. I have attached hereto, as Exhibit A, a list describing all inventions, original works of authorship, developments, improvements, and trade secrets which were made by me prior to my employment with the Company (collectively referred to as "Prior Inventions"), which belong to me, which relate to the Company's proposed business, products or research and development, and which are not assigned to the Company hereunder; or, if no such list is attached, I represent that there are no such Prior Inventions. If in the course of my employment with the Company, I incorporate into a Company product, process or service a Prior Invention owned by me or in which I have an interest, I hereby grant to the Company a nonexclusive, royalty-free, fully paid-up, irrevocable, perpetual, worldwide license to make, have made, modify, use and sell such Prior Invention as part of or in connection with such product, process or service, and to practice any method related thereto.

B. Assignment of Inventions. I agree that I will promptly make full written disclosure to the Company, will hold in trust for the sole right and benefit of the Company, and hereby assign to the Company, or its designee, all my right, title, and interest in and to any and all inventions, original works of authorship, developments, concepts, improvements, designs, discoveries, ideas, trademarks or trade secrets, whether or not patentable or registrable under copyright or similar laws, which I may solely or jointly conceive or develop or reduce to practice, or cause to be conceived or developed or reduced to practice, during the period of time I am in the employ of the Company (collectively referred to as "Inventions"), except as provided in Section 3.F below. I further acknowledge that all original works of authorship which are made by me (solely or jointly with others) within the scope of and during the period of my employment with the Company and which are protectable by copyright are "works made for hire," as that term is defined in the United States Copyright Act. I understand and agree that the decision whether or not to commercialize or market any invention developed by me solely or jointly with others is within the Company's sole discretion and for the Company's sole benefit and that no royalty will be due to me as a result of the Company's efforts to commercialize or market any such invention.

C. Inventions Assigned to the United States. I agree to assign to the United States government all my right, title, and interest in and to any and all Inventions whenever such full title is required to be in the United States by a contract between the Company and the United States or any of its agencies.

D. Maintenance of Records. I agree to keep and maintain adequate and current written records of all Inventions made by me (solely or jointly with others) during the term of my employment with the Company. The records will be in the form of notes, sketches, drawings, and any other format that may be specified by the Company. The records will be available to and remain the sole property of the Company at all times.

E. Patent and Copyright Registrations. I agree to assist the Company, or its designee, at the Company's expense, in every proper way to secure the Company's rights in the Inventions and any copyrights, patents, mask work rights or other intellectual property rights relating thereto in any and all countries, including the disclosure to the Company of all pertinent information and data with respect thereto, the execution of all applications, specifications, oaths, assignments and all other instruments which the Company shall deem necessary in order to apply for and obtain such rights and in order to assign and convey to the Company, its successors, assigns, and nominees the sole and exclusive rights, title and interest in and to such Inventions, and any copyrights, patents, mask work rights or other intellectual property rights relating thereto. I further agree that my obligation to execute or cause to be executed, when it is in my power to do so, any such instrument or papers shall continue after the termination of this Agreement. If the Company is unable because of my mental or physical incapacity or for any other reason to secure my signature to apply for or to pursue any application for any United States or foreign patents or copyright registrations covering Inventions or original works of authorship assigned to the Company as above, then I hereby irrevocably designate and appoint the Company and its duly authorized officers and agents as my agent and attorney in fact, to act for and in my behalf and stead to execute and file any such applications and to do all other lawfully permitted acts to further the prosecution and issuance of letters patent or copyright registrations thereon with the same legal force and effect as if executed by me.

F. Exception to Assignments. I understand that the provisions of this Agreement requiring assignment of Inventions to the Company do not apply to any invention which qualifies fully under the provisions of California Labor Code Section 2870 (attached hereto as Exhibit B). I will advise the Company promptly in writing of any inventions that I believe meet the criteria in California Labor Code Section 2870 and not otherwise disclosed on Exhibit A.

4. Conflicting Employment.

I agree that, during the term of my employment with the Company, I will not engage in any other employment, occupation or consulting directly related to the business in which the Company is now involved or becomes involved during the term of my employment, nor will I engage in any other activities that conflict with my obligations to the Company.

5. Returning Company Documents.

I agree that, at the time of leaving the employ of the Company, I will deliver to the Company (and will not keep in my possession, recreate or deliver to anyone else) any and all devices, records, data, notes, reports, proposals, lists, correspondence, specifications, drawings blueprints, sketches, materials, equipment, other documents or property, or reproductions of any aforementioned items developed by me pursuant to my employment with the Company or otherwise belonging to the Company, its successors or assigns, including, without limitation, those records maintained pursuant to paragraph 3.D. In the event of the termination of my employment, I agree to sign and deliver the "Termination Certification" attached hereto as Exhibit C.

6. Notification of New Employer.

In the event that I leave the employ of the Company, I hereby grant consent to notification by the Company to my new employer about my rights and obligations under this Agreement.

7. Solicitation of Employees.

I agree that for a period of twelve (12) months immediately following the termination of my relationship with the Company for any reason, whether with or without cause, I shall not either directly or indirectly solicit, induce, recruit or encourage any of the Company's employees to leave their employment, or take away such employees, or attempt to solicit, induce, recruit, encourage or take away employees of the Company, either for myself or for any other person or entity.

8. Conflict of Interest Guidelines.

I agree to diligently adhere to the Conflict of Interest Guidelines attached as Exhibit D hereto.

9. Representations.

I agree to execute any proper oath or verify any proper document required to carry out the terms of this Agreement. I represent that my performance of all the terms of this Agreement will not breach any agreement to keep in confidence proprietary information acquired by me in confidence or in trust prior to my employment by the Company. I hereby represent and warrant that I have not entered into, and I will not enter into, any oral or written agreement in conflict herewith.

10. Arbitration and Equitable Relief.

A. Arbitration. IN CONSIDERATION OF MY EMPLOYMENT WITH THE COMPANY, ITS PROMISE TO ARBITRATE ALL EMPLOYMENT-RELATED DISPUTES AND MY RECEIPT OF THE COMPENSATION, PAY RAISES AND OTHER BENEFITS PAID TO ME BY THE COMPANY, AT PRESENT AND IN THE FUTURE, I AGREE THAT ANY AND ALL CONTROVERSIES, CLAIMS, OR DISPUTES WITH ANYONE (INCLUDING THE COMPANY AND ANY EMPLOYEE, OFFICER, DIRECTOR, SHAREHOLDER OR BENEFIT PLAN OF THE COMPANY IN THEIR CAPACITY AS SUCH OR OTHERWISE) ARISING OUT OF, RELATING TO, OR RESULTING FROM MY EMPLOYMENT WITH THE COMPANY OR THE TERMINATION OF MY EMPLOYMENT WITH THE COMPANY, INCLUDING ANY BREACH OF THIS AGREEMENT, SHALL BE SUBJECT TO BINDING ARBITRATION UNDER THE ARBITRATION RULES SET FORTH IN CALIFORNIA CODE OF CIVIL PROCEDURE SECTION 1280 THROUGH 1294.2, INCLUDING SECTION 1283.05 (THE "RULES") AND PURSUANT TO CALIFORNIA LAW. DISPUTES WHICH I AGREE TO ARBITRATE, AND THEREBY AGREE TO WAIVE ANY RIGHT TO A TRIAL BY JURY, INCLUDE ANY STATUTORY CLAIMS UNDER STATE OR FEDERAL LAW, INCLUDING, BUT NOT LIMITED TO, CLAIMS UNDER TITLE VII OF THE CIVIL RIGHTS ACT OF 1964, THE AMERICANS WITH DISABILITIES ACT OF 1990, THE AGE DISCRIMINATION IN EMPLOYMENT ACT OF 1967, THE OLDER WORKERS BENEFIT PROTECTION ACT, THE CALIFORNIA FAIR EMPLOYMENT AND HOUSING ACT, THE CALIFORNIA LABOR CODE, CLAIMS OF HARASSMENT, DISCRIMINATION OR WRONGFUL TERMINATION AND ANY STATUTORY CLAIMS. I FURTHER UNDERSTAND THAT THIS AGREEMENT TO ARBITRATE ALSO APPLIES TO ANY DISPUTES THAT THE COMPANY MAY HAVE WITH ME.

B. Procedure. I AGREE THAT ANY ARBITRATION WILL BE ADMINISTERED BY THE AMERICAN ARBITRATION ASSOCIATION ("AAA") AND THAT THE NEUTRAL ARBITRATOR WILL BE SELECTED IN A MANNER CONSISTENT WITH ITS NATIONAL RULES FOR THE RESOLUTION OF

EMPLOYMENT DISPUTES. I AGREE THAT THE ARBITRATOR SHALL HAVE THE POWER TO DECIDE ANY MOTIONS BROUGHT BY ANY PARTY TO THE ARBITRATION, INCLUDING MOTIONS FOR SUMMARY JUDGMENT AND/OR ADJUDICATION AND MOTIONS TO DISMISS AND DEMURRERS, PRIOR TO ANY ARBITRATION HEARING. I ALSO AGREE THAT THE ARBITRATOR SHALL HAVE THE POWER TO AWARD ANY REMEDIES, INCLUDING ATTORNEYS' FEES AND COSTS, AVAILABLE UNDER APPLICABLE LAW. I UNDERSTAND THE COMPANY WILL PAY FOR ANY ADMINISTRATIVE OR HEARING FEES CHARGED BY THE ARBITRATOR OR AAA EXCEPT THAT I SHALL PAY THE FIRST $200.00 OF ANY FILING FEES ASSOCIATED WITH ANY ARBITRATION I INITIATE. I AGREE THAT THE ARBITRATOR SHALL ADMINISTER AND CONDUCT ANY ARBITRATION IN A MANNER CONSISTENT WITH THE RULES AND THAT TO THE EXTENT THAT THE AAA'S NATIONAL RULES FOR THE RESOLUTION OF EMPLOYMENT DISPUTES CONFLICT WITH THE RULES, THE RULES SHALL TAKE PRECEDENCE. I AGREE THAT THE DECISION OF THE ARBITRATOR SHALL BE IN WRITING.

C. Remedy. EXCEPT AS PROVIDED BY THE RULES AND THIS AGREEMENT, ARBITRATION SHALL BE THE SOLE, EXCLUSIVE AND FINAL REMEDY FOR ANY DISPUTE BETWEEN ME AND THE COMPANY. ACCORDINGLY, EXCEPT AS PROVIDED FOR BY THE RULES AND THIS AGREEMENT, NEITHER I NOR THE COMPANY WILL BE PERMITTED TO PURSUE COURT ACTION REGARDING CLAIMS THAT ARE SUBJECT TO ARBITRATION. NOTWITHSTANDING, THE ARBITRATOR WILL NOT HAVE THE AUTHORITY TO DISREGARD OR REFUSE TO ENFORCE ANY LAWFUL COMPANY POLICY, AND THE ARBITRATOR SHALL NOT ORDER OR REQUIRE THE COMPANY TO ADOPT A POLICY NOT OTHERWISE REQUIRED BY LAW WHICH THE COMPANY HAS NOT ADOPTED.

D. Availability of Injunctive Relief. IN ADDITION TO THE RIGHT UNDER THE RULES TO PETITION THE COURT FOR PROVISIONAL RELIEF, I AGREE THAT ANY PARTY MAY ALSO PETITION THE COURT FOR INJUNCTIVE RELIEF WHERE EITHER PARTY ALLEGES OR CLAIMS A VIOLATION OF THE EMPLOYMENT, CONFIDENTIAL INFORMATION, INVENTION ASSIGNMENT AGREEMENT BETWEEN ME AND THE COMPANY OR ANY OTHER AGREEMENT REGARDING TRADE SECRETS, CONFIDENTIAL INFORMATION, NONSOLICITATION OR LABOR CODE SECTION 2870. I UNDERSTAND THAT ANY BREACH OR THREATENED BREACH OF SUCH AN AGREEMENT WILL CAUSE IRREPARABLE INJURY AND THAT MONEY DAMAGES WILL NOT PROVIDE AN ADEQUATE REMEDY THEREFOR AND BOTH PARTIES HEREBY CONSENT TO THE ISSUANCE OF AN INJUNCTION. IN THE EVENT EITHER PARTY SEEKS INJUNCTIVE RELIEF, THE PREVAILING PARTY SHALL BE ENTITLED TO RECOVER REASONABLE COSTS AND ATTORNEYS FEES.

E. Administrative Relief. I UNDERSTAND THAT THIS AGREEMENT DOES NOT PROHIBIT ME FROM PURSUING AN ADMINISTRATIVE CLAIM WITH A LOCAL, STATE OR FEDERAL ADMINISTRATIVE BODY SUCH AS THE DEPARTMENT OF FAIR EMPLOYMENT AND HOUSING, THE EQUAL EMPLOYMENT OPPORTUNITY COMMISSION OR THE WORKERS'

COMPENSATION BOARD. THIS AGREEMENT DOES, HOWEVER, PRECLUDE ME FROM PURSUING COURT ACTION REGARDING ANY SUCH CLAIM.

F. Voluntary Nature of Agreement. I ACKNOWLEDGE AND AGREE THAT I AM EXECUTING THIS AGREEMENT VOLUNTARILY AND WITHOUT ANY DURESS OR UNDUE INFLUENCE BY THE COMPANY OR ANYONE ELSE. I FURTHER ACKNOWLEDGE AND AGREE THAT I HAVE CAREFULLY READ THIS AGREEMENT AND THAT I HAVE ASKED ANY QUESTIONS NEEDED FOR ME TO UNDERSTAND THE TERMS, CONSEQUENCES AND BINDING EFFECT OF THIS AGREEMENT AND FULLY UNDERSTAND IT, INCLUDING THAT ***I AM WAIVING MY RIGHT TO A JURY TRIAL***. FINALLY, I AGREE THAT I HAVE BEEN PROVIDED AN OPPORTUNITY TO SEEK THE ADVICE OF AN ATTORNEY OF MY CHOICE BEFORE SIGNING THIS AGREEMENT.

11. General Provisions.

A. Governing Law; Consent to Personal Jurisdiction. This Agreement will be governed by the laws of the State of California. I hereby expressly consent to the personal jurisdiction of the state and federal courts located in California for any lawsuit filed there against me by the Company arising from or relating to this Agreement.

B. Entire Agreement. This Agreement sets forth the entire agreement and understanding between the Company and me relating to the subject matter herein and supersedes all prior discussions or representations between us including, but not limited to, any representations made during my interview(s) or relocation negotiations, whether written or oral. No modification of or amendment to this Agreement, nor any waiver of any rights under this Agreement, will be effective unless in writing signed by the President of the Company and me. Any subsequent change or changes in my duties, salary or compensation will not affect the validity or scope of this Agreement.

C. Severability. If one or more of the provisions in this Agreement are deemed void by law, then the remaining provisions will continue in full force and effect.

D. Successors and Assigns. This Agreement will be binding upon my heirs, executors, administrators and other legal representatives and will be for the benefit of the Company, its successors, and its assigns.

Date: ______________________ ______________________

Signature

____

Print Name

Exhibit A

LIST OF PRIOR INVENTIONS AND ORIGINAL WORKS OF AUTHORSHIP

___ No inventions or improvements
___ Additional Sheets Attached

Signature of Employee: ______________________
Print Name of Employee: ______________________
Date: ______________

Exhibit B

CALIFORNIA LABOR CODE SECTION 2870
INVENTION ON OWN TIME-EXEMPTION FROM AGREEMENT

"(a) Any provision in an employment agreement which provides that an employee shall assign, or offer to assign, any of his or her rights in an invention to his/her employer shall not apply to an invention that the employee developed entirely on his/her own time without using the employer's equipment, supplies, facilities, or trade secret information except for those inventions that either:

(1) Relate at the time of conception or reduction to practice of the invention to the employer's business, or actual or demonstrably anticipated research or development of the employer; or

(2) Result from any work performed by the employee for the employer.

(b) To the extent a provision in an employment agreement purports to require an employee to assign an invention otherwise excluded from being required to be assigned under subdivision (a), the provision is against the public policy of this state and is unenforceable."

Exhibit C

[NAME OF COMPANY]
TERMINATION CERTIFICATION

This is to certify that I do not have in my possession, nor have I failed to return, any devices, records, data, notes, reports, proposals, lists, correspondence, specifications, drawings, blueprints, sketches, materials, equipment, other documents or property, or reproductions of any aforementioned items belonging to ________________, its subsidiaries, affiliates, successors or assigns (together, the "Company").

I further certify that I have complied with all the terms of the Company's Employment, Confidential Information, Invention Assignment and Arbitration Agreement signed by me, including the reporting of any inventions and original works of authorship (as defined therein), conceived or made by me (solely or jointly with others) covered by that agreement.

I further agree that, in compliance with the Employment, Confidential Information, Invention Assignment, and Arbitration Agreement, I will preserve as confidential all trade secrets, confidential knowledge, data or other proprietary information relating to products, processes, know-how, designs, formulas, developmental or experimental work, computer programs, data bases, other original works of authorship, customer lists, business plans, financial information or other subject matter pertaining to any business of the Company or any of its employees, associates, consultants or licensees.

I further agree that for twelve (12) months from this date, I will not solicit, induce, recruit or encourage any of the Company's employees to leave their employment.

Date: ______________________________ ______________________________

[Employee's Signature]

____

[Print Name]

Exhibit D

[NAME OF COMPANY]
CONFLICT OF INTEREST GUIDELINES

It is the policy ___________________ to conduct its affairs in strict compliance with the letter and spirit of the law and to adhere to the highest principles of business ethics. Accordingly, all officers, employees and independent contractors must avoid activities which are in conflict, or give the appearance of being in conflict, with these principles and with the interests of the Company. The following are potentially compromising situations which must be avoided. Any exceptions must be reported to the President and written approval for continuation must be obtained.

1. Revealing confidential information to outsiders or misusing confidential information. Unauthorized divulging of information is a violation of this policy whether or not for personal gain and whether or not harm to the Company is intended. (The At Will Employment, Confidential Information, Invention Assignment and Arbitration Agreement elaborates on this principle and is a binding agreement.)

2. Accepting or offering substantial gifts, excessive entertainment, favors or payments which may be deemed to constitute undue influence or otherwise be improper or embarrassing to the Company.

3. Participating in civic or professional organizations that might involve divulging confidential information of the Company.

4. Initiating or approving personnel actions affecting reward or punishment of employees or applicants where there is a family relationship or is or appears to be a personal or social involvement.

5. Initiating or approving any form of personal or social harassment of employees.

6. Investing or holding outside directorship in suppliers, customers, or competing companies, including financial speculations, where such investment or directorship might influence in any manner a decision or course of action of the Company.

7. Borrowing from or lending to employees, customers or suppliers.

8. Acquiring real estate of interest to the Company.

9. Improperly using or disclosing to the Company any proprietary information or trade secrets of any former or concurrent employer or other person or entity with whom obligations of confidentiality exist.

10. Unlawfully discussing prices, costs, customers, sales or markets with competing companies or their employees.

11. Making any unlawful agreement with distributors with respect to prices.

12. Improperly using or authorizing the use of any inventions which are the subject of patent claims of any other person or entity.

13. Engaging in any conduct which is not in the best interest of the Company.

Each officer, employee and independent contractor must take every necessary action to ensure compliance with these guidelines and to bring problem areas to the attention of higher management for review. Violations of this conflict of interest policy may result in discharge without warning.

8. Annual Meeting Documents

Annual Meeting

In California, Corporation Code Chapter 6 (Section 600-605) provides statutory guidelines regarding convening of meeting, notice, quorum and procedures. Corporation Code Chapter 7 (Sections 700-711) provides statutory guidelines regarding voting of shares and record date. Bylaws provide specifics regarding meetings and should parallel applicable statutes.

The main purpose of holding annual meetings is to protect the corporate identity "corporate veil" from being pieced and corporate protections lost in certain instances where a corporation is found to not have a true corporate structure. For example, electing directors annually affords protection of corporate structure. In small corporations, a written consent in lieu of annual meeting may be desirable, if allowed by applicable law.

If an annual meeting has not been held or deemed necessary in the start-up phase of a corporation, it may be advisable to hold an annual meeting approximately one year prior to initial public offering, but this should be determined by an attorney. Matters typically included for approval include: (i) election of directors, (ii) approval of stock option plan or amendment there to, (iii) ratification of appointment of auditors, and (iv) if not already included in the Articles, approval of indemnification and liability provisions, including: amendment of Articles, amendment of Bylaws, and approval of form of Indemnity Agreement.

Resolutions of Board of Directors

Resolutions of the Board of Directors are prepared to set date of meeting, record date, and matters to be approved by shareholders.

RESOLUTIONS TO BE ADOPTED BY THE BOARD OF DIRECTORS FOR CALLING OF ANNUAL MEETING

ANNUAL MEETING OF SHAREHOLDERS/STOCKHOLDERS

RESOLVED, that the 20__ Annual Meeting of [shareholders/stockholders] of the Company (the "Annual Meeting") be, and it hereby is, set for ____________, 20__, at the Company's offices at ____ [a.m./p.m.];

RESOLVED FURTHER, that the record date for persons entitled to receive notice of, and to vote at, such Annual Meeting be, and it hereby is, set at ____________, 20__.

RESOLVED FURTHER, that ___________, ___________, ___________, and ___________ be recommended for nomination at the Annual Meeting to serve as directors of the Company until the next Annual Meeting of [shareholders/stockholders] or until their successors are elected and qualified; and

RESOLVED FURTHER, that the Secretary of the Company be, and [he/she] hereby is, authorized and directed cause a Notice of Annual Meeting to be sent to the Company's shareholders/stockholders of record as of the record date and to solicit proxies for the voting of their shares with respect to the following matters: (i) election of the Company's directors for the ensuing year, (ii) [approval of [an amendment to] the Company's 20__ Stock Option Plan (the "Plan") [to increase the number of shares of Common Stock available for issuance under the Plan to ______________ (_________) shares], (iii) ratification of the Board's selection of ____________ as the Company's auditors for the fiscal year ending ________, 20__.

SELECTION OF AUDITORS

RESOLVED, that __________________, is hereby selected as the Company's auditors for the fiscal year ending __________, 20__; and

RESOLVED, that the selection of ________________ as auditors for the fiscal year ending __________, 20__ be submitted to the [shareholders/stockholders] for ratification as set forth in the foregoing resolutions.

[ELECTION OF OFFICERS

RESOLVED, that the following named persons are elected to the offices set forth opposite their names [at the annual compensation for services to be rendered to the corporation set forth opposite their titles] to serve until the next annual meeting of the Board of Directors or until their successors are duly elected and qualified:

Name	Officer	[Annual Compensation]
__________________	______________	_________________
__________________	______________	_________________]

[RATIFICATION

RESOLVED, that the [contract/lease agreement] executed on behalf of the Company by ____________, ____________ of the Company, on __________, 20__ attached hereto as Exhibit ___ be, and it hereby is, confirmed, ratified and approved as action taken by and for the Company.]

AUTHORIZATION

RESOLVED, that the officers of the Company be, and they hereby are, authorized and directed, for and on behalf of the Company, to take such action and execute such documents as they deem necessary or advisable in order to carry out and perform the purposes of the foregoing resolutions.

Dated: ____________, 20__

____

Secretary

Notice of Annual Meeting

Note record date and prepare a shareholder list as of record date. Record date is typically fixed by Board and, if so fixed, is at least 10 days but not more than 60 days prior to meeting. Be alert to stock issuances that may be processed after record date, but have an issuance date prior to the record date.

NAME OF CORPORATION
Street Address
City, State, Zip Code

NOTICE OF ANNUAL MEETING OF SHAREHOLDERS

NOTICE IS HEREBY GIVEN that the Annual Meeting of Shareholders (the "Annual Meeting") of ________________, a [California] corporation (the "Company"), will be held at the offices of the Company at ____________________________ on _________, 20__ at _____ [a.m./p.m.] for the following purposes:

1. To elect ____ directors to the Board of Directors to serve until the next Annual Meeting of Shareholders.

2. [To approve [an amendment to] the Company's 20__ Stock Option Plan].

3. To ratify the selection by the Board of Directors of ___________________ as the Company's auditors for the first year ending __________, 20__.

4. [To approve provisions relating to director liability and indemnification of agents, including amendments to the Company's Articles of Incorporation and Bylaws, and to approve the related form of indemnity agreement.]

5. To transact such other business as may properly come before the meeting or any continuation or adjournment thereof.

Only shareholders of record at the close of business on _________, 20__ will be entitled to receive notice of and vote at the Annual Meeting in accordance with the number of shares of record held in the name of each shareholder on that date.

All shareholders are cordially invited to attend the meeting.

By Order of the Board of Directors

___________________________________ ___________________________

City and State from where notice was mailed [Name]

____

____

Date of Mailing Secretary

WHETHER OR NOT YOU EXPECT TO ATTEND THE ANNUAL MEETING, PLEASE COMPLETE, DATE AND SIGN THE ENCLOSED PROXY AND RETURN IT PROMPTLY IN THE ENCLOSED ENVELOPE TO ASSURE REPRESENTA-TION OF YOUR SHARES.

Proxy Statement

The Proxy Statement is mailed with the Notice of Annual Meeting.

[NAME OF CORPORATION]
Street Address
City, State, Zip Code

PROXY STATEMENT
FOR
ANNUAL MEETING OF SHAREHOLDERS
TO BE HELD __________, 20__

THIS PROXY STATEMENT is furnished in connection with the solicitation of proxies by the Board of Directors of [Name of Corporation], a [California] corporation (the "Company"), for use at the Annual Meeting of Shareholders to be held on __________, 20__, at _____ [a.m./p.m.] local time or at any adjournment or postponement of that meeting. [The cost of solicitation of proxies by mail may be supplemented by telephone, telegram and personal solicitation by officers, directors or other regular employees of the Company. No additional compensation will be paid to such individuals.]

All proxies will be voted in accordance with the instructions contained in the proxy. If no choice is made on proxies signed and returned to the Company, such proxies will be voted in favor of the proposals set forth in the Notice of Annual Meeting attached to this Proxy Statement. Any proxies given pursuant to this solicitation may be revoked by the person giving it at any time before its use by delivering to the Company a written notice of revocation or a duly executed proxy bearing a later date or by attending the meeting and voting in person.

VOTING

The Board of Directors has fixed _________, 20__ as the record date for the determination of shareholders entitled to vote at the Annual Meeting of Shareholders. On _________, 20__ [record date], there were outstanding and entitled to vote _________ shares of Common Stock, _________ shares of Series A Preferred Stock (the "Series A Stock") and _________ shares of Series B Preferred Stock (the "Series B Stock"). [**OPTION 1**: Holders of Common Stock, Series A Stock and Series B Stock are entitled to one vote for each share of such stock held (on an as-converted basis).] **[OPTION 2: ALTERNATIVE FOR USE WHEN CONVERSION RATES ARE NOT EQUAL AND/OR WHEN CLASSES HAVE DIFFERENT VOTING RIGHTS TO ELECT DIRECTORS**: Each share of Common Stock is entitled to one vote; holders of Common Stock as a group are entitled to an aggregate of __________ votes. Each share of Series A Stock is entitled to _________ votes; holders of Series A Stock as a group are entitled to an aggregate of __________ votes. Each share of Series B Stock is entitled to ________ votes; holders of Series B Stock as a group are entitled to an aggregate of __________ votes.]

With respect to the election of directors, shareholders may exercise cumulative voting rights. Cumulative voting is permitted for all shareholders if at least one shareholder gives notice, at the meeting and prior to voting for the election of directors, of such shareholder's intention to cumulate his/her votes. Under cumulative voting, each shareholder will be entitled to cast [number of directors to be elected] votes for each share of stock held (on an as-converted basis). Each shareholder may give one director-nominee all the votes such shareholder is entitled to cast or may distribute such votes among as many nominees as such shareholder chooses. Voting on all other matters to be submitted at this meeting is non-cumulative. Unless the proxy-holders are otherwise instructed, shareholders, by means of the accompanying proxy, will grant the proxy-holder discretionary authority to cumulate votes.

PROPOSAL 1: ELECTION OF DIRECTORS

One of the purposes of the Annual Meeting is to elect members of the Board of Directors of the Company to serve until the next Annual Meeting of Shareholders or until their successors are elected and have qualified. Shares represented by executed proxies will be voted for the election of the nominees listed below, unless authority to vote in favor of the nominees is withheld. In the event that one or more of such nominees should become unavailable for election for whatever reason, the current Board of Directors will propose a substitute nominee.

Under the Bylaws of the Company, there are ______ authorized directors. The _____ nominees receiving the highest number of the affirmative votes cast at the meeting will be elected directors of the Company.

[OPTION 1 – FOR ONE-CLASS VOTE:

The Company's management intends to nominate the following persons, [each of whom currently is a member of the Company's Board of Directors,] to be elected as directors:

____

____

____

____

Biographical information regarding the nominees is available from the Company upon request.]

[OPTION 2 – FOR USE WHEN VOTING RIGHTS AS TO DIRECTORS DIFFER. MODIFY LANUGAGE TO REFLECT CIRCUMSTANCES ACCURATELY:

The Articles of Incorporation of the Company provide for the election of directors as follows: the holders of Series A Stock shall be entitled, voting as a separate class, to elect _______ director(s); the holders of the Series B Stock shall be entitled voting as a separate class, to elect _______ director(s); and the holders of the Common Stock [and the Preferred Stock] shall be entitled, voting together as one class, to elect the remaining _______ directors.

The nominees to represent the respective classes as set forth above are as follows:

NAME	**PRINCIPAL OCCUPATION**
Series A Stock (_____ Director(s))	
______________________	____________________________
______________________	____________________________

Series B Stock
(_____ Director(s))

_____________________ _________________________

_____________________ _________________________

Common and Preferred Stock
(_____ Director(s))

_____________________ _________________________

_____________________ _________________________

END OF OPTION 2]

THE BOARD OF DIRECTORS RECOMMENDS A VOTE IN FAVOR OF EACH NAMED NOMINEE.

[OPTION 1 – FOR NEWLY-ADOPTED PLANS:

PROPOSAL 2: APPROVAL OF THE COMPANY'S 20__ STOCK OPTION PLAN

On ____________, 20__, the Board of Directors approved the 20__ Stock Option Plan (the "Plan") and reserved an aggregate of ____________ shares of its Common Stock for issuance to the Company's [employees, directors and consultants] upon exercise of options granted under the Plan. The Plan was adopted to allow the Company to grant incentive stock options and supplemental stock options to attract and retain qualified persons as [employees, directors and consultants].]

[OPTION 2 – FOR AMENDMENTS/INCREASES TO PLANS:

PROPOSAL 2: APPROVAL OF AMENDMENTS TO THE COMPAN'S 20__ STOCK OPTION PLAN

On ____________, 20__, the Board of Directors approved the 20__ Stock Option Plan (the "Plan") and reserved an aggregate of ____________ shares of its Common Stock for issuance to the Company's [employees, directors and consultants]. On ____________, 20__, the shareholders approved the adoption of the Plan. On ____________, 20__, the Board of Directors amended the Plan to increase the number of shares reserved for issuance thereunder to ____________ shares, which increase is for the purpose of [increasing the number of shares available for grant under the Plan].

As of ____________, 20__, the Company has granted options to purchase an aggregate of ___________ shares of Common Stock (net of cancellations) at exercise prices ranging between $__________ and $__________ per share. Options to purchase an aggregate of ____________ shares have been exercised through ____________, 20__.

END OF OPTION 2]

[DRAFTING NOTE: MAKE SURE THAT THE FOLLOWING DESCRIPTION ACCURATELY DESCRIBES THE TERMS OF THE PLAN BEING APPROVED.]

DESCRIPTION OF THE PLAN

A copy of the Plan is attached as Exhibit A hereto. The following is a summary of the essential features of the Plan, which should be read in conjunction with the Plan itself.

GENERAL

The Plan provides for the grant of both incentive and supplemental stock options. Incentive stock options granted under the Plan are intended to be "incentive stock options" as defined in Section 422A of the Internal Revenue Code of 1986, as amended. Supplemental stock options granted under the Plan are intended by the Company not to qualify as incentive stock options under the code.

ADMINISTRATION

The Plan is administered by the Board of Directors. The Board has the power to construe and interpret the Plan and, subject to the provisions of the Plan, to determine the persons to whom and the dates on which options will be granted, the number of shares to be subject to each option, the time or times during the term of each option within which all or a portion of such option may be exercised, the exercise price, the type of consideration and other terms of the option. [The Board of Directors is authorized to delegate administration of the Plan to a committee composed of not less than three members.]

ELIGIBILITY

Incentive stock options may be granted under the Plan only to employees (including directors if they are also employees) of the Company and its affiliates. Selected employees, directors and consultants are eligible to receive supplemental stock options under the Plan. Officers who are not salaried employees of or consultants to the Company or any affiliates are not eligible to participate in the Plan.

For incentive stock options granted under the Plan, the aggregate fair market value of the shares of Common Stock with respect to which such options are exercisable for the first time by an optionee during any calendar year (under all such plans of the Company or any affiliate of the Company) may not exceed $100,000. No incentive stock option may be granted under the Plan to any person who, at the time of the grant, owns (or is deemed to own) stock possessing more than 10% of the total combined voting power of the Company or any affiliate of the Company, unless the option price is at least 110% of the fair market value on the date of grant of the stock subject to the option, and the term of the option does not exceed five years from the date of grant.

TERMS OF OPTIONS

The exercise price of incentive stock options under the Plan must be equal to at least the fair market value of the underlying stock on the date of the option grant. In some cases (see "Eligibility" above), the exercise price of options under the Plan may not be less than 110% of the fair market value of the underlying stock on the date of grant. The exercise price of supplemental options under the Plan must be equal to at least 85% of the fair market value of the underlying stock on the date of the option grant. The maximum term of options under the Plan is 10 years. Options granted under the Plan become exercisable in cumulative increments as determined by the Board. Options must be exercised within specified periods of the end of a person's relationship with the Company.

DURATION, AMENDMENT AND TERMINATION

The Board may suspend or terminate the Plan without shareholder approval or ratification at any time or from time to time. Unless sooner terminated, the Plan will terminate on _____________, 20__.

The Board may also amend the Plan at any time or from time to time. However, no amendment shall be effective unless approved by the shareholders of the Company within 12 months before or after its adoption by the Board if the amendment would: (i) modify materially the requirements as to eligibility for participation; (ii) increase the number of shares reserved for options; or (iii) modify the Plan in any other way if such modification requires shareholder approve in order for the Plan to satisfy the requirements of Section 422A(b) of the Code or to comply with the requirements of Rule 16b-3 promulgated under the Securities Exchange Act of 1934.

TAX CONSEQUENCES

The tax consequences of the grant and exercise of stock options and the sale of the stock acquired upon exercise of options are complex and have been changing with changes in the tax law. Option holders are generally informed of these consequences.

The favorable vote of shareholders holding a majority of the votes attributable to the Company's outstanding voting stock is required for approval of the Plan.

THE BOARD OF DIRECTORS RECOMMENDS A VOTE IN FAVOR OF PROPOSALS 2.

END OF OPTIONAL SECTION]

PROPOSAL [3]: SELECTION OF AUDITORS

The Board of Directors has approved, and is now submitting for shareholder ratification the selection of _________________ as the Company's auditors for its fiscal year ending _____________, 20__. [_________________ has served as the Company's auditors since the Company's inception. **ALTERNATIVELY, DESCRIBE CHANGE IN AUDITORS.]**

The favorable vote of shareholders holding a majority of the votes attributable to the Company's outstanding voting stock is required for approval of the selection of the Company's auditors.

THE BOARD OF DIRECTORS RECOMMENDS A VOTE IN FAVOR OF PROPOSAL [3].

[NOTE: THE FOLLOWING OPTION APPLIES ONLY TO CALIFORNIA CORPORATIONS AND IS DESIRABLE IF THE CORPORATION HAS NOT ADOPTED INDEMNIFICATION PROVISIONS AS CURRENTLY PROVIDED FOR BY CALIFORNIA LAW:

PROPOSAL [4]: APPROVAL OF PROVISIONS REGARDING DIRECTOR LIABILITY AND INDEMNIFICATION OF AGENTS; INDEMNITY AGREEMENT

The Board of Directors of the Company has adopted a proposal to amend the Company's Articles of Incorporation to eliminate the liability of its directors for monetary damages to the fullest extent permissible under California law and to amend the Company's Articles of Incorporation and Bylaws to broaden the indemnification provided to its directors, officers, employees and other agents. The proposed amendments to the Articles of Incorporation are set forth in Article ___ of the Restated Articles attached as Exhibit ___ hereto. The proposed amendment to the Bylaws is set forth in Article ___ of Exhibit ___ attached hereto. In addition, the Board has adopted a form of indemnity agreement in the form attached hereto as Exhibit ___ to cover the Company's directors and senior executive officers. Shareholders are requested to approve Article ___ of the Restated Articles and Article ___ of the Bylaws. Although California law does not require shareholder approval or ratification of the indemnity agreements, the Company is also submitting these agreements for shareholder ratification as a matter of good corporate practice.

The Board's actions in submitting this proposal to shareholders is prompted by changes in California law allowing the broader indemnification of agents of a corporation and the elimination of certain aspects of director liability. The Board believes approval of this proposal will enhance the Company's ability to attract and retain qualified members of the Company's Board of Directors as well as to encourage the directors, officers, employees and other agents of the Company to continue to make independent decisions in good faith on behalf of the Company.

DIRECTOR LIABILITY

Under California law, a director of a corporation is required to perform the duties of a director in good faith and in a manner the director believes to be in the best interests of the corporation and its shareholders and with the care of an ordinarily prudent person. Liability for breaches of the duty of care, including liability for monetary damages, may arise when a director has failed to exercise sufficient care and diligence in reaching decisions or in attending to his or her responsibilities to the corporation and its shareholders.

California law enables a California corporation to include a provision in its Articles of Incorporation that limits or eliminates a director's personal liability to the corporation and its shareholders for monetary damages arising out of breaches by the director of the director's duty of care.

The Company's Restated Articles include such a provision (the "Liability Provision"). The effect of the Liability Provision is to protect directors from personal liability in connection with claims made by the Company or its shareholders for negligence, gross negligence or recklessness in the directors' exercise of their duty of care. The Liability Provision does not, however, protect directors from personal liability in connection with claims made by anyone other than the Company or its shareholders.

The Liability Provision also would not protect a director if the Company or its shareholders were able to establish that the director failed to act in good faith, knowingly acted contrary to the best interests of the Company or its shareholders, engaged in intentional misconduct, knowingly violated the law, derived an improper personal benefit or illegally approved a transaction in which he/she was an interested party, approved an illegal dividend or stock repurchase, acted recklessly under circumstances where the director was aware, or should have been aware, in the ordinary course of performing his/her duties, of a risk of serious injury to the Company or its shareholder or exhibited an unexcused pattern of inattention amounting to an abdication of the director's duty to the Company. Because the Liability Provision is tied to applicable California law, the extent of the limitations with respect to the liability of directors could be expanded or otherwise modified by future changes in California law without shareholder action.

INDEMNIFICATION UNDER CALIFORNIA LAW

California law provides that a corporation may indemnify its directors, officers, employees and other agents against the expenses and cost of settlement or judgment of actions brought against such persons by third parties, provided that the person being indemnified acted in good faith and in a matter such person reasonably believed to be in the best interests of the corporation, and, in the case of a criminal proceeding, such person had no reasonable cause to believe the conduct of such person was unlawful. California law further provides that a corporation may indemnify its directors, officers, employees and other agents against the expenses of defense or settlement of actions by or in the right of the corporation (such as a shareholder derivative suit), so long as such person acted in good faith and in a manner such person believed to be in the best interest of the corporation and its shareholders, *provided* that no indemnification is payable if such person is found liable to the corporation in the performance of his/her duty to the corporation or its shareholders (except to the extent that the court involved expressly authorizes such indemnification) or if the action is settled or otherwise disposed of without court approval. Indemnification in either instance may be paid only if the director, officer, employee or other agent is successful on the merits of his/her defense in court or the indemnification is specifically authorized after a determination that indemnification is proper under the circumstances because the director, officer, employee or other agent has met the applicable standard of case described above. This determination must be made by one of the following: (1) a majority vote of a quorum of directors who are not parties to the action; (2) if such quorum is not obtainable, by independent legal counsel in a written opinion; (3) by a vote of the shareholders, with the shares of the person to be indemnified not being entitled to vote thereon; or (4) by the court in which the action is or was pending.

California law further provides that a corporation may indemnify its directors, officers, employees and other agents for breach of duty to the corporation and its shareholder beyond the limits expressly provided by California law if the corporation's Articles of Incorporation are amended to expressly permit such indemnification. If a corporation's Articles of Incorporation are so amended, indemnification remains unavailable for prohibited acts or omissions and to the extent expressly prohibited by California law. The proposed Restated Articles of the Company permit indemnification beyond that expressly permitted by the statute.

The Board of Directors has also amended indemnification provisions of the Company's Bylaws to provide that the Company shall indemnify its directors to the fullest extent not prohibited by California law and to permit the Company to provide similar indemnification to officers, employees and other agents. Such indemnification is intended to provide the full flexibility available under California law and may, under certain circumstances, include indemnification for negligence, gross negligence and certain types of recklessness.

Article ___ of the Bylaws, as amended, provides that the rights to indemnification provided in the Bylaws are not limited to those expressly provided by the California statute to the extent permitted by the Company's Articles of Incorporation. As a result, under California law and the Company's Bylaws, the Company will be permitted to indemnify its directors, officers, employees and other agents, within the limits established by law and public policy, pursuant to an express contract. Bylaw provision, shareholder vote or otherwise, any or all of which could provide indemnification rights broader than those expressly available under California law. The Board of Directors has authorized the Company to enter into such agreements should this proposal be approved.

The current Bylaws also provide that expenses will be advanced to a director upon such person's delivery of an undertaking to repay such advances if it shall be determined that the director is ultimately not entitled to indemnification under the Bylaws. Because the indemnification provisions of the Bylaws are tied to applicable California law, they may be modified by future changes in such law without further shareholder action.

In the same spirit, the Board approved indemnity agreements for the Company's directors providing them with similar protections. The form of the agreement is attached as Exhibit ___ hereto.

California corporate law and the Bylaws of the Company may permit indemnification for liabilities arising under the Securities Act of 1933 or the Securities Exchange Act of 1934. The Board of Directors has been advised that, in the opinion of the Securities and Exchange Commission, indemnification for liabilities arising under those Acts is contrary to public policy and is therefore unenforceable, absent a decision to the contrary by a court of appropriate jurisdiction.

The affirmative vote of the holders of a majority of the outstanding shares of the Company is required to approve the amendment to the Articles of Incorporation and Bylaws.

THE BOARD OF DIRECTORS RECOMMENDS A VOTE IN FAVOR OF PROPOSAL [4].

END OF OPTIONAL SECTION]

OTHER MATTERS

The Board of Directors knows of no other matters that may come before the Annual Meeting. If any other matters are properly presented at the Annual Meeting, it is the intention of the persons named in the accompanying proxy to vote, or otherwise to act, in accordance with their best judgment on such matters.

_______________, 20__ BY ORDER OF THE BOARD OF DIRECTORS
[Date of mailing.]
____
Secretary

THE BOARD OF DIRECTORS HOPES THAT THE COMPANY'S SHAREHOLDERS WILL ATTEND THE ANNUAL MEETING. WHETHER OR NOT YOU PLAN TO ATTEND, HOWEVER, YOU ARE URGED TO COMPLETE, SIGN AND RETURN THE ENCLOSED PROXY IN THE ACCOMPANYING ENVELOPE.

Proxy

The Proxy is mailed with the Proxy Statement and the Notice of Annual Meeting.

[NAME OF CORPORATION]
Street Address
City, State, Zip Code

PROXY

The undersigned hereby appoints _____________ and ____________ and each of them, as the attorneys and proxies of the undersigned, with power of substitution, to vote all shares of the stock of _________________, a [California] corporation (the "Company"), which the undersigned is entitled to vote at the Annual Meeting of Shareholders of the Company to be held at the offices of the Company, __________________, on ___________, 20__ at _____ [a.m./p.m.], and at any continuation or adjournment thereof, with the same force and effect as the undersigned might or could do if personally present thereat, as set forth below and in their discretion upon any other business that may properly come before the meeting.

1. To elect directors of the Company, whether by cumulative voting or otherwise, to serve until the next Annual Meeting of Shareholders and until their successors are elected.

Nominees:

____
____
____
____

[OPTION 1: WHEN ALL SHAREHOLDERS VOTE AS ONE CLASS:

☐ WITH AUTHORITY to vote for nominees listed above (except as marked below)

☐ WITHHOLD AUTHORITY as to the following nominees:

END OF OPTION 1]

[OPTION 2: DIFFERENT VOTING RIGHTS AMONG CLASSES:

☐ WITH AUTHORITY to vote for all nominees listed above (unless such authority is withheld below), as applicable pursuant to the Proxy Statement distributed to the Shareholders herewith (the "Proxy Statement").

☐ WITHHOLD AUTHORITY as to the following nominees, as applicable pursuant to the Proxy Statement:

END OF OPTION 2]

1. [To approve [the amendment of] the Company's 20__ Stock Option Plan (check one box).

☐ FOR ☐ AGAINST ☐ ABSTAIN]

2. [To ratify the appointment of ____________________ as auditors for the Company for the fiscal year ending ____________, 20__ (check one box).

☐ FOR ☐ AGAINST ☐ ABSTAIN]

3. [To approve the provisions regarding director liability and indemnification of agents as fully described in the Proxy Statement.

☐ FOR ☐ AGAINST ☐ ABSTAIN]

THIS PROXY IS SOLCITED ON BEHALF OF THE BOARD OF DIRECTORS. SHARES REPRESENTED BY THIS PROXY WILL BE VOTED IN ACCORDANCE WITH SPECIFICATIONS MADE HEREIN. IF NO SPECIFICATION IS MADE AS TO ANY INDIVIDUAL ITEM HEREIN, IT IS INTENDED THAT SHARES REPRESENTED BY THIS PROXY WILL BE VOTED FOR THE ELECTION OF THE NAMED NOMINEES AND FOR THE OTHER PROPOSALS SPECIFIED HEREIN.

Both of said attorneys and proxies or their substitutes as shall be present and act at the meeting, or if only one be present and act then that one, shall have and may exercise all of the powers of both of said attorneys and proxies hereunder.

The undersigned hereby acknowledges receipt of (a) the Notice of Annual Meeting of the Shareholders to be held on ___________, 20__ and (b) the accompanying Proxy Statement.

WITNESS the signature of the undersigned this ______ day of __________, 20__.

____
[Name of Shareholder]

____
[Signature]

____
[Title, if applicable]

NUMBER OF SHARES HELD:

Common Stock _________

Series A Preferred Stock _________

Series B Preferred Stock _________

Script

Attachment to script includes formula for calculation of cumulative voting, if allowed by applicable law, and discussion of cumulative voting ramifications.

SCRIPT FOR ANNUAL MEETING OF [SHAREHOLDERS/STOCKHOLDERS] OF [NAME OF CORPORATION]

[Annual Meeting Date]

[Chair]: Good [morning/afternoon]. I am [Name], and I am [Title] of [Name of Corporation]; and will act as chairman of this meeting. I am very happy to welcome you to the [Name of Corporation] 20__ [shareholders/stockholders] meeting. Before I call the meeting to order, I would like to introduce to you the members of the Board and the business team who are with us today.

The other members of the Board are: [Names].

The other officers of the Company here today are: [Names].

I would also like to introduce [Name of Auditors], the Company's auditors, who is/are available to respond to appropriate questions.

1. CALL TO ORDER

[Chair]: The meeting now officially comes to order. We propose to proceed with the formal business of the meeting set forth in your notice of annual meeting and proxy statement. After the formal part of the meeting, we will review the Company's recent business activities and give you an opportunity to ask any questions you may have.

2. LIST OF [SHAREHOLDERS/STOCKHOLDERS] AND PROOF OF MAILING OF NOTICE

[Chair]: Will the secretary please report at this time with respect to the mailing of the notice of the meeting and the [shareholders/stockholders] list.

[Secretary]: I have at this meeting a complete list of the [shareholders/stockholders] of record of the Company's capital stock on [Record Date], the record date for this meeting.

I also have with me an affidavit certifying that on [Date], a notice of annual meeting of [shareholders/stockholders'] of the Company was deposited in the United States mail to all [shareholders/stockholders] of record at the close of business on [Record Date].

3. INSPECTOR OF ELECTION

[Chair]: At this time I'd like to introduce [Name of Inspector of Election]. I am appointing [Name] to act as inspector of election at this meeting. [Name] has taken and subscribed to the customary oath of office to execute his/her duties with strict impartiality, which will be filed with the records of the meeting. [His/her] function is to decide upon the qualifications of voters, accept their votes, and, when balloting on all matters are completed, to tally the final votes.

Will the Secretary please report at this time with respect to the existence of a quorum?

4. ANNOUNCEMENT OF QUORUM PRESENT

[Secretary]: I have been informed by the inspector of election that proxies have been received for [Number] of the [Number] shares of common stock and for [Number] of the [Number] shares of Series A Preferred Stock [on an as-converted basis] and for [Number] of the [Number] shares of Series B Preferred Stock [on an as-converted basis] outstanding on the record date, which represents approximately [Number]% of the total number of outstanding shares. This constitutes a quorum for the meeting today and we may now carry out the official business of the meeting. Are there any additional proxies to be submitted to the inspector of election at this time?

[If yes, collect and deliver to inspector.]

5. CONSIDERATION OF BUSINESS LISTED IN NOTICE OF MEETING

[Chair]: We will now proceed with the formal business of this meeting.

There are [Number] proposals to be considered by the [shareholders/stockholders] at this meeting.

6. ELECTION OF DIRECTORS

[Chair]: The first item of business today is the election of directors to serve until the next annual meeting and until their successors are elected. The nominees for directors of the Company are: [Names]. Is there any discussion? [Pause]. Nominations for director are now closed.

7. APPROVAL OF THE ADOPTION OF THE COMPANY'S 20__ STOCK OPTION PLAN

[Chair]: The second item of business today is the approval of the adoption of the Company's 20__ Stock Option Plan, as described in the proxy statement relating to this annual meeting. Is there any discussion? [Pause].

8. APPROVAL OF AMENDMENT TO THE ARTICLES OF INCORPORATION

[Chair]: The third item of business is the approval of the amendment to the Articles of Incorporation to increase the number of authorized shares of common stock of the Company to an aggregate of [Number] shares. Is there any discussion? [Pause].

9. AMENDMENTS TO THE COMPANY'S 20__ STOCK OPTION PLAN

[Chair]: The fourth item of business today is the approval of the Company's 20__ Stock Option Plan, as amended, as described in the proxy statement relating to this annual meeting. Is there any discussion? [Pause].

10. **RATIFICATION OF INDEPENDENT AUDITORS**

[Chair]: The fifth item of business today is the ratification of the selection of [Auditors] as the independent auditors of the company for the fiscal year ending [Date]. Is there any discussion? [Pause].

That was the final proposal for today's meeting. The Secretary will now describe the voting procedures.

11. **DISTRIBUTION OF BALLOTS AND VOTING**

[Secretary]: Voting is by proxy and written ballot. You do not need to vote in person if you have already sent in your signed proxy or if you have submitted your signed proxy at this meeting. Is there anyone present, whether or not you already submitted a proxy, who now wants to vote in person? [If yes, distribute ballots and say: "After you complete your ballot, please give it to the inspector of election and register your name with [him/her]."]

[Secretary]: Each share of common stock [and each share of Series A Preferred Stock and each share of Series B Preferred Stock] is entitled to [one] vote. [If an election to cumulate votes has been made, the following: "In voting for directors, each share of common stock is entitled to [Number of Directors being elected] votes"].

12. **ANNOUNCEMENT OF RESULTS OF VOTING**

[Chair]: May we have the results of the voting?

[Secretary]: The report of the inspector of election covering the proposals presented at this meeting are as follows:

1) The proposal to elect [Names] as directors of the company are carried. [If election is by cumulative voting, say instead: "The [Number of Directors being elected] nominees with the highest number votes are: [Names]."

2) The Company's 20__ Stock Option Plan has been approved.

3) The amendment to the Articles of Incorporation to provide for an increase in the number of authorized shares of common stock to an aggregate of [Number] shares has been approved.

4) The Company's 20__ Stock Option Plan, amended, has been approved.

5) The appointment of [Auditors] as independent auditors for the fiscal year ending [Year] has been ratified.

[Chair]: Is there any other business to come before this meeting? [Pause]. This concludes the formal portion of our meeting. [After adjournment, we will make a presentation regarding the Company's recent business and then entertain any questions from [shareholders/stockholders].

[Chair]: Is there any discussion? Is there any opposition to adjournment?

This meeting is adjourned.

Inspector of Election

An Oath of Inspector of Election must be prepared and signed at or prior to the annual meeting and included as an exhibit to the Minutes of the annual meeting. It is recommended that you use a tabulation worksheet to determine quorum, keeping track of returned proxies. In addition, the Certificate and Report of Inspector of Election must also be prepared and attached as an exhibit to the Minutes of the annual meeting.

OATH OF INSPECTOR OF ELECTION

STATE OF CALIFORNIA }
} ss.
COUNTY OF __________ }

_________________ declares and says that:

I, _______________, the undersigned duly-appointed Inspector of Election of ______________, do solemnly swear that I will fairly and impartially perform my duties as Inspector of Election at the Annual Meeting of Shareholders of __________________, to be held this ____ day of ___________, 20__ and will faithfully and diligently canvass the votes cast at such meeting on all matters as may be properly voted upon at such meeting and honestly and truthfully report the results of said voting.

____
[Name]

[NAME OF CORPORATION]

CERTIFICATE AND REPORT OF INSPECTOR OF ELECTION

I, _______________, the undersigned duly-appointed Inspector of Election at the Annual Meeting of Shareholders of ______________ (the "Company"), held on __________, 20__, do hereby report:

1. The number of shares of stock of the Company issued and outstanding and entitled to vote upon such matters as were properly brought before said meeting was __________ shares of Common Stock, _________ shares of Series A Preferred Stock and __________ shares of Series B Preferred Stock.

2. There were present at said meeting, in person or by proxy, shareholders holding ________ shares of Common Stock, __________ shares of Series A Preferred Stock and _________ shares of Series B Preferred Stock, or __________ shares on as-if-converted basis, equal to ____% of all such shares outstanding and entitled to vote, which constitute a quorum.

3. I received the votes of the shareholders at said meeting.

4. I canvassed the votes and the vote on the election of the ______ nominees to serve as the Board of Directors until the next Annual Meeting of Shareholders and until their successors are elected and qualified was:

	For	**Withheld**
____________________________	____________________	________________
____________________________	____________________	________________

____________________________	____________________	________________
____________________________	____________________	________________

On that basis, the nominees were elected as directors.

5. I canvassed the votes, and the vote on the approval of [the amendment of] the Company's 20__ Stock Option Plan (the "Plan") was ____________ votes for to __________ votes against with __________ votes abstaining; on that, the [amendment to the] Plan was approved.

6. I canvassed the votes and the vote on the ratification of the appointment of [Auditors] as auditors for the fiscal year ending ___________, 20__, was __________ votes for to __________ votes against with __________ votes abstaining; on that basis, the appointment was ratified and approved.

7. I canvassed the votes and the vote on the approval of the liability and indemnification provisions, including amendments to the Articles of Incorporation and Bylaws, and the approval of the form of indemnity agreement was __________ votes for to __________ votes against with _________ votes abstaining; on that, the provisions and related amendments were ratified and approved.

____

[Name]

[NAME OF CORPORATION]
A [CALIFORNIA] CORPORATION
ANNUAL SHAREHOLDERS MEETING
[DATE OF MEETING]

		No. of Shares	As-If-Converted
1)	Proxies received		
	(a) Common Stock	______________	
	______________		
	(b) Series A Preferred Stock	______________	______________
	(c) Series B Preferred Stock	______________	______________
Total:		______________	______________
2)	Less: Checked shares (proxy filed, but Shareholder present and voting in Person):		
	(a) Common Stock	______________	
	______________		
	(b) Series A Preferred Stock	______________	______________
	(c) Series B Preferred Stock	______________	______________
Total:		______________	______________
3)	Total shares represented by proxy		
	(a) Common Stock	______________	
	______________		
	(b) Series A Preferred Stock	______________	______________
	(c) Series B Preferred Stock	______________	______________
Total:		______________	______________
4)	Plus: shares at meeting voting in		

person:

(a) Common Stock ______________ ______________

(b) Series A Preferred Stock ______________ ______________

(c) Series B Preferred Stock ______________ ______________

Total: ______________ ______________

5) Total shares at meeting:

(a) Common Stock ______________ ______________

(b) Series A Preferred Stock ______________ ______________

(c) Series B Preferred Stock ______________ ______________

Total: ______________ ______________

6) Total shares issued and outstanding on [record date]

(a) Common Stock ______________ ______________

(b) Series A Preferred Stock ______________ ______________

(c) Series B Preferred Stock ______________ ______________

Total: ______________ ______________

7) Number of shares (as-if-converted) necessary for quorum

____

8) Quorum present Yes ☐ No ☐

Certified List of Shareholders

A list of shareholders as of record date will also be prepared and attached as an exhibit to the Minutes of the annual meeting.

STATE OF CALIFORNIA }
} ss.
COUNTY OF __________ }

_________________ declares and says that:

1. [He/she] is the Secretary of __________________, a [California] corporation (the "Company"), having its principal office in the State of California.

2. Attached hereto is a list of shareholders of record, as of __________, 20__, of the Company, with their names and the total number of voting shares they held of record as of such date set forth opposite their names.

I declare under penalty of perjury the foregoing to be true and correct.

Executed as of __________, 20__ at ____________, California.

____
Secretary

Certificate of Mailing

A Certificate of Mailing will also need to be prepared and attached as an exhibit to the Minutes of the annual meeting.

[NAME OF CORPORATION]
CERTIFICATE OF MAILING OF
NOTICE OF ANNUAL MEETING OF SHAREHOLDERS

[NAME] declares and says that:

1. [He/she] is the Secretary of ____________________, a [California] corporation (the "Company");

2. On __________, 20__ [he/she] caused a written Notice of Annual Meeting of Shareholders of the Company, together with a Proxy Statement and Proxy, copies of which are attached hereto, to be mailed, postage prepaid, addressed to each shareholder of record on __________, 20__, entitled to vote, at the last known address appearing on the records of the Company, or given to the Company for the purpose of notice.

I declare under penalty of perjury that the foregoing is true and correct.

Executed as of ___________, 20__ at _____________, California.

____
Secretary

Ballot

In California, Section 708(e) provides that ballots are optional, unless requested by a shareholder for election of directors.

[NAME OF CORPORATION]
A [CALIFORNIA] CORPORATION
ANNUAL MEETING OF SHAREHOLDERS
______________, 20__
BALLOT

I, the undersigned, hereby vote _________ shares of stock, on a common-equivalent basis, of ____________ in the following manner:

ELECTION OF DIRECTORS

Nominees	For	Withheld
______________	______________	
______________		
______________	______________	
______________		
______________	______________	
______________		

[PROPOSITION

To approve [the amendment of] the Company's 20__ Stock Option Plan.

☐ FOR ☐ AGAINST ☐ ABSTAIN]

[PROPOSITION

To ratify the appointment by the Board of Directors of ______________ as the auditors for the fiscal year ending _________, 20__.

☐ FOR ☐ AGAINST ☐ ABSTAIN]

[PROPOSITION

To approve provisions regarding direct liability and indemnification of agents, including amendments to the Articles of Incorporation and Bylaws, and to approve the form of indemnity agreement.

☐ FOR ☐ AGAINST ☐ ABSTAIN]

____

[Print Name]

____

[Signature]

Minutes of Annual Meeting

The Minutes of the annual meeting are usually prepared before the actual meeting based on proxies returned. If no shareholders attend meeting, Minutes may be executed after the meeting.

MINUTES OF ANNUAL MEETING
OF SHAREHOLDERS OF
[NAME OF CORPORATION]

THE 20__ ANNUAL MEETING OF SHAREHOLDERS OF [Name of Corporation], a [California] corporation (the "Company"), was held at the offices of the Company, _________, 20__, at [Time].

CALL TO ORDER

[Name] served as Chairman of the meeting. The Chairman introduced [Officers, Directors and/or Accountants] to the shareholders present at the meeting. The meeting was called to order at [Time] by the Chairman. [Name] served as Secretary of the meeting.

PRESENTATION OF LIST OF SHAREHOLDERS

The Secretary presented to the Chairman a certified list of the shareholders of record as of the close of business on [Record Date], showing opposite each shareholder's name the number of shares held by such shareholder. A copy of the certified list is attached hereto as Exhibit A and incorporated herein by reference.

PRESENTATION OF PROOF OF DUE CALLING OF MEETING

The Secretary then presented to the Chairman a certificate, signed by the [Secretary], stating that on [Date], [Name] caused to be deposited in the United States mail, postage prepaid, addressed to each of the shareholders of record as of the close of business on [Record Date], a Notice of Annual Meeting, a Proxy Statement and Proxy, all in forms attached to said certificate. A copy of the certificate with attachments is attached hereto as Exhibit B and incorporated herein by reference.

INSPECTOR OF ELECTION

[Name] was appointed Inspector of Election. A copy of the duly subscribed oath of the Inspector of Election is attached hereto as Exhibit C and incorporated herein by reference.

ANNOUNCEMENT OF A QUORUM PRESENT

The Secretary announced that a quorum [of each class] of the Company's stock was present. The Chairman declared the meeting to be duly constituted for the transaction of business and asked if there were any additional proxies to be submitted.

CONSIDERATION OF BUSINESS

The Chairman then stated that the formal business for the meeting would proceed.

ELECTION OF DIRECTORS

The first item of business was the election of directors to serve until the [Year] Annual Meeting and until their successors are elected. [Names of Directors] were nominated as directors. [The Chairman then inquired whether there were any further nominations.] [A shareholder gave notice of his/her intention to cumulate votes.] There being no discussion, the Chairman proceeded with the next item of formal business.

APPROVAL OF [AMENDMENT TO] THE [YEAR] STOCK OPTION PLAN

The [second] item of business considered by the shareholders was the approval of the [adoption of/amendment to] the Company's [Year] Stock Option Plan. The Chairman then asked if there was any discussion. There being no discussion, the Chairman proceeded with the next item of formal business.]

RATIFICATION OF SELECTION OF INDEPENDENT AUDITORS

The [third] item of business considered by the shareholders was the ratification of the selection by the Company's Board of Directors of [Auditor] as independent auditors for the fiscal year ending [Date]. The Chairman asked if there was any discussion. There being no discussion, the Chairman proceeded with the next item of formal business.

DISTRIBUTION OF BALLOTS AND VOTING

The Chairman then asked if any persons wished to vote in person.

ANNOUNCEMENT OF RESULTS OF VOTING

The Inspector of Election then submitted the report, a copy of which is attached hereto as Exhibit D. The [Secretary] thereupon declared that:

(1) [Names] were elected directors of the Company for the ensuing year and until their successors are elected and qualified;

(2) the [approval of/amendment to the] [Year] Stock Option Plan was approved; [and]

(3) the selection of [Auditors] to serve as the Company's auditors for the fiscal year ending [Date] was ratified; [and]

[The Chairman asked if there was any other business to come before the meeting.]

ADJOURNMENT OF MEETING

There being no further business to come before the meeting, the meeting was adjourned.

____
Secretary

APPROVED:

____
Chairman

Exhibit A – Certified List of Shareholders
Exhibit B – Certificate of Mailing
Exhibit C – Oath of Inspector of Election
Exhibit D – Report of Inspector of Election

UNANIMOUS WRITTEN CONSENT
[IN LIEU OF ANNUAL MEETING]
OF THE SHAREHOLDERS OF
[NAME OF CORPORATION]

The undersigned, as the record owners of [Number of Shares] shares of stock, being all of the outstanding shares entitled to vote of [Name of Corporation], a [California] corporation, do hereby consent by this writing to the adoption of the following resolutions:

ELECTION OF DIRECTORS

RESOLVED, that the following named persons are hereby elected to serve as the directors of the corporation to hold office until the next annual meeting of shareholders or until their successors are duly elected:

[Name of Directors]
[Name of Directors]
[Name of Directors]
[Name of Directors]

RATIFICATION

RESOLVED, that all proceedings of the Board of Directors and all acts taken by members of the Board of Directors or by officers of this corporation on behalf of the corporation [since the last annual meeting of shareholders] since _______, 20__, are hereby confirmed, ratified and approved as actions taken by and for the corporation.

The undersigned hereby consent to the foregoing resolutions and direct that this Written Consent be filed with the minutes of the proceedings of the shareholders of this corporation and that pursuant to Section 603 of the California General Corporation Law [and the Bylaws of this corporation], said resolutions shall have the same force and effect as if they were adopted at a meeting at which the undersigned were personally present.

Name	Holding Number of Shares	Signature
____________	____________________	____________________
____________	____________________	____________________
____________	____________________	____________________
____________	____________________	____________________

9. Stock Purchase Agreement

SAMPLE STOCK PURCHASE AGREEMENT

OF

____

THIS FOUNDER STOCK PURCHASE AGREEMENT (the "Agreement") is made as of the _____ day of __________, 20__, by and between ____________________, a CALIFORNIA corporation (the "Company"), and ________________ ("Purchaser").

WHEREAS, the Company desires to issue, and Purchaser desires to acquire, stock of the Company as herein described, on the terms and conditions hereinafter set forth; and

WHEREAS, the issuance of common stock hereby is in connection with a compensatory benefit plan for the employees, directors, officers, advisors or consultants of the Company and is intended to comply with Rule 701 promulgated by the Securities and Exchange Commission under the Securities Act of 1933, as amended (the "Act").

NOW, THEREFORE, IT IS AGREED between the parties as follows:

1. PURCHASE AND SALE OF STOCK. Purchaser hereby agrees to purchase from the Company, and the Company hereby agrees to sell to Purchaser, an aggregate of ______________ shares of the Common Stock of the Company (the "Stock") at ________ per share, for an aggregate purchase price of ___________ payable in cash.

The closing hereunder, including payment for and delivery of the Stock shall occur at the offices of the Company immediately following the execution of this Agreement, or at such other time and place as the parties may mutually agree.

2. REPURCHASE OPTION

(a) In the event Purchaser's relationship with the Company (or a parent or subsidiary of the Company), whether as an employee, director or consultant, terminates for any reason (including death or disability), or for no reason, with or without cause, then the Company shall have an irrevocable option (the "Repurchase Option"), for a period of ninety (90) days after said termination, or such longer period as may be agreed to by the Company and the Purchaser, to repurchase from Purchaser or Purchaser's personal representative, as the case may be, at the original price per share indicated above paid by the Purchaser for such Stock ("Option Price"), up to but not exceeding the number of shares of Stock that have not vested as of such termination date in accordance with the provisions of Section 2b below as of such termination date.

(b) _______________ (_______) shares of the Stock will vest immediately upon issuance thereof to Purchaser. The remaining ______________ (_______) shares will initially be subject to the Repurchase Option. On ________, 20__ (the "Vesting Anniversary Date") _______________ (_______) shares of the Stock shall vest and be released from the Repurchase Option. Thereafter, ____ of _______________ (_______) shares of the Stock shall vest and be released from the Repurchase Option on a monthly basis measured from the Vesting Anniversary Date, until all the Stock is released from the Repurchase Option (provided in each case that the Purchaser's relationship as an employee, director or consultant of the Company (or a parent or subsidiary of the Company) has not been terminated prior to the date of such release).

3. **Exercise of Repurchase Option.** The Repurchase Option shall be exercised by written notice signed by an officer of the Company or by any assignee or assignees of the Company and delivered or mailed as provided in Section 16a. Such notice shall identify the number of shares of Stock to be purchased and shall notify Purchaser of the time, place and date for settlement of such purchase, which shall be scheduled by the Company within the term of the Repurchase Option set forth in Section 2a above. The Company shall be entitled to pay for any shares of Stock purchased pursuant to its Repurchase Option at the Company's option in cash or by offset against any indebtedness owing to the Company by Purchaser (including without limitation any Note given in payment for the Stock), or by a combination of both. Upon delivery of such notice and payment of the purchase price in any of the ways described above, the Company shall become the legal and beneficial owner of the Stock being repurchased and all rights and interest therein or related thereto, and the Company shall have the right to transfer to its own name the Stock being repurchased by the Company, without further action by Purchaser.

4. **Adjustments to Stock.** If, from time to time, during the term of the Purchase Option there is any change affecting the Company's outstanding Common Stock as a class that is effected without the receipt of consideration by the Company (through merger, consolidation, reorganization, reincorporation, stock dividend, dividend in property other than cash, stock split, liquidating, dividend, combination of shares, change in corporation structure or other transaction not involving the receipt of consideration by the Company), then any and all new, substituted or additional securities or other property to which Purchaser is entitled by reason of Purchaser's ownership of Stock shall be immediately subject to the Repurchase Option and be included in the word "Stock" for all purposes of the Repurchase Option with the same force and effect as the shares of the Stock presently subject to the Repurchase Option, but only to the extent the Stock is, at the time, covered by such Repurchase Option. While the total Option Price shall remain the same after each such event, the Option Price per share of Stock upon exercise of the Repurchase Option shall be appropriately adjusted.

5. **Corporate Transaction.** In the event of (a) a sale of substantially all of the assets of the Company; (b) a merger or consolidation in which the Company is not the surviving corporation (other than a merger or consolidation in which shareholders immediately before the merger or consolidation have, immediately after the merger or consolidation, greater stock voting power); (c) a reverse merger in which the company is the surviving corporation but the shares of the Company's common stock outstanding immediately preceding the merger are converted by virtue of the merger into other property, whether in the form of securities, cash or otherwise (other than a reverse merger in which stockholders immediately before the merger have, immediately after the merger, greater stock voting power); or (d) any transaction or series of related transactions in which in excess of 50% of the Company's voting power is transferred ((a) through (d) being collectively referred to herein as a "Corporate Transaction"), then the Repurchase Option may be assigned by the Company to any successor of the Company (or the successor's parent) in connection with such Corporate Transaction. To the extent that the Repurchase

Option remains in effect following such a Corporate Transaction, it shall apply to the new capital stock or other property received in exchange for the Stock in consummation of the Corporate Transaction, but only to the extent the Stock is at the time covered by such right. Appropriate adjustments shall be made to the price per share payable upon exercise of the Repurchase Option to reflect the effect of the Corporate Transaction upon the Company's capital structure; provided, however, that the aggregate Option Price shall remain the same.

6. TERMINATION OF REPURCHASE OPTION. Sections 2, 3, 4 and 5 of this Agreement shall terminate upon the exercise in full or expiration of the Repurchase Option, whichever first occurs.

7. ESCROW OF UNVESTED STOCK. As security for Purchaser's faithful performance of the terms of this Agreement and to insure the availability for delivery of Purchaser's stock upon exercise of the Repurchase Option herein provided for, Purchaser agrees, at the closing hereunder, to deliver to and deposit with the Secretary of the Company or the Secretary's designee ("Escrow Agent"), as Escrow Agent in this transaction, three (3) stock assignments duly endorsed (with date and number of shares blank) in the form attached hereto as **Exhibit A**, together with a certificate or certificates evidencing all of the Stock subject to the Repurchase Option; said documents are to be held by the Escrow Agent and delivered by said Escrow Agent pursuant to the Joint Escrow Instructions of the Company and Purchaser set forth in **Exhibit B**, attached hereto and incorporated by this reference, which instructions shall also be delivered to the Escrow Agent at the closing hereunder.

8. RIGHTS OF PURCHASER. Subject to the provisions of Sections 7, 9, 12 and 14 herein, Purchaser shall exercise all rights and privileges of a shareholder of the Company with respect to the Stock deposited in escrow. Purchaser shall be deemed to be the holder for purposes of receiving any dividends that may be paid with respect to such shares of Stock and for the purpose of exercising any voting rights relating to such shares of Stock, even if some or all of such shares of stock have not yet vested and been released from the Repurchase Option.

9. LIMITATIONS ON TRANSFER. In addition to any other limitation on transfer created by applicable securities laws, Purchaser shall not assign, hypothecate, donate, encumber or otherwise dispose of any interest in the Stock while the Stock is subject to the Repurchase Option. After any Stock has been released from the Repurchase Option, Purchaser shall not assign, hypothecate, donate, encumber or otherwise dispose of any interest in the Stock except in compliance with the provisions herein and applicable securities laws. Furthermore, the Stock shall be subject to any right of first refusal in favor of the Company or its assignees that may be contained in the Company's Bylaws.

10. RESTRICTIVE LEGENDS. All certificates representing the Stock shall have endorsed thereon legends in substantially the following forms (in addition to any other legend which may be required by other agreements between the parties hereto):

(a) "THE SHARES REPRESENTED BY THIS CERTIFICATE ARE SUBJECT TO AN OPTION SET FORTH IN AN AGREEMENT BETWEEN THE COMPANY AND THE REGISTERED HOLDER, OR SUCH HOLDER'S PREDECESSOR IN INTEREST. A COPY OF WHICH IS ON FILE AT THE PRINCIPAL OFFICE OF THIS COMPANY. ANY TRANSFER OR ATTEMPTED TRANSFER OF ANY SHARES SUBJECT TO SUCH OPTION IS VOID WITHOUT THE PRIOR EXPRESS WRITTEN CONSENT OF THE COMPANY."

(b) "THE SHARES REPRESENTED BY THIS CERTIFICATE HAVE NOT BEEN REGISTERED UNDER THE SECURITIES ACT OF 1933 AS AMENDED. THEY MAY NOT BE SOLD, OFFERED FOR SALE, PLEDGED OR HYPOTHECATED IN THE ABSENCE OF AN EFFECTIVE REGISTRATION STATEMENT AS TO THE SECURITIES UNDER SAID ACT OR AN OPINION OF COUNSEL SATISFACTORY TO THE COMPANY THAT SUCH REGISTRATION IS NOT REQUIRED."

(c) "THE SHARES REPRESENTED BY THIS CERTIFICATE ARE SUBJECT TO A RIGHT OF FIRST REFUSAL OPTION IN FAVOR OF THE COMPANY AND/OR ITS ASSIGNEE(S) AS PROVIDED IN THE BYLAWS OF THE COMPANY."

(d) Any legend required by law.

11. **Investment Representations.** In connection with the purchase of the Stock, Purchaser represents to the Company the following:

(a) Purchaser is aware of the Company's business affairs and financial condition and has acquired sufficient information about the Company to reach an informed and knowledgeable decision to acquire the Stock. Purchaser is purchasing the Stock for investment for Purchaser's own account only and not with a view to, or for resale in connection with, any "distribution" thereof within the meaning of the Act.

(b) Purchaser understands that the Stock has not been registered under the Act by reason of a specific exemption therefrom, which exemption depends upon, among other things, the bona fide nature of Purchaser's investment intent as expressed herein.

(c) Purchaser further acknowledges and understands that the Stock must be held indefinitely unless the Stock is subsequently registered under the Act or an exemption from such registration is available. Purchaser further acknowledges and understands that the Company is under no obligation to register the Stock. Purchaser understands that the certificate evidencing the Stock will be imprinted with a legend which prohibits the transfer of the Stock unless the Stock is registered or such registration is not required in the opinion of counsel for the Company.

(d) Purchaser is familiar with the provisions of Rules 144 and 701, under the Act, as in effect from time to time, which, in substance, permit limited public resale of "restricted securities" acquired, directly or indirectly, from the issuer thereof (or from an affiliate of such issuer), in a non-public offering subject to the satisfaction of certain conditions. Rule 701 provides that if the issuer qualifies under Rule 701 at the time of issuance of the securities, such issuance will be exempt from registration under the Act. In the event the Company becomes subject to the reporting requirements of Section 13 or 15(d) of the Securities Exchange Act of 1934, the securities exempt under Rule 701 may be sold by Purchaser ninety (90) days thereafter, subject to the satisfaction of certain of the conditions specified by Rule 144 and the market stand-off provision described in Section 12 below.

In the event that the sale of the Stock does not qualify under Rule 701 at the time of purchase, then the Stock may be resold by Purchaser in certain limited circumstances subject to the provisions of Rule 144, which requires, among other things: (i) the availability of certain public information about the Company and (ii) the resale occurring following the required holding period under Rule 144 after the Purchaser has purchased, and made full payment of (within the meaning of Rule 144), the securities to be sold.

(e) Purchaser further understands that at the time Purchaser wishes to sell the Stock there may be no public market upon which to make such a sale, and that, even if such a public market then exists, the Company may not be satisfying the current public current information requirements of Rule 144 or 701, and that, in such event, Purchaser would be precluded from selling the Stock under Rule 144 or 701 even if the minimum holding period requirement had been satisfied.

(f) Purchaser further warrants and represents that Purchaser has either (i) preexisting personal or business relationships, with the Company or any of its officers, directors or controlling persons, or (ii) the capacity to protect his own interests in connection with the purchase of the Stock by virtue of the business or financial expertise of himself or herself or of professional advisors to Purchaser who are unaffiliated with and who are not compensated by the Company or any of its affiliates, directly or indirectly.

12. MARKET STAND-OFF AGREEMENT. Purchaser shall not sell, dispose of, transfer, make any short sale of, grant any option for the purchase of, or enter into any hedging or similar transaction with the same economic effect as a sale, any Common Stock or other securities of the Company held by Purchaser, including the Stock (the "Restricted Securities"), for a period of time specified by the underwriter(s) (not to exceed one hundred eighty (180) days) following the effective date of a registration statement of the Company filed under the Act. Purchaser agrees to execute and deliver such other agreements as may be reasonably requested by the Company and/or the underwriter(s) which are consistent with the foregoing or which are necessary to give further effect thereto. In order to enforce the foregoing covenant, the Company may impose stop-transfer instructions with respect to Purchaser's Restricted Securities until the end of such period.

13. SECTION 83(B) ELECTION. Purchaser understands that Section 83(a) of the Code, taxes as ordinary income the difference between the amount paid for the Stock and the fair market value of the Stock as of the date any restrictions on the Stock lapse. In this context, "restriction" includes the right of the Company to buy back the Stock pursuant to the Repurchase Option set forth in Section 2a above. Purchaser understands that Purchaser may elect to be taxed at the time the Stock is purchased, rather than when and as the Repurchase Option expires, by filing an election under Section 83(b) (an "83(b) Election") of the Code with the Internal Revenue Service within thirty (30) days from the date of purchase. Even if the fair market value of the Stock at the time of the execution of this Agreement equals the amount paid for the Stock, the 83(b) Election must be made to avoid income under Section 83(a) in the future. **Purchaser understands that failure to file such an 83(b) Election in a timely manner may result in adverse tax consequences for Purchaser**. Purchaser further understands that an additional copy of such 83(b) Election is required to be filed with his/her federal income tax return for the calendar year in which the date of this Agreement falls. Purchaser acknowledges that the foregoing is only a summary of the effect of United States federal income taxation with respect to purchase of the Stock hereunder, and does not purport to be complete. Purchaser further acknowledges that the Company has directed Purchaser to seek independent advice regarding the applicable provisions of the Code, the income tax laws of any municipality, state or foreign country in which Purchaser may reside, and the tax consequences of Purchaser's death. Purchaser assumes all responsibility for filing an 83(b) Election and paying all taxes resulting from such election or the lapse of the restrictions on the Stock.

14. REFUSAL TO TRANSFER. The Company shall not be required (a) to transfer on its books any shares of Stock of the Company which shall have been transferred in violation of any of the provisions set forth in this Agreement or (b) to treat as owner of such shares or to accord the right to vote as such owner or to pay dividends to any transferee to whom such shares shall have been so transferred.

15. NO EMPLOYMENT RIGHTS. This Agreement is not an employment contract and nothing in this Agreement shall affect in any manner whatsoever the right or power of the Company (or a parent or subsidiary of the Company) to terminate Purchaser's employment for any reason at any time, with or without cause and with or without notice.

❖ MISCELLANEOUS.

(a) Notices. Any notice required or permitted hereunder shall be given in writing and shall be deemed effectively given upon personal delivery or sent by telegram or fax or upon deposit in the United States Post Office, by registered or certified mail with postage and fees prepaid, addressed to the other party hereto at his address hereinafter shown below its signature or at such other address as such party may designate by ten (10) days' advance written notice to the other party hereto.

(b) Successors and Assigns. This Agreement shall inure to the benefit of the successors and assigns of the Company and, subject to the restrictions on transfer herein set forth, be binding upon Purchaser, Purchaser's successors, and assigns. The Repurchase Option of the Company hereunder shall be assignable by the Company at any time or from time to time, in whole or in part.

(c) Attorneys' Fees; Specific Performance. Purchaser shall reimburse the Company for all costs incurred by the Company in enforcing the performance of, or protecting its rights under, any part of this Agreement, including reasonable costs of investigation and attorneys' fees. It is the intention of the parties that the Company, upon exercise of the Repurchase Option and payment of the Option Price, pursuant to the terms of this Agreement, shall be entitled to receive the Stock, in specie, in order to have such Stock available for future issuance without dilution of the holdings of other shareholders. Furthermore, it is expressly agreed between the parties that money damages are inadequate to compensate the Company for the Stock and that the Company shall, upon proper exercise of the Repurchase Option, be entitled to specific enforcement of its rights to purchase and receive said Stock.

(d) Governing Law; Venue. This Agreement shall be governed by and construed in accordance with the laws of the State of California. The parties agree that any action brought by either party to interpret or enforce any provision of this Agreement shall be brought in, and each party agrees to, and does hereby, submit to the jurisdiction and venue of, the appropriate state or federal court for the district encompassing the Company's principal place of business.

(e) Further Execution. The parties agree to take all such further action(s) as may reasonably be necessary to carry out and consummate this Agreement as soon as practicable, and to take whatever steps may be necessary to obtain any governmental approval in connection with or otherwise qualify the issuance of the securities that are the subject of this Agreement.

(f) Independent Counsel. Purchaser acknowledges that this Agreement has been prepared on behalf of the Company by the Chief Executive Officer of the Company, and that the Chief Executive Officer does not represent, and is not acting on behalf of, Purchaser. Purchaser has been provided with an opportunity to consult with Purchaser's own counsel with respect to this Agreement.

(g) Entire Agreement; Amendment. This Agreement constitutes the entire agreement between the parties with respect to the subject matter hereof and supersedes and merges all prior agreements or understandings, whether written or oral. This Agreement may not be amended, modified or revoked, in whole or in part, except by an agreement in writing signed by each of the parties hereto.

(h) Severability. If one or more provisions of this Agreement are held to be unenforceable under applicable law, the parties agree to renegotiate such provision in good faith. In the event that the parties cannot reach a mutually agreeable and enforceable replacement for such provision, then (i) such provision shall be excluded from this Agreement, (ii) the balance of the Agreement shall be interpreted as if such provision were so excluded and (iii) the balance of the Agreement shall be enforceable in accordance with its terms.

(i) Counterparts. This Agreement may be executed in two or more counterparts, each of which shall be deemed an original and all of which together shall constitute one instrument.

IN WITNESS WHEREOF, the parties hereto have executed this Agreement as of the day and year first written above.

NAME OF CORPORATION
By: ____________________________
PURCHASER:
By: ____________________________

EXHIBIT A
JOINT ESCROW INSTRUCTIONS

____
____
____

Ladies and Gentlemen:

As Escrow Agent for ____________________, a California corporation ("Corporation") and ________________ ("Purchaser"), you are hereby authorized and directed to hold the documents delivered to you pursuant to the terms of that certain Founder Stock Purchase Agreement dated as of ____________, 20__ ("Agreement"), to which a copy of these Joint Escrow Instructions is attached as Exhibit A, in accordance with the following instructions:

1. In the event Corporation or an assignee shall elect to exercise the Repurchase Option set forth in the Agreement, the Corporation or its assignee will give to Purchaser and you a written notice specifying the number of shares of stock to be purchased, the purchase price, and the time for a closing thereunder at the principal office of the Corporation. Purchaser and the Corporation hereby irrevocably authorize and direct you to close the transaction contemplated by such notice in accordance with the terms of said notice.

2. At the closing, you are directed (a) to date the stock assignments necessary for the transfer in question, (b) to fill in the umber of shares being transferred, and (c) to deliver the same, together with the certificate evidencing the shares of stock to be transferred, to the Corporation against the simultaneous delivery to you of the purchase price (which may include suitable acknowledgment of cancellation of indebtedness) for the number of shares of stock being purchased pursuant to the exercise of the Repurchase Option.

3. Purchaser irrevocably authorizes the Corporation to deposit with you any certificates evidencing shares of stock to be held by you hereunder and any additions and substitutions to said shares as specified in the Agreement. Purchaser does hereby irrevocably constitute and appoint you as his/her attorney-in-fact and agent for the term of this escrow to execute with respect to such securities all documents necessary or appropriate to make such securities negotiable and complete any transaction herein contemplated, including but not limited to any appropriate filing with state or government officials or bank officials. Subject to the provisions of this paragraph 3, Purchaser shall exercise all rights and privileges of a shareholder of the Corporation while the stock is held by you.

4. This escrow shall terminate upon the exercise in full or expiration of the Repurchase Option, whichever occurs first.

5. If at the time of termination of this escrow you should have in your possession any documents, securities, or other property belonging to Purchaser, you shall delver all of the same to Purchaser and shall be discharged of all further obligations hereunder; provided, however, that if at the time of termination of this escrow you are advised by the Corporation that any property subject to this escrow is the subject of a pledge or other security agreement, you shall deliver all such property to the pledge holder or other person designated by the Corporation.

6. Except as otherwise provided in these Joint Escrow Instructions, your duties hereunder may be altered, amended, modified or revoked only by a writing signed by all of the parties hereto.

7. You shall be obligated only for the performance of such duties as are specifically set forth herein and may rely and shall be protected in relying or refraining from acting on any instrument reasonably believed by you to be genuine ad to have been signed or presented by the proper party or parties. You shall not be personally liable for any act you may do or omit to do hereunder as Escrow Agent or as attorney-in-fact for Purchaser while acting in good faith and in the exercise of your own good judgment, and any act done or omitted by you pursuant to the advice of your own attorneys shall be conclusive evidence of such good faith.

8. You are hereby expressly authorized to disregard any and all warnings given by any of the parties hereto or by any other person or corporation, excepting only orders or process of courts of law, and are hereby expressly authorized to comply with and obey orders, judgments or decrees of any court. In case you obey or comply with any such order, judgment or decree of any court, you shall not be liable to any of the parties hereto or to any other person, firm or corporation by reason of such compliance, notwithstanding any such order, judgment or decree being subsequently reversed, modified, annulled, set aside, vacated or found to have been entered without jurisdiction.

9. You shall not be liable in any respect on account of the identity, authorities or rights of the parties executing or delivering or purporting to execute or deliver the Agreement or any documents or papers deposited or called for hereunder.

10. You shall not be liable for the outlawing of any rights under any statute of limitations with respect to these Joint Escrow Instructions or any documents deposited with you.

11. Your responsibilities as Escrow Agent hereunder shall terminate if you shall cease to be Secretary of the Corporation or if you shall resign by written notice to each party. In the event of any such termination, the Corporation shall appoint any officer or assistant officer of the Corporation as successor Escrow Agent and Purchaser hereby confirms the appointment of such successor as his/her attorney-in-fact and agent to the full extent of your appointment.

12. If you reasonably require other or further instruments in connection with these Joint Escrow Instructions or obligations in respect hereto, the necessary parties hereto shall join in furnishing such instruments.

13. It is understood and agreed that should any dispute arise with respect to the delivery and/or ownership or right of possession of the securities held by you hereunder, you are authorized and directed to retain in your possession without liability to anyone all or any part of said securities until such dispute shall have been settled either by mutual written agreement of the parties concerned or by a final order, decree or judgment of a court of competent jurisdiction after the time for appeal has expired and no appeal has been perfected, but you shall be under no duty whatsoever to institute or defend any such proceedings.

14. Any notice required or permitted hereunder shall be given in writing and shall be deemed effectively given upon personal delivery, including delivery by express courier, or five (5) days after deposit in the United States Post Office, by registered or certified mail with postage and fees prepaid, addressed to each of the other parties entitled to such notice at the following addresses, or at such other addresses as a party may designate by ten (10) days' advance written notice to each of the other parties hereto.

CORPORATION: ____________________
____
____

PURCHASER: ____________________
____
____

ESCROW AGENT(S): ____________________
____
____

15. By signing these Joint Escrow Instructions, you become a party hereto only for the purpose of said Joint Escrow Instructions; you do not become a party to the Agreement.

16. You shall be entitled to employ such legal counsel and other experts as you may deem necessary to properly advise you in connection with your obligations hereunder. You may rely upon the advice of such counsel, and you may pay such counsel reasonable compensation, therefore. The Corporation shall be responsible for all fees generated by such legal counsel in connection with your obligations hereunder.

17. This instrument shall be binding upon and inure to the benefit of the parties hereto and their respective successors and permitted assigns. It is understood and agreed that references to "you" and "your" herein refer to the original Escrow Agents. It is understood and agreed that the Corporation may at any time or from time to time assign its rights under the Agreement and these Joint Escrow Instructions.

18. This Agreement shall be governed by and interpreted and determined in accordance with the laws of the State of California, as such laws are applied by

California courts to contracts made and to be performed entirely in California by residents of that state.

Very truly yours,

NAME OF CORPORATION

By ____________________________

PURCHASER

____

ESCROW AGENT(S):

____

AND

____

EXHIBIT B
STOCK ASSIGNMENT SEPARATE FROM CERTIFICATE

FOR VALUE RECEIVED, ____________________ hereby sells, assigns and transfers unto ______________________, a California corporation (the "Company"), pursuant to the Repurchase Option under that certain Founder Stock Purchase Agreement, dated _______________ by and between the undersigned and the Company (the "Agreement"), _________________ (________) shares of Common Stock of the Company standing in the undersigned's name on the books of the Company represented by Certificate No. ____ and does hereby irrevocably constitute and appoint the Company's Secretary to transfer said stock on the books of the Company with full power of substitution in the premises. This Assignment may be used only in accordance with and subject to the terms and conditions of the Agreement, in connection with the repurchase of shares of Common Stock issued to the undersigned pursuant to the Agreement, and only to the extent that such shares remain subject to the Company's Repurchase Option under the Agreement.

Dated: ________________, 20__

____

(Signature)

____

(Print Name)

EXHIBIT C
ELECTION UNDER SECTION 83(b)

Director of Internal Revenue
Internal Revenue Service
Fresno, CA 93888

Re: Election under Section 83(b) of the Internal Revenue Code of 1986, as amended

Gentlemen:

After consulting with, or having had the opportunity to consult with, my personal tax advisor this statement constitutes an election pursuant to Section 83(b) of the Internal Revenue Code of 1986, as amended from time to time (the "***Code***").

If this election also or only relates to the receipt of property from the exercise of an "incentive stock option" as defined in Section 422(b) of the Code, then the undersigned hereby elects, pursuant to the provisions of Sections 55-56 and 83(b) of the Code to include in alternative minimum taxable income for the undersigned's current taxable year, as compensation for services, the excess, if any, of the fair market value of that portion of the property described below that is property received from the exercise of an "incentive stock option" at the time of transfer over the amount paid for such property.

The undersigned also elects pursuant to Section 83(b) of the Code to include in gross income for the taxable year in which the undersigned disposes of some or all of the property described below that is property received from the exercise of an "incentive stock option" in a transaction which fails to satisfy the requirements of Section 422(a)(l) of the Code (a "disqualifying disposition"), as compensation for services, the excess, if any, of the fair market value of the disposed property at the time of transfer to the undersigned over the amount paid for such property.

The undersigned intends that this election has the maximum permissible effect and only apply to property for which the election can be made. If the description of the property overstates the property that can be covered by this election, then this election shall only apply to that portion of the property described below for which this election can be made.

Pursuant to Treasury Regulation Section 1.83-2, the following information is submitted:

1. **Name:** ____________________________
Lesley Jones ("***Purchaser***")
Address: ____________________________
123 Santana Row, #2343
Social Security Number: ____________________________
2. **Property Description:**____________ shares of Common Stock (the "***Stock***") of ___________________ (the "***Corporation***").
3. The date on which property was transferred is ___________________.
4. The taxable year for which the election is made is the calendar year 20__.
5. **Restrictions:** If, on or before _________, 20__ the employment of the Purchaser by the Corporation terminates for any reason, the Corporation shall have the option to repurchase some or all of the property (depending upon the date of such termination) for a price equal to the cost of the property repurchased.
6. The fair market value at the time of transfer of the Stock, determined without regard to any restriction other than a restriction which by its terms will never lapse, is _________ (_______ shares having a fair market value of _______ per share).
7. **Purchase Price:** _______________ shares at _______ per share.

A copy of this statement has been furnished to the Corporation and the transferee of the Stock, if different than Purchaser.

Dated: _________________, 20__

Very truly yours,

____

10. Contract for Services Agreement

CONTRACT FOR SERVICES

This agreement is entered into on ________, 200__, between ____________ (Company), having a principle place of business at ______________________________________ (address), and ________________ (Contractor), having a principle place of business at ____________________ ____ __________.

1. Contract Term. This Agreement is effective commencing on ______________, and will continue in effect until _______________, unless terminated sooner in accordance with Paragraph 9 of this Agreement (Project Conclusion Date).

2. Independent Contractor Relationship. The parties intend that the relationship between them is solely an independent contractor relationship, and that no employer-employee relationship shall exist. Both parties expressly acknowledge and agree that Company does not have the right to control the manner or method by which Contractor will perform the services described in this Agreement.

3. Contractor Services. Contractor agrees to render the following services to Company:

   ____
   ____
   ______________________________________. (Work Product).

   a) Contractor will promptly perform the above-described services at the Contractor's principal place of business referenced above or at other location of Contractor's choosing, during times of Contractors choosing, so long as services are completed no later than the Project Conclusion Date. This section may be amended from time to time with the written consent of the Company and the Contractor by attaching to this Agreement a schedule detailing additional Work Product.

   b) The parties agree that Contractor need not personally render the services described in this paragraph. Contractor may, at Contractor's own expense, hire employees and/or agents to assist in the performance of such services. In that event, Contractor acknowledges Contractor's full responsibility for payment of wages and other compensation to all employees and/or agents of Contractor. Contractor agrees to maintain workers' compensation insurance for such employees and/or agents, as required by law, and assumes full and sole responsibility for the payment of all federal, state and local taxes, withholding, and insurance obligations relating to such employees and/or agents.

4. Compensation. In consideration for the services to be performed under this Agreement, Company agrees to pay Contractor fees of an amount not to exceed $_________. The Contractor will be paid within thirty (30) business days after receipt of Contractor's bi-weekly or monthly invoice that details completion of the Work Product (and/or milestones achieved and number of hours worked, if applicable). The parties agree that Contractor is solely responsible for all costs and expenses incurred by Contractor in connection with performance of the work described in this Agreement.

5. Contractor's Obligations. Apart from obligations detailed elsewhere in this agreement, Contractor agrees to furnish all other necessary equipment and supplies required to perform services under this Agreement, at Contractor's own expense, except for any (Company) products that must be provided by the Company in order for the Contractor to perform the agreed-upon work.

   a) Contractor agrees that Contractor is responsible for paying all required federal, state and local taxes relating to Contractor's business, and that Company has no responsibility for any such payments. In particular, the parties agree and understand that because of the independent contractor relationship between them, Company will not withhold any social security or income taxes or make any unemployment or disability insurance contributions on behalf of Contractor. Further, Company will not obtain workers' compensation insurance of behalf of Contractor, Contractor's employees and/or agents.

   b) Contractor nor its employees shall not hold its self out as an agent of the Company. Contractor shall not bind the Company in any way.

   c) Contractor agrees that for a period of twelve (12) months immediately following the termination of its relationship with the Company for any reason, whether with or without cause, Contractor shall not either directly or indirectly solicit, recruit, or encourage any of the Company's employees to leave their employment, or take away such employees, or attempt to solicit, induce, recruit, encourage or take away employees of the Company, either for Contractor or for any other person or entity.

   d) Contractor agrees to indemnify and hold Company harmless against any and all liability claimed or imposed, including reasonable attorneys' fees, arising from any act or failure of Contractor, Contractor's employees and/or assistants, in connection with performance of the services described in this Agreement.

6. Ownership Rights. It is understood and agreed that Work Product which is being developed by Contractor under this Agreement shall be considered a "Work Made for Hire" as that phrase is defined by the U.S. copyright laws and shall be owned by and for the express benefit of Company. In the event it should be

established that such work does not qualify as a Work Made for Hire, Contractor agrees to and does hereby assign to Company all of its right, title, and interest in such work product including, but not limited to, all copyrights, patents, trademarks, and other proprietary rights. Both during the Term of this Agreement and thereafter, Contractor shall fully cooperate with Company in the protection and enforcement of any intellectual property rights that may derive as a result of the services performed by Contractor under the terms of this Agreement. This shall include executing, acknowledging, and delivering to Company all documents or papers that may be necessary to enable Company to publish or protect said inventions, improvements, and ideas.

7. Representations and Warranties. Contractor represents and warrants to Company that it is free to enter into this Agreement and that its performance thereunder will not conflict with any other agreement to which the Contractor may be a party. Contractor further represents and warrants to Company that Work Product is unique and original, is clear of any claims or encumbrances, and does not infringe on the rights of any third parties.

8. Confidentiality. Contractor recognizes that during the course of its work with Company, Contractor may have occasion to conceive, create, develop, review, or receive information which is considered by Company to be confidential or proprietary, including information relating to inventions, patent, trademark and copyright applications, improvements, know-how, specifications, drawings, cost data, process flow diagrams, customer and supplier lists, bills, ideas, and/or any other written material referring to same (Confidential Information). Confidential Information includes proprietary information of third parties received by the Company for which the Company, its employees and contractors have a duty to maintain the confidentiality of such information. Both during the term of employment and thereafter:

a) Contractor agrees at all times during the term of this Agreement and thereafter, to hold in strictest confidence, and not to use, except for the benefit of the Company, or to disclose to any person, firm or corporation without written authorization of the Board of Directors of the Company, any Confidential Information of the Company, and

b) Contractor agrees to maintain in confidence such Confidential Information unless or until: (1) it shall have been made public by an act or omission of a party other than itself; or (2) Contractor receives such Confidential Information from an unrelated third party on a non-confidential basis, whichever shall first occur, and

c) Contractor agrees to use all reasonable precautions to ensure that all such Confidential Information is properly protected and kept from unauthorized persons or disclosure. If requested by Company, Contractor agrees to promptly return to Company all materials, writings, equipment, models, mechanisms, and the like obtained from or through Company including, but not limited to, all Confidential Information, all of which Contractor recognizes is the sole and exclusive property of Company, and

d) Contractor agrees that it and its employees and agents will not, during the term of this Agreement with the Company, improperly use or disclose any proprietary information or trade secrets of any current or former employer or other person or entity, and that Contractor will not bring onto the premises of the Company any unpublished document or proprietary information belonging to any such employer, person, or entity unless consented to in writing by such employer, person or entity, and

e) Contractor agrees that it will not: (1) directly or indirectly utilize such Confidential Information in its own business; (2) manufacture and/or sell any product that is based in whole or in part on such Confidential Information; or (3) disclose such Confidential Information to any third party.

f) Upon, request, Contractor agrees to promptly return to Company any materials obtained from or through Company, including all memoranda, drawings, patent, trademark and copyright applications, specifications, and process or flow diagrams including any copies, notes, or memoranda made by Contractor that, in any way, relate to Field or Confidential Information disclosed or transmitted to Contractor by Company.

9. Termination of Agreement. This Agreement may be terminated, at the Company's or Contractors option with 30 days written notice.

10. Arbitration. The parties understand and agree that any and all controversies between them will be submitted for resolution to final and binding arbitration to be held in San Mateo County, California. Such arbitration will be in accordance with the California Arbitration Act. (Code of Civil Procedure Section 1280 et seq.) Both parties expressly waive their entitlement, if any, to have controversies between them decided by a court or jury.

11. Entire Agreement. This Agreement constitutes the entire agreement between the parties regarding the subjects covered. No other agreement, understanding, statement or promise, other than those contained in this Agreement, is part of the agreement of the parties; no other agreement, understanding, statement or promise regarding the subjects covered will be effective or binding on the parties. Any modification to this Agreement will be effective or binding on the parties. Any modification to this Agreement will be effective only if in writing and signed by the parties.

12. Governing Law. This Agreement will be governed by and construed in accordance with the laws of the State of California.

13. The parties agree to the terms and conditions set forth above.

By:

____
Name:
Title:

Date:____________________________

____
Social Security or Taxpayer ID #

COMPANY

____
Name:
Title:

Date:____________________________

In conclusion, the documents included in this Appendix are provided as general templates to assist you in organizing and structuring your business operations. While these templates serve as a useful starting point, they should not be considered as a substitute for professional legal advice. We strongly recommend that you customize these documents to suit your specific needs and consult with a qualified attorney to ensure that they are compliant with applicable laws and tailored to your particular circumstances. This approach will help safeguard your interests and ensure that your business's legal framework is robust and effective. Use these resources wisely to support and enhance your business's structural and legal foundations.

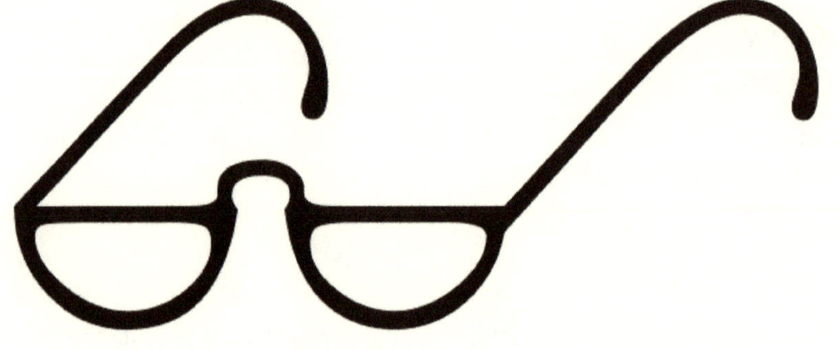

Resources

The Empire Builders and Blueprint Series

Welcome to the Resource section of the Empire Builders Series: Masterclasses in Business and Law. Here, we provide a carefully curated collection of practical tools and materials designed to complement the strategies and insights discussed throughout the series. This section is your gateway to deeper understanding and application, offering everything from sample agreements and checklists to detailed case studies and guidelines. Whether you're forging a new business, protecting intellectual property, or planning for expansion, these resources are intended to empower you with the necessary tools to effectively implement and navigate the complex landscape of business and law. Embrace these resources as your companion in building and sustaining a robust empire.

Empire Builders Series: Masterclasses in Business and Law

In the dynamic world of business, where innovation intersects with opportunity, success often hinges not only on creativity but also on a deep understanding of the legal and operational landscapes. The Empire Builders Series is meticulously designed to arm aspiring entrepreneurs, seasoned business owners, creative professionals, and legal experts with the comprehensive knowledge and strategies needed to navigate these complexities and build lasting empires.

Each book in the series serves as a foundational pillar, offering expert guidance and actionable insights in specific areas of business and law; tailored to foster growth, innovation, and success in today's competitive marketplace:

1. **Brick by Brick**: This guide acts as your blueprint for building a business from the ground up. It offers essential strategies, legal insights, and operational tactics crucial for establishing a solid foundation for any business venture.
2. **Mark Your Territory**: Dive deep into the world of trademarks with this essential guide, designed to help you protect and effectively leverage your brand in today's competitive market.
3. **From Idea to Empire**: Transform your entrepreneurial dreams into reality with this exhaustive guide to business planning. Learn how to craft a compelling business plan that not only attracts investors but also sets the stage for a successful enterprise.
4. **Beyond the Pen**: Safeguard your creative works and master the intricacies of copyright law with this expert guide, tailored specifically for writers, artists, musicians, and digital content creators.
5. **Legal Ink**: Demystify the complex legal landscape of publishing with practical advice on negotiating contracts and protecting intellectual property, essential for authors and publishers.

The Empire Builders Series stands as a testament to the power of knowledge and the importance of mastering the strategic and legal aspects of business management. Each book is designed not merely to inform but to inspire action and lead to success. Embark on this journey to build your empire, one masterclass at a time.

Brick by Brick:
The Entrepreneur's Guide to Constructing a Company

The first book in the Empire Builders Series: Masterclass in Business and Law is "Brick by Brick: The Entrepreneur's Guide to Constructing a Company."

Summary: "Brick by Brick" is an indispensable resource for entrepreneurs who are poised to transform their innovative business ideas into successful enterprises. This comprehensive guide meticulously outlines the complexities of business formation, providing detailed, step-by-step instructions and vital insights into the legal, operational, and strategic aspects of starting and running a thriving company.

Part 1: Laying the Foundation – Focuses on selecting the appropriate business entity, delving into the legal implications of each option and the economic considerations vital for establishing a solid foundation for your business.

Part 2: Operational Mechanics – Discusses the operational aspects of setting up partnerships and LLCs, navigating corporate governance, maintaining corporate records, and managing capital and shareholder relationships effectively.

Part 3: Advanced Strategic Planning – Offers insights into managing structural changes, handling stock and ownership issues, expanding operations across state lines, and deploying tax strategies to ensure compliance and optimize financial performance.

Part 4: Implementation Tools and Resources – Provides practical tools such as sample agreements, startup task checklists, and comprehensive guidelines for drafting business plans and the incorporation process, enabling entrepreneurs to effectively implement their business strategies.

"Brick by Brick" not only serves as a guide but acts as a complete blueprint for building a robust business capable of thriving in today's competitive market. It arms aspiring entrepreneurs with the necessary knowledge and tools to navigate the complexities of business formation. From drafting your first business plan to preparing for incorporation, this book delivers invaluable insights and practical advice to establish a strong foundation and sustain growth.

Mark Your Territory:
Navigating Trademarks in the Modern Marketplace

The second book in the Empire Builders Series: Masterclass in Business and Law is "Mark Your Territory: Navigating Trademarks in the Modern Marketplace."

Summary: "Mark Your Territory" provides an indispensable resource for anyone involved in the branding and legal aspects of their business, offering a comprehensive guide to understanding, acquiring, and effectively managing trademarks. This book is crucial for ensuring that trademarks, which are vital assets to any business, are properly protected and leveraged.

Part 1: Fundamentals of Trademarks – Introduces the basics of trademarks, including their legal framework, the process of trademark selection and registration, and their importance in identifying business sources and ensuring product quality.

Part 2: Strategic Trademark Management – Focuses on the ongoing management of trademarks, detailing strategies for maintaining rights, monitoring for infringements, addressing challenges in digital marketing, and managing global trademark portfolios.

Part 3: Advanced Topics in Trademarks – Delves into more complex issues such as preventing trademark dilution, managing renewals, understanding the specific needs of service marks in advertising, and navigating the intricacies of trademark licensing and emerging legal trends.

Part 4: Practical Tools and Resources – Provides practical aids like sample trademark filings, management checklists, and insightful case studies, equipping readers with tangible tools and real-world examples to apply the concepts discussed effectively.

Designed for entrepreneurs, business owners, and legal professionals, "Mark Your Territory" equips readers with actionable strategies and essential tools for effective trademark management. It ensures that readers can maintain their brand's uniqueness and legal protections, thus securing a competitive edge in the marketplace.

From Idea to Empire:
Mastering the Art of Business Planning

The third book in the Empire Builders Series: Masterclass in Business and Law is "From Idea to Empire: Mastering the Art of Business Planning."

Summary: "From Idea to Empire" offers an indispensable roadmap for entrepreneurs eager to transform their innovative ideas into successful businesses. This comprehensive guide equips readers with a strategic blueprint for drafting robust business plans that attract investors and serve as a roadmap for navigating the transition from startup to thriving enterprise.

Part 1: Conceptualizing Your Business – This section lays the groundwork by assisting readers in defining their business vision, understanding market needs, analyzing competitors, and setting clear business objectives. It also guides readers in selecting an effective business model that aligns with their long-term goals.

Part 2: Strategic Planning – Delve into creating detailed marketing strategies, operational plans, and financial projections. This part covers risk management and technological integration, ensuring the business plan is both innovative and executable.

Part 3: Articulating Your Plan – Focuses on the actual drafting of the business plan, including how to write an engaging executive summary, develop compelling proposals, and master communication and negotiation tactics with potential investors and partners.

Part 4: Execution and Review – Outlines the necessary steps to launch the business successfully, monitor its performance, and make adjustments based on real-world feedback and market dynamics. This section also explores strategies for sustainable growth and long-term viability.

"From Idea to Empire" is more than a mere planning manual; it's a strategic guide that provides budding entrepreneurs with the necessary knowledge, tools, and confidence to build a business capable of facing today's market complexities. With practical advice, real-world examples, and essential resources, this book is a vital tool for anyone ready to evolve their business concept from idea to a profitable empire.

From Idea to Empire: Abridged Edition

The third book in the Empire Builders Series: Masterclass in Business and Law is "From Idea to Empire: Abridged Edition."

Summary: "From Idea to Empire: Abridged Edition" delivers the essential roadmap for turning business ideas into successful enterprises—streamlined for readers seeking concise and actionable insights. While the original edition provides an expansive resource with success stories and detailed case studies, this abridged version focuses solely on the strategic elements of business planning, offering the tools needed to conceptualize, design, and execute a winning business strategy.

By eliminating supplementary stories and focusing on the practical frameworks, this edition is perfect for readers eager to dive straight into the mechanics of business planning without distraction. It provides the knowledge required to develop robust business models, articulate compelling proposals, and successfully launch and grow a business in today's dynamic marketplace.

Part 1: Conceptualizing Your Business – Laying the Foundation – In this section, readers learn how to define their business idea, identify market needs, analyze competitors, and set clear objectives. It introduces essential business models and helps entrepreneurs align their vision with long-term goals.

Part 2: Strategic Planning – Mapping the Path to Success – Here, readers will discover how to design effective marketing strategies, operational plans, and financial projections. Topics like risk management and technological integration are covered to ensure every business plan is both realistic and innovative.

Part 3: Articulating Your Plan – Communicating with Precision and Impact – This section emphasizes the importance of clarity in communication. Readers will learn how to craft compelling executive summaries, develop strong proposals, and master negotiation strategies for working with investors and partners.

Part 4: Execution and Review – Launching and Scaling with Purpose – The final section covers essential steps for launching a business successfully, monitoring performance, and making real-time adjustments. It also addresses strategies for sustainable growth, long-term resilience, and market adaptation.

About This Edition:
The Abridged Edition is crafted for readers who prefer a focused, no-frills approach to business planning. By presenting the core methodologies from the original book in a concise format, this version allows entrepreneurs to absorb key concepts quickly and efficiently. Whether you're a first-time entrepreneur or a seasoned business owner, this streamlined guide provides the essential tools needed to transform an idea into a thriving business.

Why This Edition Matters:
"From Idea to Empire: Abridged Edition" underscores that great business planning doesn't require lengthy explanations—it requires clear strategies and actionable frameworks. This edition emphasizes the importance of focus, discipline, and adaptability in building a successful business.

Designed to complement busy entrepreneurs, it delivers the same powerful strategies as the original book but in a more accessible format. Readers can quickly refer to specific sections, apply the knowledge, and move forward with confidence in their business endeavors.

"From Idea to Empire: Abridged Edition" is the perfect companion for entrepreneurs who need to move swiftly from concept to execution. With straightforward advice and practical insights, this edition equips readers to create robust business plans and take decisive action toward building their own empire.

Beyond the Pen:
Copyright Strategies for Modern Creators

The fourth book in the Empire Builders Series: Masterclass in Business and Law is "Beyond the Pen: Copyright Strategies for Modern Creators."

Summary: "Beyond the Pen" serves as a crucial guide for artists, writers, musicians, and digital creators who seek to effectively navigate the complexities of copyright law and protect their creative assets. This comprehensive resource provides a deep dive into the mechanisms, legal frameworks, and strategic practices necessary to safeguard intellectual property in today's rapidly evolving digital landscape.

Part 1: Understanding Copyright Law – This section lays the groundwork by covering the essentials of copyright, including how to register works, the extent of legal protection available, and the nuances of international copyright laws. It equips creators with the crucial knowledge needed to assert and defend their rights.

Part 2: Navigating Use and Fair Use – Focuses on the vital concept of fair use, offering real-world scenarios and detailed guidance on how to handle copyright infringements and resolve disputes effectively without compromising creative freedom.

Part 3: Licensing and Monetization – Explores strategic approaches to structuring and managing licensing agreements, understanding diverse revenue models, and handling collaborations, ensuring creators can monetize their works effectively while maintaining control over their usage.

Part 4: Copyright in the Digital Age – Addresses the challenges and opportunities presented by new technologies, digital rights management, and online content sharing platforms. This part also examines the impact of social media on copyright and anticipates future trends that could influence creators' rights.

"Beyond the Pen" is more than just a legal manual; it is a strategic resource that empowers creators to protect, manage, and prosper with their intellectual property in today's interconnected market. Packed with practical examples, expert advice, and actionable strategies, this book is an indispensable tool for anyone looking to navigate the legal challenges and seize the opportunities in the modern creative landscape.

Legal Ink:

Navigating the Legalese of Publishing

The fifth book in the Empire Builders Series: Masterclass in Business and Law is "Legal Ink: Navigating the Legalese of Publishing."

Summary: "Legal Ink" offers an indispensable guide for authors seeking to navigate the complex world of publishing contracts. This comprehensive book demystifies legal jargon and provides a clear roadmap to understanding and managing the intricacies of publishing agreements effectively.

Part 1: The Grant of Rights – This section explains the various types of publishing rights, offering guidance on how to negotiate and manage these rights effectively to safeguard the author's interests.

Part 2: Your Obligations – Details the commitments authors must uphold under publishing contracts. It emphasizes the implications of these obligations for an author's literary career and advises on managing multiple contractual commitments.

Part 3: Getting Your Book to Market – Covers the practical aspects of the publishing process from the final manuscript preparation to marketing and distribution. This part ensures authors understand the steps involved and their roles in bringing their book to market.

Part 4: Follow the Money – Breaks down the financial components of publishing contracts, including advances, royalties, and accounting clauses. It offers crucial advice on how to negotiate for fair compensation.

Part 5: Parting Ways – Discusses strategies for effectively managing the conclusion of a publishing agreement, including rights reversion and contract termination, providing tactics for authors to regain control of their work.

"Legal Ink" acts as more than just a guide—it's a strategic tool for any author looking to deeply understand and master the legal framework of publishing contracts. With this book, writers are equipped to make informed decisions, negotiate better terms, and ensure their rights are protected throughout their publishing journey. It is an essential resource for anyone looking to confidently handle the legalities of publishing and secure the success of their work in the competitive marketplace.

In conclusion, the Resource section of the Empire Builders Series serves as a valuable extension of the learning journey you've embarked upon. By utilizing these carefully chosen tools and materials, you are better equipped to apply the principles and strategies discussed in the series to real-world scenarios. Each resource has been tailored to enhance your understanding and effectiveness in the realms of business and law, ensuring you have the practical support necessary to navigate challenges and seize opportunities. We hope these resources prove instrumental in helping you build and sustain your business empire, transforming knowledge into actionable success.

The Empire Blueprint Series:
Case Studies for Business Success

Welcome to the Case Studies section of The Empire Blueprint Series: Case Studies for Business Success. This collection serves as an essential companion to the theoretical knowledge presented in the earlier volumes. Here, we delve into real-world applications and successful business practices through detailed case studies, showcasing how various entrepreneurs and businesses have navigated challenges, seized opportunities, and achieved success in their respective fields.

In this series, you will encounter a variety of scenarios that illustrate the practical implementation of business strategies and legal frameworks. Each case study not only highlights successes but also discusses the obstacles faced and lessons learned along the way. Whether you're a budding entrepreneur, a seasoned executive, or a legal professional, these insights will provide you with invaluable perspectives and tools to enhance your own business endeavors.

Each book in the series includes:

1. **70 Case Studies in Vision, Strategy, and Personal Branding**: This volume explores the journeys of entrepreneurs who have effectively crafted their visions and built strong personal brands. It highlights strategies for aligning personal values with business goals and creating a lasting impact in the marketplace.

2. **70 Case Studies in Leadership, Innovation, and Resilience**: This volume examines leaders who have driven innovation and fostered resilience within their organizations. The case studies showcase their approaches to overcoming challenges and inspire others to cultivate a culture of adaptability and forward-thinking.

3. **74 Case Studies in Growth, Digital Presence, and Legacy Building**: This volume delves into the strategies employed by businesses that have successfully navigated digital transformation and growth. It emphasizes the

importance of establishing a strong online presence and building a legacy that resonates with future generations.

Each case study in The Empire Blueprint Series: Case Studies for Business Success is crafted to offer actionable insights and inspiration for readers. By examining these real-world examples, you will gain a deeper understanding of the strategies that drive business success and how to apply these lessons to your own ventures.

70 Case Studies in Vision, Strategy, and Personal Branding: The Foundations of Success, Volume 1

The first book in The Empire Blueprint Series: Case Studies for Business Success is "70 Case Studies in Vision, Strategy, and Personal Branding: The Foundations of Success," Volume 1

Dive deeper into the essential elements of business success with Volume 1: 70 Case Studies in Vision, Strategy, and Personal Branding. This volume not only presents a wealth of real-world examples but also serves as a practical toolkit for aspiring entrepreneurs and seasoned professionals alike. Here, you will find a curated collection of resources designed to complement the case studies and enhance your understanding of effective business practices.

From strategic planning templates and personal branding frameworks to time management guides and storytelling techniques, these resources empower you to implement the insights gleaned from the case studies. Explore practical tools for optimizing your online presence, launching impactful marketing campaigns, and engaging audiences across various platforms.

With a focus on innovation and adaptability, this resource section is your go-to companion for navigating the complexities of today's business landscape. Whether you're looking to craft an inspiring vision, develop effective strategies, or build a standout personal brand, the materials provided will equip you with the actionable insights needed to achieve meaningful success. Embrace the tools and inspiration within these pages, and take your entrepreneurial journey to new heights.

70 Case Studies in Leadership, Innovation, and Resilience: building a Thriving Enterprise, Volume 2

The second book in The Empire Blueprint Series: Case Studies for Business Success is "70 Case Studies in Leadership, Innovation, and Resilience: Building a Thriving Enterprise," Volume 2

Enhance your understanding of effective leadership with Volume 2: 70 Case Studies in Leadership, Innovation, and Resilience: Building a Thriving Enterprise. This resource section is designed to complement the rich insights presented throughout the volume, providing you with practical tools and frameworks to elevate your leadership journey.

Within this section, you'll find a variety of resources that address the core themes of this book—leadership, innovation, and resilience. From templates for developing effective communication strategies to guides on fostering a collaborative corporate culture, these materials are crafted to support your growth as a leader. Explore negotiation techniques, emotional intelligence assessments, and frameworks for ethical leadership that will help you build trust and loyalty within your teams.

The resources also include practical tips for embracing digital transformation and integrating innovative technologies into your business practices. Learn how to leverage these tools to drive growth, enhance customer engagement, and maintain a competitive edge in today's dynamic market.

With a focus on creating lasting value and building a legacy, this section equips you with actionable insights and strategies to navigate challenges with confidence. Whether you are an entrepreneur launching a new venture or an executive steering an established enterprise, these resources will empower you to lead with purpose and resilience.

Dive into these valuable tools and insights, and discover how to turn challenges into opportunities, fostering an environment where innovation and sustainable growth thrive.

74 Case Studies in Growth, Digital Presence, and Legacy Building: Strategies for Long-Term Success, Volume 3

The third book in The Empire Blueprint Series: Case Studies for Business Success is "74 Case Studies in Growth, Digital Presence, and Legacy Building: Strategies for Long-Term Success," Volume 3

Unlock the secrets to sustainable success with Volume 3: 74 Case Studies in Growth, Digital Presence, and Legacy Building: Strategies for Long-Term Success. This resource section is designed to enhance your understanding and application of the powerful insights shared throughout the volume, providing you with practical tools and strategies for thriving in today's competitive landscape.

In this section, you'll find a wealth of resources that align with the key themes of this book—growth, digital engagement, and legacy building. From templates for strategic goal-setting and growth frameworks to guides on optimizing digital marketing efforts, these materials will help you implement the actionable insights gained from the case studies.

Explore best practices for storytelling and community engagement in the digital realm, along with practical tips for leveraging social media to amplify your brand's presence. Discover frameworks for navigating the complexities of innovation and operational efficiency, ensuring your business not only grows but flourishes sustainably.

The resource section also emphasizes the importance of legacy building, offering tools for effective succession planning and community involvement. Learn how to align your everyday decisions with your long-term vision, ensuring that your enterprise leaves a lasting impact for future generations.

Whether you are an entrepreneur embarking on a new venture, an executive scaling operations, or a professional seeking to elevate your digital presence, these resources will empower you to lead with purpose and confidence. Dive into the practical tools and insights provided here, and equip yourself to navigate challenges, innovate boldly, and create a meaningful legacy.

In conclusion, the Resource section of the Empire Builders Series and Empire Blueprint Series serves as valuable extensions of the learning journey you've embarked upon. By utilizing these carefully chosen tools and materials, you are better equipped to apply the principles and strategies discussed in the series to real-world scenarios. Each resource has been tailored to enhance your understanding and effectiveness in the realms of business and law, ensuring you have the practical support necessary to navigate challenges and seize opportunities. We hope these resources prove instrumental in helping you build and sustain your business empire, transforming knowledge into actionable success.

L. A. Moeszinger also known as simply "L" is the face behind the AuthorsDoor Leadership Program: AuthorsDoor Series: *Publisher & Her World*, AuthorsDoor Advanced Series: *Publisher & Her World*, and AuthorsDoor Masterclass Series: *Publisher & Her World.* The program comprises, books, courses, and workbooks. The courses expand upon the books. The workbooks go into further detail, outlining step-by-step instructions. Courses are *free*; books and workbooks are available for purchase on Amazon and other retailer sites. She has been launching the careers of self-publishers since 2009, and she also writes the AuthorsRedDoor.com blog on writing, publishing, and marketing. L is also the co-founder of The Ridge Publishing Group and its imprints.

She is an American author, publisher, and creator who resides in Coeur d'Alene, Idaho, with her husband and two dogs. She writes under the pseudonyms: Ann Patterson and Ann Carrington for her business law pieces; L. A. Moeszinger for her writing, publishing, and marketing pieces; Lori Ann Moeszinger for her biblical books and personal pieces; and a handful of others for her Manhattan Diaries series. She believes strongly in faith, blessings, and working her butt off . . . and she thinks one of the best things about being an author-publisher—unlike the lawyer she used to be—is that she can let her passion out.

About the Author

Parent Website: https://www.RidgePublishingGroup.com and

blog site https://www.PublisherAndHerWorld.com

Publisher Website: https://www.GuardiansofBiblicalTruth.com and

blog site https://www.Jesus-Says.com

Author website: https://www.LAMoeszinger.com and New Youniversity sites:

https://www.NewYouniversity.com, https://www.ManhattanChronicles.com

Bridge Website: https://www.AuthorsDoor.com and

blog site https://www.AuthorsRedDoor.com

Entertainment website: https://www.EthanFoxBooks.com and

blog site https://www.KidsStagram.com

Want More?

The ideas in this book are expanded upon throughout the AuthorsDoor Leadership Program of books, courses, and workbooks. Follow our Facebook page. Join our Facebook private group. Watch our YouTube channels: AuthorsDoor Group, Authors Red Door #Shorts, and Publisher and Her World at Ridge Publishing Group. Listen to our Podcast channel: Publisher's Circle; or

email me: *Hello@AuthorsDoor.com*

AuthorsDoor Hubs

Get insights from the articles we write on our *website* (AuthorsDoor.com). You'll find more publications to help authors sell better, pitch better, recruit better, build better, create better, and connect better. You are also invited to visit our *blog* and find out what we're talking about now. Sign up for our *AuthorsDoor Leadership Program Newsletter* and join the conversations going on there with our private community (Publisher's Circle); visit:

www.AuthorsRedDoor.com

Publisher & Her World Blogs

Enter a world where the sometimes shocking and often hilarious climb to the top as an author-publisher is exposed by a true insider. Faced with on-going trials and tribulations of the world of self-publishing, L. A. Moeszinger is witty and sometimes brutally candid in her postings. If you enjoy getting the inside scoop on the makings and thoughts behind self-publishing, this is the blog for you!

www.PublisherAndHerWorld.com

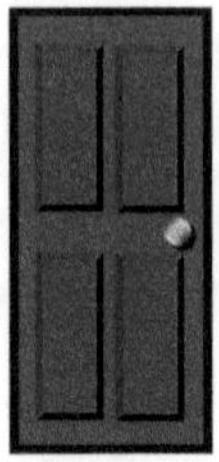

This
book was art
directed by John Jared.
The art for both the cover and the
interior was created using pastels on toned
print making paper. The text was set in 10 point Times
New Roman, a typeface based on the sixteenth-century type designs
of Claude Garamond, redrawn by Robert Slimback in 1989.
The book was printed at Amazon and IngramSpark.
The Managing Editor was Jack Clark. The
Production was supervised by
Jason Reed and Ed
Warren.

www.ingramcontent.com/pod-product-compliance
Lightning Source LLC
Chambersburg PA
CBHW031837200326
41597CB00012B/184

* 9 7 8 1 9 5 6 9 0 5 2 7 4 *